DATE DUE

~~OC 25 '99~~			
~~DE 14 '99~~			
MY 20 '02			
~~DE 10 '02~~			
~~FEB 11 2003~~			
~~OC 7 '03~~			
~~FE 10 05~~			
~~AP 18 05~~			
~~FE 12 08~~			
MR 2 4 '10			

DEMCO 38-296

Inside the Vatican

Inside the Vatican

THE POLITICS

AND ORGANIZATION OF

THE CATHOLIC CHURCH

THOMAS J. REESE

HARVARD UNIVERSITY PRESS

Cambridge, Massachusetts
London, England

Copyright © 1996 by The Woodstock Theological Center
All rights reserved
Printed in the United States of America
Third printing, 1997
Library of Congress Cataloging-in-Publication Data
Reese, Thomas J., 1945–
  Inside the Vatican : the politics and organization of the Catholic
  Church / Thomas J. Reese.
     p. cm.
  Includes bibliographical references and index.
  ISBN 0-674-93260-9 (alk. paper)
  1. Catholic Church—Government—History. 2. Catholic Church—
  Doctrines—History. 3. Vatican City—History. 4. Papacy—History.
  5. Councils and synods. 6. Church management. I. Title.
  BX1802.R44 1996
  262'.13—dc20
  96-26641

Contents

Preface

WHEN I TOLD my friends I was writing a book about the Vatican, they were skeptical. For most of them, the Vatican is a mysterious place, as impenetrable as a thick cloud of incense. Those who know a little about the Vatican warned that I would never be able to get any information out of it and, if I wrote the book, I was bound to get into trouble. At the same time, they all wanted to read the book as soon as it was finished.

The Vatican holds a fascination for Catholics and non-Catholics alike. It is an institution rich in history and intrigue that still makes headlines as it attempts to govern the Catholic church and mold world events according to its own vision.

As a political scientist and a Jesuit priest, I was always curious about the workings of the present-day Vatican. But in 1972 when Aaron Wildavsky suggested the church as an object of research for my doctoral dissertation, I demurred, wanting to study "real" politics first. The book that emerged from my dissertation, *The Politics of Taxation* (1980), led me to three exciting years in Washington as a writer for *Tax Notes* and a lobbyist for Taxation with Representation, a public interest tax reform organization. In November 1978, I kicked the Washington dust off my feet and moved to New York City to become associate editor of *America,* a weekly magazine published by Jesuits in the United States, where for seven years I wrote about politics, economics, and anything else that struck my fancy.

When the American Catholic bishops began preparing pastoral letters on peace and economic justice, I had all the excuse I needed to turn my journalistic and political science skills toward examining the government and politics of the Catholic church. Ultimately this led me back to Washington to the Woodstock Theological Center at Georgetown University, where I wrote

Archbishop: Inside the Power Structure of the American Catholic Church (1989) and *A Flock of Shepherds: The National Conference of Catholic Bishops* (1992). The first examines politics and governance in the local church, while the second looks at the church on the national level.

Inside the Vatican completes the series by examining the politics and organization of the church at the highest level, although it is not necessary to read the earlier books to understand this one. This is not a work of history, theology, or canon law, although these disciplines are sometimes used to explain how and why the Vatican operates as it does today. Rather, I examine the governance of the church from the perspective of social science. As part of my research, I spent the academic year of 1993–94 in Rome interviewing more than a hundred people working in the Vatican, including thirteen cardinals. (All quotations of Vatican officials are from these interviews unless otherwise noted.) I was surprised and pleased by the number of people who were willing to talk about their work in the Vatican. But while most allowed the interviews to be taped, very few wanted their names to be used. This in itself says much about politics in the Vatican.

I have tried to be objective in my reporting and have allowed those interviewed to speak for themselves. What opinions and conclusions I express are my own and certainly are not infallible. Some readers may be shocked by what they read, but the church has always admitted that it has more sinners than saints. The human face of the church is found not just in the pews but also in the Vatican. Over the centuries the Vatican has changed, along with the papacy it serves, and it will continue to change in the next century. My hope is that this book will contribute to a better understanding of this important institution so that it can evolve to meet the needs of the church and the world in the next millennium.

Many people deserve thanks for their kindness and help during this project. R. Scott Appleby, John Coleman, S.J., Jerry Filteau, Thomas Green, Gene Hemrick, Bishop James Malone, James Provost, and Robert Trisco read early versions of the manuscript and gave helpful suggestions. I am especially grateful to those both in the United States and Rome who were willing to be interviewed. Since most want to remain anonymous, I cannot thank them by name, but I still want to acknowledge my debt to them. Without their help this book could not have been written. I also wish to thank Nora O'Callaghan, Eugene Rooney, S.J., and Joseph Tylenda, S.J., of the Woodstock Theological Center Library and Julie Delong and Katherine Nuss of the Catholic News Service (CNS) library. CNS reporters John Thavis and Cindy Wooden were generous in sharing their experience and hospitality with me in Rome. As the notes indicate, I am greatly indebted to CNS's reporters, who have covered the Vatican with distinction through the years.

The Woodstock Theological Center provided a supportive environment for my research, and I am especially grateful to the director, James Connor, S.J., Elizabeth Kostelac, and Adoreen McCormick. My research assistants, Ina Saal, Lara Winner, and Yu-Chen Fan, were also meticulous and generous in their work. Encouragement and companionship came from my Jesuit colleagues in the United States and Rome, especially those I lived with at the Woodstock Jesuit Community and Villa Malta. Financial support for my research came from the Woodstock Theological Center, the Woodrow Wilson International Center for Scholars in Washington, D.C. (for a 1994–95 fellowship), and anonymous donors. Finally, my thanks to Joyce Seltzer, my editor at Harvard University Press, for helping me make this book interesting and accessible to a wide audience, and to Mary Ellen Geer for an excellent job of copy editing. In spite of all this help, I take full responsibility for everything in the book.

Thomas J. Reese, S.J.
Woodstock Theological Center
July 31, 1996

Inside the Vatican

Introduction

As the world moves toward the year 2000, there are few institutions we can point to that have played a major role in shaping practically every one of the last twenty centuries. In fact, there are few organizations that have been around that long. One of the most prominent is the Christian church. For almost two thousand years Christianity has intimately touched the personal lives of millions of individuals, whether rich or poor, powerful or powerless, famous or unknown. Even those who are not members of the church find it impossible to ignore because they are often forced to define themselves through their opposition to certain Christian teachings and practices.

Christianity has had an impact on family life, economic transactions, political alliances, artistic achievements, and the way in which we understand the meaning of life and human purpose. It has formed cultures and changed the course of history. Its teachings touch areas as private as sexual fantasies and as public as nuclear war. It preaches salvation to sinners and everlasting life with God for the faithful.

Christianity has accomplished this not as an abstract philosophy but as a community of believers who are organized as a church. The church has been the means by which new members (both converts and those born to Christian parents) are socialized into the community as the faith is passed on from generation to generation. Through the church individual Christians have also joined forces to meet their religious and social needs and to have a corporate impact on the world that has been both lasting and widespread.

In the Catholic form of Christianity, church organization is based on episcopal leadership of dioceses, the geographical units into which the church divides the world. In these local faith communities Christians live their faith and interact with the world. But these local churches do not exist in isolation; through their bishops they are united to one another and to the church of Rome. The leadership of the bishop of Rome, the pope, in this communion of churches has through the centuries unmistakably influenced the life of the church and the lives of individual Christians. Even the day on which we will begin the third millennium is due to Pope Gregory XIII, who in 1582 established the calendar in use throughout the world.

The role of the papacy through the centuries has varied tremendously: comforting Christians during the Roman persecutions, accepting imperial support from Emperor Constantine and his successors, confronting kings and other secular rulers, converting and civilizing the barbarian hordes, patronizing the arts, condemning heretics, calling the Crusades, and mediating disputes among nations. Some popes protected local churches from political rulers, while others sold benefices to the highest bidders. The popes have been saints and scoundrels, warriors and peacemakers, reformers and corrupters. Their actions have both united and divided the church.

The papacy is not just a quaint artifact of history irrelevant to the world of today. The present pope, John Paul II, will undoubtedly go down in history as one of the most influential leaders in the second half of the twentieth century. His support of the dissident Solidarity movement in Poland began the avalanche that swept Communism from Eastern Europe and the Soviet Union and freed the persecuted Catholic church. He has been an articulate voice for social justice, peace, and human rights in his visits to almost every corner of the world, from Alaska to South Africa. In his teaching he has also been a staunch defender of the traditions and practices that he believes are essential to the life of the church and society at large. That the papacy continues to have great relevance to the world today is obvious in the extensive coverage it is given by the news media.

Despite all this, the proper role of the papacy today is a hotly debated topic within the Catholic church itself. It is also a sticking point in ecumenical relations among the Christian churches. Many complain that the church has become excessively centralized, with local bishops behaving like branch managers of a multinational corporation where directives from the top are expected to be obeyed without question. Others feel that, in a world of moral and political chaos, a firm hand is needed at the helm. Papal leadership becomes more important than ever as communications and technology turn the world into a global village.

Within the Catholic church, the papacy's influence is all-pervasive. During 68 papal visits to 112 countries, millions have turned out to listen to and pray with the pope during his first seventeen years in office. Even when he is not physically present, he controls much of what is going on in the church even at the parish level. Recently, for example, a papal commission completed *The Catechism of the Catholic Church,* a publication that will direct the religious education of adults and children into the next century. Papal opposition to married clergy and women priests has determined who will and will not lead parish communities in worship each Sunday. And practically every prayer uttered during those worship services has been approved in Rome, not only in its original Latin version but also in its various translations. Thus Rome decided that "man" would continue to be used to refer to humanity in Scripture readings at Mass and in *The Catechism of the Catholic Church.* Vatican regulations also determine how difficult it is for divorced Catholics to get annulments before they can be married again in the church.

Vatican officials also select, often without consultation with the local church, the bishops who govern these churches. By appointing papal loyalists as bishops, Rome can ensure that Vatican policies will be observed at the diocesan level. These bishops see to it that pastors, seminary professors, and other church employees support papal teachings. When necessary, Vatican officials intervene and demand that dissident theologians either recant or lose their right to teach. And in 1995, despite protests from his local French supporters, even a bishop, Jacques Gaillot, was deposed for being out of line with Vatican directives.

Papal actions and teachings are decisive not only to Catholics but to others because of their reverberations in the world outside the Catholic church. Participation in ecumenical dialogues by Catholics is both encouraged and controlled by the papacy. Papal teachings on birth control and abortion have demographic and environmental effects that are widely condemned by those supporting population control and "reproductive freedom," and widely endorsed by conservatives espousing "family values." Vatican diplomats successfully opposed the inclusion of abortion rights language in a UN document at the 1994 Cairo conference on population and development. Papal opposition to the Persian Gulf war angered some and pleased others. Vatican opposition to economic sanctions against Iran, Iraq, Libya, and Cuba has gone against American foreign policy goals. Vatican views on arms control, Third World debt, capitalism, religious freedom, and refugees are an integral part of the international discourse in which the Catholic church is a unique participant. The impact of papal actions on the world has led practically every nation except China and Vietnam to exchange ambassadors with the Holy See. Catholic and non-Catholic nations alike believe it is in their self-interest to have representation in the Vatican. And when popes speak at the United Nations, it is an event of major international importance.

Despite the importance of the papacy for the Catholic church and its prominent role in international affairs, its internal workings are little known to Catholics, to world leaders, or to the world at large. This is partly a result of the secretive nature of the Vatican, which sees little advantage to letting others know its internal operations. Nor does it have confidence that it will be treated fairly by outside observers. General ignorance of the Vatican is bred by the uniqueness of this institution that is like no other, with its unusual laws, structures, goals, procedures, personnel, and culture. An observer of the Vatican can quickly become lost in technical jargon, theological concepts, bureaucratic byways, and canonical procedures that have no parallel in secular society or in other churches. The confusion is increased as personnel, policies, procedures, and structures evolve and change, for this is a living institution, not one frozen in time.

Unfamiliarity with the workings of the Vatican has led many political leaders into unforeseen difficulties. The Clinton administration suffered an embarrassing confrontation with the Holy See at the Cairo conference when the Vatican delegation successfully opposed the U.S. delegation's language on abortion. The Reagan administration was thrown off guard by Vatican opposition to economic sanctions against the imposition of martial law in Poland in 1981. This ignorance is not limited to political leaders. When they come to Rome, bishops are just as confused about Vatican decision making when confronted by a papal bureaucracy with overlapping jurisdictions and secretive procedures. Maneuvering through this maze without a friendly guide is difficult for insiders and almost impossible for outsiders. Even within the Vatican itself, people in one office often do not know what is happening in another.

A comprehensive analysis of the papacy as it operates today is long overdue. Knowledge about this complex, contemporary, and living organization is important to Catholics and non-Catholics alike, to those who love the papacy and those who fear it. Understanding how the papacy operates is especially important today as it approaches the end of this millennium and tries to prepare itself for the next. That the papacy has evolved and changed during the last two millennia is a historical fact. That it will continue to evolve and change is without doubt. Although many in the past have predicted the end of the papacy and of Christianity, both have outlived their doom-saying critics. The papacy of the future will undoubtedly have an impact both on the future of Christianity and on human history as a whole.

The Holy See is a unique organization because it pursues spiritual and secular goals at an international level. Its organizational complexity arises from the fact that the pope plays many roles in order to fulfill these goals. He is the bishop of Rome, the sovereign ruler of the State of Vatican City, and the successor of St. Peter as head of the college of bishops. As bishop of Rome, he is directly responsible for the spiritual needs of the 2.6 million Catholics in the diocese of Rome, just as every bishop throughout the world is responsible for the spiritual needs of the people in his local church. As monarch of Vatican City, a 108.7-acre independent state with fewer than 500 citizens, the pope is a civil chief of state like any other monarch of a small state recognized under international law. And as head of the college of bishops, which includes all the bishops of the world, the pope leads and directs the Catholic church over which he and the college are the supreme authority.

The papacy touches the moral and spiritual lives of millions of people through the pope's pastoral visits to scores of countries, his comprehensive teachings on doctrine and morals, his appointment of bishops, and his supervision of local churches. His decisions can foster unity in a multinational and multicultural church by reminding far-flung local churches that they are part of one communion. His decisions can also divide the church when he insists on teachings or practices that alienate and estrange portions of the faithful. His episcopal appointments have been greeted with joy by some and consternation by others. His strong voice has reminded richer local churches of their responsibility to help less fortunate local churches. Because of his role within the Catholic church, the pope's constituency is global, and he works for peace and human rights throughout the world. As the leader of this constituency he is a force to be reckoned with. When he focuses his attention and energy on specific issues, he can sometimes marshal the attention and energy of the entire church to further his objectives.

Essential to the pope in doing his work and accomplishing his goals are the offices housed at the Vatican. The name "Vatican" comes from the ancient Roman name for the hill and land around it on which St. Peter's Basilica, the Apostolic Palace, and the Vatican museums are built. The Vatican City State takes its name from this hill. The Roman curia is the complex of offices, housed in or near the Vatican, that help the pope in governing the universal church. The term "see" in Holy See (Santa Sedes) refers to "seat" (as in the seat of government) or "diocese." Although Holy See originally referred to the diocese of Rome, the seat of St. Peter, it is now more commonly used to refer to the pope and the Roman curia. Purists would limit the term "Vatican" to the Vatican City State, but I, like those working in Rome, also use it to refer to the Roman curia and the Holy See.

The Vatican, like any organization, is a system by which people, resources, and technologies are organized through structures and procedures to achieve goals within a given environment.[1] Therefore, in order to understand the Vatican, we must look at its structures and procedures, its people and their goals, its resources and technologies, and the environment in which it operates. As a living institution, it must and does respond when any of these factors changes. Thus, an important purpose of the historical material in this book is to show that the Vatican has changed its structures and procedures over time not simply because of different popes but because of the changing environment within which the church operated.

Understanding the Vatican requires looking at it from many angles. Too often observers focus on one aspect of the Vatican, such as the personality of the pope, and try to explain everything from that perspective. Although the personality of the pope is certainly important, the papacy is as much an institution as an individual. It is an organization made up of a variety of people pursuing different goals while working together in Vatican structures that have evolved over the centuries. It is also a vital institution in which the structures are changing under the impact of new people, new historical circumstances, and new goals.

Most Vatican officials are diocesan priests and members of religious communities who have given up family and alternative careers to work for the church. They have gone through an extensive indoctrination and training that appeals to the highest ideals of service and commitment based on Christian faith and principles. Most also have specialized training in theology, canon law, or diplomacy. The people who work in the Vatican are a key to understanding the Vatican itself. Their goals, their values, their professional and personal culture are part of the unique character of this institution.

Beyond the geographical boundaries of the Vatican is the larger world community in which the papacy operates. The papacy interacts with an ever-changing secular environment—political, social, economic, and cultural—that demands sophisticated knowledge and skills. As a religious institution, the papacy also exists in a theological and religious environment with which it constantly interacts. Sometimes this external world is supportive, sometimes it is threatening, but at all times it is the source of the money, people, technology, and ideas the papacy needs to lead the Catholic church. Sometimes forces in the larger environment crash upon the papacy like invading armies that cannot be kept out and force change. Willingly or unwillingly, the Vatican is shaped by the world in which it operates, while at the same time the Vatican tries to shape this world according to its ideals and values.

In responding to the world around it, the Vatican uses structures and procedures that are unique: the college of cardinals, the synod of bishops, congregations, councils, secretariats, tribunals, papal diplomats, the State of Vatican City, the Code of Canon Law. Most of these structures have their roots centuries deep in history, and yet church structures and procedures are constantly evolving. Changes in structures and procedures have been particularly noticeable since the Second Vatican Council as Paul VI and John Paul II have attempted to reorganize the Vatican to deal with the contemporary church and the modern world.

In order to achieve its spiritual and temporal goals, the Vatican must operate in the real world. It has to buy equipment and office supplies, pay salaries, and cover the costs of telephone, utilities, printing, travel, and other items. Limits on funds mean limits on activities. The Vatican requires a stable and dependable financial organization to raise money and spend it wisely, but financial scandals and mismanagement have repeatedly blemished the papacy. Vatican finances have traditionally been hidden from view, but recently more information has become available that sheds light on how the Vatican manages its finances and how such management affects its policies.

Understanding the Vatican as a complex organization in a complicated and changing environment requires an awareness of many factors. Sometimes an event in the external environment, such as Italian reunification in 1870, changes the papacy against its will. Sometimes individuals, especially the popes themselves, have a deep impact on the Vatican because of their ideas and skills. Sometimes it is structures that provide the mechanism for processing information and making decisions that have an impact on millions. Looking at the total picture, despite its sometimes Byzantine complexity, is essential for understanding such a unique organization.

Visiting the Vatican for the first time can be an overwhelming experience for anyone. The pilgrim or tourist is dwarfed by gigantic columns and high ceilings. Everywhere one turns there is a piece of history or a priceless work of art. The journalist's first impression of the Vatican is likewise daunting. Hardly anyone will speak on the record, and separating fact from rumor is an art, not a science. Nor is the bishop who comes to Rome for the first time at all sure what he will find. He knows he must pray at the tombs of the Apostles and see the pope, but then he wanders from office to office hoping for assistance or at least sympathy. Even a newly elected pope, like John Paul I or John Paul II, can be intimidated by the strangeness and the complexity of the internal operations of the Vatican.

If the visitor sneaks past the Swiss Guards in their colorful uniforms and the security guards in their plainer attire, he can look into offices where ambassadors discuss UN documents, where theologians nervously await examination, where millions of dollars are transferred from the First to the Third World, where the appointment of a new American archbishop is decided, where the ethics of arms sales are debated, and where penalties for pedophile priests are discussed. Dressed in cassocks or black suits, the priests and religious, like millions of their secular counterparts, process paper for their superiors. The decisions that come out of these offices can change people's lives, cause international incidents, and control the way the Christian message is presented to the world.

Since the pope is central to the Vatican, it is appropriate to begin this inquiry by looking at the pope's roles as the bishop of Rome, civil monarch of Vatican City, and head of the college of bishops. Ensuing chapters will describe the roles of ecumenical councils, episcopal conferences, synods of bishops, and the college of cardinals in the governance of the church. I will also examine the Roman curia—its people, culture, organization, procedures, and finances. I will then look at how the pope uses the Roman curia to have an impact outside the Vatican, especially in the selection of bishops, the control of theologians, and papal relations with secular rulers. Finally, I conclude by examining how the papacy and the Vatican might be reorganized to serve the church and the world in the twenty-first century.

Many people would like to look over the walls of the Vatican to find out what is going on inside: the Catholic or other Christians who want a peek into the engine room, the ambitious cleric who is tempted to higher office, the journalist who despairs of peeling the Vatican onion, the bishop who wants an affirmative response to his request, the world leader who wants to know with whom he is dealing, the church reformer who needs data to support his conclusions, the intellectually curious who delight in Chinese puzzles and Byzantine politics.

The pope sits on St. Peter's chair (Santa Sedes). This is an uncomfortable chair because the man sitting in it is burdened with the enormous spiritual, political, and social concerns of people all over the world. It is a throne from which it is easy to fall from grace. It is a highly visible chair that makes its occupant the target of cranks, prophets, pundits, reformers, and even assassins. The pope and those trying to understand the papacy and prepare it for the next millennium face a monumental task. The salvation of souls and the future of humankind will be influenced by decisions made inside the Vatican.

∼ 1

Papal Roles

"YOU ARE PETER, and upon this rock I will build my church"—these were the words of Jesus when he commissioned a Galilean fisherman as the leader of the Apostles (Matthew 16:18). The difference between this simple ceremony and today's papacy is so great that Peter would have a difficult time comprehending it, yet Catholics acknowledge the pope as the successor of St. Peter. Bishop of Rome, head of the college of bishops, and chief of state of Vatican City—all of these papal roles belong to the pope who is the successor of St. Peter.

The papacy has traveled a long distance in almost two thousand years: from the shores of the Lake of Galilee to the shores of the Tiber, from a fishing boat to a Renaissance palace where the pope reigns as a sovereign monarch, from a one-man show to a complex international institution. This institution has numerous offices and commissions and about three thousand employees who help the pope in his ministry. This complexity reflects the multiple roles and interests of the pope. The pope is bishop of Rome, the primate or chief bishop of Italy, the patriarch of the West,[1] the absolute monarch of the Vatican City State, and the head of the college of bishops and of the Catholic church. His role as head of the college of bishops and of the Catholic church is the principal focus of this book, but this role cannot be properly understood without seeing it in the context of his other roles, especially his role as bishop of Rome and monarch of Vatican City.

The pope is bishop of Rome because of Peter's decision to settle in Rome, the capital of the Roman empire. The church, the world, and Middle East politics would be very different today if Peter had become the bishop of Jerusalem and the papal states had once included Israel, Jordan, and Lebanon. But Peter did move to Rome and became the first bishop of Rome, with his successors in Rome inheriting his role as head of the college of bishops.

As the bishop of Rome, the pope must look after the pastoral needs of about 2.6 million Catholics living in the diocese of Rome, which covers the city of Rome and its suburbs. The diocese of Rome is structured like other large dioceses in the world: it has parishes, schools, religious education programs, social services, and a cathedral. It also has a seminary, a priests' council, a pastoral council, a council of pastors, and an episcopal council.[2] Serving in the parishes are diocesan priests, who permanently belong to the diocese of Rome. Religious—Dominicans, Franciscans, Jesuits, and others—also serve in parishes, schools, and other ministries, although as members of religious communities these priests, sisters, and brothers would not spend their whole lives working in Rome.

Although St. Peter's is the largest and most famous church in Rome, it is not the cathedral of the bishop of Rome. It is simply the church built over the tomb of St. Peter. The pope's cathedral is St. John Lateran, built on a site given to the popes by Emperor Constantine in the fourth century. The popes lived there for a thousand years and moved to the Vatican only after returning from Avignon in the fourteenth century. Next to the cathedral is the sixteenth-century Lateran Palace, which now houses the curia or offices of the vicariate of Rome.

During the last four centuries, when the popes have been occupied with governing the papal states and the universal church, they have delegated the pastoral care of the Rome diocese to a vicar. From 1871 to 1929 the popes did not even visit their diocese because they refused to set foot on Italian soil in protest against the seizure of the papal states. The postwar growth in the population of Rome and its expansion into the suburbs have made it even more difficult for popes personally to care for the Romans.

Today, the diocese of Rome is divided into two vicariates: the vicariate of Rome and the Vatican vicariate. The Vatican vicariate contains only one parish, St. Ann's, for people living and working within the Vatican. It also contains St. Peter's Basilica, which serves the pastoral needs of pilgrims and tourists as well as being the principal church for papal ceremonies. The vicar for the Vatican is the archpriest of St. Peter's, Cardinal Virgilio Noè.

The Roman vicariate contains more than 330 parishes with about 450 diocesan and 500 religious priests serving Catholics in Rome. The vicar of Rome,

Cardinal Camillo Ruini, is assisted by two archbishops and six bishops who are each responsible for different regions or pastoral concerns in Rome. Together they form an episcopal council. Cardinal Ruini deals with the day-to-day affairs of the vicariate, although he is expected to consult with the pope on major questions. The cardinal was the general secretary of the Italian bishops' conference before becoming the vicar for Rome. The pope has also appointed him president of the Italian bishops' conference, although this is a violation of the rule that only diocesan bishops can be presidents of bishops' conferences.

The vicariate curia with about 150 employees is separate from the Roman curia and is overseen by a general secretary. He is responsible for the pastoral formation of the clergy, religious, and laity and for the training of teachers and catechists. There are several offices in the curia including ones for evangelization and catechetics, for worship and sacraments, for social and charitable works, for personnel, and for finances. There is also a tribunal to handle marriage annulments for Catholics living in Rome.[3]

As the bishop of Rome, the pope faces many of the same pastoral problems faced by other bishops in Western Europe: religious indifference, low church attendance, anticlericalism, and declining numbers of priests and religious. A study by the University of Turin, commissioned for the diocese of Rome, found that 80 percent of Romans consider themselves Catholic but more than 70 percent of these Catholics condone birth control, divorce, cohabitation, and premarital sex. Fewer than half believe in an afterlife or believe that Christianity is the one true religion.[4] The vicar of Rome, Cardinal Ruini, in 1994 went so far as to refer to Rome as a de-Christianized city. The pope clearly has much work to do in his own backyard.

Despite his heavy workload, Pope John Paul II has attempted to give personal attention to his diocese and has acted more like the bishop of Rome than many of his Italian predecessors. Unlike his predecessors, this non-Italian pope has not cultivated the old aristocratic families of Rome that had traditionally been aligned with the papacy. As bishop of Rome, John Paul has continued to follow certain traditions. For example, on December 8, the feast of the Immaculate Conception, the pope lays a wreath at the pedestal of the statue of Mary in the Piazza di Spagna while a local fireman climbs to the top of the column to crown the statue. John Paul has also broken new ground. In 1986, he became the first pope to visit Rome's main synagogue. In 1992, he convoked an eight-month-long synod for the diocese of Rome, only the second synod in its modern history. There he called for pastoral attention to families and young people as well as concern for those who suffer the most:

"the sick, the neglected, the elderly who live alone, the unemployed, the immigrants—people, families and social categories who for various reasons are afflicted by material and moral poverty."[5]

At the beginning of his pontificate, John Paul spent a half-day each month at the Lateran Palace, the headquarters for the diocese of Rome, so that he could get to know diocesan personnel and issues. He also committed himself to visiting every parish in Rome. "I try to visit Rome's parishes—on average about 15 a year—in the period between the Solemnity of All Saints [November 1] and Easter," he told a meeting of the college of cardinals in 1994. "With God's help I have now been able to fulfill my pastoral duty towards 233 out of the 323 parishes."[6]

The personal attention that the pope gives to visiting Roman parishes is similar to his earlier practice as a bishop in Poland.[7] It also anticipates on the diocesan level his pastoral visits to local churches around the world. John Paul wants to pastor the world the same way he pastors his diocese. The pope clearly enjoys these parish visits, but he is also presenting himself as a model for other bishops in the church.

In visiting parishes in the suburbs of Rome, the pope is away from the tourists, priests, and religious who crowd his ceremonies in the Vatican. In the suburbs he meets ordinary Italian churchgoers in their neighborhoods and churches. These suburban parishes are often more alive and crowded than the churches in the center of Rome, where the Sunday liturgies are often lightly attended. The suburban churches are more lively, with congregational singing at liturgies crowded with families. At these parishes, altar girls were frequently present long before they were officially approved by the Vatican. The pope, like many American bishops, quietly ignored this violation of church practice and did not banish the girls from the sanctuary.

The parish visits, taking three to four hours on a Sunday morning, are timed to get the pope back to St. Peter's for the Angelus at noon. In preparation for the visit he meets with the parish priests and diocesan officials to learn about the parish. Often these meetings are working lunches or dinners in his Vatican apartment. On arriving at the parish, he first greets those waiting outside, moving along the police barricades shaking hands, touching people, and blessing them. He visits with the children in the parish catechetical center, where he sometimes sings songs with them and answers questions. "Are you happy being pope?" he was asked at one parish. "You can see I am," the pope responded. "You don't need a sad pope. The pope must be joyful and happy."[8]

Then he enters the church and celebrates the Eucharist with the community. The Vatican press office releases the text of his homily, but journalists accompanying him note that he sometimes ignores the text when speaking. "You see a more spontaneous and relaxed pope during these visits," explained one Roman journalist who has followed the pope closely. "He really seems to enjoy them."[9]

As bishop of Rome, the pope is also the primate or principal bishop of Italy, and thus he plays a larger role in the Italian church than he does in other countries. He has made 122 pastoral trips visiting 247 cities, towns, and villages all over Italy.[10] He has spoken out on numerous social and religious issues. For example, he strongly criticized the Mafia in southern Italy in 1993, and the Mafia struck back by setting off a bomb next to his cathedral.

Some Italians would like to see the pope play a less dominant role in the Italian church, especially because he is not an Italian. The pope's activity in Italy goes well beyond what would be considered appropriate for a primate in any other country, and the deference shown to him by the Italian bishops is greater than would be shown to a primate by the bishops of another country. This additional deference is partly due to history but is also a result of the fact that he is not only primate but also head of the universal church. As pope he appoints the bishops, something other primates cannot do.

The pope's dominance can be seen in his relationship to the Italian bishops' conference, where he appoints its president. In 1985 the Italian conference held an election in keeping with its constitution, and Cardinal Marco Cé of Venice and Cardinal Carlo Martini of Milan received the most votes. John Paul II set aside the election and appointed his vicar for Rome as president, a controversial practice he has continued ever since. In other countries the president would not be appointed by the primate but would be elected by the bishops, and the primate would have one vote just like any other bishop. Traditionally, the Italian bishops' conference has followed the lead of the pope on Italian church and political issues. Whether a conference in other countries would defer to the local primate or not would depend on personalities and particular historical circumstances. Many countries, like the United States, do not even have a primate.

Although John Paul has clarified the administrative and financial distinction between the diocese of Rome and the Vatican, he does not have a separate staff to help him in his work as primate of Italy.[11] Instead he uses the vicar for Rome and the Roman curia. Thus the Secretariat of State, not the Italian bishops' conference, conducts most negotiations with the Italian government over church-state issues. Likewise curial officials, especially Italian curial officials, are intimately involved in discussing Italian church and political issues.

The election of the first non-Italian pope in centuries has affected the role of the papacy in Italian political life. John Paul II does not have the detailed knowledge and interest in Italian affairs that Italian popes have had. Paul VI, for example, had long-standing personal contacts with leaders in the Christian Democratic party even before becoming pope. Even though John Paul II has periodically called for Catholic unity in Italian politics and has opposed the division of Italy proposed by the Lombard League, some Italian observers say that papal involvement in Italian affairs has declined under this Polish pope. It is too early to tell whether the presence of non-Italian popes will eventually liberate the Italian church so that it becomes less dependent on the pope and the Roman curia for leadership on Italian church and political issues.

Various Italian cardinals and bishops spoke out before the 1994 Italian election, and although most were sympathetic to the reformed and renamed Christian Democratic party, few thought that this was an effort led by the pope. Many Italian bishops have friends and relatives who are Christian Democrats and hoped that the reformed party could be a vehicle for implementing Catholic social teaching. Other Italian bishops prefer to keep all politicians at a distance rather than become tainted by close association with a group that the people do not trust. These bishops see the destruction of the Christian Democratic party as an opportunity to free the church from an alliance that has become anachronistic. With the Italian party system in chaos as a result of the indictment of scores of political leaders, the stage is set for a new relationship between church and state in which the Italian church stays aloof from entanglements with one political party.

Since they live in Rome, popes have been especially concerned about local politics, at times governing the city and at other times being at the mercy of Rome's rulers. Today, city officials (none of whom were practicing Catholics in 1994) have a love-hate relationship with the church, recognizing it as the principal reason for Rome's thriving tourist industry while at the same time seeing it as a tax-exempt consumer of services. The diocese of Rome must deal with the city of Rome on a variety of questions concerning city services, zoning laws, building permits, social services, and repair of historic churches.

Relations between the Vatican and the city government were cozy during much of the postwar period, when the church worked in partnership with Christian Democratic politicians against the Communists. In 1976, however, a Communist-Socialist coalition in the city council elected a Communist mayor in Rome. At first the council blocked construction of new churches in the Roman suburbs, but later relented. More recently, the city sent the pope a bill for $1 million for blocking off streets during the repair of St. John Lateran after the Mafia had bombed it. The government even tried to evict

Mother Teresa's Missionaries of Charity from a city-owned former monastery where the sisters were running a shelter for the homeless. City officials, who wanted the building for offices, quickly backed down in the face of an international outcry.

John Paul II gets along with the Communist mayor better than did his two Italian predecessors, Paul VI and John Paul I. In 1994 he reported that "relations between the Apostolic See and the authorities of the capital and the Italian State have been marked by cordiality and mutual respect."[12] At the same time, he has used his annual visits with city officials to lecture them on the problems of the city: lack of housing, neighborhoods without essential services, and the unmet needs of the elderly, handicapped, unemployed, illegal workers, transients, AIDS sufferers, the mentally ill, drug addicts, and juvenile delinquents.[13]

Monarch of Vatican City

Although Vatican City is surrounded by the city of Rome, it is not part of Italy. The State of Vatican City is a sovereign state recognized under international law. When a person is elected bishop of Rome and pope, he also automatically becomes the head of Vatican City. The city state is as much a burden as a benefit to the popes. As ruler of Vatican City the pope is the last absolute monarch in Europe, with supreme legislative, judicial, and executive authority. He also controls all the assets of the Vatican, since this is a state economy without private property other than personal possessions of the employees and residents. The Vatican does not consider its monarchical government a model for other nations. Rather, its purpose is to provide an internationally recognized territory where the Holy See can operate in total freedom, without political interference.

With 108.7 acres, Vatican City is the smallest independent state in the world. For centuries the papal states included large parts of Italy. The role of the pope as a secular ruler began when the Byzantine empire lost control of Italy as a result of the barbarian invasions. With the collapse of civil order, the people turned to the pope for leadership. Sometimes the popes were successful in protecting their people through negotiations or arms. Pope Leo the Great talked Attila the Hun out of attacking Rome in 452. Three years later, Leo could not keep the Vandals from looting Rome, but he got them to agree not to burn it or massacre its people.

In 590, Gregory the Great became the de facto ruler of Italy. As a layman he had been the prefect of Rome and therefore had experience as a civil administrator. As pope he paid soldiers, appointed generals, negotiated treaties, and fed the people. He did all this before the papal states even existed; he did it in the name of the emperor. He also tried to convert the Lombards, not only to save their souls but also in the hope that this might keep them from sacking Rome. The emperor opposed this strategy as treason to the empire; he believed that the only good barbarian was a dead barbarian.

As the empire declined and as the barbarians became Christian, the popes began dealing with rulers other than the distant and weak emperor. Faced with Lombards to the north of Rome and an unsympathetic and weak imperial government to the south, Pope Zacharias turned to Pepin, the de facto ruler of the Franks under the feeble Merovingian dynasty. Pepin wanted to be king and was looking for political legitimacy. With the pope's backing, the old king was deposed and Pepin was elected. In exchange, Pepin not only defended Rome against the Lombards, he also presented the pope with the papal states in 773. His son Charlemagne was later crowned by Pope Leo III at St. Peter's in the year 800.

For the next eleven hundred years the popes struggled through diplomacy and war to keep or regain the papal states. The names and nationalities of the players constantly changed, but the geopolitics remained constant. Since the papal states were in the middle of Italy, the popes did not want the same power controlling northern and southern Italy. When one giant became all-powerful in Italy, the papacy suffered.

Why were the papal states so important to the papacy? The popes realized that the good will of monarchs was a very weak foundation for the freedom of the papacy. Time and time again kings, nobles, or mobs threatened or attacked popes. Whoever controlled the police and military in Rome could control the papacy. Without constitutional government and the rule of law, the only way to stay free was to have your own army. The papal states, therefore, were a necessary foundation for papal independence and church freedom.

The papal states also provided revenues for the papacy. No institution can operate without money, and land was the primary source of revenues during the medieval period. Without an independent source of revenues, the popes would have to go hat in hand to kings and thus lose their independence.

The wealth and political power of the papacy ultimately proved to be a two-edged sword. Although it did provide revenues for the church and some independence in a time of absolute monarchs, it also attracted ambitious and corrupt clerics and laypersons who bought and sold favors and severely damaged the church. For these individuals the power and riches of the papal states became an end in themselves and not a means to preserve the independence of the church. Clerical ambition and corruption led to numerous fights over who would be pope, and this divided the church. Ultimately this corruption contributed to the Reformation and the fracturing of church unity, which still exists today.

The fall of the papal states in 1870 during the unification of Italy proved to be an unanticipated blessing for the papacy and the church. At that time the papal states consisted of 16,000 square miles of Italy (larger than the combined areas of Massachusetts, Connecticut, and Rhode Island). After their fall, Pius IX told the French ambassador, "All that I want is a small corner of earth where I am master. This is not to say that I would refuse my states if they were offered to me, but so long as I do not have this little corner of earth, I shall not be able to exercise my spiritual functions in their fullness."[14]

Although Pius IX would have accepted a return of the papal states, no modern pope would want the headache or the distraction of governing a large chunk of Italy. In 1929, Pius XI turned down additional extraterritorial land during the negotiations that led to the normalization of relations between the Vatican and Italy in the Lateran Treaty. He wanted only enough to guarantee his independence. In addition to the 108.7 acres that make up Vatican City, there are buildings in Rome that enjoy extraterritoriality by agreement with Italy. These include the major basilicas (St. John Lateran, St. Paul's Outside the Walls, St. Mary Major), Vatican office buildings outside Vatican City, the Jesuit curia, and the Lateran Palace.

The Vatican has few citizens or residents. Citizenship is normally given on a temporary basis to persons performing a particular function for the Holy See. In 1994 there were only 474 citizens, about half of whom were in the Vatican diplomatic service. Another 101 were members of the Swiss Guard (who lose Vatican citizenship when they return to Switzerland), and around 47 were cardinals working or retired in the Vatican. The remaining citizens are almost equally divided between clerics and laity working in the Vatican.[15] Few people actually reside in Vatican City, although this number will increase with the completion of Santa Martha, a 131-room residence in the Vatican for employees and visitors. The residents and citizens pay no taxes except for a few small user fees.

Under international law, Vatican City could have a navy and an air force, but has neither, only a small heliport. The Swiss Guard, which is responsible for protecting the pope, is the closest thing the Vatican has to an army. In 1970 Paul VI unilaterally disarmed and abolished the Noble Guard, the Palatine Guard, and the Pontifical Gendarmes, whose functions had become mostly ceremonial.

The Secretariat of State conducts the foreign relations of Vatican City, but foreign ambassadors are accredited not to Vatican City but to the Holy See. Thus even if the pope lost Vatican City as a sovereign state, as head of the Catholic church he could still exchange diplomatic representatives with countries. While the international agenda of the Holy See deals with many nations on issues of justice, peace, and human rights, the Vatican City's agenda is primarily with Italy on such prosaic issues as the price of water and electricity.

The Vatican has its own laws, but as a matter of convenience it normally follows Italian legal practices (for example, for inheritance and contracts) unless for some special reason it deviates from Italian law. It uses the Italian lira as its normal currency and has the right to mint a small number of coins that are interchangeable with lire. Like any other government, the Governatorato (governorship) of the city state collects garbage, puts out fires, and manages the state-owned buildings, stores, and museums. It has a police force, postal service, gardens, apartment buildings, offices, and a railroad station. It has more employees than citizens and is one of the few governments on earth that makes a profit. The budget of the Governatorato is about $130 million a year, which is separate from the budget of the Holy See and that of the diocese of Rome.

The pope delegates the governance of Vatican City to the Pontifical Commission for the Vatican City State, which is made up of five cardinals headed by Cardinal Rosalio José Castillo Lara. The commission meets a few times a year to establish administrative and financial policies for the city, but the real power lies with the Venezuelan president, Cardinal Castillo.[16] "The president is just like a prime minister," explains Cardinal Castillo. "In the name of the Holy Father, he has to rule."

The cardinal has been a very active and hard-working president, although until 1995 he also had two other full-time jobs as head of the Vatican Bank and head of the finance office of the Roman curia (the Administration of the Patrimony of the Apostolic See, or APSA). In 1995 the pope turned APSA over to another prelate. The pope is not interested in the administrative details of civil government and trusts the cardinal, who meets with him every month or two. According to the cardinal, he brings to the pope "only important things for great decisions" like the building of a $20-million residence for clerical visitors and employees in the Vatican. This building was unsuccessfully opposed by the Vatican's Roman neighbors, who feared it would block their view of St. Peter's.

Under the president is the special delegate who, like a city manager, deals with the day-to-day affairs of Vatican City. The current delegate is a layman,

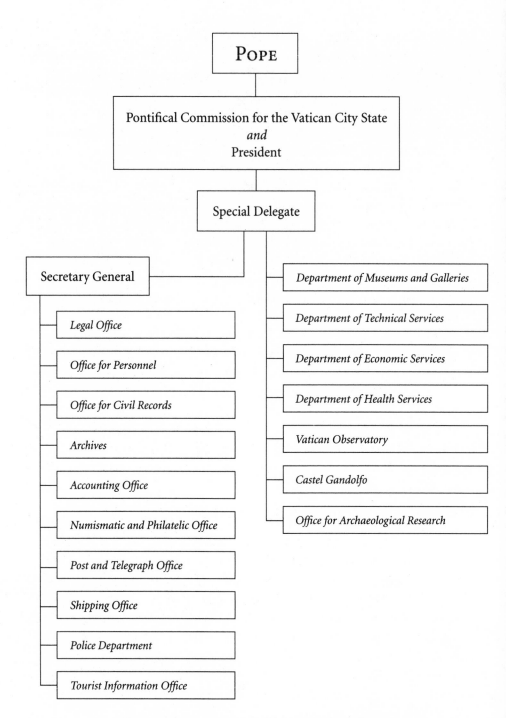

ORGANIZATION OF THE VATICAN CITY STATE

Marquis Giulio Sacchetti, a descendant of a Roman noble family long associated with the papacy. Most of the other officials and the 1,300 employees in the Governatorato are also lay and Italian. Only about 70 are priests or religious. Every day the president meets with the delegate, the general secretary, and the vice secretary "to decide or to approve the main things that come up," explains Cardinal Castillo. He also meets every two weeks with the heads of the major departments and offices in a council of administration. There is also a committee of consultors, practically all lay experts from outside the Vatican, to advise the president.

Under the delegate are the secretary general and four major departments: museums and galleries, technical services, economic services, and health services. Also under the delegate are the Vatican observatory, the papal villa at Castel Gandolfo, and an office for archaeological research. The secretary general, Msgr. Giorgio Corbellini, oversees about 180 people working in offices dealing with personnel, legal affairs, accounting, records and archives, shipping, tourists, mail, and commemorative stamps and coins.

Most Americans and Germans think Vatican City is inefficiently run, but in comparison with Italian bureaucracies it operates fairly well and its profits help finance the Roman curia. The Vatican museums, with 250 employees, are better maintained and have more visitors than most Italian museums. These museums are world renowned, with more than two million visitors coming every year to view an extensive and exquisite collection of paintings, statues, and artifacts. Likewise, the Vatican post office is very efficient: it handles not only official mail coming in and out of the Vatican, but also letters, postcards, and packages mailed by thousands of tourists and Romans. About 20 million pieces of mail leave the Vatican each year. Its postal rates are the same as those in Italy, but residents of Rome trust its services more than the Italian mail when sending a letter outside Italy. Vatican international mail is flown to Switzerland, where it is sorted and then sent around the world.

The Governatorato also has a technical services department with 380 employees including carpenters, electricians, plumbers, gardeners, cleaners, mechanics, and other technicians necessary to maintain the equipment, buildings, streets, and grounds at the Vatican and at the extraterritorial properties of the Holy See. Maintenance is a difficult and expensive project, given the age of the buildings and their historical and artistic value that cannot be compromised. This department also maintains the telephones, water pipes, and the electrical system. The water and power are purchased from Italy and the phone system is connected to the Italian system. The Vatican telephone system was computerized in 1992 and handles 12 million phone calls going in and out of the city each year. The switchboard operators handle 2,000 calls a day in several languages.

Also part of the technical services department is the "Floreria," which is responsible for the physical preparation of papal events in the Vatican. It sets up chairs and platforms for audiences and liturgies in St. Peter's Basilica and St. Peter's Square, as well as for private audiences in the palace. The Floreria also provides furniture from its stores for Vatican offices and cardinals' residences.

The department of economic services of the Governatorato, with 129 employees, runs the most popular services of the Vatican: a supermarket, a gasoline station, a clothing store, and an electronics store. These facilities are open only to Vatican employees and religious houses in Rome, but "everyone in Rome seems to have a friend who will purchase things for them in the Vatican," reports a Vatican employee. Although the prices are often significantly lower than prices in Rome, these services make a profit for the Vatican because the sales are not subject to Italian tariffs or taxes. Thus highly taxed items like gasoline, liquor, and tobacco are much cheaper in the Vatican but are also big money makers. The American Cardinal Edmund Szoka has argued that the sale of cigarettes by the Vatican is wrong, but he is still a voice crying in the wilderness since the Vatican is in the middle of Italy, where heavy smoking is still common.[17]

The Vatican has a 100-member department of health services that provides comprehensive health care for all Vatican employees and a pharmacy where medicines, including some not available in Italy, can be purchased. Vatican medical personnel provide first aid for medical emergencies involving tourists and visitors. Vatican public health inspectors also check the water, restaurants, and other areas of the Vatican.

Also in the Governatorato is the Vatican fire department, consisting of about a dozen men, 500 hydrants, but no fire engine (the streets are too narrow). The fire department is rather recent by Vatican standards, going back to only 1941 when Pius XII feared bomb damage during the war. Only one bomb fragment actually landed inside Vatican City. Fires are rare in the Vatican, where so much is built of stone and marble, but because of the extensive collections of artwork, books, and archives, a fire would be catastrophic. The firemen depend on smoke detectors and constant vigilance. In case of need, the Roman fire department will come to their assistance. Like firemen everywhere, the Vatican firemen also rescue kittens, not from trees, but from the top of the colonnade surrounding St. Peter's Square.[18]

The *corpo di vigilanza* is a 120-person police force under the Governatorato that provides security to the Vatican. It is separate from the Swiss Guard, which is responsible for the protection of the pope and attached to the Papal Household. There is little violent crime inside the Vatican these days, although in 1986 an attempted armed robbery did occur in the cashier's office. An employee scared off the robbers by setting off the alarm. A more serious problem is theft by insiders. In 1994 four ancient Greek vases worth millions of dollars were stolen from the Vatican museum. They were taken from a locked display case in a section of the museum closed to the public. Three were later recovered. Even the papal palace is not immune from theft: some commemorative coins and jewel-studded gold pectoral crosses were stolen in the time of Paul VI. One Vatican employee involved in planning the caper was not fired for his crime but instead was banished to Vatican Radio's transmission facility outside Rome.

Pickpockets in St. Peter's Square are a more common problem. Under the Lateran Treaty, the Vatican normally allows Italian authorities to exercise police power in St. Peter's Square. The treaty also provides that, at the request of the Vatican, Italy will punish crimes that are committed in Vatican City. The Vatican jail consists of one small room normally used for storage. Vatican officials do not want the bother or the expense of dealing with criminals. The worst crime in recent memory was, of course, the attempted assassination of John Paul II in St. Peter's Square in 1981. Although the crime was committed in Vatican City, the Italian police apprehended the assassin, who was tried and punished in Italy. Under the Lateran Treaty an attack on the pope is punishable by the same penalties as an attack on the president of Italy.[19]

A month after the assassination attempt, Vatican security guards conducted a silent protest by refusing to carry their 7.65-caliber Beretta pistols; they were demanding better training and equipment to protect the pope. Although Vatican officials are naturally reluctant to discuss security, the attempt on John Paul's life has increased security measures in the Vatican. Just outside the Vatican are heavily armed Italian police. Metal detectors are used to screen visitors to the pope's Wednesday general audience. Some closed-circuit television cameras have also been installed. Most areas of the Vatican are restricted to residents and employees. Anyone needing to visit an office in the Vatican must get a special pass that the gate keepers do not issue without first calling to make sure the visitor is expected.

Vatican City is both an asset and a headache to popes. It provides a politically independent base for the papacy and a historically majestic platform for public events. However, it is an inefficient workplace that serves better as a museum than as the headquarters of the largest multinational organization in the world. It projects an image of mystery and tradition, but also the image of a wealthy and archaic institution that belongs in another century. This is further accentuated by the costumes and dress of those who work in the Vatican.

Modern popes have not been interested in governing Vatican City but have delegated the responsibility to others so that they could devote their attention to the church. Nevertheless, problems in Vatican City periodically arise that require the pope's attention—whether this involves restoring the frescoes in the Sistine Chapel, constructing buildings, or dealing with employee unrest. While no pope is likely to abandon Vatican City, modern popes would prefer not to worry about such matters as maintaining buildings and dealing with labor problems.

Head of the College of Bishops

Although Vatican City provides the pope with an independent state to operate from, the reason he is pope derives not from Vatican City but from the fact that as bishop of Rome he is the successor of St. Peter as head of the college of bishops. This role is a unique one, without any secular or religious counterparts, and it is not easily understood either inside or outside the Catholic church. The most common mistake is to see the pope as the chief executive from whom the bishops receive their authority, just as regional managers would in a secular corporation. In this view a diocese is like a Burger King franchise: the pope sets policy and gives the orders, and the bishops follow them. At the other extreme, the pope is seen as simply the first among equals who presides over meetings of the college of bishops. Both extremes were rejected at Vatican II. The council stressed the role of the local bishop in his diocese, where he is the vicar of Christ for his people, while at the same time affirming the pope's universal jurisdiction.

Vatican II also taught that the bishops are responsible not simply for their dioceses, but that as a college they have a role in the governance of the universal church. On the other hand, the council stressed that the pope is the head of the college of bishops, which cannot act without his approval. Thus it tried to find a middle ground by stressing both collegiality and papal primacy. Collegiality is important, but the pope has the last word and can often act on his own.

This theological balancing act is easier in theory than in practice, and since Vatican II, the Catholic church has been attempting to come to terms with it. The actual working out of the relationship of the pope to the college of bishops is very important to the life of the church. Extreme decentralization could cause a fracturing of the church if individual bishops went their own way without concern for church unity. The ability of the pope to intervene directly in local disputes in an emergency has sometimes resolved problems that were tearing the church apart at the local level. On the other hand, overcentralization stifles local creativity, making it impossible for bishops to respond to the needs of local churches. Papal interference in local affairs can itself cause division. Ecumenical efforts will also fail if Protestant and Orthodox churches feel that any reunion with the Catholic church will mean the loss of their autonomy to a papal power center.

The role of the college of bishops in the governance of the universal church is extremely important if decisions made at the highest level are to be responsive to the reality of the local churches. The bishops have a responsibility for the entire church, not just their local churches. History shows that depending on one man to look out for the good of the church, without any checks and balances, is a risky business. On the other hand, public disagreements between the bishops and the pope can cause confusion and disorder in the church, and a divided church has a more difficult time surviving in a hostile environment.

Maintaining Christian unity has never been easy in the church, but it is an essential responsibility of the pope and the college of bishops. From the very beginning, disagreements over how to interpret and live the message of Jesus have threatened Christian unity. Local communities could be divided internally or could be at odds with neighboring communities over what is an orthodox interpretation and what is heresy.

The very first dispute in the Christian community involved the treatment of Gentiles. All the original disciples of Jesus were Jews. Paul wanted to make disciples of the Gentiles but did not want to force Gentile Christians to be circumcised and follow the Jewish dietary laws. James of Jerusalem was not happy about including Gentiles in the Christian community, which was then still seen as part of the wider Jewish community. If Gentiles were admitted, they would have to observe all the Jewish laws. Peter played a pivotal role in this dispute. He was not as innovative as Paul nor as austere as James, but everyone respected and liked him. At first hesitant about welcoming the Gentiles, he finally backed the position of Paul and brought the rest of the community with him. At the council of Jerusalem, James and Paul agreed to a compromise. The Gentiles must observe the part of the Levitical code that applied to resident aliens in Israel: they must refrain from illicit marriages and from the eating of blood or animals sacrificed to idols. Peter played a pivotal role in maintaining the unity of the church by getting the two sides to compromise.

In later disputes, when bishops or local communities were divided, people liked to have the church of Rome, the church of Peter and Paul, on their side. Popes as early as St. Clement at the end of the first century would write letters to other communities encouraging certain beliefs and practices while discouraging others. Early popes could not demand obedience, but they could influence debates within the church and the college of bishops. As time went on, Rome became a court of appeals to deal with disputes in local communities and disputes between bishops. Heretics were condemned, and a tradition of church teaching developed. When the papacy failed in its role of fostering unity as a result of either corruption or authoritarianism, church unity often broke down. Reform of the papacy came too late to prevent the Protestant Reformation in the sixteenth century.

In the early church, the local communities were still highly autonomous, electing their own bishops and following their own customs. A practice developed of notifying Rome when a new bishop was elected because these local communities wanted to be in communion with the church of Rome. This later grew into the need for Roman approval of episcopal selections and then Roman appointment of bishops. Unity was also fostered through mandating uniform practices in liturgy, church law, and seminary training. Doctrinal unity was encouraged through papal teaching and through suppression of dissent.

These practices have continued into the twentieth century, when the Vatican has suppressed theologians who are out of step with the papacy, first during the Modernist period (around 1907) and even more so today. Theologians who disagree with the pope on birth control, married clergy, and women priests have been removed from teaching positions in seminaries and Catholic faculties. John Paul II has also appointed bishops who agree with him on these issues even over the objections of local churches. Whether such actions will unify the church or further divide it remains to be seen.

On the other hand, beginning with John XXIII, popes have been active in attempting to heal the breach between Catholics and Christians of other churches. At no time since the Reformation have Protestants and Catholics been on better terms with each other. Although many believe that the ecumenical movement is now stalled, it could not have made the tremendous progress it has without papal support.

The papacy has also played a critical role in gaining independence for the church from civil authorities. From the very beginning Christians have been in conflict with government leaders. Jesus was executed by the Roman governor in Jerusalem. His early disciples were persecuted by Roman authorities, who used emperor worship as a unifying ideology within the empire. Persecution ended with Emperor Constantine in 313, but instead of exchanging state persecution for freedom, what the church got was state interference. After Christianity became the official religion, emperors and kings competed with church leaders for control of the church, its personnel, its beliefs, and its property. The papacy became central in the struggle over whether civil leaders or church leaders would control the church.

Constantine immediately began interfering in the operation of the church because he wanted to use Christianity as the spiritual basis of his empire. It was therefore politically important that the church be united. He summoned the first ecumenical council at Nicea (325) to foster church unity on doctrine and governance. "In Constantine's view, the security of the empire and the unity of the Church were inseparably linked," writes the historian Odilio Engels.[20] Constantine considered himself, not the pope, to be the leading figure in the church.

Sometimes imperial interference came at the request of the Christians themselves. When disputes arose in local Christian communities, one of the parties would often appeal to the civil authorities. For example, when two bishops claimed the see of Carthage, one appealed to Constantine, who appointed the pope and three bishops from Gaul to examine the case. This committee was not meant to decide the case but to make a recommendation to the emperor. The pope transformed the committee into a church synod headed by himself, with fifteen Italian bishops. The synod backed one of the candidates and excommunicated the other. The loser again appealed to Constantine. Constantine did not consider the pope's decision final, but called a council to resolve the issue.

Later emperors continued to interfere in church life both in Rome and around the empire. Sometimes the emperors had theological views they wanted imposed out of conviction, as when Empress Theodora used her money and influence to make Vigilius pope in 537 after he promised to reject the council of Chalcedon (451). At other times the civil authorities simply wanted to force the Christian factions to stop squabbling so that there would be peace and unity in the empire. But as the Byzantine emperors lost control over the pope, they encouraged and sometimes forced the patriarchs of Constantinople to be independent of Rome. The resulting divisions are still with us today.

In the West, kings and emperors attempted to run the church, and papal influence waxed and waned depending on the international political climate and the degree to which political leaders needed papal support. During this period, the papacy swung between periods of corruption and reform. Despite periods when corrupt people led the papacy, many Catholic reformers saw increasing the power of the papacy as a way of liberating the local church from political control and corruption. The pope was more likely than the king to put the spiritual interests of the church ahead of political concerns of the state. In fights between the local clergy and the nobility, the pope usually sided with the clergy while the king sided with the nobility. It was also likely that a bishop would have more independence under a distant pope than under a local king. Protestant reformers, on the other hand, stressed local church autonomy in response to papal corruption and centralization. This approach led to more church divisions as the Protestant community continued to splinter without a Petrine figure to foster unity.

The fall of the European monarchies, the expropriation of church property, and the fall of the papal states combined to establish a new external environment for the church. Although at first suspicious of church links to the old monarchies, democratic states eventually granted the church more autonomy over its internal affairs than the church had had under Catholic monarchs. This increased freedom went hand in hand with increased authority for the papacy, especially in the appointment of bishops, because papal diplomats often negotiated the church-state agreements.

It is somewhat ironic that the papacy became stronger within the church as Europe became more secular. Without Catholic kings to oppose it, the papacy's power and influence in the European and the Latin American church continued to grow through the nineteenth and twentieth centuries. It also grew stronger in mission territories with the decline of the colonial powers. The persecution of Christians by Fascists and Communists also increased the papacy's influence as Catholics saw the need for unity in the face of these enemies. John Paul successfully used the papacy to help liberate the church in Eastern Europe. The pope continues to work for a freer church in China, Cuba, and Vietnam. He also defends the rights of Catholic minorities in other Third World countries, especially where Muslim regimes deny religious freedom to the church. These papal efforts have made many local churches grateful for a friendly voice in Rome and supportive of a strong papacy.

While the role of the pope as a civil governor has declined, his role as bishop of Rome and head of the college of bishops has been strengthened. At the same time, there have been strong voices in the theological community arguing against the centralizing trend in the church. These voices gained some prominence at Vatican II, which was the best example of collegiality in action during this century. The council itself urged the use of collegial structures, such as episcopal conferences and the synod of bishops, which have grown in influence since Vatican II. Collegial structures for governance in the church have a long and complex history that cannot be ignored when looking at the papacy.

~ 2

The College of Bishops

DESPITE THE GROWING centralization of authority in the papacy over the centuries, there have been countervailing forces in the church that represent a more collegial form of government. Among these have been regional and national interests as expressed through collegial groupings of local bishops. In the past these bishops gathered in provincial and national councils, whereas today they are more likely to meet as episcopal conferences.

From the earliest days of Christianity, individual bishops have wanted to exercise their authority in union with neighboring bishops. As early as the second century in Asia Minor and Italy, bishops met in councils or synods (originally the terms were synonymous) in the nearest major city (metropolis).[1] The Council of Nicea (325) organized the church geographically into dioceses and provinces that matched imperial boundaries and ordered bishops to meet on a province level twice a year. As Brian Daley noted, "Meetings were so frequent that the pagan historian Ammianus Marcellinus wryly observed that the public transportation system, during the reign of Constantius II (337–361), was paralyzed by Christian bishops traveling to and from their synods at the imperial expense."[2]

Provincial councils modeled themselves on the rules of procedure of the Roman Senate, with the presiding bishop (metropolitan) in the role of the emperor. The councils decided both doctrinal and disciplinary issues.[3] They met to deal cooperatively with all the problems that confronted them, whether these involved lapsed Christians, heretics, wayward clerics, or disagreements over doctrine. Provincial councils elected bishops, consecrated them, and acted as courts of appeals for those excommunicated by a local bishop. Representatives from the provincial councils also met on a regional level.

In the time of Leo the Great (440–461), the competence of these councils was restricted not so much by subject matter as by their ability to reach consensus. If a provincial council could not reach agreement, the matter went to a regional council. When consensus was lacking there, the matter could go to Rome or an ecumenical council.

Secular leaders, kings or emperors, often called the regional or national councils and determined who could attend. The ruler set the agenda, and the council's conclusions, if approved by the king, were enforced by the civil authorities. In Germany, the ruler was even referred to as the vicar of Christ and the teacher of bishops.[4] Decisions of foreign councils could be rejected. Charlemagne, for example, refused to recognize the Second Council of Nicea (787).

By the eleventh century, popes were successfully claiming the right to convoke local and national synods, to appoint legates to preside over them, and to review their actions. This was a challenge to the civil ruler's control over these councils as well as local episcopal autonomy. With the rise of papal influence and the increasing role of ecumenical or worldwide councils, regional councils became less frequent and less important. Although the Council of Trent (1563) continued to mandate the calling of provincial councils every three years, Sixtus V (1585–1590) required local and national councils to send their decrees to Rome for approval before they could be promulgated. Despite the requirement, few provincial councils were called. The 1917 Code of Canon Law reduced the requirement to once every twenty years, restricted the councils' authority, and made their calling cumbersome.[5]

Episcopal Conferences

The rise of nation states and the separation of church and state in nineteenth-century Europe led to the need for mechanisms by which the bishops of a country could deal with their governments on a variety of issues. Bishops began meeting on a regular basis to develop plans and to form a united front in dealing with their governments. By calling these gatherings conferences rather than councils, the bishops bypassed the restrictions imposed by canon law. Historians note that a very broad range of concerns marked these regional and national meetings, as the conferences attempted to deal with the century's rapid social, economic, political, and cultural changes.[6] For the most part, these conferences (unlike councils) dealt with public policy issues and had no authority over church issues. The independence of the local bishop and the authority of Rome were not to be challenged.

The Second Vatican Council (1962–1965) made episcopal conferences not only possible but absolutely necessary. The council called for reform, but the church had to find systems to manage change in a way that avoided chaos. For example, after the council, liturgies were put in the vernacular. The pope and the Roman curia could not do translations for every language in the world; it was simply too much for them to handle and they did not have the expertise. On the other hand, if each bishop did a translation for his diocese, there would be more than 150 English translations of the Mass in the United States alone. Some mechanism between these two extremes had to be found that could deal with church issues on a national scale.

Many council fathers had had positive experiences with episcopal conferences, and the bishops decided that conferences could be a useful vehicle for implementing the council reforms and dealing with other church issues. The theological status and teaching authority of episcopal conferences were debated, but their practical necessity was recognized by all.[7]

Without deciding the theological issues, the Second Vatican Council encouraged episcopal conferences and described them as "an assembly in which the bishops of a given nation or territory jointly exercise their pastoral office by way of promoting the greater good which the church offers mankind." Using canonical language, the council allowed for limited juridical authority for episcopal conferences: "Decisions of the episcopal conference, provided they have been made lawfully and by the choice of at least two-thirds of the prelates who have deliberative vote in the conference, and have been reviewed by the Apostolic See, are to have juridically binding force in those cases and in those only which are prescribed by common law or determined by special mandate of the Apostolic See, given spontaneously or in response to a petition from the conference itself."[8] Which specific responsibilities would be given to conferences by common law and special mandates was to be determined by practice and by the revised Code of Canon Law after the council.

When discussing the code, it is important to note that bishops are not "given" authority or power by the code or by the pope. Bishops have their authority because they are bishops, just as priests have sacramental power because they are priests. Likewise, the conference's power is derived not from the pope but from the bishops themselves exercising episcopal authority in their particular churches. The Holy See, however, can regulate episcopal authority for the good of the universal church.[9] In practice, canon law so restricts the authority of bishops and conferences that it often looks as if they receive what little authority they have from the Holy See.

The interrelationship among episcopal conferences, the Holy See, and the diocesan bishops was an area of tension during the code revision. As the code went through a series of drafts during the revision process, the authority of the conference was gradually reduced in each draft, because of fears that the conferences would threaten the autonomy of individual bishops or jeopardize church unity by exaggerating nationalism.[10]

Under the final version of the 1983 Code of Canon Law, some actions by a conference can be legally binding. However, the Holy See must review all such decrees of a conference.[11] In theory the review is meant to make sure that the decrees are not contrary to universal church law, but in practice this "review" gives Rome an absolute veto over conference decrees. The review of decrees by Rome has delayed the promulgation of some decrees. Tension between the Vatican and bishops of various parts of the world also arises when Rome uses the reviewing process to force changes in a decree. As James Provost notes:

It [review] is designed as a safeguard to assure that decisions of particular councils [or conferences] are not contrary to general church law. It has also been used, however, for other purposes, including that of imposing on local churches a discipline which they themselves had not voted to assume, for in the "review" of the decrees changes have been made which were not the work of the council [or conference] in question but which must be promulgated with the authority of that council [or conference] since they appear in the final version of the decree.[12]

The 1983 Code of Canon Law contains about eighty-four canons that permit legislative action by episcopal conferences.[13] The cases mentioned are a combination of major and minor issues. The requirement that the Vatican review most decisions of episcopal conferences has allowed the Roman curia to keep conferences on a tight leash.

The Vatican and episcopal conferences tend to downplay their conflicts. During its thirty-year history, the National Conference of Catholic Bishops (NCCB) has been in disagreement with Rome over regulations dealing with annulments, the age of confirmation, lay preaching, altar girls, alienation of church property, the role of retired bishops in the bishops' conference, terms for pastors, inclusive language in liturgical books and *The Catechism of the Catholic Church,* granting the chalice to the laity on Sundays, and other liturgical issues.[14] The Vatican has also had problems with some of the early drafts of pastoral letters of the U.S. bishops. Nor does the Vatican like the open and consultative process used by the NCCB in drafting pastoral letters. Most of these differences were eventually worked out, but when the Vatican was adamant, the NCCB backed down. The NCCB has become even more conciliatory as John Paul II has remade it through the appointment of bishops more in keeping with his views.

Ecumenical Councils

Unlike episcopal conferences and regional councils, an ecumenical council in union with the pope is the supreme authority in the church on matters of doctrine and governance. The term "ecumenical" here means universal as opposed to regional or local. Canon law stipulates that an ecumenical council must be called by the pope; it must be presided over by him or his legate; and its decisions do not have force until approved and promulgated by the pope. Papal teaching makes clear that a council is not superior to the pope, nor can a council judge or impeach a pope. In fact, all of these precepts have been violated by councils in the course of church history.[15]

Early ecumenical councils involving bishops from all over the Roman empire were a logical extension of the idea of metropolitan and regional councils of bishops once persecution ended and more distant travel was possible. It was not until the ninth century that ecumenical councils were distinguished as such from regional synods.[16] In the East, the bishops from the Black Sea to Egypt had met in a series of synods at Antioch in the second half of the third century. These synods provided a model for the first ecumenical council in Nicea in 325, where these bishops constituted the vast majority of the participants since few Western bishops attended.

Emperor Constantine convoked the Nicene Council and presided over its sessions. The emperor was considered the representative of Christ the king. The council followed Roman senatorial procedure, which had also been used in local councils. The place of the most important senator, the *princeps senatus,* was given to the representative or legate of the bishop of Rome. The pope's legate played an increasingly important role at the councils because he often represented the views not only of the pope but of the absent Western bishops, who might have already met in a Roman synod to discuss the issues being dealt with by the council. The influence of the popes and their legates at the councils grew over time and sometimes came in conflict with the views of the emperors.

Constantine's successors continued to call councils, including the first seven ecumenical councils (from 325 to 787) accepted by both Catholic and Orthodox churches. Not every council called by an emperor attained ecumenical status, however. Sometimes the participants could not reach agreement or the whole church did not accept their decisions. According to later papal canonists, a council achieved ecumenical status only if a pope accepted its decisions.

These early councils in the East proved very important for church unity by developing consensus on Trinitarian and Christological doctrine as exemplified in the Nicene Creed, which is still acknowledged today by most Christians. Councils condemned heresies (Arianism, Nestorianism, and Monophysitism) and approved the veneration of images (an example of inculturation by Gentile Christians). They also legislated matters of church governance and discipline (such as ecclesiastical boundaries, the frequency of local synods, or the precedence given to the bishop of Constantinople).

After the division between Catholic and Orthodox Christians, the pope took over the role of the emperor at ecumenical councils in the West. He called the council, set its agenda, and approved and promulgated its decrees. This was a logical development of the synodal practice in Rome where the popes called bishops from Italy to make important decisions. Membership was expanded to include bishops from outside Italy, especially under Gregory VII (1073–1085). The popes held councils at the Lateran in 1123, 1139, and 1179 that later generations upgraded to ecumenical status. The Fourth Lateran Council (1215) was the first in the West to see itself as a successor of the earlier ecumenical councils.

The four Lateran councils, the two councils at Lyons, and another at Vienne continued to condemn heresies, define doctrine (for example, transubstantiation), and legislate for the church (they required Catholics to go to confession and Communion once a year and established rules for papal conclaves). They also dealt with political-religious affairs such as confirming the Concordat of Worms, calling a crusade, and deposing emperors. Although the papal role at these councils was dominant, Gregory VII (1073–1085) also asserted his right to act independently of a council by issuing laws for the whole church and deposing bishops. This centralizing trend continued through the Avignon Exile (1309–1377).

In the face of a corrupt and centralized papacy, reformers looked to a council to reform the church and the papacy. Although papal candidates promised to call councils, they procrastinated once they were elected. Various civil leaders (Frederick II, Philip IV of France, and Louis IV of Bavaria) also played with the idea of appealing to a general council against the real or alleged abuse of papal power. Problems reached a crisis level in 1378, with the election of a pope and an anti-pope. Those seeking unity and reform developed the theory of conciliarism, which placed a universal council above the pope.[17]

In 1409 the Council of Pisa, led by cardinals from the two camps, deposed both popes as schismatics and elected a third. Rather than uniting the church, this strategy further divided it. Gregory XII, the pope in Rome, called his own council at Cividale, but attendance was so sparse that he abandoned it. In 1414 the anti-pope John XXIII summoned the Council of Constance, which under the leadership of the German King Sigismund ultimately deposed him and the other popes. The council entered into negotiations with Gregory, who agreed to abdicate as long as he was able to first convoke the council since he could not accept one called by John XXIII. This was acceptable to the council, and in July of 1415 Gregory convoked the council and then resigned.

In its decree *Haec Sancta,* the Council of Constance affirmed the superiority of a general council over the pope. This council was acknowledged as ecumenical, but whether Martin V confirmed this decree is disputed. In any case, papal canonists never acknowledged conciliar supremacy and power to depose a legitimate pope. They argued that it was the voluntary resignation of Gregory XII that made the election of Martin V legal.

Although Constance decreed the calling of councils at fixed intervals as a counterbalance to papal absolutism, this did not happen. The next council, called by Eugene IV, met in Basel, Ferrara, Florence, and Rome (1431–1447) to work toward union with the Eastern churches, but it had difficulty operating at times because of low attendance. When the council disbanded in Basel, some attendees moved to Pisa where they elected an anti-pope in 1439. At the next council, the Fifth Lateran Council (1512–1517), papal supremacy was once again in place. One of its decrees condemned the Council of Pisa. The Council of Trent (1545–1563) condemned Protestant errors and legislated reform of the church. The reforms came too late to head off the Protestant Reformation, but they did strengthen the papacy within what was left of the Catholic church.

The defining of papal infallibility and papal primacy at Vatican I (1869–1870) led many Catholics to believe that another council would never be needed since the pope could now do whatever was necessary for the church. The calling of Vatican II (1962–1965) by John XXIII surprised almost everyone. Although it did not challenge papal primacy, it did bring again to the fore the role of the college of bishops in the governance of the church. Collegiality became an acceptable concept at Vatican II, while those disappointed by papal actions after Vatican II began to speak again of conciliarism.

The membership of ecumenical councils has varied over time. Today most theologians and canonists would argue that only bishops have a right to participate and vote in council meetings, although others (including laypersons) can be invited to attend and permitted to vote. Some theologians see the bishops attending a council as representatives of their local churches, while others see them as successors of the apostles. This has practical as well as theological implications. Under the 1917 Code of Canon Law, for example, titular bishops (bishops without sees) were not guaranteed a deliberative vote. On the other hand, the 1983 code says that all bishops have the right and duty to take part with a deliberative vote, even if they do not lead a local church.

Not every bishop must attend a council for it to be considered ecumenical. Only a small portion of the episcopacy attended the early Eastern councils. At Ephesus (431) there were only 153 bishops, while twenty years later at Chalcedon there were 600.[18] In the West, not all the bishops attended, nor were they all invited. At the Council of Vienne (1311–1312), only a limited number of bishops were invited after the king of France, Philip the Fair, had cleared their names.

The first seven ecumenical councils in the West included abbots and representatives of religious orders as well as princes and their ambassadors. From 1215 onward, the college of cardinals had a special place at the councils, even though many of them were not bishops. At the Council of Constance, delegates from the universities and princes attended and voted. Voting followed a system used in medieval universities, where each nation (Germany, France, England, Italy, and Spain) had one vote.[19] At Trent and Vatican I voting was limited to bishops and heads of religious orders. Vatican II followed a similar system, although laypersons and non-Catholics were allowed in as observers.

Before the first session of the Second Vatican Council, preparatory commissions of curial officials and outside experts were established to prepare draft documents for consideration by the council.[20] Except for the draft on liturgy, the council fathers jettisoned those documents and established working committees to prepare their own drafts. The decision of the council to ignore the advice of curial officials marked a turning point in the council. Numerous official and unofficial "periti" or experts were present to advise the bishops and help draft speeches and documents. Debates on the documents were long and exhausting since Vatican II was the largest (2,860 participants) and the most international council in the church's history. Latin was the official language of the council, but some discussions occurred in language groups and in episcopal conferences, which also suggested names for committees and other jobs.

In the assembly, the council members voted "placet" (yes), "non placet" (no), or "placet iuxta modum" (yes with reservations or amendments). The drafting committees then took the "modi" or amendments and worked with them in revising the text. Votes on individual amendments occurred rarely, unlike under Robert's Rules of Order. The drafting committee's job was to come up with a text that would be acceptable to the largest number of participants. The goal was not majority support but overwhelming consensus. As a result, texts were often the result of compromise. Issues failing to achieve consensus were often described with ambiguous language and left open for future resolution.

Many in the Roman curia saw the council as a threat to church stability and unity, especially after it rejected their direction at its initial session. Many in the council saw the Roman curia as obstructionist. These debates aside, clearly the council was able to act independently of the Roman curia. Its committees, although slow-working, were able to produce documents that have had a significant impact on the life of the church. This was possible because the council fathers had at their disposal experts who were not members of the curia. The council also had sufficient time to discuss issues, develop drafts, debate them, revise them, and ultimately come to consensus on what the council wanted to say. Four sessions over a 38-month period provided time for the council to do its work and develop consensus.

Although curial officials could not always get their way at the council, the pope was very influential and could sway uncertain votes one way or the other. Opposing sides solicited papal support, but often the pope would hold off until discussion had matured. When Paul VI did intervene, it was frequently to help expand consensus through compromises aimed at winning conservative support. In some instances, for example on discussions of the role of the papacy, Paul VI was forceful in intervening and requiring changes in texts and the inclusion of an "Explanatory Note" appended to *Lumen Gentium,* the Dogmatic Constitution on the Church. At other times Paul VI intervened to remove certain topics from the agenda, such as clerical celibacy and birth control.

Vatican II caused a revolution in church thinking and practice from the papacy to the local parish. The council touched almost every aspect of church life from liturgy to political action, from seminary education to catechetics. In the process, it implicitly admitted errors on the part of the Roman magisterium. As Avery Dulles writes:

Vatican II quietly reversed the earlier positions of the Roman magisterium on a number of important issues . . . the *Constitution on Divine*

Revelation accepted a critical approach to the Bible, thus supporting the previous initiatives of Pius XII and delivering the church once and for all from the incubus of the earlier decrees of the Biblical Commission. In the *Decree on Ecumenism,* the council cordially greeted the ecumenical movement and involved the Catholic church in the larger quest for Christian unity, thus putting an end to the hostility enshrined in Pius XII's *Mortalium animos.* In church-state relations, the *Declaration on Religious Freedom* accepted the religiously neutral state, thus reversing the previously approved view that the state should formally propose the truth of Catholicism. In the theology of secular realities, the *Pastoral Constitution on the Church in the Modern World* adopted an evolutionary view of history and a modified optimism regarding secular systems of thought, thus terminating more than a century of vehement denunciation of modern civilization.[21]

Vatican II's sixteen documents became normative for the church, and although a few reactionaries like Archbishop Marcel Lefebvre rejected some texts, the debate soon centered not on their legitimacy but on their interpretation. After the council, opposing sides in church debates would quote the council documents against each other without acknowledging that the documents had sometimes deliberately been made ambiguous to gain consensus at the council. As the council passes from living memory with the deaths of the participants, this tendency to read the documents in an ahistorical fashion is increasing.

Throughout history, collegial structures in the church have evolved and changed, and they will continue to evolve in the next millennium. Today's episcopal conferences have their historical roots in the provincial and regional councils of the past, which had much more power and responsibility than conferences do today. Giving more power to these conferences would be not a novelty but a return to ancient traditions so that they would be more like patriarchal synods.

Ancient councils adopted the secular procedures of the Roman senate. In keeping with this tradition, today's episcopal conferences and ecumenical councils might well learn from modern secular legislative bodies. This does not imply an uncritical acceptance of secular political procedures, but it would require an honest and professional analysis of collegial structures that have parallels in secular society. Comparative legislative studies, for example, have shown the importance of periodic sessions, committees, staff, and parliamentary procedures. They have also focused on the role of legislatures in controlling bureaucracies and the abuse of executive power. A system of checks and balances is important in any institution, even in the church, where the presence of human error and sin is well documented by history.

For the participants at Vatican II, the council was a Spirit-filled event that was the high point of their lives. But the council was also so exhausting and time-consuming that few saw it as a viable organ for ongoing governance of the church, especially when they had dioceses to take care of. Today, however, the increasing speed and ease of international travel make it easier for ecumenical councils to become a regular instrument of governance in the church. Holding an ecumenical council once every twenty-five years will not be too difficult in the twenty-first century. Although an ecumenical council can be expensive and cumbersome, given the large number of bishops in the church (4,100 at the end of 1994), there are ways to reduce the size of the council—for example, excluding the 732 retired bishops. Limiting council membership to diocesan bishops (bishops who head local churches) would bring the number down to 2,331 bishops. Future councils will have to have better structures for lay input, and they will need to include the full participation of all Christian churches if they are to be truly ecumenical.

There is no enthusiasm in the Roman curia for another council. Nor are the bishops calling for another council. On the other hand, Peter Hebblethwaite once predicted that John Paul II would call a council for the year 2000 since he had done everything else during his papacy. But John Paul appears to be comfortable in consulting the college of bishops outside a council setting. For example, in his 1995 encyclical *Evangelium Vitae,* he stressed that he consulted the college of bishops by mail and he repeatedly declared that the judgment he was expressing was "taught by the ordinary and universal magisterium." While the calling of a council during John Paul's papacy becomes less and less likely, the church has to be open to ecumenical councils in its future if it is to be true to its past. Having a council once every twenty-five years would allow each generation of bishops to share their experiences, reflect on the state of the church, and act collegially.

~ 3

The Synod of Bishops

THE BISHOPS WHO ATTENDED Vatican II liked the experience of having a role in the governance of the universal church and looked for ways to continue this after the council.[1] Some feared that once they went home, the Roman curia would again become dominant in the church, a fear that proved prophetic. The bishops wanted an institutionalized method for continuing their involvement in the governance of the church, and Melkite Patriarch Maximos IV suggested a synod of bishops, modeled on those of the Eastern churches, that would be "the supreme . . . executive and decision-making council of the worldwide church. All the Roman departments must be subject to this."[2] Before these discussions could mature, Paul VI issued a document creating the synod of bishops with a much more limited scope.[3] The document defined the synod's authority and structure.[4] The council followed Paul's lead and incorporated his ideas in its document *Christus Dominus.*

With elected delegates from episcopal conferences, the synod of bishops is the closest thing to an international representative institution in the Catholic church. In the absence of an ecumenical council, the synod of bishops is the institutionalized voice of the college of bishops. If the college is to speak and act on important issues facing the church and the world, it will be through the synod of bishops. As a result, the successful functioning of this institution is important to the life of the church.

Liberal Catholics hoped and conservatives feared that the synod would be a check on the authority of the Roman curia, but that has not been the case. Liberals have been disappointed with the synod as a weak instrument for expressing different views in the church. They feel that the Roman curia controls the synod and that the college of cardinals may take over its role as adviser to the pope. Vatican officials and the pope, on the other hand, have a very positive view of the synod of bishops. According to John Paul II, delegates represent their local churches at the synod, which is an instrument of collegiality "at the service of all the local churches." He says that "the synod expresses collegiality in a highly intense way, even while it does not equal that achieved by the [ecumenical] council."[5]

The role of the synod is strictly defined as advisory to the pope unless he endows it with deliberative power.[6] He calls the synod, specifies the issues to be discussed, determines its agenda, presides over its sessions either in person or through his appointed delegate, and can suspend or dissolve it. In order for any of its recommendations to take effect, he must approve them. Thus the synod can play as large or small a role in the church as the pope likes.

To understand how the synod of bishops functions in the church, it is necessary to examine the three types of synods: ordinary, extraordinary, and special.[7] The membership and operations of the synod depend on the type of synod convoked.

The "ordinary" synod is the most common, with nine having been called between 1967 and 1994. Immediately after Vatican II there was great enthusiasm for frequent meetings of the synod of bishops as a means of continuing the work of the council. At the first extraordinary synod in 1969, the bishops recommended having meetings of the ordinary synod of bishops every two years. Gradually this was extended to every four years because the bishops felt that it was impossible to prepare for and digest the work of the synods so quickly.[8] Ordinary synods take place at the Vatican, normally in October, and last about a month.

For ordinary synods, each bishops' conference elects one to four bishops, depending on the size of the conference.[9] The Union of Superiors General also elects ten religious priests, usually the superiors general of religious orders like the Jesuits, Franciscans, and Dominicans. New delegates are elected for each ordinary synod.

In the election of delegates, the conferences are encouraged to choose bishops with expertise in the topic of the upcoming synod. The National Conference of Catholic Bishops (NCCB) has often elected as one of its four representatives the chair of the conference committee most closely related to the topic of the synod. Others elected have been acknowledged experts on the topic of the synod.[10] The U.S. bishops also always elect their president, and they tend to elect cardinals, recognizing that cardinals have more influence in Rome.

The pope must ratify the elections of synod delegates.[11] In the past, the NCCB immediately announced whom it elected, but now it waits until the names have been confirmed. When the names come into the synod secretariat from all over the world, it sends them to the Secretariat of State for clearance. In a few cases the Vatican has not been happy with the theological views of some of those elected, "but this Holy Father does not take that too much into consideration," explains an official. "If the delegate is elected legitimately by the conference, then 99 percent of the time he is approved."

About fourteen patriarchs and metropolitans from the Eastern Catholic churches attend an ordinary synod as ex officio members. Since many of these prelates were originally elected by their synods, the democratic character of the synod is preserved while at the same time the traditional governance structures of the Eastern churches are respected. About thirty cardinal heads of offices of the Roman curia also attend as ex officio members. These officials bring an expertise to the synod, but they do not represent local churches because they are appointed by the pope. Since they are always available in Rome to advise the pope, their presence in the synod is not essential to its purpose as a consultative body.

Finally, the pope increases the size of the synod by 15 percent through the appointment of additional bishops or clerics as voting members. Most of the appointees are bishops, although the pope appointed the Jesuit superior general to the African synod because so many Jesuits are working in Africa and he had not been elected by the Union of Superiors General. Although critics assert the pope appoints only loyalists who will not criticize papal policies, Vatican officials say that the pope uses these appointments to make the synod more representative. "It really is a balancing act to try to get as much a representation of the church at large," explains a Vatican official. "The pope looks at all the delegates who have been elected, then he says, 'Well, there are not enough from this background or from this continent.' Or 'this voice is too much to the right and this one is too much to the left.' If he sees a particular problem, maybe this person could add a dimension that other persons could not because this person is involved in the other side. It really is a balancing act to add to the richness of the exchange." The size of the ordinary synods has been slowly growing over time. The first in 1967 had only 197 members, but by 1994 the membership had grown to 244. Except for the first synod in 1967, all the ordinary synods have had a majority of the participants from Third World countries.[12]

An "extraordinary" synod is the least common type of synod, having taken place only in 1969 and 1985. Its members include many who attend an ordinary synod: curial officials, patriarchs and metropolitans from the Eastern churches, representatives (three, not ten) from the Union of Superiors General, and papal appointees (15 percent). Also attending are the presidents of episcopal conferences rather than elected representatives from episcopal conferences. Since episcopal conferences usually elect their presidents, the democratic and representational character of the synod is maintained. An extraordinary synod is smaller (146 members in 1969 and 165 in 1985) and less representative of larger conferences than an ordinary synod. Since the total number of delegates is smaller, the pope appoints fewer under the 15 percent rule.

In theory, an extraordinary synod deals with issues that need immediate and quick attention. An extraordinary synod can be convened quickly since no elections are needed, a process that could take a year if the episcopal conferences wait for their next regular meeting to elect delegates. In fact, the ordinary synod process could have taken care of the issues dealt with at the 1969 and 1985 synods without much difficulty. And the amount of time between the convocation of the 1969 extraordinary synod and its assembling was greater than that for the 1967 ordinary synod.[13]

"Special" synods deal with issues of a particular region or nation.[14] For example, there have been special synods for Holland (1980),[15] Europe (1991),[16] Africa (1994),[17] and Lebanon (1995). Other special synods are planned for the Americas, Asia, and perhaps Oceania before the year 2000.

The special synods need not take place in Rome, but they normally do. The Lebanon synod was originally going to be held in Lebanon, but concern for security prevented the pope from going there. There was some discussion about having the African synod meet in Africa, but the council for the secretariat finally recommended meeting in Rome for logistical and political reasons (choosing one African country over another would be controversial).

The membership of a special synod is drawn from the patriarchs, bishops, and religious of the particular territory. If the synod is for a small area such as Holland and Lebanon, all the bishops can attend. For the European synod, the presidents of episcopal conferences were ex officio members, and in the election of delegates special rules gave Eastern Europe more representation than it would have under the rules for an ordinary synod. For the African synod, every country was represented. Numerous bishops attended ex officio: all the African cardinals and the presidents of the various episcopal conferences. The larger national conferences elected additional delegates.

Heads of curial offices that have responsibility for the matters to be treated at the special synod also attend. At the Dutch synod there were five cardinal prefects. The head of every major curial office attended the African synod. The pope may also appoint additional members, including bishops from outside the territory, to give the synod representation from the whole church.

Although the pope picks the topic for a synod, he seeks suggestions from the bishops. One of the last things an ordinary synod does before adjourning is to recommend possible topics for the next synod.[18] After the synod, the general secretariat writes to the episcopal conferences, the Roman curia, and the Union of Superiors General for suggestions. They are asked to send three possible topics and to rank them in order of choice. The recommendations of the synodal members, the episcopal conferences, and the Roman curia are gathered and analyzed by the general secretariat of the synod and its council, which meets in Rome two or three times a year.

Council of the Synod Secretariat

Before going home, the delegates at each ordinary synod elect twelve members to serve on the Council of the General Secretariat of the Synod of Bishops.[19] Three members of the synod are elected from each continent: Africa, Asia, Europe, and the Americas. (Australia and the Pacific islands are included in Asia, and the Americas are considered one continent by Europeans.)[20] The council members are elected by all the synod members, not just by the members from their continent.[21] Usually those elected are from different countries, but once two Brazilians were elected from the Americas and two Filipinos were elected from Asia. Someone from the United States has always been elected. Cardinal John Krol was elected to the first council in 1972, and from the year 1974 onward Cardinal Joseph Bernardin has been elected except at the 1990 synod when Cardinal James Hickey was elected.

Those elected to the council have been prominent prelates in the church, including eight archbishops who later became cardinals: Joseph Bernardin of Cincinnati, Joseph Cordeiro of Karachi, Godfried Danneels of Mechelen-Brussel, Roger Etchegaray of Marseilles, Aloisio Lorscheider of Santo Angelo, Simon Pimenta of Bombay, Eduardo Pironio of Mar del Plata, and Hyacinthe Thiandoum of Dakar. Prominent cardinals who have been elected to the council include Evaristo Arns of São Paulo, James Hickey of Washington, Basil Hume of Westminster, John Krol of Philadelphia, Carlo Martini of Milan, Jaime Sin of Manila, and Karol Wojtyla of Krakow. Cardinal Wojtyla was a member of the council from its inception until he was elected pope in 1978.

The pope appoints three additional members to get more balance on the council, according to Cardinal Jan Schotte, the general secretary:[22]

> In these elections by continent, an Oriental bishop will never be elected because they are a minority and everybody votes for the members of the conferences. So the pope always appoints an Oriental bishop to have also the input of the Oriental churches. Nobody from the Roman curia gets elected. They vote for the people who are in the territories, so the Holy Father appoints somebody from the Roman curia, because the heads of the departments are also members of the synod, to make it complete. Then he appoints somebody either to balance out a situation in a certain continent, or to bring in a certain expertise.

The Vatican official most frequently appointed to the Council of the General Secretariat is the prefect of the Congregation for the Doctrine of the Faith. John Paul has appointed Cardinal Joseph Ratzinger to every council from 1981, when he was still cardinal archbishop of Munich, to 1994. In 1994, Cardinal Eduardo Martinez Somalo, prefect of the Congregation for Institutes of Consecrated Life and Societies of Apostolic Life, was appointed to the council that followed the synod on consecrated life. Paul VI also appointed the prefect of the Congregation for the Doctrine of the Faith, Cardinal Franjo Seper, to the council in 1975, after the synod on evangelization and before the synod on catechesis. For other synods, Paul VI appointed other Vatican officials with particular expertise on the topic of the just completed synod or on the topic of the next synod.[23]

Special synods have their own pre-synodal councils whose members are appointed by the pope. For the African synod, the pope chose bishops who were elected leaders in Africa: the presidents of the regional episcopal conferences and the president of the continental conference. As a result, the members of the council kept changing during the preparatory process because of new elections. From the curia, Cardinal Jozef Tomko, prefect of the Congregation for the Evangelization of Peoples, was appointed to the council for both the African and Asian synods. For the forthcoming synod for the Americas, the pope has appointed fourteen bishops from North and South America, including the presidents of a number of bishops' conferences. He also appointed two Vatican prelates: Cardinal Bernardin Gantin, prefect of the Congregation for Bishops and president of the Pontifical Council for Latin America, and Bishop Cipriano Calderón Polo, vice president of the council.

After studying the recommendations for synod topics, the Council of the General Secretariat reports its findings to the pope and makes its recommendation. Although the pope normally chooses one of the topics proposed by the council, he can ignore all their recommendations in selecting the topic.[24] Before the 1990 synod, the council recommended spirituality, youth, or religious as possible topics. The pope, however, chose another topic: the formation of priests.[25]

Sometimes the pope modifies the topic to give it a particular direction. For example, the council recommended "Reconciliation and Renewal" as the topic for the 1983 synod, which the pope changed to "Reconciliation and Penance." The change to "penance" narrowed the focus of the synod, since "renewal" could have gone beyond the individual to include institutional reforms. The council for the African synod recommended "the church in Africa and her evangelizing mission," to which the pope added "toward the year 2000," an orientation he would give to other special synods.

Because of the need to have topics of interest to the whole church, the issues discussed at ordinary synods, although important, are of such a general nature that the discussions are often more theoretical than practical.[26] The first two ordinary synods discussed more than one topic, but this was so difficult that later synods concentrated on only one topic.

Ordinary synods have discussed the following topics:

1967: Challenges to faith; revision of the Code of Canon Law; seminaries; mixed marriages; liturgy.[27]
1971: Ministerial priesthood and justice in the world.[28]
1974: Evangelization in the modern world.[29]
1977: Catechesis in our time.[30]
1980: The Christian family.[31]
1983: Penance and reconciliation in the mission of the church.[32]
1987: The vocation and mission of the lay faithful in the church and in the world.
1990: The formation of priests in circumstances of the present day.
1994: The consecrated life and its role in the church and in the world.

As can be seen from the list of synodal topics, many were aimed at particular constituencies in the church: priests (1967, 1971, 1990), families (1980), laity (1987), and religious (1994). Others have dealt with pastoral problems and the strategies and programs to deal with them: faith (1967), justice (1971), evangelization (1974), catechesis (1977), and penance and reconciliation (1983).

The two extraordinary synods also had topics of general interest:

1969: The collegiality of the bishops with the pope; the role of episcopal conferences.[33]

1985: The twentieth anniversary of the conclusion of the Second Vatican Council.[34]

The 1969 topic of episcopal conferences was appropriate for an extraordinary synod since the presidents of the episcopal conferences attended ex officio. The presidents had special knowledge and interest in episcopal conferences and could advise the pope accordingly.

The 1985 extraordinary synod took on a different character under John Paul II when he explained its purpose as reliving the experience of Vatican II, exchanging information concerning the application of the council at the local and universal level of the church, and promoting further study of ways to incorporate Vatican II into the life of the church.[35] The emphasis was not on advising the pope but on giving the synod members an opportunity to relive the experience of the Second Vatican Council and to share experiences with one another. Whether any two-week meeting could recreate the experience of the council is doubtful, but the synod did provide a platform for the bishops to celebrate and reaffirm the council and exchange information.

Preparing for a Synod

A critical factor in determining the procedures and success of any synod is the amount of time given for preparation. The synod for Africa, for example, was convoked in January of 1989 but did not meet until April of 1994 because the African bishops insisted on a long process of local consultation. This allowed the African bishops plenty of time to follow consultative procedures even more extensive than those of an ordinary synod. Many observers thought this was the best-prepared synod yet. On the other hand, the synod for Europe, which began on November 28, 1991, was convoked in April 1990. The theme of the synod was not even set until six months before the synod met.

An extensive process of preparation has gradually been developed for ordinary synods to gather information and opinions before the start of the synod. "The synod is not an event that is limited to 30 days," explains Cardinal Schotte. "It is essential, if you want to preserve the integrity of the synod, that it not be just a meeting of bishops, but that it be a meeting of bishops coming together after they have deeply reflected together with the people on the topic, so that what they bring into the synod is really the input of the whole church, of everybody, priests, religious. If we isolate the synod into a meeting that lasts 30 days then we have totally missed the point about the nature of the synod."

Central to the preparatory process is the general secretariat of the synod of bishops and its fifteen-member council. The general secretariat sees to the preparation of the synod, the smooth functioning of the synod while it is in session, and any post-synodal work that is required. As a permanent body with archives, it also provides the institutional memory of the synod.

The key staff person is the general secretary, who has direct access to the pope on synod business and often interprets the mind of the pope to the council and synod delegates. All the general secretaries (Wladyslaw Rubin, 1967–1979; Jozef Tomko, 1979–1985; Jan Schotte, 1985–) have been promoted to the cardinalate. Rubin and Tomko were moved to other jobs after being made cardinals because the general secretary was not considered an important enough job for a cardinal. John Paul has so far kept Cardinal Schotte as general secretary, which is another indication of the importance the pope places on the synod. The secretariat has a small permanent staff (about six priests and four support staff), which is augmented by additional people when needed.

The general secretariat does the staff work, but the Council of the General Secretariat of the Synod makes the decisions subject to the approval of the pope. The council also makes suggestions for improving synodal procedures. For example, in 1975 it concluded that because of the increasing number of bishops not fluent in Latin, simultaneous translation was clearly necessary. The council meets two or three times a year, generally for three or four days. The meetings, chaired by the general secretary, usually begin with presentations made by the general secretary or experts selected by him. The presentations are followed by a round-table discussion. Cardinal Schotte explains how it works: "I suggest one or two or four alternatives that we can do, but then the council can talk about it and discover a fifth or sixth possibility, or takes one of the ones that I have suggested. It is all very flexible, very open, and very collegial."

The council often finds it helpful to break into language groups (usually French and English even though the documents are often in Italian) for discussions. Then they come back to the plenary session to share the results of the small group meetings. Rarely would there be a vote in these sessions. Rather, the council members discuss a topic and then the person who wrote the text takes notes and says, "OK, I know what you mean. I will write it up." Or the council gives instructions to the general secretary to implement its decisions.

After the pope chooses the synod topic, the general secretariat consults experts who help the council draw up a "lineamenta," a preliminary document outlining topics to be treated at the meeting.[36] The purpose of this background paper is to stimulate discussion and generate responses from the bishops' conferences. Often the experts are from Roman universities, but sometimes they are experts or bishops from outside Rome. Before the lineamenta is sent to the conferences, the Council of the General Secretariat reviews it, modifies it, and submits it to the pope for his approval.

For the African synod, the African council members drafted the preparatory documents. As one Vatican official reports, the African council members "knew the situation more than anybody. For that reason the secretary general bent over backwards to try to get them more involved in things as bishops. So they did major portions. There were times when two bishops would come up here from Africa so that they could compare texts and come up with a completed document. They did a lot of work. The Africans really worked for this synod."

The lineamenta for an ordinary synod is translated into seven languages (English, French, German, Italian, Spanish, Portuguese, and Latin) and sent to episcopal conferences, the Roman curia, and the Union of Superiors General for official comment. Other groups might be asked for official comments depending on the topic of the synod. For example, the superiors general of women's communities were asked to comment on the lineamenta for the synod on consecrated life.

The lineamenta normally includes a description of the issues together with a series of questions aimed at stimulating responses from episcopal conferences, although individual bishops and others can also respond. Bishops can consult with experts and the wider community. Depending on the topic and the time available, a bishop might get reactions to the lineamenta from his priests' council, pastoral council, religious educators, seminary professors, theologians, canon lawyers, or other experts. The lineamenta also generates discussion in the Catholic press and in theological journals.

The lineamenta provides the first public indication of the direction the synod might take. Liberal critics have often seen it as a curial document aimed at directing and controlling discussion in the synod, but recent lineamenta have usually come from the council and the general secretariat. The secretariat staff frequently make the point that the synod, the council, and the secretariat are not part of the Roman curia. They also insist that the purpose of the lineamenta is to stimulate discussion and suggestions and not to set the agenda of the synod.

The curia does, however, provide input into the preparatory process by submitting information and suggestions to the council. Members of the council from the curia are also an important channel of information to and from the curia on the preparation process. The contribution from the curia varies depending on the topic of the synod. For the African synod, the Congregation for the Evangelization of Peoples was involved through its prefect, Cardinal Tomko, who was on the council, but the congregation's staff was not very involved. For the synod for Lebanon, the Congregation for the Oriental Churches was very much involved both through its prefect, Cardinal Achille Silvestrini, who was a member of the council, and through its staff. On the other hand, for the synod on consecrated life, Cardinal Martinez Somalo, prefect of the Congregation for Institutes of Consecrated Life, was not a member of the preparatory council but was a member of the follow-up council.

"The one [from the curia] who is always involved is Cardinal Ratzinger [prefect of the Congregation for the Doctrine of the Faith] because of the doctrinal elements that have to be treated," according to one official. Cardinal Ratzinger has input as a member of the Council of the General Secretariat and through his direct access to the pope, with whom he meets almost every week. When asked by journalists about the upcoming 1985 extraordinary synod, John Paul replied, "Oh, I leave that sort of thing to Cardinal Ratzinger."[37] This response indicates that when it comes to ideas and topics for the synod, Cardinal Ratzinger plays a key role, perhaps even overshadowing the general secretary and his council.

Another contribution from the curia is the holding of pre-synodal symposiums on the topic of the synod. The Council for the Laity first did this by bringing together lay leaders from around the world for a symposium before the 1987 synod on the laity. Prior to the 1991 European synod, the Council for Culture held a similar symposium to which it invited Christian cultural leaders from Western and Eastern Europe. Because of the limited time given to preparing for the European synod, this symposium proved an important source of ideas and experts.

The responses to the lineamenta sent to the general secretariat of the synod from around the world are voluminous and in many different languages.[38] The most important responses come from episcopal conferences, but others come from the Roman curia, religious communities, and individual bishops.

The percentage of episcopal conferences responding varies with every synod: 75 percent in 1974, 67 percent in 1977, 50 percent in 1980, 43 percent in 1983, 54 percent in 1987, 64 percent in 1990, and 65 percent in 1994.[39] The episcopal conferences respond in a variety of ways to the lineamenta, according to Cardinal Schotte:

> Some of the answers that are sent in the name of the conference are done by the conference itself, where the bishops have discussed in plenary assembly the text that they are sending in, have voted upon it, amended it. Others are done by the president of the conference, without consulting the others, because he says, "I know how they think. They have elected me so they must trust me." Still others set up a committee of experts, so the answer is not the answer of all the bishops but of a committee of experts of the bishops' conference, and that is totally different.

Episcopal conferences are usually given only six to nine months to respond to the lineamenta, which critics say is too short a time for a serious response. Having synods every four years, rather than every three, would provide more time for responses if Rome distributed the lineamenta earlier. For the 1994 synod, the bishops had a full year to respond. A shorter period is difficult for episcopal conferences that normally meet only once or twice a year and have other agenda at their meetings. It would take many months for bishops to consult in their dioceses and then work through their conference committees to develop a conference response that would be discussed and voted on in a conference assembly. This is especially true of a large conference like the U.S. conference. As a result, the NCCB often sends responses from its relevant committees rather than from the full assembly.

The responses from episcopal conferences are supposed to be secret, but friendly bishops sometimes leak them to journalists. Critics charge that the responses are kept secret so that Rome can ignore those recommendations that it does not like. Ideally, Rome should allow each conference to decide whether its response becomes public. Making the responses public would allow the whole church to participate in the discussions and help delegates prepare for the synod by seeing what other conferences have said.

The general secretariat staff divides the responses into two groups: the official responses and unofficial observations. The official responses are those from episcopal conferences, the Roman curia, the Union of Superiors General, and others who were asked for an official response. The unofficial observations are those from individual bishops or anyone else who sends in comments. The staff organizes and analyzes the responses and prepares an "instrumentum laboris" or working paper for the synod. The secretariat takes on additional staff, including professors and graduate students from Roman universities, to help sift through the material.

This is not an easy task nor a neutral process. John G. Johnson, a canon lawyer who has studied the workings of the synod, writes: "Episcopal conferences can supply the secretariat with reams of information in their reports. Winnowing out the chaff (repetitions, observations not germane to the issue, and the like) from the grain (important questions raised by one or another of the particular churches) so as to prepare a modest working paper is difficult; it is always possible for someone to eliminate worthwhile suggestions because they conflict with one's own presuppositions."[40] In this process of winnowing, the staff would be especially reluctant to push forward recommendations that they know the pope or important Vatican officials oppose. But, as a Vatican official reports, "all the responses, all the observations are made available to the council members so they can pick and choose what they want. The member might say, 'I would like to see the responses from my continent.' He can take anything he wants and look it over, and then he is better prepared to concentrate on the text that is before him."

To come up with ideas for the instrumentum laboris, the council meets for more consultation. "I usually split up the council into three language groups so that they can discuss more deeply," reports Cardinal Schotte. "Each group returns with a set of observations and proposals that in general assembly we work on together and produce something. In drafting the working papers, we work with some experts in our office, but it is the council who reviews the drafts, makes suggestions, and decides what to change. Then the final draft goes to the Holy Father for approval, but the major work is done with the collaboration of the members of the council."

The instrumentum laboris or working paper is not a draft of the final synod document but a further attempt to focus the discussion of the synod topic. It is sent to the synod delegates and made public, and thus it generates additional discussion throughout the church. The public response to the instrumentum laboris has usually been more positive than to the lineamenta, indicating that the secretariat and council take seriously the suggestions they receive. On the other hand, there are often complaints that the ideas of one or another conference do not make it into the working paper. It is normally the liberals who are complaining.

Finally, at least thirty days before the opening of the synod, a report on the topic to be treated is distributed to the delegates. The report is written by the synod's "relator," who is a bishop appointed by the pope. The relator has the key leadership role at the synod since his job is to facilitate discussion and foster consensus on the synod's conclusions. He is assisted by a papally appointed special secretary (as distinguished from the general secretary), who is an expert on the topic of the synod.[41] The Council to the Secretariat of the Synod of Bishops officially goes out of business with the start of the synod, although its members as individuals can still be influential.

Synod Deliberations

On the opening day of the synod, after celebrating the Eucharist in St. Peter's, the delegates gather in the synodal hall, a modern auditorium with a sloping floor and equipment for simultaneous translations. Pope John Paul II has usually attended the meetings of each synod except when he was recovering from a fall at the end of the 1994 African Synod. He does not normally speak during the synod but listens to the presentations, although at the 1994 synod he "frequently read his breviary during synod proceedings."[42]

All but the ceremonial sessions of the synod are closed to the public and the media. Besides the delegates, certain priests, religious, laypersons, and non-Catholic observers approved by the pope are permitted to attend, address the assembly, and participate in small group meetings, but they cannot vote. The representatives from non-Catholic religions are normally nominated by their respective international organizations.[43] The only *periti* or experts allowed in the synod meetings are those appointed by the pope. Some conferences and bishops bring experts with them, but they have no official standing.

A president (or presidents) appointed by the pope chairs the meetings. The president first recognizes the general secretary, who gives a report on the work of the secretariat and its council since the last synod, with emphasis on the preparations for the synod. Then the relator summarizes and explains his report.[44] The relator's summary is followed by eight-minute speeches in which each delegate is allowed to express his views on the synod's topic. The observers are often given more than eight minutes to speak and tend to be the only speakers applauded by the bishops.[45] Mother Teresa spoke at the 1985 extraordinary synod and went way beyond her time limit, but no one dared to cut her off. Simultaneous translations, which vary in quality, are provided by individuals recruited by the secretariat from people in the curia or universities in Rome. Speakers are asked to present a written copy of their speeches in advance to help the translators.

The speakers are called upon by the president, who uses a list prepared by the general secretariat based on those who have asked to speak.[46] Some of the conferences, such as the NCCB, organize their presentations so that each delegate speaks on a particular aspect of the topic in the name of the conference. The rules give such delegates precedence over those speaking only in their own name. The regulations governing the synod insist that a bishop represents not only himself but also his conference.[47] He must express the views of his conference even if they are contrary to his own, which he can also give. Synod regulations also instruct him to follow the views of his conference when voting unless, after hearing the discussions, in good conscience he judges another view to be for the good of the church. But if his conference gives him a binding mandate, he should follow it unless it is against his conscience.[48]

The number of initial speeches at synods has been steadily increasing: 77 in 1969, 82 in 1971, 86 in 1974, 141 in 1977, 162 in 1980, 177 in 1983,[49] and more than 200 in 1994. Many bishops and observers complain that these opening speeches are boring and repetitive. The long series of eight-minute speeches does not encourage either debate or the coherent development of ideas, since speakers have prepared texts (often written before they arrive in Rome) and have no idea what the other speakers will say. At best, the interventions provide a striking picture of the variety of opinions and experiences in the church and allow the voices of the local churches to be heard. At worst, the speeches can be highly repetitive, boring, and time-consuming. Few bishops pass up the opportunity to speak, although they may submit written interventions for distribution.

At the end of about two weeks of speeches, the relator makes a presentation summarizing the main points of the speeches, a task that can be quite challenging. The bishops then go into small groups (circuli minores), using his report and questions as a jumping-off point for discussions. At the 1994 synod there were fourteen groups: four English, three French, three Spanish-Portuguese, two Italian, one German, and one Latin (made up primarily of East Europeans). With 244 members plus 75 observers, this meant an average of 23 persons in each small group.

At the beginning of their meeting, the members of each group select a moderator to chair their discussions. These moderators sometimes work with the president in determining synodal procedures, timing, and the actual conducting of debates.[50] The members also choose one of their group (called the group relator) to present their views to the assembly.[51] According to the participants, the most fruitful interchanges at a synod occur during these small group sessions. The give-and-take of the discussions in the small groups is freer than in the assembly, since the groups are more compact and the language is common. At the same time, the members are from a variety of countries and cultures.[52]

The group relators present the small group reports to the assembly. Afterward, individual responses to the reports are usually limited to five minutes. If the synod is going to make recommendations to the pope, the bishops then return to their small groups for a second series of meetings to formulate a list of "propositions" or recommendations.[53] At the 1980 synod Cardinal Ratzinger, the synod relator, had his experts draft propositions based on the results of the first series of small group meetings and suggested that these propositions be discussed in the second series of meetings. The group representatives rejected this plan and insisted that the propositions be drafted by the delegates in the small groups rather than by staff.

In the last week of the synod, the recommendations from the small groups are consolidated by a drafting commission that is headed by the president and includes the synod relator, secretary, group relators, and assistants whom the president might appoint. While they are working on their draft, the assembly deals with other business or hears reports from Vatican officials on other topics. Reports from curia officials followed by a question and answer period have become a regular part of the synod. Although the reports (or their summaries) are usually made public, the questions and answers are not.

Sometimes bishops complain that suggestions coming out of the language groups do not make their way into the commission's draft. Cardinal Schotte counters by noting that what comes out of one language group may not have wider support: "If it came up in one language group, it means that only 8 percent of the synod favored it. If you take a vote and it does not get a majority . . . or the eleven other reports of the language groups do not talk about it, then you cannot push it in because it is not a consensus topic. So you work toward a consensus of the whole."

The drafting commission then offers its text to the assembly for debate. The official text is in Latin, although translations may be available. Sometimes the delegates discuss the text in the language groups, but if this happens, time becomes limited for debate in the assembly. The drafting commission then makes revisions as a result of the discussions and debate, but ultimately the full synod must vote on the draft. The procedures for voting on texts are the same as those used at ecumenical councils: placet (yes), non placet (no), and placet iuxta modum (yes with amendments or reservations). If a delegate votes "placet iuxta modum," he must submit his amendment or reservations in writing in Latin.

The drafting commission is supposed to accept modi that will increase consensus, but accepting or rejecting amendments is at the discretion of the commission. This places a great deal of power in the hands of the drafting commission. Often most of the modi are dropped, with the drafters reporting that they cancel each other out by making diametrically opposed recommendations. Ultimately the quality of the commission's work is judged by whether it can get agreement from the assembly. Reports indicate that most documents or propositions pass overwhelmingly at the end, but some close votes can occur as the text is developing. Consensus is often achieved by dropping controversial recommendations. It is also achieved under great pressure as time is running out. "The last week is hectic because they are trying to deal with all the propositions," reports a Vatican official. "Sometimes there are many amendments. The staff has to go through them, and they are up all hours of the night trying to get everything done to meet the deadline the following morning."

The commission can bring specific amendments to the floor for a vote or can have the assembly vote on whether to drop sections of the text, but no one can simply offer an amendment from the floor. To be approved, an item needs a two-thirds vote of the assembly, but to be rejected it needs only a majority vote. This voting procedure encourages consensus decision making by making it easier to drop something than to add something. But the voting procedure is subject to some manipulation. For example, bishops on the commission who were opposed to a proposal might suggest that it be offered as an amendment rather than placed in the text since it would need a two-thirds vote to be adopted. On the other hand, those favoring an idea would want it in the original text where it could be kept by a simple majority voting against its deletion.

Post-Synodal Documents

As the synod is currently structured, if the delegates want to issue a document, they are forced to write, amend, and approve it in the last few days of the meeting. "The final week of the synod is just deadly," reports one Vatican official. "It is chaos." The time constraints make it very difficult to write and approve a document. With the synod coming to a conclusion, the delegates are forced to accept a draft text or have nothing. Many bishops do not think this is a good way to write important documents.

The 1971 synod wrote and approved two major documents, one on justice and the other on priesthood. Paul VI was not happy with parts of the statement on justice. He allowed it to be published but did not give it papal approval as he did the statement on priesthood. Three years later the synod delegates were unable to agree on a document on evangelization. Two special secretaries drafted two different documents, and although a committee of bishops (including Cardinal Karol Wojtyla) tried to merge them into a single document, the assembly rejected the results. Instead the synod approved a short message to the people of God that was drafted in one evening. Paul VI took the input from the synod and used it in writing his apostolic exhortation on evangelization, *Evangelii Nuntiandi.*

The favorable response to this exhortation encouraged the 1977 synod to adopt the practice of issuing a short pastoral "message to the people of God," while at the same time making a series of recommendations to the pope who would later write a document using their suggestions. "The procedure into which the synod of 1974 had stumbled was freely chosen by the synod of 1977," explains Father Johnson.[54]

The message is drafted by a committee of four bishops (one elected from each continent)[55] and then discussed and voted on by the assembly. Not infrequently, the first draft is severely criticized. It is supposed to be inspiring and pastoral in tone, but often it is criticized for being heavy and ponderous. In 1980 the drafters complained that their text was inspiring in the original but lost a great deal when it was translated into Latin for discussion in the assembly.

Officially the propositions or recommendations of the synod are secret unless released by the pope, but they are usually leaked to the Italian press within a week of the close of the synod. The 1977 synod made 34 "propositions" or proposals on catechetics, and John Paul II responded soon afterward with *Catechesi Tradendae.* He did the same after the 1980 synod on the family using the 43 synod propositions. Joseph A. Selling found that at least 15 percent of the pope's apostolic exhortation *Familiaris Consortio* was taken directly from the 1980 synodal text.[56]

John Paul II uses the Council of the General Secretariat of the Synod of Bishops to help in drafting his post-synodal documents. This council, having been elected during the just completed synod, may be composed of different people than the ones who prepared for the synod. The new council prepares for the next synod and deals with post-synodal business of the just completed synod.

As a Vatican official explains, "The council comes up with a post-synodal document, which is raised because of the pope's signature to an apostolic exhortation. To be honest with you, he rarely, very seldom, changes a lot of stuff we send him." At the 1983 synod Archbishop Jozef Tomko, then general secretary, reported that the council drafted the pope's apostolic exhortation *Familiaris Consortio.*[57] Even if the council does not draft the post-synodal document, it has significant input, according to Cardinal Schotte: "It is the council that looks at all the material after the synod and prepares some suggestions to the Holy Father, saying, 'Don't forget that. This should be stressed because it is in the documents.' They also review the different drafts that the Holy Father prepares."

Subsequent ordinary synods have observed this pattern of synod recommendations followed by a papal document. Surprisingly, the extraordinary synod of 1985 was able to produce a document even though it met for only two weeks, half the time of an ordinary synod. This "relatio finalis" or final report described the situation in the church twenty years after Vatican II. Much credit for accomplishing this feat was given to the relator, Cardinal Godfried Danneels of Belgium, and the secretary-theologian, Walter Kasper of Germany.[58]

The council also recommends to the pope ways of implementing the recommendations of the synod. Cardinal Schotte reports that after the synod on the laity called for a study of ministry, the council

> suggested that the Holy Father set up a commission to study the question of ministry. The council suggested this not be another commission with people from all over the world, because the synod had already done that discussion, but that he appoint a commission of the people from the departments of the Roman curia that have a direct interest in the topic.
>
> There was another [synod request] for clarification of the criteria for the approval of international movements. The Council of the Secretariat said, "Let's suggest to the Holy Father that he ask the Pontifical Council for the Laity to work that out." So that was transferred to the Council for the Laity and they are working on that.

Effectiveness of the Synod

How effective the synod of bishops has been is hotly debated. The synodal and post-synodal documents have been a means of articulating synodal and papal positions on a variety of issues. Some have had more impact than others. Certainly *The Catechism of the Catholic Church*, recommended by the 1985 extraordinary synod and written by a post-synodal commission, will have a lasting impact. Other documents have had impact on targeted areas such as evangelization, the church's social teaching, and seminary education. Some question whether there is much that is new in these documents. Selling concludes, for example, that there was nothing in the exhortation following the

1980 synod that was not already part of pre-synodal teaching and practice: "It appears that *Familiaris Consortio* could have been written even if the synod had not taken place."[59]

Judging collegial bodies by their documents and their conclusions may be illusory, according to Francis X. Murphy: "What tradition seems to indicate is that frequently the solutions arrived at in such gatherings are not half as important as the fact that the problems troubling the church should be honestly debated; and that all their implications be thoroughly investigated by the residential bishops involved in the pastoral conduct of the church."[60] Some fear, however, that ecclesiastical mores prohibit any frank discussion or honest debate that might appear critical of the pope and his policies. Yet it is difficult to advise someone without pointing out what he is doing wrong. Such deferential attitudes also limit the freedom of synodal delegates to criticize the curia, whose job it is to carry out the pope's will. Without honest and open discussion, the synod becomes a showcase for unity rather than a creative source of new ideas.

Those who had hoped (or feared) that the synod would be a strong liberal voice against the conservatism of the Roman curia have been disappointed (or pleased). The synod has not become a platform for critical comments aimed at either the pope or the curia. Without the help of outside experts like those available at Vatican II and with only a month to work in, the synod members have not come up with many new or creative suggestions for the pope. Often the synodal members give the impression that the purpose of the synod is not to advise the pope but to get his advice; they will raise issues and questions and then ask the pope to clarify matters in his post-synodal apostolic exhortation. Vatican officials also play an active role at the synods. As a result, the synod has become as much a way for the pope and curia to influence the delegates (and through them the local churches) as a way for the local churches to advise the pope.

The pope's presence at all the assembly meetings indicates his regard for the synod, although his reading of his breviary during the 1994 synod must have been disconcerting to speakers. Although in theory the bishops can say anything they want at the synod, in practice they tend to be very deferential to the pope and his views. No one wants to be portrayed in opposition to the pope. This deferential attitude affects the entire synodal process, from the preparatory stage to the writing of the post-synodal document. Deference has become so strong that critics say that the pope does not get honest advice because bishops fear to disagree with him.

Some bishops, both liberal and conservative, complain that going to the synod is a waste of their time and that very little gets done. Perhaps the synod's most important function has been to bring together bishops from all over the world so that they can share ideas and experiences both inside and outside the synodal hall. It is a reminder to each of them that they are part of an international church that must maintain unity while at the same time adapting to local cultures. The simple act of meeting, making friends, praying, and worshipping together is an ecclesial act of the highest importance, even if on the practical level little is accomplished. The unity of the church symbolized by the synod is clearly an essential element in the eyes of John Paul. While liberal critics complain that this unity crosses the line into uniformity, the pope's intention is to use the synod to send a clear and unanimous message to the church and the world on critical issues of justice, faith, and church discipline. The very success of this effort to use the synod as a showcase for unity has reduced the synod's ability to be an uninhibited adviser to the pope.

The secrecy of the synod is frequently denounced. Secrecy is supposed to encourage the delegates to express their views freely, which may be relevant for delegates from countries with dictatorial regimes. Secrecy also protects the freedom of the pope to disregard the suggestions. But secrecy makes it impossible for episcopal conferences to know how well their delegates represented them at the synod. Nor does it allow the church at large to share in the experience of the synod.

Many in the Vatican see problems with making the synod more open. "This business of having everything out in the open is not all that beneficial," says one Vatican official, "because then people can't always say what is on their mind because they are always fearful that it is going to make headlines back home. On the other hand, some want it that way, which is the other problem." Others complain that some bishops are posturing even without the media present, but their audience is the Vatican rather than the folks back home. Whatever the case, the synod's secrecy breeds rumors and suspicions. And despite the current requirement of secrecy, some information inevitably leaks to the press. It would be better to have accurate information available to everyone. For example, conferences could be allowed to make public their responses to the lineamenta, and the synod's recommendations to the pope (or at least most of them) could be published.

The director of the Vatican press office is the official spokesperson for the synod with the press.[61] Official press conferences are held periodically during the synod. For example, the general secretary usually gives a press conference at the beginning of the synod describing the preparation for the synod. The relator might give a press conference after his oral report to the assembly (in

1994 his opening presentation to the synod was televised for the press for the first time). Delegates from various language groups are also presented at press conferences. But the press office and the synod secretariat do little to facilitate contact between members of the press and other synodal delegates.[62] Requests to set up cameras for interviewing delegates in a room near the synodal hall have been denied. Reporters have to wait outside Vatican territory and grab delegates as they come through the gate.

Summaries of the speeches, prepared by the speakers or the synod staff, are released to the press in half a dozen languages, a daunting task given the number of speeches. These summaries often drop the more controversial comments of the speakers either because the speaker does not want them made public or because the staff judges them too controversial. At more recent synods, more and more full texts have been released either by the individual bishops or by the press office.[63] A press spokesman (usually a priest) for each language is appointed who briefs the press at the end of each session. Often the spokesman is afraid to give any more information than is in the press summaries. At the African synod, the English-language press person taped his presentation to protect himself from being incorrectly quoted by the press or being challenged by higher officials.

Other suggestions for improving the synod, besides having less secrecy, have included allowing bishops to bring their own experts into the synod hall so that they have input from others beyond the Vatican staff. Another suggestion is having the synod meet in two sessions with time in between for more study and consultation. It has also been suggested that the synod "be in session for longer periods of time, and more frequently—even, ultimately, six months each year. This would include general working sessions, study commissions, and special task forces."[64] It would also be helpful to have some means by which delegates could offer amendments from the floor. Some have even advocated expanding the membership to include "men and women, clerical, religious, and lay" from local churches, although others object that this would dilute the role of the synod as representative of the college of bishops.[65]

Although the structure of the synod has improved incrementally over the last thirty years, it is inherently weak because it meets for such a short period without preparatory work having been done by synod committees. Studies of secular legislatures indicate that strong legislative bodies require a staff independent of the executive, ongoing committees to do preparatory work, and a continuity of membership to develop experience and expertise. In all these areas the synod system is weak. The synod secretariat is not independent of the executive, and the council could use the help of standing committees made up of synodal members. Some members, like Cardinal Bernardin, provide continuity because their conferences continually reelect them. These members have experience and expertise in both the issues and the procedures of the synod. Currently, the most permanent members of the synod are Vatican officials who attend ex officio.

Dropping the curial officials from membership in the synod of bishops would emphasize the synod's role as representing local churches. They would attend as observers or staff, which would more clearly distinguish them from the delegates who represent the local churches. Curial officials are always available to give the pope advice. The synod, however, is an opportunity for him to hear from the bishops in the local churches. Reducing the number of papal appointees at a synod would also allow for greater representation from local churches.

Structural changes will have little effect on the results of the synod as long as an excessively deferential attitude holds sway. A striking example of this deference is the extent to which the speakers quote John Paul. Since the purpose of the synod is to advise the pope, it is a little strange for the bishops to quote the pope to himself since he certainly knows what he has said. Some bishops use quotations to bolster their case with other bishops by citing the pope as an authority. But for many bishops the purpose of the synod is not to advise the pope but to provide a forum where they can affirm their loyalty. Many bishops seem so overwhelmed by the pope's presence that they think it improper to give him advice. At the same time, it would be erroneous to believe that the bishops are intimidated into adopting positions at the synod that they oppose. A large majority of the bishops clearly support the same positions as the pope. This has become increasingly true as he has changed the episcopacy through his appointment of new bishops.

That collegial bodies like the synod, episcopal conferences, and ecumenical councils will continue to evolve is certain, but how they will evolve is less certain. Under a less forceful pope, bishops might be more willing to speak up. Likewise, a gradual loosening of the restraints on episcopal conferences could occur without endangering church unity. A less centralized church would also improve chances for reunion with Protestant and Orthodox churches. Technological advances in communications and travel have made it possible for the college of bishops to take on a new life in this century. But technology also provides the means by which a more centralized papacy can exercise greater control over local churches. New technologies in the twenty-first century might enable the college of bishops to exercise its collegial role more easily. Could an ecumenical council meet in cyberspace? Certainly much of the preparatory work for conferences, synods, and councils could be done today through the Internet. On the other hand, these technologies might also permit a greater centralization of power in the Vatican. But for the church to be truly Catholic, the college of bishops must have an important role in the governance of the church.

~ 4

The College of Cardinals

IN ADDITION TO the synod of bishops, John Paul II has used the college of cardinals as a consultative body that meets in Rome to advise him. The most important role of the college of cardinals, of course, is to elect the pope. In asking the college to act as an advisory body, John Paul has resurrected a role for the college that it has not exercised for four centuries. When cardinals meet to elect a pope, it is called a conclave. When they meet to advise the pope, it is called a consistory. The term "consistory" originally referred to the room where the Byzantine emperor met with his imperial council.

The college of cardinals goes back so far in history that its origins are obscure.[1] Originally the term "cardinal" referred in any diocese to a cleric (deacon, priest, or bishop) who was incardinated to a new position as opposed to the one for which he was originally ordained.[2] In Rome, cardinal deacons were deacons who had been moved and put in charge of social services for the eighteen regions of Rome. Originally, cardinal priests were priests temporarily incardinated to certain shrines or basilicas for special liturgical services. The same was true for the bishops from the seven dioceses surrounding Rome when they came for special liturgical services in St. John Lateran, the cathedral of Rome.

Since it was normally the more talented or trusted who were assigned these duties, it was natural that these clergy became important advisers to the pope. Eventually the cardinal priests became permanently responsible for their churches in Rome, but as their curial responsibilities grew, others took over their pastoral responsibilities. Likewise, the social work of the cardinal deacons was turned over to others. The cardinal bishops worked for the pope in Rome but continued to have pastoral responsibility for their dioceses until 1962 when John XXIII (1958–1963) relieved them of any jurisdiction over these dioceses.

Eventually the distinction among the three types of cardinals became more honorific than real.[3] There were bishops who were cardinal priests and cardinal deacons, and priests who were cardinal bishops and cardinal deacons. Men who were neither deacons, priests, nor bishops were also made cardinals.[4] Although the names of these "orders" are still used, Pope John XXIII made all the cardinals bishops so that they would have precedence over patriarchs at the Second Vatican Council. Today all cardinals are bishops except for a few priests who did not wish to become bishops because they were already over 80 years of age at the time of their appointments.

In the eleventh century, Leo IX (1049–1054) began appointing prelates in distant lands as cardinals. Such cardinals were usually required to resign their sees and take up residence with the pope. During the Western Schism, it became common for these cardinals to reside with the pope without resigning their sees. Someone else would administer their diocese while the cardinal collected the revenue. The Council of Trent outlawed this abuse. Beginning in the sixteenth century, as the college of cardinals grew larger and the importance of the consistory declined, it became more common for cardinals to remain in residence in their dioceses.[5] Today the cardinal deacons are curial officials; the cardinal bishops are senior curial officials; and the cardinal priests are curial cardinals or diocesan bishops living outside Rome.

The number of cardinals fluctuated over time. In the twelfth century there were positions for about 28 cardinal priests and 18 cardinal deacons in Rome, plus the 7 cardinal bishops for a total of 53. The actual number was normally between 20 and 30, although a few times it fell below 10. In 1586 Sixtus V set the maximum number of cardinals at 70 in imitation of the 70 chosen by Moses (Exodus 24:1) and by Jesus (Luke 10:1). From 1856 until 1958, the actual number of cardinals was generally between 60 and 70, although at the death of Pius XII there were only 55 cardinals. John XXIII ignored this limit, and the college grew to more than 80 cardinals. In 1970 Paul VI reformed the college of cardinals by increasing the number of electors to 120, not counting those over 80 years of age who are excluded as electors.

From their position as the principal clergy of Rome with certain liturgical responsibilities, it was a logical development for the cardinals to become the principal advisers to the pope. This appears to have been the case as early as the reign of Leo IX (1049–1054). Their role as advisers was strengthened when they became the sole electors of the pope in 1059. This led to claims in the late eleventh century that "the powers of St. Peter belonged not to the pope alone, but collectively to the pope and the cardinals."[6] Claims were also made that the power of the papacy fell to the college of cardinals during an interregnum.

In the early centuries when faced with a complex or difficult issue, the pope would often call a provincial council consisting of bishops from Italy. In 1141, instead of calling a council, Innocent II consulted a consistory of cardinals to get their advice on the teachings of Abelard, who had been condemned by the Council of Sens. The practice caught on, and fewer provincial councils were held until they practically disappeared by the end of the twelfth century.[7] As the number of provincial councils declined, popes consulted the cardinals who were closer to home. Ecumenical councils were also called, but they were rare.

A majority of the cardinals would not have been bishops at this time, so they did not represent the college of bishops as the synod of bishops does today. Despite that, the college of cardinals came to be seen as a kind of senate of the church. In many dioceses, some of the clergy (like the canons of the cathedral) acted as a kind of senate, electing and advising the bishop. In Rome, the college of cardinals acted as a senate not just for the diocese of Rome but for the whole church. Not surprisingly, being in Rome, the cardinals also looked to the old Roman senate as a model for themselves, especially because they dealt with the governance of the papal states. The 1983 Code of Canon Law dropped the term "senate" and refers to the cardinals as a "special college."

As time went on and as papal business increased, the practice of consulting the college of cardinals in consistory became common. At first it met monthly, but by the beginning of the thirteenth century it was meeting three times a week, on Monday, Wednesday, and Friday.[8] The pope consulted the cardinals on matters of doctrine and church discipline as well as political affairs. A study of the college of cardinals recounts: "It was in consistory that the pope received the ambassadors and the notabilities of the Christian world. It was in consistory that the measures to be taken against heresy and for organizing the crusades were decided. Lastly, it was in consistory that difficulties arising from the administration of the states of the church were settled, the appointment of bishops agreed upon, major excommunications pronounced, and saints canonized."[9]

In many ways the pope and the cardinals functioned as a papal court similar to the royal courts of Europe during the Middle Ages, but the elective nature of the papacy gave to the college of cardinals a unique role not enjoyed by the nobility in most nations. In exchange for electoral support, papal candidates made deals and promises that increased the power of the cardinals. In the second half of the thirteenth century their power grew because of the brief reigns of the popes (twelve popes in forty years) and long interregnums when the cardinals governed the church and the papal states. The college considered itself the successor of the apostolic college.

At some fourteenth- and fifteenth-century conclaves, detailed agreements or "capitulations" were drawn up limiting the power of the pope and increasing the power of the cardinals. All the cardinals would agree to observe the capitulation if elected, but once elected the new pope usually repudiated the contract. For example, in 1352 all the cardinals signed a document agreeing that whoever was elected would limit the college to twenty cardinals and give half of the revenues of the Roman church to the cardinals. After his election Innocent VI, who had signed the document, declared the agreement invalid. Eugenius IV did the same thing in 1431 after his election. In 1562 Pius IV forbade all such pacts, and the current rules state that the pope is not bound by any promises he made to get votes, even if he promised under oath.[10]

The use of the consistory as an instrument of governance declined in the sixteenth century as issues became more numerous and complex and as the popes consolidated their power over the cardinals. The Reformation brought so many issues before the pope that the consistory system collapsed under the weight of them. Committees of cardinals (called congregations) were formed to study different issues and report back to the pope in consistory.

As the congregation system developed into a bureaucracy, consistories became formal events for the canonization of saints and the creation of cardinals. At these later consistories there was a pro forma consultation with the cardinals on decisions (canonization of saints or appointment of new cardinals) that had already been made. Consistories as a means of consulting with the cardinals were suppressed by Sixtus V in 1588. Consistories with all the cardinals would have been difficult to hold in any case after the Council of Trent (1545–1563) required that bishops reside in their own dioceses. Cardinals with dioceses could no longer live in Rome where they could be frequently consulted.

Modern Consistories

The resurrection of the consistories in 1979 as a papal method of consulting the college of cardinals was a surprise.[11] Most people had felt that the synod of bishops had taken over this consultative role, and some were proposing that the synod take over the cardinals' electoral role. After his election in 1978, John Paul told the cardinals at the conclave that he would like to meet and consult with them periodically, a suggestion that had come up in the plenary congregations of the cardinals during the interregnum. These special meetings "are one form in which episcopal and pastoral collegiality is exercised," he told the cardinals at the first meeting in 1979. He wished "to profit from advice and your many-sided experience."[12]

John Paul's decision to consult the college of cardinals led to unresolved questions about the relationship between meetings of the synod of bishops and consistories of the college of cardinals: Which is more important? Which should be consulted on what issues? Are both representative of the college of bishops? Is this the beginning of a bicameral system in the church?

These questions are especially important because John XXIII made all the cardinals bishops, with the consequence that the college of cardinals is now clearly linked to the college of bishops. In 1979 John Paul II tried to explain the difference between issues considered by the synod and those addressed by the college of cardinals. The questions to be considered by the cardinals are important, he said: "They seem to be more closely linked with the ministry of the bishop of Rome than the questions that are to be the subject of the synod of bishops." The pope went on to admit, "It is obvious that here one cannot speak of any rigorous demarcation."[13]

Three years later, he described the cardinals' meetings as "the means through which—in however brief space of time—big questions calling for prudence are discussed, having to do with today's apostolic action for the universal people of God."[14] What this means is unclear since surely the synod of bishops is prudent and discusses "big questions . . . having to do with today's apostolic action for the people of God." Finally, in 1994, John Paul put synods and consistories on almost an equal level by saying that "the development of the synodal dimension of the church, which visibly reflects the collegiality of the entire episcopate, is matched by the tradition of ordinary and extraordinary consistories."[15]

The 1983 Code of Canon Law (canon 353) makes a distinction between ordinary and extraordinary consistories. To an extraordinary consistory, the pope calls all the cardinals. To an ordinary consistory, he can call all the cardinals or only those present in Rome. The code also distinguishes two types of ordinary consistories. The most common is for "certain very solemn acts," such as canonizations, the conferral of the pallium to archbishops, or the creation of new cardinals. By the end of 1994, John Paul II had called six ordinary consistories. Part of these ceremonies is normally celebrated in public. According to canon 353, ordinary consistories are also called so that the cardinals can "be consulted on certain serious matters which nevertheless occur rather frequently." Although the first type of ordinary consistory has been called frequently, the second type has not yet been used. The pope's preferred type is the extraordinary consistory, described in the code as those called "when the special needs of the church or the conducting of more serious affairs suggests that it should be held."[16]

John Paul called his first extraordinary consistory of the college of cardinals one year after his election.[17] The timing and topics of the extraordinary consistories have been as follows:

November 5–9, 1979: the reform of the Roman curia; the church and culture; the finances of the Holy See.[18]

November 23, 1982: the reorganization of the Roman curia; Vatican finances, with special attention to the Vatican Bank; the revision of the Code of Canon Law.[19]

November 21–23, 1985: reform of the Roman curia.[20]

April 4–7, 1991: threats to human life, especially abortion; the problem of new religious sects.[21]

June 13–14, 1994: preparing for and celebrating the year 2000; a report on ecumenical relations; the International Year of the Family; the better use of retired bishops.[22]

A review of these topics shows that the early meetings (1979, 1982, 1985) tended to examine the internal organization and operations of the Roman curia. Thus at first the college of cardinals dealt with internal administrative issues, which had some logic to it since cardinals are members or heads of Vatican congregations and agencies. This may have been what John Paul meant in saying that the college would consider questions "more closely linked with the ministry of the bishop of Rome." Later consistories have taken on topics of a wider concern, topics (like abortion and threats to human life) that go beyond internal administrative issues and could have been dealt with by a synod of bishops. Perhaps because the synod process was already occupied with other topics, the pope pragmatically saw the college of cardinals as another avenue of consultation and publicity on these important topics.

Although the meetings of the cardinals are even more secretive than the meetings of the synod of bishops, some information is available. Much less preparation goes into these meetings than goes into a synod. The consistories are officially announced only about two or three months before the actual meeting. No extensive consultation is done with local churches or episcopal conferences, although there was consultation with the presidents of episcopal conferences on proposals to reform the Roman curia before the 1985 cardinals' meeting. There is no secretariat or council for the consistories as there is for the synod, although the secretary to the Congregation for Bishops is also the secretary to the college of cardinals. Preparatory documents, if there are any, are normally prepared by curial officials and not made public, although sometimes they are leaked.

Before the 1994 consistory a 23-page memorandum, "Reflections on the Great Jubilee of the Year 2000," was distributed to the cardinals by the Secretariat of State. No author was indicated, although at the consistory the pope took ownership of the document by referring to it as his. The memorandum discussed various possibilities for celebrating the year 2000. Within a couple of weeks of its distribution, excerpts from the memorandum were appearing in the Italian press, including a proposal for an interreligious meeting on Mount Sinai. What also caught the attention of the press was a proposal that the church publicly admit its past failings. The memorandum pointed to the Galileo case and to "the many forms of violence perpetrated in the name of faith—wars of religion, tribunals of the Inquisition and other forms of violations of the rights of persons."

All the cardinals, even those who are over 80 years of age, are invited to an extraordinary consistory. The number who actually attend has been between 97 and 122,[23] much smaller than the number attending a synod of bishops. The meetings are also much shorter than those of a synod. The first meeting in 1979 lasted five days; the rest have been even briefer.

The format of the meetings varies. Normally they begin with a talk by the pope, followed by presentations from various cardinals on the specific topics of the meetings. The pope takes a much more active role in defining the issues at the beginning of a consistory than he does at the beginning of a synod. In 1994, for example, the pope gave a lengthy talk in which he stressed the ecumenical dimensions of preparing for and celebrating the year 2000.[24] He also reported on his travels, Vatican finances, and the activities of various Vatican departments. Next Cardinal Angelo Sodano, the secretary of state, presented a list of suggestions for discussion that focused on the celebration of the year 2000. Among the possibilities were a meeting with Muslims and Jews on Mount Sinai and a meeting with other Christian representatives in Jerusalem and Bethlehem.

At other consistories, major addresses have been given by cardinals, usually the curial cardinal under whose jurisdiction the topic comes. For example, the president of the Prefecture of the Economic Affairs of the Holy See and the president of the Administration of the Patrimony of the Apostolic See spoke on Vatican finances in 1979. In 1991 Cardinal Francis Arinze, president of the

Council for Interreligious Dialogue, and Cardinal Jozef Tomko, prefect of the Congregation for the Evangelization of Peoples, spoke about the problem of religious sects.[25] After their presentations, five cardinals reported on the situation in their regions. At the same consistory, Cardinal Joseph Ratzinger, prefect of the Congregation for the Doctrine of the Faith, spoke about a proposed document on threats to life.[26] Another five cardinals reported on threats to life in their regions.

After the presentations, there can be general discussion or the cardinals can go into six to eight language groups for discussion. In the assembly meetings, each cardinal is recognized to speak in order of seniority. In the small groups, the discussion is more free-flowing. The language groups operate in a manner similar to those in the synod of bishops and sometimes vote on recommendations.

After the small group discussions, spokesmen for each group report back to the assembly. A general discussion by the cardinals follows, and the suggestions are gathered into a report and given to the pope. Cardinals have an additional month to send in more comments and recommendations after they have returned home and spent more time reflecting on the issues. The meeting usually concludes with a speech by the pope responding to the discussions.

Normally an extraordinary consistory does not issue public statements or documents, although the Vatican press office usually releases a communiqué describing the discussions and some of the conclusions of the meeting. Some of the prepared speeches, especially the pope's at the beginning and end of the meeting, are made public. The 1994 meeting was unusual in that it unanimously approved and released two short resolutions. One, written by Cardinal John J. O'Connor of New York, condemned abortion and artificial birth control programs sponsored by governments and international agencies. This resolution was aimed at the upcoming United Nations conference on population and development in Cairo. The other, drafted by Cardinal Bernard F. Law of Boston, called on the warring factions in Rwanda to lay down their arms. Both resolutions were introduced by Americans accustomed to drafting and passing such resolutions in their episcopal conference as a means of gaining media attention for an issue.

The results of the consistories are not as clear as those of the synods. There are no post-consistory documents like the post-synodal apostolic exhortations, although in 1995 the pope issued an encyclical, *Evangelium Vitae*, in response to the threats to human life discussed at the 1991 and 1994 consistories. Reform and reorganization of the curia were discussed three times (1979, 1982, 1985), but John Paul only made minor changes in the curia in his 1988 apostolic constitution *Pastor Bonus*. His decision to make only minor changes probably reflects the lack of consensus among the cardinals.

Vatican finances were also discussed at least twice (1979, 1982). Here John Paul has responded to complaints of residential cardinals by establishing a council of cardinals to review the finances of the Holy See, by appointing Cardinal Edmund Szoka as head of the Prefecture for the Economic Affairs of the Holy See, and by reorganizing the governance of the Vatican Bank. Cardinal Szoka has updated the internal accounting procedures of the Holy See and disclosed more financial information.

The impact of the consistories on the more general topics (religious sects, threats to life, celebrating the year 2000) is less clear. In these cases the pope or curial cardinals took the leadership role, and the consistory was less a means of consultation than a forum for publicizing these issues and encouraging residential cardinals to action on the local level.

Papal Elections

Despite the revival of the consistory system by John Paul II, the most important function of the cardinals is to elect a new pope. Healthy or sick, the pope is in office until he dies or resigns. The number of popes who may have resigned has been estimated to be as high as ten, but the historical evidence is not clear.[27] Pope Celestine V's resignation in 1294 is the most famous because Dante placed him in hell for it. Most popes have felt that resignation is unacceptable. As Paul VI said, paternity cannot be resigned.[28] In addition, Paul feared setting a precedent that would force future popes to resign. Nor did he want to encourage factions in the church to pressure popes to resign for reasons other than health. Thus, although other bishops had to resign at 75 years of age, Paul did not resign when he reached 75, nor has John Paul II. Nevertheless, the Code of Canon Law in 1917 provided for the resignation of a pope, as do the regulations established by Paul VI in 1975.

If the pope becomes sick, he can delegate a great deal of authority to some trusted person like the secretary of state or his personal secretary. If the pope goes into a coma without having clearly delegated responsibility, Vatican officials could continue to operate under their normal authority. Any decision requiring the pope's approval (the appointment of bishops or the approval of major documents) would simply have to wait. If this went on for more than a year, the church would face a crisis and the college of bishops would have to find a way to govern the church without an active pope. In earlier centuries incapacitated popes were less of a problem because the role of the papacy was limited and because doctors were more likely to kill a person with their care than keep him alive. The ability of modern medicine to keep the body alive while the mind is deteriorating will eventually present the church with a constitutional crisis.[29] If the pope were psychologically impaired, the church would be faced with a canonical nightmare. Likewise, a pope with Alzheimer's disease is not something anyone wants to contemplate. The only solution would be to get him to resign while he is still rational.[30]

There are currently no canonically acceptable procedures for removing a mentally ill or senile pope. In the good old days his staff might lock him in his rooms and run the church until he died. In the bad old days someone would poison him. Either strategy would be difficult to carry out in the full blaze of today's media attention. How many crazy popes the church has suffered through in the past is uncertain. Some who today might be classified as sociopaths governed through terror and violence. Others became senile or paranoid but continued to reign.

There are no easy solutions to this problem. How crazy does a pope have to be to be incompetent to govern? Who makes that decision? Any process for removing a pope for psychological reasons would be open to corruption, abuse, bad judgment, or misinterpretation. For example, if the decision were left to the college of cardinals, its members could be accused of being motivated by ambition rather than the good of the church. Attempting to remove a demented pope might be more destructive of church unity than leaving him in office. When Pope Urban VI (1378–1389) became psychologically unhinged after his election, attempts to deal with him led to the Great Western Schism (1378–1417). The Council of Constance succeeded in ending the Western Schism by deposing or forcing the resignations of all three claimants. Since the papacy has never acknowledged the right of an ecumenical council to remove a pope, currently the only acceptable way for a pope to be removed from office is by death or resignation.[31]

The church needs a procedure for removing a pope in extreme circumstances. The procedure should be cumbersome to discourage its use except when a wide consensus exists that the pope's removal is necessary for the good of the church. Perhaps a three-stage procedure involving the college of cardinals, the synod of bishops, and the college of bishops would be appropriate. The dean would convene the college of cardinals after a majority of the cardinals had signed a petition calling for a consistory. If two-thirds of the cardinals voted to remove the pope, a synod of bishops would be convened which would also have to support his removal by a two-thirds vote. Finally, all the bishops of the world would be polled and if two-thirds agreed, the see of

Rome would be declared vacant. The successful completion of such a complex procedure would indicate a clear consensus that a new pope was needed.

The Catholic church without a pope is difficult to imagine, and yet there were times in the history of the church when interregnums went on for years. Often wars or civil disturbances in Rome caused these lengthy interregnums. Sometimes they were caused by the cardinals, who enjoyed the power and financial rewards of running the papacy without a pope. These abuses led to rules governing an interregnum and requiring the speedy calling of a conclave.

When the pope dies, the prefect of the Papal Household informs the camerlengo (chamberlain), who must verify his death.[32] No autopsy is performed, which can lead to wild media speculation if the pope dies suddenly as occurred with John Paul I.[33] The absence of an independent autopsy is a serious failing in the interregnum regulations.

With the death or resignation of a pope, the government of the church is put into the hands of the college of cardinals according to rules set forth by John Paul II in his 1996 constitution *Universi Dominici Gregis*.[34] At the first meeting of the cardinals after the death of the pope, the first half of this document dealing with the interregnum is read and the cardinals swear to follow it and observe secrecy. If an ecumenical council or synod of bishops is in session at the time of the pope's death, it is adjourned until called back into session by the new pope.

All the cardinals in charge of departments in the Roman curia, including the secretary of state, lose their jobs when the pope dies. The only exceptions are the camerlengo (Cardinal Eduardo Martinez Somalo), the major penitentiary (Cardinal William W. Baum), and the vicar of the diocese of Rome (Cardinal Camillo Ruini). The vicar for Rome provides for the pastoral needs of the diocese of Rome and continues to have all the powers he had under the pope. The major penitentiary deals with confessional matters reserved to the Holy See, and he is allowed to continue because the opportunity for forgiveness of sins should always be available.

The camerlengo is the most important official during the interregnum.[35] On the death of the pope, the camerlengo destroys the pope's fisherman's ring and the die used to make lead seals for apostolic letters. He takes charge of and administers the property and money of the Holy See with the help of three cardinal assistants who are chosen by lot from the cardinals under age 80. During the interregnum he reports to the college of cardinals and gets their advice. He seals the pope's study and bedroom and arranges for the pope's funeral in accordance with instructions left him by the pope. He also sees to the preparation of the conclave.

Although the college of cardinals governs the church until a new pope is elected, the powers of the college are limited. It cannot change the rules governing papal elections, appoint cardinals, or make any decisions binding on the next pope. Until the conclave begins, the cardinals meet daily in a general congregation presided over by the dean of the college.[36] All the cardinals attend the general congregation, although attendance by those over 80 is optional.

Three cardinal assistants under 80 are chosen by lot, one from each order (deacon, priest, bishop), to form a particular congregation headed by the camerlengo to deal with matters of less importance. Every three days until a new pope is elected, the three cardinal assistants are replaced by others, also chosen by lot. A commission, made up of the camerlengo and the cardinals who had been secretary of state and president of the Vatican City State, is responsible for preparing lodging for the cardinals and preparing the Sistine Chapel for the election. These rules disperse power so that a few cardinals cannot control the interregnum or the conclave.

Unless circumstances prevent it, the rules require that conclaves take place in the Vatican. A number of elections in the nineteenth century were held in the Quirinal Palace (now the home of the Italian president) because it was safer from attack during the turbulent times. Civil disturbances, wars, and plagues sometimes made holding a conclave in Rome very dangerous. In July 1623, eight cardinals and forty of their assistants died of malaria in Rome during a very hot conclave.[37] Meeting outside Rome was often healthier and safer in early centuries. The most recent conclave outside Rome took place in 1800 after Pope Pius VI died as a prisoner of Napoleon. The cardinals met in Venice under Austrian protection and elected Pius VII. The cardinals considered holding the election outside Rome in 1878, the first conclave after the fall of the papal states. Since no country invited them and since the Italian government promised not to interfere, the cardinals met in the Vatican (the Quirinal Palace having been taken over by the Italian government). They have met in the Apostolic Palace in the Vatican ever since.

In the Apostolic Palace special cubicles were built to house the cardinals during the conclave. With the expansion of the college to 120 cardinals, this has been a tight fit in uncomfortable quarters with limited facilities for washing. Domus Sanctae Marthae, a $20 million residence for clerical visitors and Vatican employees, has recently been constructed inside the Vatican. The residence is a short distance from the Apostolic Palace and the Sistine Chapel, so the cardinals can live there during a conclave after the regular residents vacate the building. The 108 suites and 23 single rooms, all with private baths, are assigned by lot. While not luxurious, the building will certainly provide more comfortable quarters than the cubicles of past conclaves. *Universi Dominici Gregis* calls for tight security so that no one can speak to the cardinals as they travel between Domus Sanctae Marthae and the Sistine Chapel.

The college of cardinals sets the date and time for beginning the conclave. It cannot begin until at least fifteen days after the death of the pope in order to give the cardinals time to get to Rome. As late as 1922, cardinals from North and South America missed the conclave because of the time it took to get to Rome by boat. Today, most of the cardinals would already have gathered in Rome for the funeral of the deceased pope. The conclave must begin within twenty days, although cardinals arriving late may enter and take part in the election. Once inside the conclave, an elector may not leave except because of illness or other grave reasons acknowledged by a majority of the cardinals.

Before entering the conclave the cardinals are already discussing among themselves and their advisers the possible candidates. For example, before the first 1978 conclave, meetings and discussions had limited the viable candidates to Cardinal Giuseppe Siri and Cardinal Albino Luciani, who became John Paul I. The conclave regulations make it clear that a cardinal is not bound by any promises he makes before entering the conclave.

Although church regulations forbid the discussion of candidates before the death of a pope, private discussions among the cardinals do occur. The prohibition against discussing papal succession while the pope is still alive dates back to Felix IV (526–530), who instructed the clergy and the Roman senate to elect his archdeacon, Boniface, as his successor. The senate objected and passed an edict forbidding any discussion of a pope's successor during his lifetime.[38] Some seventy-seven years later, Boniface III convoked a synod that forbade, under pain of excommunication, all discussion of a papal successor until three days after the pope's death. The purpose of the prohibition today is to avoid political campaigns that would divide the church. In the Vatican, politics behind closed doors is preferred to public election campaigns.

Although the college of cardinals elects the pope today, this was not the rule until the eleventh century. A few early popes, including St. Peter, may have appointed their successors, but this method did not gain acceptance. In the early church, popes were usually chosen by the clergy and people of Rome in the same way that bishops in other dioceses were elected. This democratic process worked well when the church was small and united. But disagreements led to factions who fought over the papacy.

As early as 217, Rome was divided over whether the community should expel sinners and apostates who had denied the faith to avoid martyrdom. Pope

Callistus I, a former slave and failed banker, was sympathetic to the view that the church should be a home for sinners as well as saints. He also made enemies by translating the liturgy from Greek into the vulgar Latin of the people. A more conservative faction in Rome wanted to expel sinners and apostates, and they elected the first anti-pope, Hippolytus.[39]

Sometimes the elections got violent. In 366, mobs and hired thugs from opposing factions invaded churches and killed opponents by the hundreds.[40] For protection popes turned to the civil authorities to expel opponents and to keep the peace, but the civil authorities in Rome quickly started using their power to influence papal elections. As the popes grew wealthy and powerful, these struggles became more intense and began to involve political actors beyond the city of Rome.

Byzantine emperors from Justinian I (527–565) on claimed the right to approve the election of a new pope, and newly elected popes sometimes waited months for this approval before being consecrated. Imperial interference was sometimes more direct. Empress Theodora, the wife of Justinian, used her money and influence to get Vigilius elected pope in 537 after he promised to reject the council of Chalcedon (451). Vigilius had been the nuncio to Constantinople, where he got to know the imperial family. After Vigilius was elected, he did not deliver on his promise because he found the Western bishops supportive of Chalcedon. In 545 he was arrested at Mass in Rome by the Byzantine police and hauled off to Constantinople, where he tried to appease the empress. In the process he alienated Western bishops, and the bishops of North Africa excommunicated him as a heretic. He died a broken man on his way back to Rome.[41]

After the eighth century, the papal electors were limited to the Roman clergy. This followed the pattern of other dioceses where the clergy elected the bishop. The man elected pope was normally a priest. A bishop was not elected until 891 (Formosus) because it was considered improper for a bishop to leave the diocese for which he had originally been ordained a bishop. After his death in 896, Formosus's decaying corpse was dug up, dressed in pontifical robes, and put on trial by his successor, Stephen VI. After being found guilty of various crimes, including the abandonment of his former diocese to become pope, his body was tossed in the Tiber, minus the three fingers of his right hand that he had used to bless the crowds and sign documents. All of his decrees and ordinations were declared invalid.

Limiting the electors to the clergy did not stop papal elections from being influenced by money and threats from civil authorities or powerful families. Theophylact and his family were able to control papal elections during much of the tenth century. After Leo V was imprisoned, tortured, and killed in 903, the family had little trouble manipulating the papacy for decades. John XI (931–935), for example, was reputed to be the son of Pope Sergius III and Theophylact's 13-year-old daughter.[42]

In an attempt to reform the electoral process, Nicholas II (1059–1061) proposed a system whereby the cardinal bishops would meet to nominate a candidate and then invite in the cardinal priests to vote on him. This reduced the clergy to the same role as the laity—accepting the man chosen by the cardinals. In 1179, Alexander III modified this system by including all the cardinals in the election process from the beginning. Since 1179, only cardinals have voted for the pope except for the 1417 election ending the Western Schism. In this election, 30 representatives chosen from the Council of Constance joined the 23 cardinals (5 from the Roman line and 18 from the Pisa line).[43]

Who becomes a cardinal greatly affects who becomes pope since the cardinals usually elect him from their number.[44] Not surprisingly, popes tend to appoint people who are their friends or whose views reflect their own. From the Avignon period into the eighteenth century, nepotism was a common practice. The pope's appointment of like-minded cardinals attempts to ensure that his successor will not deviate radically from his policies. Cardinals used to wear wide-brimmed red hats, which led to referring to an appointment as "getting a red hat." Today they only receive a red biretta from the pope. According to proper ecclesiastical language, cardinals are not just appointed but "created" by the pope. Thus the cardinals appointed by a particular pope are sometimes referred to as his "creatures." This has led to the clerical joke that only God and the pope can create something out of nothing.

Popes have also used red hats to win support from major factions within the church who might prefer a change in direction after the pope's death. In past centuries, appointments were sometimes sold to raise money for the papacy, as occurred early in the sixteenth century when Julius II and Leo X needed funds for wars and construction. Even children and teenagers were appointed cardinals, although they could not be ordained deacons until they were 22 years of age. In 1735, Philip V of Spain insisted that his 8-year-old son, Louis Bourbon, be made a cardinal.[45] Eventually Louis gave up his red hat to marry. On the other hand, Giovanni de' Medici became a cardinal at age 13 and grew up to become Pope Leo X in 1513.

Although the pope can appoint anyone he wants as a cardinal, tradition places some limits on his choices. Some archdioceses, for example the capitals of major nations, have had cardinals for so long that it would be unusual for their archbishops not to be made cardinals.[46] John Paul has also used red hats to strengthen the church in places where it is in conflict with governments. In filling these sees, the pope's options are limited to some extent because he must find someone who would be not only a good cardinal but also an acceptable archbishop of a particular see. Likewise certain curial appointments, such as the prefects of congregations, are traditionally cardinals. The pope must find someone who can do the job, and not just someone who will vote the right way in the next conclave.

With the electors limited to the college of cardinals, in the past those who wished to influence papal elections tried to pressure the cardinals or tried to get their supporters appointed cardinals. During the sixteenth, seventeenth, and eighteenth centuries, Catholic kings considered it their right to nominate candidates whom the pope was forced to make cardinals. These became known as "cardinals of the crown." The history of the papacy is filled with stories of Roman and Italian families, French and Spanish kings, and German emperors fighting for control of the papacy and the college of cardinals. When persuasion was unsuccessful, they resorted to bribery, threats, and violence.

Catholic monarchs, following the example of the Byzantine emperors, also claimed the "right of exclusion" to block the election of candidates they judged to be inimical to their national interests. Spanish and French kings would frequently veto each other's candidates. The last use of such a veto was at the 1903 conclave, where Cardinal John Puszyna, archbishop of Krakow, reported that Emperor Franz Joseph of Austria and Hungary opposed the election of Cardinal Mariano Rampolla, one of the leading candidates. Pius X (1903–1914), elected at this conclave, abolished the right of exclusion.

According to the 1179 decree of Alexander III, the election of the pope required a two-thirds majority of those present, a law that remained in force until Pius XII made it two-thirds plus one in 1945.[47] In 1996, John Paul decreed that a two-thirds vote is sufficient if the number present is divisible into three equal parts. If not, one additional vote is required.

Divisions within the college of cardinals have sometimes made it difficult for a candidate to obtain a two-thirds majority vote. In the thirteenth century the papacy was vacant for a year and a half before the election of Innocent IV (1243–1254) and for three and a half years before the installation of Gregory X (1272–1276). In the first case the election was finally forced by the senate and people of Rome, who locked up the cardinals until a pope was chosen in 1243. Likewise, in the second case, the people of Viterbo in 1271 not only locked the cardinals in, but tore off the roof of the building and put the cardinals on a diet of bread and water.[48]

The man chosen at Viterbo, Gregory X, institutionalized this practice in 1274 with the "conclave," a word that comes from the Latin for "locked with a key." Under his system, the cardinals were locked in one room where they would sleep and vote. After three days their food was limited to one dish a meal. After eight days they would get only bread and water. These measures were quite drastic considering the age of some of the electors. Such severe regulations were not always enforced; twenty-nine conclaves since Gregory's reforms have lasted a month or more. Drastic measures have not been necessary in recent times to speed a conclave to its conclusion. The last conclave to go more than four days was in 1831; it lasted fifty-four days.[49]

According to the reforms instituted by Pope Paul VI, only cardinals under 80 years of age at the beginning of the conclave could vote for the pope. John Paul loosened this rule slightly by only excluding cardinals who turned 80 on the day before the pope died. No cardinal under 80 can be excluded from the conclave, even if he is excommunicated, unless he has been canonically deposed or, with the consent of the pope, has renounced the cardinalate. Needless to say, such cases are rare. A cardinal who had resigned and joined Bonaparte attempted to enter the 1800 conclave but was turned away.[50]

Besides the cardinals, a few people are admitted into the conclave to deal with the medical, liturgical, technical, and domestic needs of the conclave.[51] These persons must be approved by the particular congregation composed of the camerlengo and the three cardinal assistants. The cardinals may not bring personal assistants with them except a nurse for reasons of serious illness. In the past, these personal assistants were numerous and very active in the negotiations leading up to an election. Everyone allowed inside is sworn to secrecy concerning what happens in the conclave.

On the morning the conclave begins, the cardinal electors celebrate Mass in St. Peter's Basilica. In the afternoon, they gather in the Pauline Chapel in the Apostolic Palace and solemnly process to the Sistine Chapel. The cardinals take an oath to observe the rules laid down in *Universi Dominici Gregis,* especially those enjoining secrecy. John Paul added that this secrecy also applies to the cardinals who are not electors. After the 1978 conclaves, cardinal electors felt they could tell the over-80 cardinals what happened, and some of those cardinals, who had not taken the oath of secrecy, then felt they could tell others. John Paul closed this loophole.

Under the conclave rules, the cardinal electors swear not to support interference in the election by any secular authorities or "any group of people or individuals who might wish to intervene in the election of the Roman pontiff." Finally, the electors swear that whoever is elected will carry out the "*munus*

Petrinum [office of Peter] of pastor of the universal church" and will "affirm and defend strenuously the spiritual and temporal rights and liberty of the Holy See."[52]

After the oath is taken, everyone not connected with the conclave is ordered out with the Latin words "Extra omnes." The Sistine Chapel and the Domus Sanctae Marthae are closed to unauthorized persons by the camerlengo. Outside the conclave, the camerlengo is assisted by the sostituto of the Secretariat of State, who directs Vatican personnel to protect the integrity and security of the conclave.

The particular congregation is responsible for ensuring the secrecy of the election. Two trustworthy technicians sweep the area, especially the Sistine Chapel, for bugs or other electronic devices. No communication is permitted between the cardinals and the outside world. Nor are newspapers, radios, televisions, recording devices, or cameras allowed in the conclave. All telephone lines are disconnected except for one in the camerlengo's room to be used only for emergencies. Traditionally, the windows have been sealed and curtains shut to prevent signals to or from the outside. Sealed windows in the Apostolic Palace during the August 1978 conclave led to a stifling atmosphere in the summer heat. The purpose of these regulations is to insulate the cardinals from outside pressure and to preserve the secrecy of the conclave. Communications with the outside world are only permitted in cases of proven and urgent necessity acknowledged by the particular congregation. Three cardinals who might have urgent need to communicate with their offices are noted in *Universi Dominici Gregis:* the major penitentiary, the vicar general for the diocese of Rome, and the archpriest of St. Peter's.

After everyone else leaves, an ecclesiastic, chosen earlier by the college of cardinals, gives a meditation "concerning the grave duty incumbent on them and thus on the need to act with right intention for the good of the universal church, *solum Deum prae oculis habentes* [having only God before their eyes]."[53] When he finishes, he leaves the Sistine Chapel with the master of papal liturgical ceremony so that only the cardinal electors remain.

If they wish, the cardinals can immediately begin the election process and hold one ballot on the afternoon of the first day. Prior to *Universi Dominici Gregis,* there were three ways in which an election could take place. The first was by acclamation when the cardinals, "as it were through the inspiration of the Holy Spirit, freely and spontaneously, unanimously and aloud, proclaim one individual as supreme pontiff."[54] This form of election must be accepted unanimously by the cardinals. Although this method was dramatically depicted in the movie *Shoes of the Fisherman,* it appears to have never been used.

In the past a similar method, election by adoration, was used that required two-thirds of the cardinals to kneel before the candidate and proclaim him pope. This procedure led to abuses when elderly cardinals were tricked into joining in the adoration after being woken up in the middle of the night and told that a new pope had been chosen.

The second method was by delegation whereby the cardinal electors could entrust to a group of their members (an odd number not to exceed nine) the power of electing on behalf of them all. Whomever the group chose would then be pope. The decision to follow this method required unanimous consent, and the cardinals had to agree unanimously on the procedures to be followed by this committee—for example, "whether they should first propose to the entire body of electors the person whom they intend to elect, or whether they should carry out the election directly; whether all the delegates should agree upon the same person or whether they should nominate only a member of the electoral body or also someone outside it, etc."[55] The committee had to complete its work in the time set by the other cardinals or its mandate expired.

In the famous conclave of Viterbo in 1271, the cardinals ended almost three years of wrangling by delegating the choice to a committee of six cardinals, who chose an archdeacon who was not a cardinal and was on a crusade at the time. How often this method was tried is not known, but it appears to have been extremely rare, especially in recent times when unanimous consent was required to form such a committee.

In *Universi Dominici Gregis,* John Paul abolished the methods of election by acclamation and by delegation. He kept the third and ordinary form of electing the pope which is by "scrutiny," the name coming from the scrutineers who count the ballots. The regulations for this method are very detailed to eliminate any suspicion of electoral fraud. Three scrutineers are chosen by lot from the electors, with the least senior cardinal deacon drawing the names. He draws three additional names of cardinals (called *infirmarii*) who will collect the ballots of any cardinals in the conclave who are too sick to come to the Sistine Chapel. A final three names are drawn by lot to act as revisers who review the work done by the scrutineers.

Only the cardinals are allowed in the chapel during the actual election. The time in the chapel is for quiet and prayer and not campaign speeches. Negotiations and arguments are to take place outside the chapel. In 1963, Cardinal Gustavo Testa dramatically broke the rules by urging in a loud voice that the two curial cardinals sitting next to him stop their blocking maneuvers and vote for Montini.[56]

The electors use rectangular cards as ballots, with "Eligo in summum pontificem [I elect as supreme pontiff]" printed at the top. When folded down the middle the ballot is only one inch wide. Each cardinal in secret prints or writes the name of his choice on the ballot in a way that disguises his hand-writing. One at a time, in order of precedence, the cardinals approach the altar with their folded ballot held up so that it can be seen. On the altar there is a receptacle (traditionally a large chalice) covered by a plate (a paten). After kneeling in prayer for a short time, the cardinal rises and swears, "I call as my witness Christ the Lord who will be my judge, that my vote is given to the one who before God I think should be elected."[57] He then places the ballot on the plate. Finally he picks up the plate and uses it to drop the ballot into the receptacle. The use of the plate makes it difficult for a cardinal to drop two ballots into the receptacle. The first scrutineer also uses the plate as a cover when shaking the receptacle to mix the ballots.

Despite the oath, some cardinals on the first ballot cast a "complimentary" vote for their patron or someone they admire but who has no chance of being pope. As one cardinal jokingly remarked, "In the first ballot I will vote for somebody that I want—after that I will let the Holy Spirit guide me."[58] Some-times the complimentary vote will be for the senior cardinal or "favorite son" from a cardinal's country or his part of the world. In the past, electors some-times voted during early ballots for someone other than their favorite because they did not want their opponents to know their true intentions.

Valérie Pirie reports that in 1513, "Many of the cardinals, wishing to tempo-rize and conceal their real intentions, had voted for the man they considered least likely to have any supporters. As luck would have it thirteen [of the 25] prelates had selected the same candidate, with the result that they all but elected Arborense, the most worthless nonentity present."[59] At the 1559 con-clave, Cardinal La Queva secretly approached a large number of cardinals and individually asked them to vote for him on the next ballot so that he would get at least one vote during the conclave. None of them knew that others had been approached. The trick was discovered just before the vote took place. Since the cardinal was known as a practical joker, the trick caused more humor than consternation.[60]

The second vote is in earnest as cardinals begin to vote for the real candi-dates. In subsequent ballots it is important that a candidate keep increasing his tally and not stall short of the goal, as happened to the leading contenders (Cardinal Giovanni Benelli and Cardinal Siri) at the second conclave in 1978. As the tally mounts a bandwagon effect can take place as uncommitted cardi-nals turn to the candidate whose supporters continue to increase. If it is obvious who is going to win on the next vote, most cardinals will go for the winner to show their support for the new pope. Sometimes the final holdouts will cast blank votes to hide which faction is refusing to come on board.

In the past cardinals signed their names on a part of the ballot, which ensured that they did not vote for themselves or vote twice. Today the ballots are not signed, but they are first counted by the last scrutineer before being unfolded. If the number of ballots does not correspond to the number of electors, the ballots are burned without being counted and another vote is immediately taken.[61]

If the number of ballots does match the number of electors, the scrutineers, who are sitting at a table in front of the altar, begin counting the votes. The first scrutineer unfolds the ballot, notes the name on a piece of paper, and passes the ballot to the second scrutineer. He notes the name and passes the ballot to the third scrutineer, who reads it aloud for all the cardinals to hear. The last scrutineer pierces each ballot with a threaded needle through the word "Eligo" and places it on the thread. After all the ballots have been read, the ends of the thread are tied and the ballots thus joined are placed in an empty receptacle. The scrutineers then add up the totals for each candidate. Finally, the three revisers check both the ballots and the notes of the scrutineers to make sure that they performed their task faithfully and exactly.

The ballots and notes (including those made by any cardinal) are then burned unless another vote is to take place immediately. If a second vote takes place, the materials from two votes are burned at the same time. The ballots are burned by the scrutineers with the assistance of the secretary of the conclave and the master of ceremonies, who adds special chemicals to make the smoke white or black. Since 1903, white smoke has signaled the election of a pope; black smoke signals an inconclusive vote. At the 1978 conclaves the master of ceremonies, Virgilio Noè, in burning the ballots did not mix the chemicals properly so that the smoke gave confusing signals to the people in St. Peter's Square. The only written record of the voting permitted is a document prepared by the camerlengo, and approved by the three cardinal assistants, which is prepared at the end of the election and gives the results of each session. This document is given to the new pope and then placed in the archives in a sealed envelope that may be opened by no one unless the pope gives permission.

If no one receives the required two-thirds votes in the balloting on the afternoon of the first day, the cardinals meet again the next morning. From then on, there can be two votes in the morning and two in the afternoon. Each morning and afternoon, new scrutineers, infirmarii, and revisers are chosen by lot.

If after three days the cardinals have still not elected anyone, the voting sessions can be suspended for one day for prayer and discussion among the electors. During this intermission, a brief spiritual exhortation is given by the senior cardinal deacon. Then another seven votes take place followed by a suspension and an exhortation by the senior cardinal priest. Another seven votes take place followed by a suspension and an exhortation by the senior cardinal bishop. Voting is then resumed for another seven ballots.

If no candidate receives a two-thirds vote after all of these ballots, the camerlengo invites the electors to express an opinion about the manner of proceeding. It is at this point that John Paul II dramatically changed the election process by allowing an absolute majority (more than half) of the electors to waive the requirement of a two-thirds majority vote. Thus an absolute majority of the electors can decide to elect the pope by an absolute majority. They can also decide to force a choice between the two candidates who in the preceding ballot received the greatest number of votes. In this second case only an absolute majority is required.[62] As a consequence, if an absolute majority of the electors favor a candidate in the first ballot of the first day of the conclave, all they would have to do is hold firm for about twelve days through about thirty votes until they can change the rules and elect their candidate. There is no incentive for them to compromise or move to another candidate. In fact, the incentive is reversed. The majority is encouraged to hold tight, while the minority is encouraged to give in since everyone knows that eventually the majority will prevail.

John Paul II did not explain in *Universi Dominici Gregis* why he made this change. Perhaps John Paul fears a long conclave. By giving the cardinals more comfortable quarters, he reduced the discomfort factor that discouraged long conclaves. Allowing the cardinals to elect a pope with an absolute majority reduces the likelihood of a conclave going on for months. On the other hand, allowing an absolute majority to elect a pope after about twelve days increases the likelihood of a conclave lasting that long.

Although there have been long conclaves in the past, a long one today would be unusual. In the last 160 years, the two longest conclaves took only four days. One has to go back to 1831 to find a conclave lasting 54 days, or to 1800 for one that lasted three and a half months.

Recent conclaves have been shorter for a number of reasons. The fall of the Catholic monarchies has eliminated the involvement of civil authorities in papal elections. When these monarchs had opposing candidates, conclaves could become deadlocked. The fall of the papal states has also reduced the economic and political spoils available to the pope. In the past, the financial and political well-being of a cardinal and his family might be at risk if the wrong candidate was elected. Today that is no longer the case, although an out-of-favor cardinal might be sidetracked to a less influential post. Thus the economic and political consequences of the election have been substantially reduced. Finally, the mass media coverage of papal elections encourages the cardinals to act expeditiously. The whole world is watching and waiting, and the cardinals do not want to scandalize the faithful with a long conclave that might expose acrimonious divisions.

On the other hand, recent changes in the college of cardinals are likely to make it more difficult for the cardinals to arrive at a quick decision. The electoral college with 120 cardinals is now larger than it has ever been in history. A larger group normally takes longer to make a decision than a smaller group. In addition, the internationalization of the college may slow down elections as cultural and linguistic differences make communication and agreement more difficult. As time goes by, fewer cardinals will be able to communicate in Latin or Italian. The conclave rules make no provision for translators. In addition, in the past, elderly cardinals with poor health preferred a quick election so that they could return to the comforts of home. With the elimination of cardinals over 80, this factor will be reduced.

In past centuries when the popes were the head of the papal states, electoral politics involved bribes, threats, poisons, and even fist fights in the conclave. With the secular and financial rewards of capturing the papacy greatly diminished, the politics of papal elections have become cleaner if not less intense.

Although monarchs no longer interfere, the cardinals are not immune to the world political scene. The outbreak of World War I in 1914 encouraged the cardinals to turn to an experienced diplomat who had been a cardinal for only three months: Benedict XV (1914–1922). Likewise in 1939, the threat of World War II helped the candidacy of Pius XII (1939–1958), who had had a distinguished diplomatic career. In both cases the cardinals judged that a pope with diplomatic skills was important for the church at that time.

If the world is not on the brink of international crisis, the cardinals will focus on internal church issues. Thus in 1963 the central issue was the Second Vatican Council, which was still in session. The cardinals were clearly concerned about what would be the attitude of the new pope toward the council. Paul VI (1963–1978) was seen as a man who was sympathetic to the goals of the council and capable of successfully bringing it to conclusion without dividing the church. The other candidates, Ildebrando Antoniutti and Giacomo Lercaro, were seen as either too conservative or too liberal.

Likewise, in the 1978 elections of John Paul I and John Paul II, the internal life of the church was the cardinals' principal concern, although being strong anti-Communists won both of them conservative support. And even if the international scene is critical, internal church issues are also important. For example, in 1914 the future Benedict XV was considered a peacemaker in the church, as opposed to his predecessor, Pius X (1903–1914), who had persecuted the Modernists who were trying to update theology in response to modern times.

The makeup of the college of cardinals is of course critical to the election since they will choose the pope. In 1994, for the sixth time in his pontificate, Pope John Paul II created new cardinals. Of the 120 cardinals under 80 years of age at the end of 1994, the pope had named 83 percent. The rest were appointed by Paul VI, with none remaining from those created by John XXIII. John Paul has thus set the stage for the election of his successor, who will govern the church in the next millennium.

John Paul has had seventeen years to remake the college of cardinals, and the trend of his changes is clear. He has continued the internationalization of the college begun under Pius XII and Paul VI, with the result that the college in 1994 contained cardinals from more than fifty nations. As early as the twelfth century, St. Bernard of Clairvaux asked, "Is it not reasonable that they [the cardinals] be selected from every nation whose office it is to judge all nations?" Despite these sentiments, Italians dominated the college except during the Avignon period when 83 percent of the newly created cardinals were French.[63] The Council of Constance called for geographical diversity in the college, but the effect was slight as the Italians, followed by the French and the Spanish, dominated the college. Germans were usually kept out of the college because their nation controlled the empire. In the seventeenth and eighteenth centuries, approximately 80 percent of the cardinals named were Italian. Pius IX (1846–1878) and Leo XIII (1878–1903) began to broaden the makeup of the college by having only 58 percent of their appointees Italian. The next largest contingents continued to be French (13 percent) and Spanish (8 percent).[64] In 1875 Pius IX appointed the first cardinal in the Western Hemisphere, John McCloskey of New York. In 1903, 97 percent of the cardinals were European.[65] From 1903 to 1939, 53 percent of the cardinals appointed continued to be Italian.

True internationalization of the college of cardinals began under Pius XII, who was elected in 1939 by a college with 57 percent from Italy and 32 percent from the rest of Europe. The percentage of Italians appointed by Pius XII dropped to only 25 percent, with a third of his appointees from outside Europe. He appointed the first cardinals with sees in Africa, India, and China, although the African cardinal was Portuguese. When Pius XII died, only a third of the college was from Italy with another 31 percent from the rest of

Europe. The major winner was Latin America, which went from 3 percent of the college to 16 percent.

John XXIII, despite his reputation as a reformer, made the college more Italian and more curial than it had been at the death of Pius XII in 1958, although he did appoint the first native African cardinal as well as the first cardinals in Japan and the Philippines. Paul VI continued the internationalization begun by Pius XII. By increasing the size of the college to 120, Paul VI was able to increase the number of residential cardinals and the number of Asian and African cardinals. He thus decreased the percentage of cardinals from the curia, from Italy, and from the rest of Western Europe. He also made cardinals of patriarchs or archbishops from the Maronite, Melkite, Coptic, Ukrainian (Ruthenian), and Chaldean-Malabar churches. John Paul has continued these trends, especially in reducing the percentage of cardinals from Italy. He has also increased the percentage of cardinals from Eastern Europe.

Europe's control of the college has been reduced from 67 percent in 1963 at the death of John XXIII to 46 percent in 1994. About half of this loss came from the Italian bloc. The Italian church still has more cardinal electors (20 at the end of 1994) than any other national group, but its percentage of the college has fallen from 35 percent in 1963, to 24 percent at the death of Paul VI in 1978, to 17 percent in 1994 (half of what it was under John XXIII). The percentage from Western Europe (not counting Italy) went from 29 percent in 1963 to 20 percent in 1978 to 19 percent in 1994.

The major beneficiary of the internationalization of the college of cardinals under Paul VI and John Paul II has been the church of Africa, which has grown from 1 percent of the college at the death of John XXIII to 10.5 percent at the death of Paul VI to 12.5 percent at the end of 1994. Asia has increased slightly, from 7 percent to 9 percent to 11 percent. A beneficiary of the appointments under John Paul has been Eastern Europe, which now has 10 percent of the college of cardinals, up from 6 percent at the death of Paul VI. Latin America, on the other hand, has had a relatively stable percentage of the college since the changes made by Pius XII. The same is true for the United States and Canada, although with 10 electors the United States has the second highest number after Italy.

Thus, Western Europe and especially Italy have been the losers under the changes made in the college by Pius XII and his successors, while Latin America, Africa, and Asia have been the gainers. The internationalization of the college increases the chances that a pope from a Third World church will be elected, since cardinals from the Third World now control 42 percent of the college.

	February 10, 1939[a]	October 9, 1958[b]	June 3, 1963[c]	August 6, 1978[d]	November 26, 1994
Italy	56.5%	32.7%	35.4%	23.7%	16.7%
Western Europe without Italy	25.8	25.5	29.3	20.2	19.2
Eastern Europe[e]	6.5	5.5	2.4	6.1	10.0
Africa	0	1.8	1.2	10.5	12.5
Asia	1.6	7.3	7.3	8.8	10.8
Oceania[f]	0	1.8	1.2	3.5	3.3
Latin America	3.2	16.4	14.6	16.7	18.3
USA and Canada	6.5	9.1	8.5	10.5	9.2

a. At the death of Pius XI on February 10, 1939, there were 62 cardinals.

b. At the death of Pius XII on October 9, 1958, there were 55 cardinals. Before the election, two additional cardinals died: Cardinals Celso Costantini (an Italian in the Roman curia) and Edward Mooney of Detroit. Cardinals Jozsef Mindszenty and Alojzije Stepinac were unable to attend. There were 51 cardinals at the 1958 conclave electing John XXIII.

c. There were 82 cardinals at the death of John XXIII on June 3, 1963. Cardinals Jozsef Mindszenty and Carlos Maria de la Torre were unable to attend the conclave.

d. There were 114 cardinals at the death of Paul VI on August 6, 1978. Cardinal Paul Yu Pin of China died on August 16, 1978. Cardinal Boleslaw Filipiak of Poland missed the August conclave because of illness and died on October 12, 1978. Cardinal John Wright was unable to attend the August conclave because of illness but attended the October conclave.

e. Includes East Berlin.

f. Includes Australia, New Zealand, and Samoa.

In the past, the Italian bloc was extremely important since the pope was expected to be Italian. As the largest national group, the Italian cardinals could have a tremendous impact if they were united. Having fewer Italian cardinals reduces (but does not eliminate) the odds in favor of an Italian pope for two reasons: the number of potential Italian candidates is smaller, and the number of Italian cardinals backing a specific Italian candidate will be smaller. The last conclave elected John Paul II because the Italian cardinals were split between Cardinal Giovanni Benelli and Cardinal Giuseppe Siri. The only viable Italian compromise was Cardinal Giovanni Colombo, the 76-year-old archbishop of Milan, who said he would refuse if elected.

The curial cardinals constitute another important bloc in the college of cardinals. As late as 1939, almost half the cardinals were members of the curia. Pius XII reduced this percentage to 24 percent. John XXIII brought it back up to 37 percent, but Paul VI brought it down to 27 percent where John Paul II has kept it.[66] Since this bloc in the past was mostly Italian, their natural allies were the other Italian cardinals. With the internationalization of the curia under Paul VI and John Paul II, the overlap between the curial cardinals and the Italian cardinals has been reduced. At the end of 1994, only 31 percent of the curial cardinals were Italian.

The curial cardinals have many advantages when it comes to a papal election. They are more likely to be multilingual than their diocesan colleagues. The election takes place on their home turf, so they do not have to travel thousands of miles to get to the conclave. Until the conclave starts, they are living in their homes and operating out of their offices with the support of their staffs. They can invite other cardinals to their homes for dinner and informal consultations. They know the Vatican, they know how to get things done in Rome, and they understand ecclesiastical politics better than their colleagues. They are also more likely than residential cardinals to know the many members of the college. This was especially true in the past when the cardinals only met during a conclave. Since the college did not meet, the non-curial cardinals would not know very many of their colleagues. The curial cardinals, on the other hand, would get to know the other cardinals when they came to Rome for visits or meetings. This knowledge translated into power, making the curial cardinals the natural middlemen for communications within the college.

This situation has changed dramatically in recent years. The internationalization of the curia has reduced the likelihood of the curial cardinals acting as a unified bloc. The speed and ease of international travel also allow cardinals to visit each other's sees and to meet at various international meetings (Eucharistic congresses, regional gatherings of bishops, synods of bishops, and consistories). Residential cardinals also meet at plenary meetings of Vatican congregations and councils. At all these meetings cardinals can see each other in action in formal and informal settings. During these interminable meetings while listening to speeches by their colleagues, cardinals cannot help asking themselves, "Would that man make a good pope? How do I get along with him? Does he listen to me? What is his attitude toward the issues I think are important? How good was his intervention at the meeting? Does he speak my language? How would he go over in my country?" These encounters enable each cardinal to judge potential candidates personally without being dependent on the opinions of the curial cardinals. This is why some refer to the consistories as "dress rehearsals for the next conclave."

Despite the democratic nature of the college of cardinals, not all cardinals have equal influence in selecting a new pope. In most conclaves, a few cardinals play a major role in helping the college select the new pope, and they are referred to as the "great electors." They are ecclesiastical politicians respected or feared by the other cardinals. In past centuries, they often represented the interests of monarchs concerned about the outcome of the election.

While today no cardinal represents a monarch, some cardinals are the acknowledged leaders of various geographical, linguistic, or ideological factions within the church. Thus in 1978, Cardinal Aloisio Lorscheider, archbishop of Fortaleza, Brazil, and president of CELAM, was seen as the leader of the Third World cardinals, especially those from Latin America. His support for Cardinal Albino Luciani of Venice was essential to his election as John Paul I. Cardinal Lorscheider was impressed with Luciani's working-class background and his concern for the poor.[67] Nor did it hurt that Luciani favored Cardinal Lorscheider for pope. Likewise, in 1963, Cardinal Leon-Joseph Suenens was instrumental in getting liberal cardinals to abandon Lercaro and to go for Montini. In 1978, Cardinal Suenens backed Luciani.

The great electors often acted as the campaign managers of papal candidates. Thus while the candidate stayed aloof from the nitty-gritty of ecclesiastical politics, his great elector would wheel and deal and twist arms. In the past, promises of papal favors and appointments were offered for votes. During the time of the papal states, there were many financially rewarding offices. The great elector himself often sought the ultimate prize, appointment as secretary of state. Today, exchanging offices for votes would probably alienate more cardinals than it would gain. And canon law makes it clear that the pope is not bound by any promises made before his election.[68]

In the August 1978 conclave, Cardinal Giovanni Benelli, archbishop of Florence, was the great elector behind the candidacy of Cardinal Albino Luciani. Some thought that Cardinal Benelli, who was considered too young to be pope in the August conclave, hoped to become secretary of state. In the October conclave, Cardinal Benelli himself became a candidate. Cardinal Pericle Felici, a Vatican canonist, was the great elector behind the candidacy of Cardinal Giuseppe Siri, archbishop of Genoa. Cardinal Siri himself had promoted the candidacy of Cardinal Ildebrando Antoniutti, prefect of the Congregation of Religious, at the 1963 conclave in an attempt to stop Montini from being elected. In 1978, Cardinal Franz König, archbishop of Vienna, was a vocal promoter of Cardinal Karol Wojtyla from the very beginning.

Sometimes the voting results indicate strategies developed by the leaders of different factions. According to one report, on the first ballot in the August 1978 conclave, 25 cardinals voted for Cardinal Siri, the conservative candidate. Although he had the highest number of votes, he went to zero on the next ballot as his supporters moved to Luciani.[69] If this story is correct, it shows extraordinary planning and organization since these two votes occurred sequentially with no time for discussion in between. One would have to presume that the Siri supporters had been well instructed by Cardinal Felici on how to vote: they were to show their true feelings on the first vote and then move to the acceptable alternative on the second. By such a strategy they made it clear that the conservatives were an important bloc in the election of John Paul I, a bloc that would have to be reckoned with after the election. Other reporters believe that this story is untrue and was planted by conservatives after the election to exaggerate their influence in the conclave. In any case, a large chunk of Siri voters voted for Luciani by the third ballot.

When the cardinals became deadlocked, the great electors often negotiated to find a compromise candidate who would be acceptable to two-thirds of the conclave. Thus in the 1903 conclave, Giuseppe Sarto (Pius X) was a compromise between Cardinals Mariano Rampolla and Giuseppe Gotti. Likewise in 1922, the supporters of Cardinal Pietro Gasparri turned to Achille Ratti (Pius XI). As a result, Cardinal Gasparri was able to continue as secretary of state.

Who will be the great electors at the next election is uncertain because the timing of that election is uncertain. If the election occurs soon, Cardinals Joseph Bernardin, Basil Hume, Pio Laghi, Alfonso López Trujillo, Achille Silvestrini, Eduardo Martinez Somalo, Carlo Martini, Angelo Sodano, and Jozef Tomko could play this role if they are not candidates. A knowledge of languages, the respect of one's colleagues, and the willingness to play papal politics are all required of a great elector today.

Among the names mentioned in the press as possible successors to John Paul II are Cardinals Francis Arinze (who turned 64 in 1996), Joseph Bernardin (68), Giacomo Biffi (68), Bernardin Gantin (74), Pio Laghi (74), Alfonso López Trujillo (61), Jean-Marie Lustiger (70), Eduardo Martinez Somalo (69), Carlo Martini (69), Lucas Moreira Neves (70), Silvano Piovanelli (72), Camillo Ruini (65), Achille Silvestrini (73), Angelo Sodano (69), and Jozef Tomko (72). Although it is difficult to predict who will be elected pope, there are historical patterns that can help point out the most likely candidates. The ideal candidate would be a noncontroversial figure, in his mid-sixties, who is multilingual, has curial experience, and is archbishop in a nation that is not a major power.

Until *Universi Dominici Gregis,* the most important thing to remember about a papal candidate was that he needed two-thirds plus one votes to be elected pope. Even a popular candidate could be stopped if a third of the cardinals refused to go along. Thus the candidate with the least number of enemies had the best chance of being elected. This is one of the reasons why there is a Roman saying that he who goes into a conclave as the favorite, comes out a cardinal. The two-thirds requirement meant that the cardinals had to compromise and look for a consensus candidate, one who alienated the least number of people. The cardinals usually sought a moderate rather than a radical, a pragmatist rather than an ideologue. The two 1978 conclaves exemplify this point. The principal Italian candidates at the August conclave were Cardinals Siri, Luciani, and Pignedoli. The conservatives supporting Cardinal Siri would never accept Cardinal Pignedoli, and the liberals supporting Cardinal Pignedoli would never accept Cardinal Siri. Luciani had the fewest enemies.

But with the publication of *Universi Dominici Gregis* in 1996, there is no longer an incentive to compromise and find a consensus candidate. All that is needed is a candidate who can get an absolute majority of the votes after about thirty ballots have taken place. This change increases the likelihood of a more radical and ideological candidate being elected pope. It means that a pope can be elected who was opposed by just under half the cardinals.

Second, a papal candidate must be a linguist. He must know Italian or be able to pick it up quickly since he is the bishop of Rome and since Italian is the working language of the Vatican. Because many cardinals have studied or worked in Rome, Italian is usually not a problem especially for those knowing another Romance language like Spanish. English is most people's preferred second language. Spanish is useful because it is the language spoken by more Catholics than any other. And French is still important not only in France but in parts of Africa, Eastern Europe, and the Middle East. Not only are English, Italian, Spanish, and French important for a pope wanting to communicate with the church and the world, they are essential for a papal candidate to communicate with the cardinal electors. A weakness in languages would make it difficult for otherwise highly respected cardinals like Roger Etchegaray or Basil Hume to be elected.

Third, while a papal candidate does not have to be a media star, he cannot be a public embarrassment. Media access to the pope can be closely controlled, but few cardinals today would want to entrust the papacy to a cardinal who through words or deeds would be a public relations disaster. The potential for damage to the church is too great. Cardinals do not want a pope who will do or say embarrassing things that will make life difficult for them in their dioceses.

Age is a fourth factor. Of the nine popes who have lived in this century (beginning with Leo XIII), their average age at the time of election was 65 years.[70] The youngest was John Paul II at 58 (followed by Benedict XV at 59), while the oldest was John XXIII at 76. All the rest were in their sixties. This would indicate that, all other things being equal, the ideal candidate is in his mid-sixties.[71] Since half of the cardinals in 1958 were over 80 years of age, not surprisingly, they elected an elderly cardinal who became John XXIII. In 1978, after Paul VI excluded cardinals over 80 from the conclave, the average age was almost 69. In 1994, after the most recent appointments, the average age of the 120 potential electors was 70.

Since popes are elected for life, young cardinals traditionally are seen as undesirable candidates who would have pontificates of excessive length. Pius IX (1846–1878) was only 46 when elected and reigned for nearly 32 years, the longest papacy in history. The average length of a papal reign has been 7.3 years, but in this century it has grown to 10.5 years.[72] In previous centuries elderly and even sickly cardinals were preferred by cardinals who got rich selling their votes during papal conclaves. Even today, any cardinal who wants to be pope would be very reluctant to vote for someone younger than himself. One source told John Cornwell, who investigated the death of John Paul I, that the number one item of gossip at the August conclave was John Paul I's health.[73] If some of the cardinals (like Cardinal Benelli) knew he was sick, they may have chosen him as an interim pope without realizing how short his reign would be.

Being elderly or sickly is an advantage for a compromise candidate since the older he is the sooner he will die and allow the cardinals to return to elect a serious candidate. Cardinals elected as interim popes, like Sixtus V (1585–1590), have sometimes surprised their electors with their initiatives, John XXIII being the most recent and dramatic example. Of the cardinals most frequently mentioned as possible successors to John Paul II, the following are in their sixties in 1996: Cardinals Francis Arinze (who turned 64 in 1996), Joseph Bernardin (68), Alfonso López Trujillo (61), Camillo Ruini (65), Eduardo Martinez Somalo (69), Carlo Martini (69), and Angelo Sodano (69).

Fifth, nationality is clearly important since 78 percent of the popes have been Italian.[74] Prior to John Paul II, the last non-Italian pope was Hadrian VI (born in Utrecht) in 1522. Since the pope is the bishop of Rome, choosing an Italian, all other things being equal, certainly makes sense. But John Paul II has shown through his pastoral care of the people of Rome that it is possible for a non-Italian to give more attention to his diocese than have many Italian popes.

In periods of international crisis, nationality also makes a difference. Here the desire of the cardinals is to find someone who would be seen as neutral in the wars and disputes among nations. Even a cardinal who had been the nuncio to a great power could be viewed with suspicion by other nations for having become too friendly with that power. During most of papal history, Italy has not been a great power, which has allowed Italian cardinals a better opportunity to remain neutral. Today the candidacy of an American cardinal, like Bernardin, would be handicapped by the fact that he is from the world's only superpower, a country both envied and hated in many parts of the world.

Sixth, another consideration is whether the candidate works in the Roman curia or is a residential archbishop. Of the nine popes who ruled during this century, only one (Pius XII) was never the bishop of a diocese,[75] and only three (Pius X, John Paul I, and John Paul II) never served in the Vatican. The remaining five (Leo XIII, Benedict XV, Pius XI, John XXIII, and Paul V) had served in the Roman curia or the Vatican diplomatic service but were resident archbishops at the time of their elections.

The statistics indicate that the cardinals are reluctant to elect someone who has no pastoral experience as a diocesan bishop. The residential cardinals want someone who shares their experience as a bishop and is not simply a Vatican bureaucrat. On the other hand, the residential cardinal with previous high-level experience in the Roman curia appears to have an advantage as a candidate. There is currently only one cardinal who was an archbishop in the curia and is now a residential cardinal: Lucas Moreira Neves, archbishop of São Salvador da Bahia, Brazil, who turned 71 in 1996. But there are eleven cardinals in the curia who were diocesan bishops before coming to the curia: Francis Arinze (turned 64 in 1996), William Baum (70), Rosalio José Castillo Lara (74), Roger Etchegaray (74), Bernardin Gantin (74), Alfonso López Trujillo (61), Simon Lourdusamy (72), Eduardo Pironio (76), Joseph Ratzinger (69), José Sánchez (76), and Edmund Szoka (69). The poor health of Cardinals Baum and Lourdusamy would rule them out of consideration. Those in their seventies will become less viable candidates as the years progress.

Although the history of the synod of bishops is short, the fact that Karol Wojtyla was an elected member of the Council for the General Secretariat of the Synod of Bishops when he was elected pope encourages one to look at those cardinals elected to the council who were still under 75 years of age at the end of 1996: Joseph Bernardin (68), Godfried Danneels (63), Roger Etchegaray (74), Basil Hume (73), Aloisio Lorscheider (72), Carlo Martini (69), and Jaime Sin (68). If not candidates, these cardinals will certainly be influential because of the confidence placed in them by the synod.

A final variable to be considered is how the candidate compares with his predecessor. Often the cardinals look for someone who balances the weaknesses or failings of the previous pope *as perceived by the cardinals.* This phrase needs to be emphasized because the electors are not necessarily influenced by the media speculation or by public opinion. While the media might decry the papal positions on certain doctrinal issues (abortion, birth control, divorce, and women priests), these would not be issues for most of the cardinals who have been appointed by John Paul II.

With general consensus on doctrinal issues, the cardinals are more likely to focus on questions of style and personality. If the previous pope was considered weak, they will tend to look for a stronger leader. If he was considered authoritarian, they will look for someone more collegial. If he was intransigent, they might look for someone more open to change. A good administrator might be followed by a pastoral pope, and vice versa.

Thus the fat, jovial peasant and grandfatherly figure, John XXIII, followed the ascetic and austere aristocrat, Pius XII. Then the highly competent executive, Paul VI, followed the less organized John XXIII. The smiling pastor, John Paul I, followed the sad and depressed bureaucrat, Paul VI. Finally, the robust and confident John Paul II succeeded the sickly and uncertain John Paul I. John Paul II was also seen as the strong charismatic leader following the weak and introverted Paul VI. These descriptions are not necessarily accurate, but they were perceptions held by some of the cardinals at the conclaves.

When the cardinals meet in conclave after the death of John Paul II, what might they see as his weaknesses and failings that should be balanced by his successor? This is not something that cardinals talk freely about, but there are some concerns that might affect a future conclave.

Because John Paul's reign has been long, many cardinals will not want to elect another young pope. Realizing how he has reduced their power in the curia and in the college of cardinals, the Italians may see the next conclave as the last chance to elect one of their own. Likewise, although they generally agree with John Paul on the issues, the curial cardinals would like to see a pope who takes them more seriously by staying in Rome and meeting with them more frequently. Some curialists would also like to see a pope who would reduce the dominance of the Congregation for the Doctrine of the Faith over their offices.

"For some people in the Vatican, *the* pope was Pius XII," explains a longtime Vatican observer.

> He was distant, as though his feet did not touch the earth. John Paul II, going to the people and hugging them, that just does not fit with their conception of what the pope should be. Many of these people, who like John Paul's positions, do not care much for his public persona, this going out to the people, hugging the babies and traveling. They would say, "He travels all over the place. Look at the documents piling up, we're so far behind. No one is running the show back home, because every time he went on a trip, he would take cardinal secretary of state, the sostituto, etc." And then the skiing thing, they think that is just loco.

Some cardinals also complain that John Paul and the Vatican have issued too many documents and encyclicals for the church to absorb. And when the documents are controversial, the residential cardinal is on the firing line, forced to defend them even if he was not consulted in drafting them. Some residential cardinals may desire a pope who will give more power to diocesan bishops and episcopal conferences than John Paul has been willing to give. Those cardinals who feel overwhelmed by the force and power of John Paul's personality and charism may want someone a little less forceful. And if large numbers of theologians (or women) continue to feel alienated from the papacy, some cardinals will look for someone who can bridge that gap without giving in on sound doctrine. Other cardinals may feel that an even stronger hand should be taken with dissenters. All this has less to do with theology than with personality and leadership styles.

Immediately after the election of the pope, the dean of the college of cardinals asks the one elected, "Do you accept your canonical election as supreme pontiff?" After he says yes, the dean asks him by what name he wants to be called. The first pope to change his name was John II in 533. His given name, Mercury, was considered inappropriate since it was the name of a pagan god. Another pope in 983 took the name John XIV because his given name was Peter. Reverence for the first pope precluded his becoming Peter II. At the end of the first millennium a couple of non-Italian popes changed their names to ones that their people could more easily pronounce. The custom of changing one's name became common around the year 1009. The last pope to keep his own name was Marcellus II, elected in 1555.[76]

On rare occasions people have turned down the papacy. When offered the papacy at the 1271 Viterbo conclave, St. Philip Benizi fled and hid until another candidate was chosen.[77] Likewise St. Charles Borromeo (1538–1584), one of the few cardinals to be canonized, turned down the papacy. When Cardinal Giovanni Colombo, the 76-year-old archbishop of Milan, began receiving votes during the October 1978 conclave, he made it clear that he would refuse the papacy if elected.[78] But normally those approached accept.

Although during the last nine centuries the cardinals have normally chosen one of themselves to be pope, they can go outside the college of cardinals. The last noncardinal to be elected was the archbishop of Bari, who became Urban VI in 1378 when the citizens of Rome were rioting and demanding that an Italian be elected lest a French pope return the papacy to Avignon. This proved to be a disastrous choice because his unexpected election appears to have unbalanced him. The French cardinals withdrew and elected their own pope, beginning the Western Schism which lasted 40 years. During his 11-year reign, Pope Urban appointed 29 cardinals, most of whom deserted him before he died, probably of poison.[79] By the time things were resolved at the Council of Constance in 1417, the church had three prelates claiming to be pope.

Since in the past some cardinals were not bishops, sometimes a priest or deacon was chosen. A priest was last chosen in 1831 when Gregory XVI was elected.[80] Deacons have also been elected, as occurred at the famous Viterbo conclave in 1271.[81] When Cardinal Alfonso Borgia was elected as Callistus III in 1455 he was neither a priest nor a deacon, although technically not a layman because he had received tonsure. Forty percent of the cardinals at this conclave were not priests, and they were looking for someone who would not inhibit their profligate life styles.[82] Today all the cardinals under 80 years of age are bishops.

The cardinals can elect whomever they wish as pope as long as he is a baptized male. Even the baptized part is negotiable as long as the man is willing to be baptized, ordained a priest, and then consecrated bishop of Rome. John XIX and Benedict IX were laymen when elected in 1024 and 1032. Both owed their elections to bribery, and Benedict abdicated, at a price, to Gregory VI. Once a pope is elected, his election cannot be invalidated even if he bought the election.

As soon as the person elected consents to being pope, if he is already a bishop, he is immediately bishop of Rome and pope with full authority. No other ceremony is necessary. If he is not a bishop, he must be ordained immediately and then he becomes bishop of Rome. Thus Gregory XVI had to be consecrated a bishop when he was elected pope in 1831. In 752 a priest named Stephen was elected, but he died before he was ordained a bishop and therefore is not counted as a pope. Likewise Hadrian V (1276) died within five weeks of his election, never having even been ordained a priest.[83] The most exciting case, however, is that of the cardinal priest Theobaldo who was unanimously elected in 1124. While the installation was in progress, the Frangipani family broke into the assembly and at sword-point had Cardinal Lamberto of Ostia acclaimed pope: "There was a violent struggle in which Theobaldo suffered blows and severe wounds, but the outcome was that he was either forced or persuaded to resign while Lamberto was elected and installed as Honorius II."[84]

After the election (or ordination), the cardinals individually approach the new pope, pay him homage, and promise their obedience. The cardinals did this on their knees before a sitting pope until John Paul II broke with custom by greeting the cardinals standing. After the conclave, the pope used to be crowned with the tiara by the senior cardinal deacon, but John Paul I did away with that custom.

History teaches that there is no perfect method for choosing a pope. Both saints and scoundrels have been elected. Even Jesus did not do too well, since his choice, St. Peter, denied him and ran away on Good Friday. Of the 262 deceased successors of St. Peter, only 76 are listed as saints by the church, and half of these lived in the first four centuries. Only five popes during this millennium have been called saints: Leo IX (1049–1054), Gregory VII (1073–1085), Celestine V (1294), Pius V (1566–1572), and Pius X (1903–1914).[85]

The current procedures used to elect a pope are not of divine origin. Many people, including Paul VI, have suggested expanding the electorate beyond the college of cardinals. In 1973 Paul VI revealed a tentative plan to allow the Eastern-rite patriarchs and the fifteen members of the Council of the Permanent Secretariat of the Synod of Bishops to join the cardinals in electing the pope.[86] Since the council members are often cardinals, this would add only about six noncardinals to the electors. Some papal advisers argued against this change simply because it was against tradition.[87] Others supported the status quo because the cardinals, who are assigned titular churches in Rome, are considered members of the Roman clergy. This makes Rome one of the last dioceses in the Western church where part of the clergy still elect their bishop. To add noncardinal electors would violate this canonical legerdemain.

Paul VI listened to these objections and limited his reform to increasing the college to 120 cardinals and denying the vote to those over 80 years of age. These changes in themselves were revolutionary. Paul's reform upset the elderly cardinals and led Archbishop Marcel Lefebvre to say that he would not accept any pope elected by a conclave without the older cardinals present. After the August 1978 conclave, cardinals revealed that the final majority was large enough so that even if the sixteen over-80 (and therefore absent) cardinals had all voted against John Paul I, he would still have been elected. This eliminated any objections, however specious, to the election.[88]

Paul VI and John Paul II internationalized the college so that it became less curial, less Italian, and less Western European and more African and Asian. Despite these changes, the college of cardinals still does not accurately reflect the geographical diversity of the church. Latin America, for example, has 42 percent of the world's Catholics but only 18 percent of the cardinals. On the other hand, Europe has 30 percent of the world's Catholics and 46 percent of the cardinals. To make the college of cardinals more reflective of the universal church, the number of Latin American cardinals should be increased.

Limiting the college of cardinals to diocesan bishops would make the college more reflective of the concerns of local churches and local bishops, who make up the largest part of the college of bishops. Eliminating curial officials from the college would open up 31 additional slots for local churches in the college without increasing its size. It would also eliminate the current problem of giving the old pope's staff a major voice in the selection of their new boss. Nor would the new pope have to deal with cardinal prefects who had voted against him in the conclave.

Others have suggested adding laypersons to the college of cardinals. Paul VI wanted to appoint Jacques Maritain, a lay French philosopher, to the college of cardinals, but Maritain declined. At the 1994 synod of bishops, Bishop Ernest Kombo from the Congo suggested appointing a woman cardinal. While there is historical precedent for laymen in the college of cardinals, adding nonbishops to the college of cardinals would disconnect it from the college of bishops. By making all the cardinals bishops, John XXIII linked the two colleges in a new way that has some theological justification since the person they choose will be the head of the college of bishops. One or two lay cardinals would be mere tokenism, while more would dramatically change the electoral process. The more practical problem in appointing lay cardinals is determining who should be appointed. What criteria would be used in selecting the lay cardinals? Whom would they represent?

Eliminating the college of cardinals and returning to the ancient practice of having the people or the clergy of Rome elect the pope is unrealistic. The ancient democratic elections of popes were rife with dissension and mob violence. And one shudders at the thought of the people of Rome electing the pope. Not only have they elected Communist mayors in the past, but papal elections could become as corrupt as the rest of Italian politics with the papacy simply another prize for Italian politicians. Having the clergy of Rome elect the pope is also problematic. Rome has few priests who were born in Rome. If priests incardinated in Rome became the papal electors, politically ambitious clerics would flood into Rome from all over Italy and the world.

Cardinals Michele Pellegrino and Leon-Joseph Suenens have suggested that the presidents of the episcopal conferences (currently about 100) act as papal electors since they could be considered as representative of the college of bishops.[89] Such an election process would mean that the smallest conference would have the same vote as the largest. It would also intensify debate over how many bishops are needed in a nation before Rome creates a new conference.

Election of the pope by a synod of bishops would be a better alternative. Such an election would imitate the practice in many Eastern-rite churches, where synods of bishops elect metropolitans and patriarchs. The easiest system would be to recall to Rome those bishops whom their conferences had elected to the most recent ordinary synod of bishops. This would avoid potentially divisive elections and campaigns, although as a pope got older or became sick, the election of synod delegates would have more to do with the succession and less with the topic of the synod. Curial officials would not attend since their membership in a synod is based on holding offices that they lose when the pope dies. Nor would there be any papal appointees since the pope would be dead. Such a synod would be more representative of the local churches than the current college of cardinals.

During the Second Vatican Council some people wanted the council rather than the college of cardinals to choose the successor of John XXIII. At various times in history, reformers have suggested electing the pope by the college of bishops. All the bishops could attend such a council (including more than 900 retired bishops under the current Code of Canon Law). But a 3,200-member electorate, larger than the total number of cardinals who have ever lived, would be cumbersome. It would be impossible to lock up such a large group, and the divisions and politics would be difficult to hide. A council that unanimously chose a pope would certainly help church unity, but an acrimonious council with members publicly fighting for months over papal candidates would be a disaster for church unity. Picking a name out of a hat, as was done to replace Judas, might be preferable to a divisive election. Perhaps a two-stage election process might be devised whereby the college of cardinals or a synod would nominate a candidate who must be approved by the full college of bishops. But such a system would be subject to deadlock if the nominators and the college of bishops could not agree on a candidate. It would also be difficult to execute in times of war or political and social instability. History warns against complacently expecting rulers to keep their hands off the papacy. Any suggestions for reform must keep this in mind.

While there could be difficulties with papal elections carried out by a synod or ecumenical council, those defending the status quo must acknowledge that the college of cardinals has produced numerous bad popes, including those who gave disastrous leadership to the church in the centuries before the Reformation. The college was not immune to influence from civil authorities or clerics using threats, violence, and bribes, although its record in this century has been exemplary in this regard. Nor has the college's manner of proceeding always fostered church unity. The present procedures encourage continuity between papacies because the pope appoints many of the electors who will choose his successor. In general, this is good for church unity because it keeps the church from being pulled from side to side by popes with radically different agendas. On the other hand, in a rapidly changing world, excessive continuity may make it difficult for the church to respond to the signs of the times. This is especially true if the college of cardinals loses its sensitivity to the needs of local churches.

Finally, John Paul II's recent decision to allow the election of a pope by an absolute majority of the college of cardinals must be questioned. The two-thirds majority requirement encouraged compromise and consensus, virtues that are needed to maintain the unity of such a large and complex church. That this change was made with no debate or explanation is regrettable. It is almost as if the pope did not realize the consequences of what he decreed.

Synods, councils, consistories, and conclaves have a long and varied history in the Catholic church. Collegial bodies have been adapted through the centuries to a variety of situations as different leaders within the church have used them for attaining a variety of goals. Adaptation of collegial structures is still going on, as can be seen especially with episcopal conferences, the synod of bishops, and the consistory of cardinals. The proper role of these collegial bodies is debated within the church. Such debate is the natural result of living in a period when church leaders with a variety of goals are responding to a changing environment by proposing adaptations of church structures. The proper role and structure of these entities are unclear because different actors in the church have different goals and different interpretations of the environment. For example, while many have seen these collegial bodies as structures to express a plurality of views, John Paul has used them to foster unity in the church.

Since the 1960s there has been a tremendous increase in activity for collegial structures: an ecumenical council lasting almost four years, nine ordinary synods, two extraordinary synods, four special synods, five extraordinary consistories, three conclaves, and innumerable meetings of approximately one hundred episcopal conferences. Meetings of ordinary synods and of episcopal conferences are so regular and play such an essential role in the governance of the church that one must conclude that they are here to stay. But the long-term consequences of these structural changes in the church remain to be seen.

Collegial bodies—councils, consistories, conferences, and synods—operate differently from the more hierarchical and bureaucratic structures of the Roman curia. Although at one time these collegial bodies were a threat to papal power, today they are very deferential to papal wishes. This deference is reflected in theological doctrine and canonical regulations dealing with collegial structures. More important, deference to papal wishes is reflected in the attitudes of the members, who owe their appointment as bishops and cardinals to the papacy. Because of their size these collegial bodies are often unwieldy and can only accomplish limited results within the time constraints in which they operate. But they bring to church discussions an important perspective that is both local and varied. The ecclesial culture today demands consultation and discussion. Although not perfectly democratic, these structures provide a mechanism that acts as both a safety valve and a reality check within a large international church organized primarily on a hierarchical basis.

～ 5

The Roman Curia

ALTHOUGH THE COLLEGE of bishops together with the pope is the supreme authority within the church, the college rarely meets either as an ecumenical council or as a synod of bishops. As a result, while the bishops are home in their dioceses, the pope is left in Rome with the Roman curia. Until the time of Pius X, the term "Roman curia" referred to all the papal offices, but he restricted its use to those helping the pope in the governance of the universal church, as opposed to those involved in running Vatican City or the diocese of Rome.

The importance of the Roman curia in the life of the Catholic church must not be underestimated. This bureaucracy processes the appointment of bishops, sets policy concerning remarriage of divorced Catholics, decides what prayers will be used at Mass, and determines the position of the Vatican on Third World debt. The Roman curia was severely attacked during the Second Vatican Council for being backward and obstructionist. It is still the villain of liberal Catholics who would like to see more change in the church. Because of its relatively small size and vast jurisdiction, some consider it the most efficient bureaucracy in the world. Others say that it is out of touch with reality and that its procedures are archaic and inefficient. The organization and procedures of the Roman curia are not static; they are evolving today just as they have continually changed throughout the church's history, responding to different popes and to different historical situations.

Although the term "Roman curia" only came into use during the eleventh century, the popes always had assistants in their ministry.

Beginning in apostolic times, church leaders recruited helpers to assist them in their work. Deacons were recruited to take over the material needs of the community so the Apostles would have time to preach (Acts 6:1–6). Other assistants were chosen to preach the gospel and celebrate the sacraments in communities where the apostles could not visit or stay. A few helpers stayed with the apostles and assisted them directly in their ministry. For example, Peter and Paul had secretaries who helped with their correspondence (Romans 16:22 and 1 Peter 5:12). It is these secretaries who were the ancient forerunners of diocesan and Roman curias.

After the death of the Apostles, bishops in local communities also needed help in their ministry. At first, the bishop of Rome had helpers much like those of any other bishop: priests for house-churches, deacons for material assistance and for catechumens, and notaries or secretaries for correspondence and record keeping.[1] As the church moved from being a persecuted minority to a state-sponsored church, additional organization was required to deal with increased wealth and greater numbers of Christians. After 773, the pope's responsibility for the papal states required all the usual organs of civil power, but even earlier the pope's growing role in the universal church required assistants.

By the fourth century, imitating the practice of the imperial court, notaries were a permanent fixture in the papacy. As staff to the pope, these men wrote letters and kept records of correspondence and other official documents. For example, they took minutes at the Lateran Council of 649 and prepared its acts.[2] Because of the notaries' training and experience, popes sometimes sent them on diplomatic missions or to ecumenical councils in the East. The primicerius or chief notary was a close adviser to the pope.

As the papal workload increased, the notaries or secretaries took on added responsibility and became administrators delegated to do certain jobs. By the thirteenth century the Apostolic Chancellery was an important office, and the chancellor was the pope's principal adviser and assistant. The chancellery handled appointments of bishops and abbots as well as bulls and rescripts. Before becoming pope, John XXII (1316–1344) had been chancellor to the French king. He used his expertise in organizing the chancellery to handle papal business.

After the return to Rome from Avignon, the chancellery declined in importance, with the Apostolic Datary taking a preeminent role. The datary began as the official responsible for the proper dating of papal documents. He also witnessed papal signatures and eventually became the person who decided which papers would be presented to the pope for his signature. The datary's main function became conferring benefices reserved to the pope that did not have to be considered in a consistory. He had an office with assistants in the sixteenth century, but by the seventeenth century this office was also in decline.

The rise of the Secretariat of State paralleled the decline of the Apostolic Chancellery and the Apostolic Datary. Originally the secretariat was an office in the Apostolic Chancellery to deal with secret correspondence, especially diplomatic correspondence. These notaries were called secretaries and became a distinct office in the fifteenth century, originally called the office of the Privy Seal and then the Apostolic Secretariat in 1487. The chief secretary and adviser to the pope was the secretarius domesticus. After Leo X (1513–1521) created the apostolic nuncios, these diplomats reported to this secretary. The secretarius domesticus was soon eclipsed by the cardinal nephew and his staff, one of whom became known as the secretary of state. The pope chose a nephew or relative to be his chief executive in the belief that family loyalty would bind him closely to the pope.

It was not until the mid-seventeenth century that the practice became common of choosing the secretary of state from the cardinals. The suppression of the office of cardinal nephew meant that the secretary of state became the most powerful papal adviser with influence in political and religious affairs. The pope used him to direct other papal offices, and he became the equivalent of the prime minister of the papal states. After the fall of the papal states, the secretary of state remained the key Vatican figure in diplomatic and religious affairs. The Secretariat of State now has two sections, the first one handling papal correspondence and documents and the second section dealing with relations with states. The head of the first section also acts as a chief of staff for the pope in dealing with the Roman curia.

To return to the sixteenth century, the consistory system whereby cardinals as a group advised the pope was disappearing. Committees or congregations of cardinals were formed to study particular issues and report back to the pope. In response to the Reformation, the first permanent congregation, the Universal Inquisition, was established in 1542 to deal with matters of faith and heresy. Later it became known as the Holy Office, and today it is the Congregation for the Doctrine of the Faith. Next came the Congregation of the Council, established in 1564 to implement the decrees of the Council of Trent. Its successor today is the Congregation for the Clergy.

Pope Sixtus V (1585–1590) established fifteen congregations, five for governing the papal states and ten for church matters. To help the cardinals in their work, these congregations took on staff which eventually evolved into a bureaucracy. "Some thirty Congregations arose, disappeared, fused, or underwent transformation during the 17th, 18th and 19th centuries," reports Ignazio Gordon.[3] "At the end of the 19th century the Roman curia was a maze of congregations, tribunals, secretariats, and offices, whose functions were not precisely demarcated. Executive power overlapped with judicial, ecclesiastical affairs with the relics of the government of the papal states."[4] Pius X reformed this system in 1908, establishing the structure of congregations and tribunals that is still visible today. A number of new secretariats and councils were created after Vatican II. The 1988 reform of the curia simplified the terminology and the structure by turning the secretariats into councils.

The organization and structure of the Roman curia today are complex and confusing to the uninitiated. There are 1,740 people employed in the Roman curia, which includes the Secretariat of State, nine congregations, eleven councils, three tribunals, and other offices.[5] These curial agencies, known as dicasteries, organize the people who gather and process information, give advice to the pope, and implement his decisions.

Few people either inside or outside the curia understand its complex structure, overlapping jurisdictions, and Byzantine procedures. Part of the confusion arises from the complexity of the issues that the curia deals with (for example, ecumenism, evangelization, refugee assistance, international relations, bioethics). Part of the confusion comes from the complexity of the church itself, which includes many types of people (bishops, priests, religious, laity) involved in a variety of institutions (schools, hospitals, parishes, associations, missions, seminaries, religious communities, charitable institutions) doing a variety of activities (worship, education, seminary training, evangelization, charitable work, fund raising) in many different countries and cultures. And part of the complexity comes from the fact that the curia has developed through history in an ad hoc manner, responding to specific needs. It is a product of history, not management theory.

Tribunals

The curia currently has three tribunals. The Apostolic Penitentiary, headed by Cardinal William Baum, deals with excommunications reserved to the Holy See. There are currently only five reserved excommunications: for a priest breaking the confidentiality of a confession; for a priest absolving his accomplice in a sexual sin; for a person physically attacking the pope; for a bishop consecrating a bishop without the approval of the Holy See; and for a person desecrating the Eucharist. Needless to say, these cases are rare. The Penitentiary also provides internal forum solutions to certain cases that would otherwise not be resolvable in church courts. For example, the Penitentiary once privately removed the excommunication unjustly imposed by a Mexican bishop on a person defending the rights of the laity, but asked the man to attend church in another diocese. It has also ruled marriages invalid when the evidence was inadequate for such a ruling by a regular tribunal. The Penitentiary can also make valid *(sanatio)* an action that was originally invalid for some reason. The Penitentiary's work is very technical, very limited, and very secret.

The Roman Rota is the busiest of the Holy See's tribunals. In 1994 it had about 640 cases pending and issued about 100 decisions or sentences.[6] Thanks to money raised by Cardinal Edmund Szoka from the owner of Domino's Pizza, the Rota was one of the first dicasteries to be computerized in imitation of American diocesan tribunals. A well-prepared case could take six months to a year to process, but some cases take years because the judges have to request additional information and wait for its arrival. Although theoretically the Rota could judge other issues of justice in the church, all but a few of its decisions in 1994 involved marriage cases.

In panels of three, its twenty-one priest judges hear appeals from provincial tribunals that must review all annulments granted by diocesan tribunals. If the provincial and the diocesan tribunals disagree, the case goes to the Rota. A losing party in the case, the petitioner or the respondent, can also appeal even if the two lower courts are in agreement. Decisions of lower courts in nonmarriage cases can also be appealed to the Rota. For example, a pedophile priest who refused to resign could be dismissed from the priesthood after being convicted of an ecclesiastical crime in a diocesan court, but the priest could appeal the decision to the Rota. If the decision of a three-judge panel of the Rota is appealed, it usually goes to another panel of three judges within the Rota, except for some procedural points that can be appealed to the Signatura. Although canon law does not recognize judicial decisions as binding precedent, lower court judges study the Rota's published decisions (with names deleted) because they know their decisions can be overturned on appeal.

The Rota can accept annulment cases directly, bypassing local tribunals. This is sometimes done at the request of a petitioner, as was the case when former Governor Hugh Carey's wife sought an annulment of her three previous marriages. If an annulment case involves heads of state or royalty, who the Vatican fears could unduly influence local tribunals, it goes directly to Rome. The annulment for Princess Caroline of Monaco, which took ten years to process, was done by a special commission of Rota judges appointed by the pope. The Rota also has original jurisdiction in disputes between bishops and between people or institutions immediately under the pope. The few nonmarriage cases before the Rota usually involve disputes over money or contracts. One case involving a former employee suing his Austrian bishop went on for more than thirty-five years. In 1990 a rare libel case was brought to the Rota by a politician against a journalist for the Italian Catholic weekly *Famiglia Cristiana*. Since the journalist refused to respond in court, the case went nowhere.

Working for the Rota are a promoter of justice and the defender of the bond. The defender of the bond looks for reasons supporting the validity of the marriage in an annulment case. The promoter of justice is like a state attorney and acts as the prosecutor in criminal cases. He defends the law of the church and its system of justice, and also advises the judges on legal and procedural matters.

Arguing for the petitioner (and the respondent if he or she desires) is an advocate. About seventy-eight advocates are registered with the Rota. They are specially trained Italian canon lawyers, mostly laymen but a growing number of laywomen, whose fees are set by the court. "Everybody knows that you can speed up the case by paying the advocate something more" so that he will make it a priority among his cases, explains a canon law professor. "Technically that should not be done. It is not quite a bribe. It is your appreciation, your gift. It is done in a very subtle way." The German bishops' conference avoids this problem by hiring a single lawyer to handle all German cases. There is a special arrangement for U.S. cases that are assigned to advocates on a pro bono basis by the Rota. In these cases, court costs and any stipend for the advocate are paid directly to the Rota by the diocese. Individuals have the option of hiring their own lawyers at their own expense.

The Apostolic Signatura is the supreme court of the church and is composed of a panel of seven cardinals and four bishops headed by Cardinal Gilberto Agustoni. The Signatura staff is divided into two sections. The first serves the Signatura in resolving disputes over jurisdiction between church tribunals (for example, if the parties live in different jurisdictions) and in reviewing procedural appeals from the Rota. The second section serves the Signatura in its work as an administrative tribunal taking appeals from administrative decisions of Vatican congregations. For example, after the Congregation for the Clergy rules in a dispute over the removal of a pastor, the losing party (either the bishop or the priest) can appeal to the Signatura. About ten to thirty appeals are made to the Signatura each year, most of which are rejected at the staff level. Only about half a dozen cases a year are heard by the panel of cardinals and bishops, and these cases take about three years to be processed. "The presumption is that people in authority in the church, given the nature of the church and the nature of the pastoral office, are trying their best to do what needs to be done, respect people's rights, and follow the law," explains a member of the staff. "So it should be rare for a higher authority to say that a bishop or a religious superior actually violated the law."

The Signatura also receives reports from diocesan tribunals each year and reviews them to make sure their personnel are properly trained and following correct procedures. The Rota will overturn an annulment if the diocesan tribunal did not follow proper procedures—for example, by not notifying the other partner in an annulment case. "We have a duty to point out mistakes in procedures if somebody has complained about their rights being violated," explains a Rota judge. They are also sending a message to the lower tribunals. "Why don't you do it the way the code says? Then there wouldn't be any problem," argues another Rota judge. "The difference between doing a good job on these cases and doing a bad job amounts to about thirty minutes per case. In a drive for efficiency, many cases that are quite good do not turn out that way because the procedural law has not been followed."

American canon lawyers complain that Rota and Signatura officials are increasing procedural requirements to limit the number of annulments. For example, the Signatura requires that all tribunal officials not only know the law but have a degree in canon law. A more thorough examination of the Rota and the Signatura would require an extensive discussion of the church's law dealing with marriage annulments, which is outside the scope of this book. Regarding nonmarriage cases, an American canon law professor comments that "for all practical purposes there is no judicial system for vindicating rights in the church. Whenever anyone approaches me, I ask them if they want to go to great expense, take years, and maybe have to go to Rome. They usually drop it."

Congregations and Councils

Most of the important dicasteries are called congregations or councils. The difference between the congregations and the councils has more to do with prestige and authority than with organizational structure. The older congregations are higher in the Vatican pecking order than the more recently created councils, and the congregations often have better offices that are closer to St. Peter's Square. But the basic structure of councils and congregations is the same:

1. A defined area of competence based on the type of church, the type of person, or the type of issue. The division of competencies is laid out in the apostolic constitution *Pastor Bonus* (June 28, 1988).[7]

2. A committee (called a congregation or a council) whose members are appointed by the pope for five-year renewable terms. The membership of a council may include lay members, but the members of a congregation are only cardinals and bishops.

3. A prefect (for congregations) or president (for councils), appointed by the pope for a five-year renewable term, who chairs the committee and is in charge of the staff. In congregations he is a cardinal while in a council he need not be, although at the end of 1994 only two council presidents were not cardinals.

4. A secretary, who is in charge of the day-to-day operations of the staff. In a congregation he is an archbishop, while in a council he can be a priest.

5. An undersecretary, who often acts as an office manager under the secretary. He is usually a priest, but two council undersecretaries are laymen. The prefect, secretary, and undersecretary are referred to as the superiors in the dicastery.

6. A professional staff composed mostly of priests (the councils have more lay professionals than do congregations), and a support staff who are mostly Italian laypersons.

7. Consultors who are experts in the topics covered by the congregation or council, frequently professors in theology or canon law at pontifical universities in Rome. Most of the consultors to the congregations are priests, while some of the consultants to the councils are laypersons.

The nine congregations and eleven councils perform many functions assigned to them by the pope. Most of the functions can be grouped into one of two major categories: jurisdictional and promotional. Jurisdictional authority is the authority to make a decision on a particular matter that is binding on people, even bishops, under canon law.[8] The promotional role deals more with the education and persuasion of people rather than law.

A great deal of time and effort by dicasteries goes into studying how church teaching applies to particular issues and promoting activities in keeping with church teaching. To encourage study and action on certain issues, dicasteries put on conferences on topics such as AIDS, humanitarian intervention, the priesthood, or refugees. Dicastery staff also travel to conferences held by others to make presentations. They publish documents, newsletters, and other publications giving the results of their work and promoting study and action by others in the church. Some dicasteries use the media, for example through press conferences, to publicize their activities. In their promotional activities, dicasteries are similar to public policy think tanks except that they are dealing with religious issues or are taking a religious or ethical perspective on world issues. Their success depends on their credibility, the quality of their work, and their ability to attract and persuade a particular audience.

Most councils are primarily promotional, but some have jurisdictional authority. The Council for the Laity, for example, has the authority to approve the charters of international Catholic lay organizations. The Ecumenical Directory issued by the Council for Promoting Christian Unity has some canonical authority. Certainly the Council for the Interpretation of Legislative Texts resolves jurisdictional issues when its interpretations are approved by the pope. But the Council for Justice and Peace, the Council for the Family, and most other councils are purely promotional, with no jurisdiction over any persons.

The congregations have both jurisdictional and promotional activities. For example, the Congregation for Catholic Education has the canonical authority to approve or disapprove of the appointment of professors and the conferral of honorary degrees in ecclesiastical faculties chartered by the Holy See. At the same time, it is responsible for promoting better education and training of seminarians. The Congregation for the Clergy has the authority to overrule bishops when they violate canon law in dealing with their clergy, but it also promotes activities to help the spiritual lives of priests. The Congregation for Divine Worship and the Discipline of the Sacraments has the authority to approve liturgical texts, but it also encourages liturgical worship.

The division of responsibility among the various congregations and councils is complex. Some responsibilities are divided by the type of church (Oriental, Latin missionary, Latin non-missionary), some are divided by issues (ecumenism, doctrine, liturgy, or social communications), and some are divided by the people affected (bishops, clergy, religious, laity, health care workers).

The pope is head not only of the Roman (or Latin) Catholic Church, but also of about twenty Oriental Catholic churches. Some of the congregations and councils deal with issues affecting both the Latin and the Oriental churches, while others are limited to concerns of either the Latin church or the Oriental churches. The dicasteries that deal with the universal church include the Congregation for the Doctrine of the Faith, the Congregation for the Causes of Saints, and most of the councils (the Council for Promoting Christian Unity, the Council for Interreligious Dialogue, the Council for Justice and Peace, the Council Cor Unum, and the Council for the Interpretation of Legislative Texts).[9]

Except for the areas covered by these dicasteries, the Congregation for the Oriental Churches deals with the Oriental churches, which originally existed

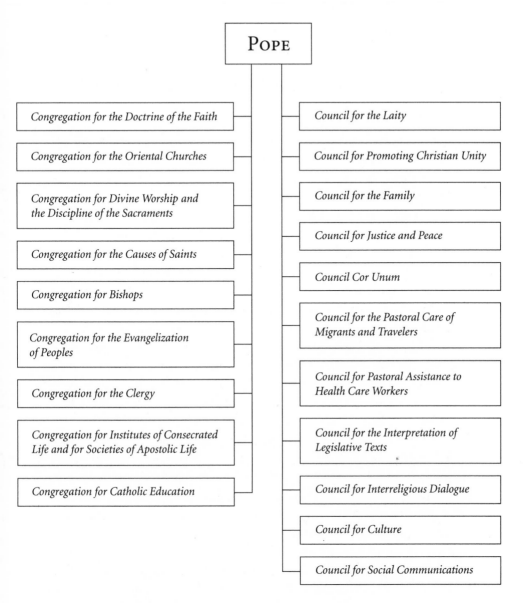

PONTIFICAL CONGREGATIONS AND COUNCILS

mostly in the Middle East and Eastern Europe but through migration spread to Western Europe and the Americas, where they are referred to as the diaspora. Most matters handled for the Latin church by the congregations for Divine Worship, Bishops, Clergy, Education, Consecrated Life, and Evangelization of Peoples would be taken care of by the Congregation for the Oriental

Churches. A separate congregation for the Oriental churches is desirable because their ancient traditions and practices are so different from those of the Latin church that a staff with special expertise and sensitivity is required. If the Oriental churches were dealt with by the other congregations, there would be greater pressure to "Latinize" them—a temptation Rome has always had in dealing with the Orientals. By having a separate congregation for them, greater respect can be given to their uniqueness and autonomy. One of the difficult tasks of this congregation is encouraging the various Oriental churches to get along together. The Syro-Malabar and the Syro-Malankara churches in India are frequently in conflict, as are the Oriental churches in Lebanon.

The Vatican divides the Latin church into missionary dioceses (mostly in Africa and Asia) and non-missionary dioceses. The Congregation for Divine Worship and the Discipline of the Sacraments and the Congregation for Institutes of Consecrated Life and for Societies of Apostolic Life are, for the most part, competent for the entire Latin church. The Congregation for Bishops and the Congregation for the Clergy deal primarily with the non-missionary Latin-rite dioceses, while the Congregation for the Evangelization of Peoples handles the work of these two congregations in mission territories. It also deals with seminaries in missionary dioceses but works in collaboration with the Congregation for Catholic Education (for Seminaries and Educational Institutions). This last congregation also deals with Catholic universities around the world.

In addition to the division of responsibility by type of church or diocese, responsibilities are also divided among dicasteries according to issues or constituencies. There are three congregations and a council that deal with the four major constituencies in the church: bishops, clergy, religious, and laity. Another council deals with health care workers, and another deals with migrants, refugees, and travelers. Questions concerning a particular group in the church would go to the proper dicastery. These divisions are not perfect or airtight. For example, the Council for the Laity deals with lay organizations that also have clerical and religious members. In addition, some controversies may involve more than one group—for example, a dispute concerning a hospital could involve the bishop of the diocese and the religious owning the hospital.

Other dicasteries are more issue-oriented, like the Congregation for the Doctrine of the Faith, Congregation for the Causes of Saints, Council for Justice and Peace, Council for Culture, Council for the Family, Council for Promoting Christian Unity, Council for Interreligious Dialogue, and Council for Social Communications. Questions dealing with specific issues would be handled by the proper dicastery. Again, the divisions are not airtight. Since the

Council for Promoting Christian Unity deals with doctrinal issues, it must work with the Congregation for the Doctrine of the Faith. Nor is the distinction between issue-oriented and people-oriented dicasteries perfect. For example, the Council for Pastoral Assistance to Health Care Workers examines issues of interest to health care workers such as AIDS, abortion, or the handicapped.

The issues assigned to a particular dicastery are further confused because for historical reasons a dicastery might have a bundle of responsibilities that have little logical connection. The Congregation for the Clergy, when originally founded in 1564 as the Congregation of the Council, was established to implement the decrees of the Council of Trent. Since the major reforms coming out of the Council of Trent had to do with the clergy, seminaries, catechetics, and church finances, the congregation dealt with these issues. Seminaries were later spun off to the Congregation for Catholic Education (for Seminaries and Educational Institutions), but the Congregation for the Clergy still deals with issues of the clergy, catechetics, and local church finances.

A more recent historical anomaly is the placement of the Commission for Religious Relations with Jews[10] under the Council for Promoting Christian Unity, despite the existence of the Council for Interreligious Dialogue which communicates with other non-Christian religions. When the Christian unity office was founded at the beginning of Vatican II, it was the only office for dialogue. Jewish groups developed a relationship with its prefect and his staff before the Council for Interreligious Dialogue was created. The Jewish groups preferred to stay with the dialogue partner they knew and were not eager to be lumped in with Muslims, Hindus, and Buddhists. Their wishes were respected.

Some responsibilities have been moved from dicastery to dicastery over time. Before the Second Vatican Council, the Congregation for the Oriental Churches dealt with the Orthodox churches because the Vatican believed that the Oriental churches in union with Rome would show the way toward reunion with the Orthodox. During the council it became clear that the Orthodox churches had a different view. They preferred to deal with the Christian unity office rather than the Congregation for the Oriental Churches, which represented the churches with which the Orthodox had had numerous conflicts.

Normally, a curial office fights to protect its turf just as in any other bureaucracy. In the 1988 reorganization, for example, the Congregation for the Clergy was able to fight off suggestions to transfer catechetics to the Congregation for Catholic Education. On the other hand, one hot potato that no dicastery really wanted was petitions for dispensations from celibacy for priests who had left the ministry. Before 1988 the Congregation for the Doctrine of the Faith dealt with dispensations, but its prefect, Cardinal Joseph Ratzinger, did not want the job. An attempt was made to give it to the Congregation for the Clergy, which did not want it either. Now these petitions are dealt with by the Congregation for Divine Worship and the Discipline of the Sacraments, which appears to have been unable to fight off the assignment.

Sometimes conflicts between dicasteries occur over which one is competent to deal with an issue. This happens especially with new issues. For example, both the Council for Pastoral Assistance to Health Care Workers and the Council for the Family wanted to deal with AIDS and drugs. The Council for the Family also tried to assert jurisdiction over sex education in religious textbooks, but it lost out to the older congregations: Doctrine of the Faith, Clergy, and Education.

Congregation and Council Members

In the strict sense, a council or congregation is not the staff but the committee of cardinals and others who meet periodically to discuss issues, make decisions within their authority, and make recommendations to the pope. Some Americans in the curia compare them to boards of trustees. Members, who must retire at age 80, are appointed by the pope for five-year renewable terms. Cardinal John O'Connor, for example, has been a member of the Congregation for Bishops since he became a cardinal.

The membership of each council and congregation varies in size and makeup. In 1995, the largest was the Congregation for the Evangelization of Peoples with 67 members, and the smallest was the Council for Social Communications with only 21 members.[11] The large size of the former congregation reflects the desire expressed at Vatican II to have diocesan bishops from many mission countries as members.

Before 1967, only cardinals were members of congregations. In response to suggestions at Vatican II, Paul VI added diocesan bishops to the congregations.[12] Councils can include as members laypersons, religious, and priests as well as bishops and cardinals. Almost half the councils have no lay members: Christian Unity, Migrants, Legislative Texts, Interreligious Dialogue, and Culture. On a few councils the laity actually outnumber the bishops and cardinals: the Council for the Laity, Council for the Family, Council for Justice and Peace, and Council Cor Unum.

There appears to be some trepidation about the presence of laity on these councils. *Pastor Bonus* insists that "matters requiring the exercise of power of governance be reserved to those in holy orders."[13] Since the councils rarely get into governance questions, this issue does not appear to have arisen. The councils for the Laity and the Family, where the largest numbers of lay members are present, both have a "committee of the president," an entity that does not exist elsewhere. These committees, which meet infrequently, appear to be safety measures to ensure clerical control. The committees can deal with governance questions and other questions that the president would rather not take to the laity. On the other hand, when consideration was given to making the Council for the Laity a congregation, one of the strongest arguments against the move was that the lay members would have to be kicked off if the council became a congregation.

Who is chosen to be on the congregations and councils is up to the discretion of the pope, although names will be recommended by the prefect or president and the Secretariat of State. Certain membership patterns are evident: 35 percent of the individuals serving on congregations and 24 percent of those serving on councils are from inside the Vatican. Those dicasteries with more than a third of their members from the curia are the Congregation for Bishops (89 percent), the Council for the Interpretation of Texts (67 percent), the Congregation for the Causes of Saints (63 percent), the Congregation for the Doctrine of the Faith (52 percent), the Council for the Pastoral Care of Migrants and Travelers (44 percent), and the Congregation for the Evangelization of Peoples (34 percent). In actual meetings the percentage from the curia would be higher because it is easier for them to attend the meetings that are held in Rome. This is especially true for Bishops, Evangelization, Doctrine, and Saints, which meet frequently during the year.

The presence of Vatican cardinals on important congregations and councils provides an interlocking directorate that has great influence over Vatican policy. The number of congregations and councils of which a cardinal is a member is a crude measure of his influence in the Vatican. The ten cardinals sitting on the most congregations and councils are all curial cardinals who are heads of dicasteries. Prefects and presidents are often ex officio members of other congregations and councils with jurisdictions related to theirs. The prefect for the Congregation for the Doctrine of the Faith, for example, is a member of almost every dicastery touching on doctrinal issues: Oriental Churches, Divine Worship and Sacraments, Bishops, Evangelization, Education, Christian Unity, and Culture. Likewise, the prefect of the Congregation for the Evangelization of Peoples, the president of the Council for Promoting Christian Unity, and the president of the Council for Interreligious Dialogue are all on one another's dicasteries. The prefect of the Congregation for the Oriental Churches, the president of the Council for Promoting Christian Unity, and the president of the Council for Interreligious Dialogue are members of one another's dicasteries. The prefects of the congregations for the Clergy and Education are on each other's congregations, and the secretaries of the councils for the Laity and the Family are also members of each other's councils. These are all dicasteries whose jurisdictions sometimes overlap.

Vatican officials see the membership of presidents and prefects on each other's congregations and councils as an important vehicle of communication and coordination. This is especially important for dicasteries operating in the same area, for example, the Congregation for the Doctrine of the Faith and the Council for Promoting Christian Unity; or the Congregation for the Evangelization of Peoples and the Council for Interreligious Dialogue. Thus when the Congregation for the Doctrine of the Faith is discussing a document from the Council for Promoting Christian Unity, the president of the council is present and participates in the discussion.

If a dicastery head is at the plenary meeting of another dicastery, he can object if it attempts to do something that touches the competence of his dicastery. For example, Cardinal Jozef Tomko, prefect of the Congregation for the Evangelization of Peoples, raised a point of order at a meeting of the Council for Interreligious Dialogue when a document on dialogue and evangelization was discussed. "In the first plenary meeting on this draft," explains Cardinal Tomko, "I said, 'Please, the matter is mixed. So we must have not simply my opinion here. No, no. My congregation must be involved deeply.'" Experts and staff from the two dicasteries met to prepare a new draft that was eventually published as a joint document of both dicasteries. The congregation has been fairly successful in getting the council to give equal time to evangelization whenever it speaks of interreligious dialogue. On the other hand, some have complained that the council has not been as successful in getting the congregation to give equal time to interreligious dialogue when it speaks of evangelization.

Semi-retired cardinals (between the ages of 75 and 80) in the Vatican make up another important bloc on the congregations and councils.[14] Since they no longer have administrative responsibilities, they can pay closer attention to the agenda of meetings if their health allows it. This is especially important for congregations that meet frequently in ordinary sessions like the Congregation for the Doctrine of the Faith, the Congregation for the Evangelization of Peoples, the Congregation for Bishops, and the Congregation for the Causes of Saints.

Cardinals and bishops living outside Rome are also members of congregations and councils. These members are chosen to some extent because of the topic areas of the dicastery. There is also an attempt to have members from different continents and cultures. Cardinals and bishops from missionary lands make up about half of the Congregation for the Evangelization of Peoples. Patriarchs and other bishops from the Oriental churches are appropriately on the Congregation for the Oriental Churches. The Council for Interreligious Dialogue has members from countries with large Muslim, Hindu, or Buddhist populations. The Council for Promoting Christian Unity tends to have bishops from countries with large Protestant populations. A number of bishops on the Congregation for Institutes of Consecrated Life are themselves members of religious orders.

Often, the interests and expertise of a cardinal are reflected in the congregation or council to which he is appointed. For example, Cardinal Anthony Bevilacqua has been interested in immigrants since his days as a young priest, and he was put on the Council for Migrants and Travelers. There are many Catholic hospitals in the Archdiocese of New York, and Cardinal O'Connor was appointed to the Council for Pastoral Assistance to Health Care Workers. As archbishop of New York he is also head of the Catholic Near East Welfare Association, and therefore he was put on the Congregation for the Oriental Churches. Cardinal William Keeler has a long history of involvement in the ecumenical dialogue with Protestants and Jews, and he became a member of the Council for Promoting Christian Unity. Cardinal Roger Mahony, a leading episcopal spokesman on issues of justice and peace, is on the Council for Justice and Peace. Coming from Los Angeles, which includes Hollywood, he easily fits on the Council for Social Communications, as does Cardinal O'Connor from New York. Some membership appears to follow historical patterns. For example, the cardinal archbishop of New York has usually been a member of the Congregation for Bishops since the time of Cardinal Francis Spellman.

The bishop members who are not cardinals also appear to be chosen for their competence and interests as well as their Roman connections. These members are an interesting group to watch, since they are likely candidates for future promotion. For example, Archbishop Joseph Bernardin of Cincinnati was a member of the Congregation for Bishops before being sent to Chicago where he became a cardinal.

The lay, religious, and priest members of councils are appointed because of their expertise or involvement in particular organizations. As with bishops, there is an attempt to have members from different continents and cultures. The lay members of the Council for the Laity tend to be leaders of Catholic lay organizations. The lay members of the Council for the Family are married couples, many of whom are active in the pro-life and natural family planning movements. The Council for Justice and Peace has members who are experts in economics, politics, and the church's social teaching. The Council Cor Unum has representatives from Catholic charitable organizations such as Catholic Relief Services and Caritas. The Council for Pastoral Assistance to Health Care Workers has people from religious communities and lay associations dealing with health care. And the Council for Social Communications has the presidents of three international Catholic communications groups.

The high percentage of curial members on councils and congregations ensures that the curia's views will have a strong voice at the meetings. In addition, since it is the curia that helps the pope screen and select candidates, vocal critics of the curia are not likely to be appointed. But the increased presence of outsiders also means that the voices of at least some local churches will be heard at a high level in the Vatican.

Congregation and Council Meetings

Periodically the members of a congregation or council meet in Rome. Meetings are of two types: ordinary and plenary. Ordinary meetings convene only the members of the congregation or council who happen to be in Rome, whereas all the members are called to Rome for a plenary meeting. To consider the appointment of bishops, the Congregation for Bishops meets about nineteen times a year and the Congregation for the Evangelization of Peoples meets about nine times a year. The Congregation for the Doctrine of the Faith meets once a month to study doctrinal issues in ordinary session. And the Congregation for the Causes of Saints meets in ordinary session to consider evidence for beatifications and canonizations whenever a cause is ready for its consideration.

According to *Pastor Bonus,* congregations and councils are to meet in plenary session at least once a year if possible "to deal with questions involving general principles, and for other questions which the prefect or president may have deemed to require treatment."[15] This schedule is unrealistic according to Vatican officials because of the amount of staff time that goes into preparing each meeting. In addition, there is the cost of travel, housing, and simultaneous translations.

How often a dicastery actually meets in plenary session is up to its head. The trend is to meet every three years rather than every year. Some, like the Congregation for the Oriental Churches and the Congregation for the Causes of Saints, do not meet in plenary session. The Oriental congregation feels that the Oriental churches have too little in common to profit from a plenary meeting. The congregation's critics say that a plenary meeting would provide a forum for the one thing the Orientals have in common: complaints about their treatment by the congregation. The Congregation for the Causes of Saints does not believe that there are any new policy issues to consider since the saint-making process was reformed in 1983.[16]

The agenda and procedures of the plenary meetings vary over time and from congregation to congregation. At a plenary meeting, the members might (1) hear a report on the activities of the dicastery since the last plenary; (2) review the draft of a document being prepared in the dicastery; (3) discuss a major policy question to give direction to the staff or to make a recommendation to the pope; (4) present and listen to addresses on general issues of concern to the dicastery in a symposium-like setting.

Thus the Congregation for the Doctrine of the Faith meets for a week every year or two, and, as a cardinal member explains, "all the subjects treated during the year are presented in a summary with the discussions on the policy in general." Sometimes a major document is also discussed, but the congregation deals with so many documents that most of them are handled in the ordinary meetings. The fewer documents a dicastery issues, the more likely they are to be reviewed in a plenary meeting. Recent documents on religious community life and on religious formation were discussed in plenary session by the Congregation for Consecrated Life before they were released. The Congregation for the Evangelization of Peoples, which meets every two or three years, has approved documents on missionary formation, priests, and catechists.

When considering a document in plenary session, the members discuss it, make changes, and ultimately vote. "Generally, one tries to come to a document with practical unanimity," explains a cardinal. "Otherwise, it has to be revised. The effort always in the congregations is to come to a certain agreement. But there is not a strict rule because the final permission [to publish] is given by the Holy Father. Therefore, this is preparatory. The practice is that the judgment is given by each one and presented to the Holy Father for the final decision. The Holy Father would know who was for and who was against. The cardinal prefect will present the situation."

In the plenary meetings, the prefect (for simplicity I will use "prefect" as a generic term to refer to both prefect and president) also seeks advice on general policy. For example, the Congregation for Consecrated Life discussed the nature of authority in religious communities and whether a brother could be a superior over the priests in his community. The Vatican position has been that non-clerics should not have authority over clerics. This is particularly an issue for Franciscans because their founder, St. Francis, was not a priest, but it also has had implications for other orders with brothers like the Jesuits. Likewise, the Congregation for Divine Worship discussed whether there was a need for new Eucharistic prayers and decided there was not a need at the present time. When the U.S. bishops asked for permission to develop new Eucharistic prayers, the congregation's staff responded that it could not give permission until the members could revisit the question at the next plenary. The staff indicated that it thought the members would reverse themselves, but Rome was not eager to have additional Eucharistic prayers.

Finally, some of the plenary meetings are like symposia on different topics with presentations being made by members, staff, or consultants. This is especially the case with the councils. Americans find the European style of most of these meetings very frustrating because long-winded papers, which could easily have been distributed before the meeting, are presented with little time for discussion. Frequently even if the papers have been distributed ahead of time, the author still reads the paper to the audience. The papers from the plenary meetings are sometimes made public to foster wider interest and understanding of the issues. This is especially true of councils that are trying to promote interest and activity by church people in specific areas. But discussion of controversial topics is rarely made public.

Although some prefects do provide time for discussion at their plenary meetings, critics feel that an agenda full of presentations without discussions is a strategy to avoid controversial topics and to keep outside members from questioning dicastery practices and policies. Some members complain that the meetings are orchestrated so that the conclusion of the meeting is predestined from the beginning. Canadian Cardinal Edouard Gagnon complained that he came to a meeting of the Council for the Family, before he was made president of the council, "and the final report of the meeting was the paper that we were given at the beginning. What was given to us as the plan of the meeting, that was the conclusion. We had come here from different continents and we had not [made any difference]. I talked about that with the Holy Father and I told him, I do not think I will come to the next meeting because it is useless. We come here, a big expense for the Holy See, and it is useless because what we end up with is what we started with."

The frequency, style, and usefulness of plenary meetings vary from dicastery to dicastery. Since they meet in secrecy, it is not possible to evaluate them completely. According to participants, some meetings appear to have an impact on the documents and policies of the dicastery while others involve mind-numbing discussions that go nowhere. Debate can be intense over issues or the implementation of decisions that have been delegated to the dicastery by the pope, but it would be considered improper for the members to discuss changing policy on a matter on which the pope has spoken. Since the members as a group never sit with the pope to discuss the issues of their dicastery, they must take signals from Vatican officials about what is appropriate and what is not.

Dicastery Office Organization and Procedures

Since the members come to Rome infrequently, the dicastery office handles most of the work of the congregation or council. In each office there is a president or prefect, a secretary, an undersecretary, and professional staff as well as some nonprofessional staff.[17] The prefect (or president) and the secretary are the key officials in the direction of the dicastery. They, together with the undersecretary who acts as an office manager, are referred to as the superiors. All policy decisions are made by the superiors, and no letter or document leaves the office without the signature of at least one of them.

Professional staffs vary in size, but none are very large by secular government standards.[18] Only three dicasteries had more than 30 professionals, including typists and technicians, listed in the 1994 *Annuario Pontificio*: the Congregation for the Doctrine of the Faith (32), the Congregation for the Evangelization of Peoples (34 plus an equal number for its mission societies), and the Congregation for Institutes of Consecrated Life and Societies of Apostolic Life (31). Some dicasteries have fewer than 10 professionals: the Council Cor Unum (6), Council for the Family (8), Council for Interreligious Dialogue (9), Council for the Interpretation of Legislative Texts (7), and Council for Pastoral Assistance to Health Care Workers (7). Some offices have professionals under short-term contracts who are not listed in the *Annuario*, but their numbers are not large.

The professional staffs are organized in a variety of ways. The smaller the staff, the more the organization of the dicastery will be ad hoc, depending on the language skills and expertise of the current staff. The larger staffs require more formal organization.

Dicasteries that distribute large sums of money, like the Congregation for the Oriental Churches and the Congregation for the Evangelization of Peoples, have an administrative or financial office that screens grant applications and distributes money. These congregations also have affiliated agencies housed in their offices for distributing money raised through special collections: the Catholic Near East Welfare Association and the Society for the Propagation of the Faith.

Some dicasteries, like the Congregation for the Clergy, are organized primarily by language. Here the English-speaking staff would handle matters dealing with every aspect of the congregation's work in the English-speaking world. Likewise, the staffs of the Congregation for the Evangelization of Peoples and the Congregation for Bishops are divided by nations and geographical regions where the language would usually be the same. The staff of the Congregation for the Oriental Churches is organized by ritual churches. Thus specific officials will deal with all the correspondence in a particular language, region, or ritual church no matter what the topic. Such organization allows the staff to work in their native language on issues confronting local churches, which reduces the likelihood of miscommunication between the Vatican and the local churches.

Many in these dicasteries like working on a number of different issues in their own language. "That's what I like about my work," says a canonist in the Congregation for the Clergy. "I get on my desk all that the congregation can do. Not just selling church property or just catechesis. I have that and also a variety of clergy cases." "It is a very rewarding task working here because you are like a general practitioner as distinguished from a specialist," agrees an official in the Congregation for the Evangelization of Peoples. But there are problems with this organizational structure. "It is an extremely difficult task because we have so few personnel. We don't have the expertise, we haven't had the chance to be a specialist in seminaries, in appointment of bishops, and in the problems of bishops, clergy, and religious. We have not had the time. So it is a real battle trying to keep up to date."

If the language skills of the superiors are weak, they are dependent on the staff for interpreting and writing correspondence. The staff can determine how the Vatican and the local church perceive each other. The staff can also influence the tone of a letter. For example, one English-speaking church official reported receiving very insulting letters from a prefect whose English was weak. The tone changed when the American priest in the congregation returned to his diocese.

Other dicasteries are organized primarily by topic area rather than language. Here experts deal with specific issues in a number of languages. For example, the Congregation for Catholic Education has offices for ecclesiastical faculties, universities, seminaries, and schools; each of the four offices is headed by a *capo ufficio,* a head of office.

The Congregation for Divine Worship and the Discipline of the Sacraments is large enough to be divided into two major sections, one dealing with liturgy and the other dealing with canonical issues relating to the sacraments (they used to be two separate congregations). Each section is further divided by topics (liturgical texts and pastoral liturgy in one section, and marriage cases and laicizations in the other). The Congregation for Institutes of Consecrated Life and Societies of Apostolic Life has two undersecretaries, one for religious and one for secular institutes. It also has offices for monastic religious, discipline (dispensation, exclaustrations, dismissals of individuals), religious constitutions, conferences of major superiors, and finances. Even in a small dicastery, like the Council for Pastoral Care of Migrants and Travelers, individuals might specialize in specific topics such as refugees, migrants, gypsies, or seafarers.

Even if on paper the dicastery is divided into offices by topic, in actuality language often becomes dominant because each dicastery must deal with correspondence in a variety of languages and sometimes the person in the office does not know the language. "I do English work for two or three departments of the congregation," explained one American canonist. "On a flow chart that would turn into an ink spot."

On the other hand, a dicastery organized by language or territory would also have individuals who are experts in specific topic areas. Often these experts are Italians who have been on the staff for a long time and know the history behind various policies. For example, the Congregation for the Clergy has officials who specialize in catechetics and in church finances. In the Congregation for the Evangelization of Peoples there is a person who handles juridical issues. As the undersecretary describes it, "Each staff person handles the question of bishops, clergy, seminaries, education, schools in his territories. If there are specific canonical problems, then they will consult our juridical expert." Such officials provide expert advice and make sure that all the language groups are following the same policies. Sometimes these officials are referred to as *capi ufficio,* heads of offices, but often they are only one-person offices and may also be responsible for a language group.[19]

"If it's a routine thing, it would come to me," explains an American who handles English correspondence in a congregation. "I would know how we handle it as a rule. I would write it up and pass it to the undersecretary. If it's very complicated or it's questionable that it could be approved, then there would be some people I would consult. I would probably write it up and ask them to look at it and give me an opinion."

The Council for Promoting Christian Unity has an interesting way of dealing with the complexity of working in a number of languages with a host of dialogue partners on a variety of issues, while at the same time keeping its staff to a limited size. Each member of the staff specializes in a language, a dialogue partner, and an issue. For example, an English-speaking official would naturally deal with English correspondence and with the Anglicans as his dialogue partner. On the other hand, correspondence from Lutherans could come in English or German. The Lutheran expert, who might also deal with German correspondence, would be consulted by the English-speaking official on correspondence from Lutherans in the United States. Finally, since the dialogues cover a number of issues (for example, ministry, primacy, Eucharist, social justice, common training for seminarians), each staff person follows a particular issue that is the topic of dialogue with a number of partners in more than one language. This division of labor requires constant interaction and communication among the staff because three staff people might have to work together on one letter.

Correspondence coming into a dicastery is normally opened and read by the undersecretary. Most correspondence is routed upward to the secretary and the prefect, who initial it to indicate that they have seen it. Then the secretary or undersecretary assigns it to the appropriate person on the staff. The archivist gives a protocol number to each incoming letter, and notes its date, author, diocese of origin, and topic. If it is a new topic, the archivist gives it a new protocol number and opens a new file. If it deals with an ongoing case, he places it in the existing file. He also keeps track of who has the file. In some offices the archivist still works with large ledgers and file cards, but computerization of the process is spreading in the curia.

Often the prefect or secretary writes brief instructions on the letter, telling the official what should be done with it. The official then drafts a response that passes through the undersecretary and secretary to the prefect. The undersecretary and secretary note on the draft any suggested changes. "The secretary can read everything that passes through him and give his opinion," explains an official, "but the real work is done by the underlings." If the secretary's knowledge of the language is weak, his review can be cursory. The prefect will then accept the draft, make his own revisions, or send it back for more work. Correspondence from the dicastery is signed only by the secretary or the prefect. Very important letters and documents are signed by both the secretary and the prefect. A copy of the final letter, together with the marked-up drafts, becomes a part of the permanent file. If a problem arises, there is a record of who recommended what wording.

For more complicated issues, the prefect or secretary might hold a staff meeting to discuss the letter or document. Some dicasteries have general staff meetings to which all the professionals are invited. In others (especially the larger ones), only the pertinent staff who are directly involved or the heads of offices meet with the secretary and the prefect to discuss the issue. Offices with general staff meetings tend to have a higher morale because the staff is better informed and more involved in the work of the dicastery. On the other hand, some feel the general meetings are a waste of time because staff are called to meetings when they could be doing their own work. Without general staff meetings, officials in the same dicastery often do not know what their fellow officials are doing. Some secretaries and prefects prefer this because it maintains a higher level of secrecy when information is shared only on a "need to know" basis.

If the question raised by the letter needs more study, the superiors can send it to a consultor. Each dicastery has official consultors appointed by the pope because of their expertise in the areas of the dicastery and their loyalty to Vatican policy. The dicasteries also consult other experts whom they trust. Often these consultors are theology and canon law professors at pontifical universities in Rome, where they are readily accessible. Modern communications technology makes it possible to consult experts outside Rome, but this is not very common.

The Congregation for the Doctrine of the Faith is unusual in that it has monthly meetings of its consultors, chaired by the secretary, to discuss issues and documents under consideration by the congregation. The consultors who are expert in the topic under consideration (scripture, morals, ecclesiology, and so forth) are invited to this meeting, and the secretary reports the results of the discussion to the prefect.

Consultors are also used in the drafting of major documents. The idea for the document might originate with the pope, the prefect, the members of the congregation, or the staff. But the staff is so busy with its normal work that the drafting of documents is often contracted out to one or more experts. The drafts are reviewed and critiqued by the staff and by other consultors.

Consultors provide invaluable expertise and advice to Vatican dicasteries. They are an inexpensive resource since they receive very little pay for their work. It is considered an honor to be consulted by a Vatican dicastery. Some Roman professors are so heavily consulted that it interferes with their teaching, but university officials encourage them to accept the work because it brings prestige to the professor and his school. Critics object that the Vatican screens out scholars who disagree with it on issues like birth control and married priests. By restricting consultation to those who are in basic agreement with Vatican policy, the Vatican gets only a limited sampling of views held by experts around the world.

Interdicasterial Consultation

A dicastery would usually consult other dicasteries on a document or issue that touches their areas of concern. Comments from other dicasteries can lead to changes in a document. Cardinal Edward Cassidy, president of the Council for Promoting Christian Unity, reports that in the council's first draft of the *Ecumenical Directory,*

> we probably took more cognizance of the situation in Europe, where mixed marriages have become almost the norm. We were reminded, and I think rightly so, that this is not the case throughout the whole church. So it is good to have this input from different sources so that someone like the Congregation for the Evangelization of Peoples could say to us, "We wouldn't be happy with the way you said that because this could be taken in our new churches, which are not yet fully established, as an encouragement." They would not be happy to encourage mixed marriages. We were not encouraging them, but we were saying, if you look at Germany that is the reality.

Dicasteries might also be consulted on other topics that touch their area of competence. Although the Congregation for the Evangelization of Peoples is competent for seminaries in mission countries, it might consult experts in the Congregation for Catholic Education to see how it is handling a similar issue in non-mission countries. For example, Education instituted a process of visitations of seminaries which Evangelization wanted to imitate in its territory. Likewise, the Congregation for the Oriental Churches and the Council for Promoting Christian Unity are in regular contact to try to find ways of dealing with Oriental Catholics and the Orthodox without upsetting either. On questions of religious education, three congregations are in communication: Clergy, which handles catechetics; Education, which handles schools; and Doctrine, which handles issues of orthodoxy. Likewise, when it comes to dealing with a dissident theologian who is a religious, Education, Consecrated Life, and Doctrine might work together.

Sometimes superiors of two dicasteries have to work together because the division between their jurisdictions is not clear. For example, communities or movements that include both religious persons with vows and married persons might turn either to the Congregation for Consecrated Life or to the Council for the Laity, depending on whether they see themselves as a lay organization with religious associates or a religious organization with lay associates. Which dicastery an organization should deal with is not always clear, and conflicts can occur if two dicasteries are dealing with similar organizations in different ways.

If two dicasteries disagree over jurisdiction, the matter is settled by the Secretariat of State.[20] "The Secretariat of State calls a meeting if there is disagreement between the Congregation for the Oriental Churches and a Latin-rite congregation, between Evangelization and Interreligious Dialogue, between Doctrine and Christian Unity, between Doctrine and others because Doctrine is often involved," explains an official of the Secretariat of State. "The Secretariat of State sets the ground rules or arbitrates."

Pastor Bonus provides for permanent interdicasterial commissions when there is the need for continuing discussion of an issue by a number of dicasteries. The members of these commissions are appointed by the Secretariat of State, but the staff will come from the dicasteries. In 1995 there were five such commissions listed in the *Annuario Pontificio*. One interdicasterial commission deals with the church in Eastern Europe, where dicasteries need to work together to respond to the rapidly changing situation. This commission has the secretary of state as its president and includes as members the secretary and undersecretary for relations with states, and the secretaries of the Congregation for the Oriental Churches, the Congregation for the Clergy, the Congregation for Institutes of Consecrated Life, and the Council for Promoting Christian Unity.

Another interdicasterial commission deals with issues touching religious in missionary lands. The prefect of the Congregation for the Evangelization of Peoples presides over the commission, which includes as members the prefect and secretary of the Congregation for Institutes of Consecrated Life, and the secretary and undersecretary of the Congregation for the Evangelization of Peoples. This commission became necessary when *Pastor Bonus* transferred jurisdiction over the internal community life of missionary religious from the Congregation for the Evangelization of Peoples to the Congregation for Consecrated Life, which has staff with expertise in the canon law and spirituality of religious communities. The apostolic work of missionary religious remains under the jurisdiction of the Congregation for the Evangelization of Peoples.

"It's a little awkward," admits a canonist in the Congregation for Consecrated Life. "Which part of you is your apostolate and which part of you is your religious life? There are some practical ramifications. The bishops of mission territories are under Evangelization. Religious work in the missions in collaboration with the bishops. Sometimes there is funding that comes through Evangelization. We do not have money to give to the missions." Mother Teresa opposed splitting religious between the two congregations and got an exception for the Missionaries of Charity, so that her community remains completely under Evangelization. The Maryknoll priests also stayed under Evangelization because they are not vowed religious, but the Maryknoll sisters now must deal with the Congregation for Consecrated Life.

Another interdicasterial commission on priestly formation is chaired by the prefect of the Congregation for Catholic Education and includes the prefects and secretaries from Oriental Churches, Evangelization, and Consecrated Life—all the dicasteries that would deal with religious or diocesan seminaries. Another interdicasterial commission was secretly formed to study what to do with priests who have molested youngsters.

Recently interdicasterial cooperation has resulted in the issuing of important joint documents by some dicasteries. The Council Cor Unum and the Council for Migrants and Travelers issued a joint document in 1992 on refugees that received very favorable international attention. In 1994, the Congregation for Catholic Education and the Council for Culture issued a joint document on the role of Catholics in universities. The Council for Interreligious Dialogue and the Congregation for the Evangelization of Peoples issued a joint document in 1991 on evangelization and interreligious dialogue. Despite these successes, everyone in the curia agrees that there is a need for better interdicasterial communication and coordination. This need is felt especially by dicasteries whose jurisdiction overlaps that of other dicasteries. "We are not experts in seminaries, and yet we have seminary problems and seminary responsibilities," comments an official in the Congregation for the Evangelization of Peoples. "We have doctrinal problems, yet we are not experts in doctrine. So we could use greater consultation in these areas."

A group of American canonists visiting the curia were struck by how little communication there is between dicasteries. "They were curious to find out what we found out at other offices," explained a canonist. "It got so that we were bringing information that you would think would have gone by interdepartmental memo or something. There is more communication at my university than there is at this international headquarters. So it's very striking that they live in an isolated little world."

In the Vatican, talking to anyone outside the office is normally restricted to the prefect, secretary, and undersecretary. Typically, interdicasterial communication is done by letter or by the superiors talking to each other. Or the superiors might assign a person from each dicastery to work on an issue together. A lower official cannot simply telephone his counterpart in another office. An official who did get a call from another official would be reluctant to divulge much information without checking with his superiors.

One of the few offices that works systematically at interdicasterial communication is the Council for Promoting Christian Unity. Periodically during the year it invites dicastery secretaries to a conference where ecumenical issues are reported and discussed. For example, someone from the council reports on a dialogue, and then there is time for discussion and questions. This system has been very successful in disseminating information about various dialogues and in helping the curia become more ecumenically minded.

The Council for Culture also puts on a yearly conference on the relationship of culture to some aspect of church life or theology. Often someone from another dicastery makes a presentation on how culture relates to his field. "Every year I invited one of the dicasteries," explains Cardinal Paul Poupard, president of the Council for Culture. "One year faith and culture, Ratzinger [prefect of the Congregation for the Doctrine of the Faith]. One year Mayer [then prefect of the Congregation for Divine Worship], and this time liturgy and culture. Another time Tomko [prefect of the Congregation for the Evangelization of Peoples], evangelization and culture. Another time, Silvestrini [then secretary for relations with states], politics and culture. And Arinze [president of the Council on Interreligious Dialogue], interreligious dialogue and culture. Willebrands [then head of the office on ecumenism], ecumenism and culture." Cardinal Poupard realizes that he has no authority to force his council's ideas on other parts of the curia; he can only persuade. By asking dicastery heads to speak on the relationship of culture to their area of responsibility, he makes them think about the issue. These high-profile speakers also give credibility within the curia to the council's position that the cultural aspect of issues is important. When he explained these conferences to the pope at a lunch, the Holy Father laughed and said, "Oh, you are inculturating the curia."

In the past, although a Vatican office might circulate a draft document within the curia, it would never circulate a draft outside the curia in the way that the American bishops circulate drafts of pastoral letters. Wide circulation of Vatican drafts is still unusual, but it is beginning to occur in some instances. Members of a council or congregation outside Rome might be sent drafts for written comments between plenary meetings, and they in turn might confidentially ask experts in their dioceses or country for comments.

An unusually public consultation process was used for *Ex Corde Ecclesiae*, a document on Catholic universities by the Congregation for Catholic Education. The initiative for this document came directly from John Paul II early in his reign. A draft was circulated to about twenty or thirty institutions in 1983, and the reactions were mostly favorable since these were people the congregation knew would be in basic agreement with its goals. Around 1984 another draft was distributed widely so that any university could comment on it. "That is when they got the negative reaction," explains an American familiar with the history of the document. "The major universities, not just in the U.S., but throughout the world said to the congregation, 'You do not understand who we are.' They received a pile of comments on this draft about fifteen inches high. Not all negative, but heavily negative."

The universities suspected that the purpose of the document was to restrict academic freedom and to tighten the hierarchy's control over the universities. They feared that the draft would not be changed and that the consultation process was simply for show. Much to their surprise, the congregation distributed a fifty-page report that accurately and openly summarized the negative responses to the draft. This was followed by a meeting in Salamanca to which university representatives from around the world were invited to discuss the draft. This meeting convinced university officials that the congregation was at least listening, if not in full agreement with them. The congregation even agreed to have a commission of university representatives review future drafts. The final document from the congregation was much closer to the position of the universities than the original draft.

When it comes to documents that touch on matters of doctrine, there is one office in the curia that is always consulted: the Congregation for the Doctrine of the Faith. It is often still referred to by its old name, "the Holy Office." Although *Pastor Bonus* speaks of all dicasteries being equal, in the Vatican some are more equal than others. Doctrine of the Faith acts as the gatekeeper on doctrinal questions, reviewing everyone else's documents.[21] On the record, everyone says how helpful it is to have the Congregation for the Doctrine of the Faith reviewing their documents. Some even acknowledge that their documents were improved by the process. Off the record, there are complaints of excessive delays and nit-picking about doctrinal issues.

"The Congregation of the Faith, nobody likes them or the way they work," complains a Vatican official. "They do a lot of stupid things because they are secretive. They will put out documents that are really not very sound or good. If they had done a bit of consultation before, they could have eliminated some of the wrong things and made a much better document. They are so committed to secrecy. They are terrified of journalists, paranoid about leaks. They only consult with their own little group." Another Vatican official complained that congregation staff would insist on adding redundant qualifying phrases throughout their documents to make sure that no one could interpret the text in an unorthodox manner.

Most Vatican officials find the congregation's staff reasonable if overworked because they are reviewing so many documents. Many curial officials say that the congregation's suggestions made their documents better. "Cardinal Ratzinger gave us good suggestions of how to formulate the document on interreligious dialogue and evangelization," reports Cardinal Tomko. "I think that we follow here in Rome a very collegial spirit. We are also careful. It does take time."

"We have a very close cooperation with the Doctrine of the Faith since we are constantly dealing with theological questions in our dialogues," explains Cardinal Cassidy, president of the Council for Promoting Christian Unity. "For the ARCIC [Anglican Roman Catholic International Commission] document or the question of [revoking] the condemnation of Luther, we need to deal with all of these questions together with the Congregation for the Doctrine of the Faith."

After reviewing a dicastery's document, the Congregation for the Doctrine of the Faith might raise questions or make suggestions. The dicastery can then respond to these issues in a dialogue with the congregation. The congregation raised a number of concerns about a document of the Council for Social Communications, according to its president, Archbishop John Foley: "We accepted some of them without any question. We could see what they meant. Three points we thought would create problems and I pointed out why. Cardinal Ratzinger said, 'Fine, I can see that.' So there is a very good spirit within the Holy See and it is very cooperative. I have never found any difficulty. The only difficulty is time."

The revised *Ecumenical Directory* took a long time getting through the congregation. "We really did not have very much trouble with them," reports Cardinal Cassidy. "What the Doctrine of the Faith was concerned about was particularly the first chapter, since we were speaking about the doctrinal theological basis of ecumenism. Certainly it improved as a result of that consultation because we were able to be more precise, to see perhaps some of the difficulties that we might not have foreseen in writing our part. Our difficulty was not a question of having problems with [the congregation] but of going right through the whole thing very carefully, number [section] by number [section], until everybody was happy that that was the best way at this time of stating it."

The Congregation for the Doctrine of the Faith is often accused of being a roadblock to ecumenism, but Cardinal Cassidy denies this while admitting the different perspectives of the two dicasteries:

The Doctrine of the Faith has the job of defending the doctrine, so naturally there is a difference between our approach which is promoting Christian unity and the Doctrine of the Faith which has not got the job of promoting Christian unity but has certainly not got the job of stopping Christian unity. And it does not try to do that. But it would look at it from a different angle. Whereas we would perhaps want to push ahead, they would also say, "Wait a minute, don't forget that you have to see what is the effect of this on the whole church. You have got abuses, you have got difficulties."

So a happy balance has to be found between wanting to go ahead, but not also creating serious problems for the church. This is not a tension, I would not say that, that would not be the right word, but two different ways of looking at a question. I think that is good because we might go too far in our enthusiasm of doing something, without keeping in mind that there are other questions, other aspects that have to be considered.

Others are not so generous in their evaluation of the work of the Congregation for the Doctrine of the Faith. Cardinal Gagnon, a conservative French Canadian, had a run-in with Cardinal Ratzinger when he was head of the Council for the Family. "[Peter] Hebblethwaite [a journalist] wrote that we had meetings regularly, Cardinal Ratzinger and Monsignor [Carlo] Caffarra and myself, to have *Humanae Vitae* declared a dogma," recalls Cardinal Gagnon. "I can tell you that in all my years of work here I have never been able to meet Cardinal Ratzinger to talk with him about theological problems concerning the family. That was the main reason I left the Council for the Family. He disauthorized me when I sent a letter to the American bishops about certain text books." The letter criticized the treatment of sex education in *The New Creation* series. "I have been a teacher of moral theology more years than he has. But I am an ignorant person for him. It is annoying. I have studied those problems of the family. He is a very nice man, but there is a profound conviction that they are the only ones who know."

Within the curia, criticism of the Congregation for the Doctrine of the Faith is muted. According to Cardinal Cassidy, if the two prefects cannot agree, "it would have to go to the Holy Father. But normally we come to an agreement. We are all working for the same boss so, in a way, that's why we need to try to find a way in which we can say things together. The Holy See can't speak with three or four voices. It has to speak with one voice, so you have to work it out. Normally it takes time, but you come to a decision, you come to an arrangement by which everybody is able to say yes, fine."

Reforming Curial Structures

The organization and procedures of the Roman curia centralize power in the hands of dicastery superiors. The most important superiors are the heads of key dicasteries who also sit on a number of councils and congregations. The congregation and council system gives the appearance of allowing the participation of noncurial prelates and even lay people in the government of the church. In reality, their impact is limited since plenary meetings are rarely held, and the most important dicasteries (Bishops, Doctrine of the Faith, and Evangelization of Peoples) do their work primarily in ordinary sessions attended only by prelates living in Rome. When plenary meetings do take place, the agenda is tightly controlled, Vatican officials make up a large percentage of the membership attending, and Vatican policies are rarely challenged. "What you have to remember," said a Scottish priest to a colleague in Rome for a meeting, "is that they know that we eventually have to go home."

There is a need for new structures in the church to counterbalance the centralized power of Vatican officials. For example, rather than using congregations and councils as Vatican decision-making bodies, it might be better to convert them into oversight committees composed totally of outside members. For example, the members of the Congregation for Divine Worship could be the elected chairmen of liturgical committees of episcopal conferences. Such a selection process would ensure that the members represent the local churches and have expertise in the appropriate field. These committees might even become an integral part of the synod of bishops. The role of the oversight committees would be to review and critique the work of their dicasteries from the perspective of the local church. The committees would report their recommendations directly to the pope for his consideration.

The organizational structure and procedures of the Vatican will continue to evolve into the next millennium just as they did during the last two. Offices merge and split, open and close. The Congregation for Divine Worship and the Discipline of the Sacraments was once two congregations. They were merged in 1975, split again in 1984, and united again in 1988. One of the shortest-lived dicasteries was the Council for Dialogue with Unbelievers created in 1965 by Paul VI, who was concerned about modern atheism. In 1993, after the fall of Communism, John Paul II merged it with the Council for Culture. The same fate may be in store for the Council for Pastoral Assistance to Health Care Workers once its president, Cardinal Fiorenzo Angelini, passes from the scene.

Anachronisms, like having catechetics in the Congregation for the Clergy, need to be addressed. Minor changes in competencies of dicasteries could also provide clearer lines of responsibility in the curia. For example, having one dicastery deal with the marriage cases currently handled by the Congregation for the Doctrine of the Faith and by the Congregation for Divine Worship and the Discipline of the Sacraments would simplify matters. The same dicastery could also handle laicizations from the priesthood. This would free up these two congregations for their principal work. Nor does it make much sense to have the electronic press and photographers serviced by the Council for Social Communications while the print media are handled by the Vatican press office.

At the same time, new phenomena in the church (such as lay movements, communities of laity and religious, personal prelatures, and concerns about ecumenism, culture, justice, and communications) require new structures and procedures. Currently these concerns are being forced into old structures that never anticipated them or placed in new offices that relate illogically to older offices. Confusion in dealing with new phenomena is not surprising, nor are temporary ad hoc responses necessarily bad. For example, the Council for Justice and Peace provides an institutionalized base for experts focused on these issues. But in the long run, it is more important that the Secretariat of State and other dicasteries integrate justice and peace into their agenda than that this council continue to exist as an independent office. The same is true for the Council for Culture and the Council for Social Communications. But as long as other curial offices ignore these issues, these offices will be necessary.

In the next millennium, the distinction between missionary and older churches will become anachronistic, and the need for a separate Congregation for the Evangelization of Peoples will be questioned (unless missionaries go to extraterrestrial locations!). Any reunion with Protestant or Orthodox churches would also require major rethinking of the curia's structure. The Orthodox would certainly not accept being placed under the Congregation for the Oriental Churches.

The organizations connected to the papacy have evolved through history. Often these structures have been copied from secular governments—the Roman senate, the Byzantine imperial court, the French chancery. Learning from secular experience is not contrary to Vatican tradition but very traditional. Today the church could learn from experts in government and business management as well as from the legislative committees and boards that oversee government and nongovernmental bureaucracies.

Past developments in technology have also caused changes in the Vatican, and new technological developments are having an impact on the Vatican today. First typewriters, then photocopiers, and now computers for word processing, accounting, and database management are changing the way the Vatican offices are run. The telephone and fax machine are reluctantly being accepted as a way of doing business. The Vatican bureaucracy is slower at adopting new technologies than are businesses and First World governments because of the costs and the lack of technical sophistication of those at the top. Only a few offices currently have their computers connected in local area networks, but a few Vatican technicians are dreaming of a paperless Vatican connected to local churches through the Internet.

New technologies make it possible for wider and quicker consultation with local churches, although officials can delay responding to a fax or e-mail just as easily as they now delay answering an airmail letter. Improved technology could also lead to greater centralization if the Vatican becomes more efficient in processing the huge amounts of data that pour into it every day. Someday a high-tech inquisitor in the Congregation for the Doctrine of the Faith may want software designed to scan the writings of theologians for unorthodox views. On the other hand, the sharing of information will become increasingly difficult for the Vatican to control.

The proper structures and procedures of the curia are highly dependent on what role the church wants the pope to exercise in the next millennium. His role has changed over time, and it is likely to change further depending on the environment in which the church operates. If the church is seen as a communion of churches, then a more decentralized structure is possible where greater liberty and authority are given to local churches. This would reduce the demands on the curia and increase the role of episcopal conferences and local bishops. But it is unlikely that the structure of the Roman curia will ever be simple as long as Catholics from multiple cultures speaking many languages face a host of complex issues. Concern for unity in the church will ultimately turn all faces toward Rome as the home of the one whose principal ministry is to foster unity. This is especially true as the world itself becomes more interconnected through travel, communications, and trade.

The structure and procedures of the Roman curia are only part of the story. Prefects, presidents, and other officials appointed by the pope to run these offices set the tone more than any organizational table. No matter what the procedures or how the organizational chart is drawn, the curia is run not by robots but by people who are unique individuals.

~ 6

Vatican Officials

THE POPE CANNOT GOVERN a one-billion-member church by himself. He cannot even relate individually to the approximately 4,000 bishops in the world. The Roman curia that assists him in his work is not simply a series of mechanized offices and bureaucratic procedures. These offices are inhabited by real people who help the pope in his ministry to the universal church. These curial officials, whom he chooses or inherits from his predecessor, are an integral part of his team. Without them he cannot function.

The importance of the officials in the Roman curia should not be underestimated. Like civil servants in a government, Vatican officials gather and process information, prepare memoranda, answer correspondence, draft documents and speeches, advise the pope, carry out his decisions, and make decisions on issues that he has neither the time nor the interest to follow. Their attitudes, skills, and decisions have an impact on the life of the church and the church's relationship to the world.

Comments on the curia by Vatican officials are often full of contradictions, as if they are caught in a love-hate relationship with other members of the curia that bounces from admiration to ridicule. According to its inhabitants, the Vatican is a place full of saints and sinners, workaholics and clock watchers, the brilliant and the incompetent, loyal servants and ambitious clerics, petty tyrants and kind pastors. It is a place where too many documents are produced and nothing gets done. It is a place of tension and laughter, legalism and flexibility, idealism and ambition, hierarchy and personal relations, a place where history is made and tradition paralyzes the present. All of this blends together to make the Vatican the unique place it is.

Early in this century, the people working in the curia were mostly Italians. The Vatican was an Italian preserve, and non-Italians were not actively recruited. Pius XII first began to recruit non-Italians to the curia, and after Vatican II, internationalization of the curia was a major goal of Paul VI. Paul and the bishops at Vatican II felt that non-Italians were necessary for the curia to reflect the universal nature of the church. Reformers hoped that internationalizing the curia would make it more open to the outside world. On a practical level, the decline of Latin as the universal language of the church meant that curia offices had to have an international staff to communicate with local churches in their native languages.

The change has been dramatic. The greatest immediate impact after Vatican II was at the top as more non-Italian prefects were appointed to head up congregations. In 1961, 10 of the 11 congregations were headed by Italian cardinals, but by 1970 Italians headed only 4 of 12.[1] On the staff level, non-Italians were especially strong in the offices created after Vatican II, but their numbers were increasing in the older congregations as well. In 1961, 80 percent of the congregations' professional staff (including typists and technicians) was Italian; by 1970 the percentage had dropped to 65. Since the staffs got bigger during this period, many of the new employees were non-Italian. In the early years after Vatican II, internationalization did not have as great an impact on the Secretariat of State, which already was one fourth non-Italian in 1961. In fact, the Secretariat of State became more Italian between 1961 and 1970.

The internationalization of the curia has continued since 1970 but at a much slower pace. In 1994, one-third of the congregations still had Italian prefects and 3 of the 11 councils had Italian presidents. Italians still dominate the

Percentage of Officials Who Are Italians

	1961	1970	1994
Prefects of Congregations	91%	33%	33%
Presidents of Councils	n/a	n/a	27[a]
Congregation Professional Staff	80	65	54
Council Professional Staff	n/a	n/a	49
Secretariat of State	76	80	66

a. Cardinal Roger Etchegaray, a Frenchman, is counted twice since he headed two councils in 1994.

professional staff, but their numbers continue to decline. Two-thirds of the Secretariat of State's staff, 54 percent of the congregations' staffs, and 49 percent of the councils' staffs were Italian in 1994.[2] The non-professionals—porters, messengers, and so forth—are still practically all lay Italians.

Italians are more influential than their numbers indicate. Italian is the working language of the curia, which gives them an advantage. As a group, they also tend to have longer tenures in the curia and to be more knowledgeable and experienced in its ways. Non-Italians in the curia are quick to criticize their Italian counterparts. "The Italians really know how to live, but they don't know how to get anything done" is a typical comment from an American working in a council. "To get anything done is really a workout. You've got to know your way around. An Italian knows whom you talk to and what to do. If you yourself go as an American, forget it, they will kill you."

But many Americans are also quick to defend their Italian colleagues. "The Italians are the ones that are making it go," explains another American. "Many of them are in subordinate positions in congregations. They are doing all the paperwork, getting things all set, doing the real thinking and argumentation that goes into something while others take the credit."

Most agree, including the Italians, that internationalizing the curia has been good by bringing people with different experiences and perspectives into the curia. But some non-Italians adapt to curial ways to the point where they lose their national identity. "Some of the worst people here are not Italians but foreigners who have been Italianized," says an official in the Secretariat of State. As Karl Rahner wrote in 1972, "members of the curia become quickly Romanized, lose any real contacts with their countries of origin and become more Roman than the Romans."[3]

Prefects and Presidents

Although the nationalities of the top Vatican officials may have changed, their backgrounds have changed less dramatically. In 1961, only two of the ten prefects of congregations had been diocesan bishops before becoming cardinals.[4] The other congregations were headed by Vatican careerists, most of whom had been in the Vatican diplomatic corps. Nuncios, after serving in major European capitals, often became cardinal prefects when they returned to Rome. This pattern still persists for Vatican congregations. In 1994, only three of the nine prefects were former diocesan bishops and the rest were careerists, with four from the diplomatic service. The pattern of appointments for council presidents is different. Of the eleven council presidents in 1994, only two were from the Vatican diplomatic corps while seven had been diocesan or auxiliary bishops and one had been a diocesan priest before his appointment. The hope was that the appointment of non-careerists as prefects, presidents, and secretaries would bring a more pastoral orientation to the curia. But according to one study, half of the heads of curial offices in 1995 had each logged more than thirty-five years of service to the Holy See.[5]

Critics claim that some diocesan bishops are brought to Rome not because of their qualifications, but because they are having pastoral, political, or legal problems in their dioceses. They are given positions in the Vatican to get them out of their dioceses. Some have even been given titles without real jobs, the most famous being Emmanuel Milingo, a charismatic archbishop who held public healing services and exorcisms in Africa. He was removed from his archdiocese and made special delegate of the Council for Migrants and Travelers in 1984. Unusual titles like delegate, vice president, or referendario are sometimes signals that a position has been created for such a bishop.

Vatican gossips have also laid this charge against prominent non-careerists such as Cardinals Joseph Ratzinger, Edmund Szoka, Alfonso López Trujillo, and José Sánchez. For example, a number of critics point to the furor caused in Detroit when Cardinal Szoka closed a large number of inner-city parishes. These accusations undermine the authority of their targets by downgrading their qualifications for their jobs. In fact, Cardinal Ratzinger is a highly qualified theologian and Cardinal Szoka has done wonders in modernizing Vatican accounting practices. Both have made enemies in their jobs. But some prelates brought to Rome appear to have few qualifications for their positions.

Despite the changes in nationality and backgrounds, surprisingly few of the prefects have any expertise in the areas of their appointments. In the years since Vatican II, no expert in liturgy has ever headed the Congregation for Divine Worship. Only one prefect of the Congregation for Catholic Education has been an educator. No prefect of the Congregation for the Oriental Churches was an Eastern Catholic or an orientalist. No prefect of the Congregation for the Evangelization of Peoples was a missionary or from a mission country. No prefect of the Congregation for the Causes of Saints was a historian or an expert in spirituality. Only one prefect of the Congregation for Religious was a religious.

Prefects with expertise in their area before their appointment are noteworthy exceptions: Joseph Ratzinger, a former professor of theology, was appointed to the Congregation for the Doctrine of the Faith; Johannes Willebrands, a renowned ecumenist, to the Council for Promoting Christian Unity; Francis Arinze, who wrote his doctoral dissertation on native African religion, to the Council for Interreligious Dialogue; Fiorenzo Angelini, a health care expert, to the Council for Pastoral Assistance to Health Care Workers; John Foley, a newspaper editor, to the Council for Social Communications; Giuseppe Casoria, an expert canonist, to the Congregation for Divine Worship and the Discipline of the Sacraments; and Rosalio José Castillo Lara, Vincenzo Fagiolo, and Julián Herranz, expert canonists, to the Council for the Interpretation of Legislative Texts. Clerical canonists are clearly the experts most easily found to head dicasteries.

For some prefects, diplomatic experience is very helpful to their job as a dicastery head. Cardinal Achille Silvestrini, an experienced diplomat, brings valuable skills to the Congregation for the Oriental Churches since most of these churches are in Eastern Europe and the Middle East, where politics and religion are intertwined. When dealing with refugee and migration problems, Archbishop Giovanni Cheli, president of the Council for Migrants and Travelers, benefits from his experience as the Holy See's observer at the United Nations.

Those who come up through the ranks of the diplomatic service also get to know the general business of Vatican dicasteries by dealing with them on the specific problems and issues from the nunciatures. "Was I ready?" asks a cardinal who had worked in the diplomatic service for decades and was a nuncio in three countries before becoming a prefect. "No one is ready for a job like this. I knew what was the expectation and what more or less is the competence of this congregation because working for the Holy See, you have a general knowledge. This congregation had communicated with me [while a nuncio] on all the aspects of its work that we are taking care of."

"It is like a train," continues the cardinal. "I had been almost forty years representing and working for the Holy See abroad. The instructions are just to change this locomotive from the railroad system that I was working in and place it in another one. It is always Holy See and church service." As the locomotive analogy indicates, sometimes officials are appointed to a particular office simply because that is the one that became vacant at the right time. "It's just the luck of the draw," explains an official of the National Conference of Catholic Bishops. "It's whoever happens to be around. There isn't a great effort to match up competencies."

Some officials even argue against the appointment of prefects with expertise. One curial official compared it to civilian control of the military, except that here it is pastoral control of experts. In defending this practice some, who do not like Cardinal Ratzinger, refer to the perils of having a German professor in charge of the Inquisition. They would prefer a pastor or a simple bureaucrat.

Generalists—diocesan bishops or curial officials—heading Vatican offices are similar to generalists or politicians holding cabinet-level appointments in civil governments. They are appointed because of their loyalty to the pope and their pastoral or curial experience. What they bring to the job is not expert knowledge but pastoral prudence, political skills, and an understanding and support for papal policies. Such a prefect brings to curial discussions political and pastoral insights based on years of experience as a bishop or a Vatican official. He can stop staff initiatives that he considers impractical or counterproductive. He can direct staff attention into fields he considers important and fruitful. His political skills within the curia and his standing with the pope are essential in making sure that his dicastery has a voice in matters that touch many dicasteries.

Many prefects and presidents work hard to develop expertise in the area of their responsibility. They learn from the secretary and the staff about the projects already under way in the dicastery. "You come into an office which has already been functioning since the Second Vatican Council," says Cardinal Edward Cassidy, explaining how he learned his job as president of the Council for Promoting Christian Unity. He noted that his predecessor, Cardinal Willebrands, was very helpful, as were the secretary and undersecretary who had been in the office for many years. "You have to learn from your staff and from the people with whom you are working. That was not a very difficult experience. Each one has his or her own field of activity, and I had to pick up knowledge from all of them in their own activities as we went along, as each thing happened." Those who do not take advice from their staff and other experts usually make a mess of it.

Some prefects are strikingly honest in admitting their lack of expertise. One participant at a meeting chaired by Cardinal Giuseppe Casoria, prefect of the Congregation for Divine Worship, reports that Cardinal Casoria "came to the table and sat there at the beginning of the meeting and said, 'I don't know anything about liturgy. I leave it to these experts and I will sit here.' He would give an occasional *ferverino* about how we must all love God and all work together, but as far as the issues he didn't enter into any of them." Cardinal Casoria's appointment came three years before his retirement. He was an expert in the canon law of marriage, which is dealt with in one section of the congregation. He knew he was at the end of his career and saw no reason to become an expert in liturgy, which is dealt with by the other section of his congregation.

Some appointments, like Cardinal Casoria's, are made to reward a man for years of service. Becoming a prefect or president is the cap to their careers. This pattern is seen with prefects appointed a few years before reaching the retirement age of 75, as was the case with Cardinals Casoria and Augustin Mayer at the Congregation for Divine Worship and Cardinal Corrado Bafile at the Congregation for the Causes of Saints. These appointments allowed them to become cardinals, to retire with a bigger pension, and to be members of congregations and councils until they turned 80. A few appointments are made to get people out of their current job. For example, Archbishop Jean Jadot was moved from being apostolic delegate in the United States to being president of the Council for Interreligious Dialogue, a position that did not require making him a cardinal.

Ultimately, it is the pope who appoints the prefects to five-year renewable terms, and he can appoint anyone he wishes. John Paul II, for example, brought back Cardinal Silvio Oddi, who had been forced into retirement by Paul VI, and made him prefect of the Congregation for the Clergy. Cardinal Oddi voted for John Paul II at the 1978 conclave. Later John Paul II called Edouard Gagnon back to Rome to head up the Council for the Family, even though Gagnon had quit the curia in disgust and was not liked in the Secretariat of State. "A month before" being called back to Rome by the pope, reports Cardinal Gagnon, "a cardinal asked that I be secretary of his congregation, and the Secretary of State [Agostino Casaroli] said, 'Gagnon will never come back.'" Both Cardinals Oddi and Gagnon were friends of the pope and very popular with conservative Catholics. They proved to be controversial and outspoken members of his curia.

Turnover in dicastery heads, except through death or retirement, is very low. Most dicastery heads are reappointed at the end of their five-year terms or given another position of similar rank. In 1995, 8 of the 20 dicastery heads had served more than ten years in office; another 7 had served for five years. Cardinal Ratzinger has been a prefect the longest, since 1981.

Although in the past newly elected popes sometimes exiled their enemies, more recent popes (John XXIII, Paul VI, and John Paul II) have rarely replaced dicastery heads, not even those who voted against them in the conclave. Only by 1985 had John Paul II replaced all the congregation prefects he inherited from Paul VI in 1978. It was another four years before the last Paul VI appointee, Cardinal Johannes Willebrands, was replaced in the Council for Promoting Christian Unity. It is unheard of for prefects or presidents to be fired, and rarely does anyone, like Cardinal Oddi, get "retired" early. Despite having Alzheimer's disease, Cardinal Wladyslaw Rubin remained for some years as prefect of the Congregation for the Oriental Churches. Getting rid of controversial or incompetent prelates would be considered un-Christian by some and difficult to explain to the media. Sometimes officials are reassigned to less important positions. For example, in 1981 Cardinal James Knox was moved from head of the Congregation for Worship to the Council for the Family. The Vatican Library, the Vatican Archives, and the Fabrica of St. Peter's have also been used as places for cardinals who are not trusted in more important jobs. This has caused difficulties for the professional staff of the library and the archives.

As time goes on, a new pope fills vacancies resulting from retirements or deaths. As part of Paul VI's reform of the curia in 1970, dicastery heads are required to submit their resignations at age 75. They are often allowed to continue serving one or two additional years until the next consistory, when the pope will create new cardinals and make new assignments in the curia.[6] Voluntary early retirements are rare since alternative employment for cardinals and archbishops is not available inside or outside the church. The church does not know what to do with unemployed archbishops and cardinals.

Secretaries and Undersecretaries

In the past, a prefect often left the running of his congregation to its secretary. This was especially the case when prefects did not retire at 75 and continued in office when they were old or sickly. Unless they are ill or close to retirement, prefects and presidents today tend to be much more hands-on than in the past. But the secretary of a congregation or council is still a key figure in the Vatican curia.[7] Some documents require his signature as well as the prefect's. While the prefect has many meetings and other duties outside the office, the secretary focuses solely on the business of the dicastery.

As late as 1967, 95 percent of the secretaries were Italian.[8] Many in the past were from the diplomatic service. Today, most of the secretaries are still careerists, but only a few are Italian and from the diplomatic service. In 1994, only about 25 percent of the secretaries were Italian and fewer were from the diplomatic service.[9] Only one secretary had been a diocesan bishop before being appointed. More than half of the council secretaries, who do not have to be bishops, were promoted from the staff or consultors of their own offices. They were thus knowledgeable in the work of their offices before their appointments. Promotion from within is rare in congregations, however. All but one of the congregation secretaries, who are archbishops, came from outside their congregations.

The pope appoints secretaries after consultation with the secretary of state and the pertinent prefect or president. The prefect "doesn't have much say," explains a congregation secretary. "These are decisions made by the secretary of state. They may ask him, but he may not get the person he wants. He may get a person he wouldn't particularly want. There are certain checks and balances, which is not bad. You don't want people that clash. On the other hand, you don't want people that always agree either. Sometimes it is good to have differences." Normally the prefect gets someone who is acceptable to him, but not always. "The secretary was appointed without consulting the prefect," reports another Vatican official. "He was furious. The man had no qualifications. He was appointed here to get him out of another office." As with prefects, some secretaries are appointed as a reward for long service rather than because of their expertise in a particular field.

Just as with prefects and secretaries, so too have more non-Italian under-secretaries *(sotto-segretario)* been appointed in the curia. As late as 1967, 94 percent of the undersecretaries were Italian. In 1994, only 35 percent were Italian.[10] Promotion from within is very common for the position of under-secretary, who acts as the office manager in the dicastery. In 1994, practically all the undersecretaries in the congregations and about half the undersecre-taries in the councils had been promoted from within. About a third of the undersecretaries were Italians, with a higher concentration in the congrega-tions than in the councils. The prefect (or president) and secretary present three names to the Secretariat of State when the undersecretary's position becomes vacant, but the pope is still free to choose whomever he wants. The prefect's and secretary's recommendations carry weight in this appointment unless the Secretariat of State has a candidate it wants to promote.

The undersecretaries are usually priests, although two are laymen. Since most undersecretaries have been promoted from within, they know the history behind policies, the abilities of the staff, and the experts who can be consulted on different issues. Although they cannot decide policy, they can influence what kind of information gets to their superiors. The prefect (or president), secretary, and undersecretary are referred to as the dicastery's superiors who can make decisions, while those under them are the staff whose work is always reviewed by the superiors. Only the superiors can sign correspondence from the office.

Professional Staff

The professional staff in the councils and congregations are mostly priests. Some professionally trained women religious also work in dicasteries, for example, as canon lawyers in the Congregation for Institutes of Consecrated

Life and for Societies of Apostolic Life. Some lay professionals, mostly Italian, are hired to work on a permanent basis in the curia, usually at financial work. A few lay professionals (including women) also work on substantive issues in the councils for the Laity, the Family, Justice and Peace, Cor Unum, Migrants and Travelers, Interreligious Dialogue, Health Care Workers, and Communications.

"We would like more lay professionals," says a council secretary. "We have been very fortunate with the laypeople we have. It is not always easy to get them because it involves a certain sacrifice financially, and opportunities for advancement are not great." Only two laymen have become undersecretaries (in the councils for Communications and Laity). In 1995, of the 21 *capi ufficio* in the congregations and councils, none were laypersons. Few laity even rise to the rank of *minutante* (1 out of 10) or *aiutante di studio* (6 out of 42). These are the three highest ranks below an undersecretary. Most laity only get as high as *addetto di segreteria,* the next rung down on the ladder, but even here they are a small minority. The same pattern is true of religious women, although they are more likely than laypersons to work in congregations. Most of the *scrittori* or typists are religious women or Italian laywomen.[11]

The curia's priests, who make up the bulk of the professional staff, are unmarried men who have gone through the normal intellectual and spiritual formation for priests in a seminary. Most priests working in the curia also have advanced degrees usually in canon law or theology or are working on them at pontifical universities in Rome. While most of their peers were destined to work in parishes, these priests ended up in the church's bureaucracy, but their vocation, life style, and culture are first and foremost those of a priest. Like other priests, they have given up family, secular careers, and their freedom and dedicated their lives to serve God as ministers in the Catholic church. The greatest criticism within the curia is directed at those who through ambition and careerism forget that they are priests and servants of the church.

Ecclesiastical Academy Graduates

The priests working in the curia can be divided into those who are long-term careerists and those who are planning to stay only five or ten years. The elite of the Vatican civil service are the diocesan priests who attended the Pontifical Ecclesiastical Academy, where they were trained for the Vatican diplomatic service. The academy is the West Point of the Vatican civil service, with room for a student body totaling only thirty-two priests. Earlier in this century, students had to be from noble families. In the 1950s the academy's student body was 75 to 80 percent Italian, but in 1994 only six students were Italians according to an academy administrator. The rest came from nineteen different countries, many in the Third World. Students for the academy are recruited by the Secretariat of State. "If they apply, we generally don't want them," reports an American in the Secretariat of State. "Don't call us, we'll call you."

Most of the students are recruited within a few years after ordination. "We look for someone who can do the academic work, for someone who is happy being a priest, and hopefully a good priest," he continues. "We also look for someone who has common sense. You can be Einstein, but you also have to have someone who can figure out that if the plumbing is broken then maybe it is a good idea to call a plumber." Another essential quality is loyalty to the Holy See. Anyone who is known to question decisions or theological views coming from the Vatican would not be invited to the academy.

When a candidate for the academy or for the curia from a particular country is sought, trusted members of the curia from that country would be consulted. "When the sostituto [head of the first section of the Secretariat of State] is looking for some Americans to come and work in the curia," explains an official at the U.S. bishops' conference, "he goes to his Americans in the diplomatic corps and says, 'Would you suggest somebody?'"

Nuncios and trusted diocesan bishops are also asked to suggest candidates when a person is needed from a particular country. Recommendations are also sought from the rectors of the national colleges, such as the North American College in Rome. These are not colleges in the American sense but in the European sense, that is, residences where students live while attending universities in Rome. Only three or four academy students in 1994 had not studied in Rome before entering the academy. Having lived in Roman colleges, these students already know some Italian and have absorbed some of the Roman atmosphere. Having watched them for three or four years, their rectors would know whether they have the qualities necessary for Vatican service. Very few Americans in the service of the Holy See did not first live at the North American College.

One priest, who had returned to Rome to do graduate studies after two years working in a parish, tells of getting a phone call from the highest ranking person from his country in the Secretariat of State. "He asked me if I could come over and talk to him," he recalls. His first reaction was, "What did I do? Someone wrote some nasty letter about me." When asked to accept an appointment to the academy, he was so surprised that "I fell off my chair." Since the monsignor did not know him personally, the priest presumes his name was put forward by a good friend in the diplomatic service with whom he had gone to the seminary. He was given 24 hours to respond.

He immediately called his bishop, who because of the time difference was in bed. His bishop had already been consulted and wanted him to accept, but the bishop said, "The decision is yours. If you say no, I will defend you. I won't let them pressure you." He accepted, a decision that meant a lifetime commitment to Vatican service. Some who are approached do say no because they do not want to leave their countries or because they prefer parish work. Many Vatican officials also complain that "many times the bishops have good candidates, but they prefer to keep them for their dioceses."

The course of studies at the academy normally takes four years, the first two being spent getting a licentiate in canon law at one of the Roman universities. Often the students will also get a doctorate in canon law or theology, although some avoid the Gregorian University because it is the toughest academically. If they already have a doctorate, they can get through the academy in two years. The students also do a two-month internship during their last two summers, first in the Secretariat of State and the following summer in a nunciature.

Academy classes are in the afternoon so that they do not conflict with university classes in the morning. The students have academy courses in languages, international law, diplomatic history, ecclesiastical diplomacy, and diplomatic writing (how to write reports and correspondence). There would also be shorter courses or individual lectures on a variety of other topics. For example, there is a brief course in bookkeeping since the secretary usually keeps the books at the nunciature. These academy lectures are highly practical in orientation and are often given by members of the Vatican diplomatic service or members of the Roman curia. For example, the prefect or secretary of a congregation would give a talk to the students on the work of his congregation.

Academy courses are not aimed toward getting an academic degree. At the completion of the course of studies, there is a comprehensive oral and written examination. "They give you a problem and you write a report on it," explains a former student. "You then go before a board, which consists of five people, and they ask you questions for a half hour or so. Generally, if you are admitted to the exam, you pass the exam."

In addition to the academic work, the students are expected to absorb the culture and atmosphere of the Vatican diplomatic service. "It is hoped that in the time in the Accademia by being exposed to how things are done, at least in Italian society, that those characteristics will also rub off," explains an official in the Secretariat of State. "So by serving formal meals every day, you would learn which fork to use. That is part of the formation at the Accademia, but it is not etiquette 101 and then you move to etiquette 102. It's done in a very Latin way."

Spiritual and personal formation is also emphasized through frequent contact between the students and the academy staff. The graduate should be "a priest with human and Christian virtues to a high degree," explains an academy official.

> Of course, you need somebody who is very prudent, who has a very good equilibrium, who has a very good disposition for human relations. Someone who is not only able to talk to anybody, but who is able to have a dialogue with anybody: a man, a woman, a Catholic, a non-Catholic, Christian, non-Christian, believer, non-believer, government officials. That's very important. Somebody who has a very good equilibrium, a lot of common sense, a lot of prudence, who is able to hear others, who is able to dialogue and to solve problems in a peaceful way. I should say that's more or less. It's impossible to find somebody who has all this.

After completing his training, a graduate is sent to work in a nunciature as an assistant to a nuncio, with whom he lives. In a sense, his training does not stop but continues under the supervision of the local nuncio, who reports on his work to the Secretariat of State. "Normally for approximately 18 to 20 years, you are in an auxiliary position," explains an official in the Secretariat of State. "And if you are out in the field, you are usually someplace for three years at a time and then moved somewhere else. Ideally, everyone comes back to Rome for a term in the Secretariat of State," although non-Italians are more likely to be brought back because skill in their native language is needed in the secretariat.

Although such a career gives the papal diplomats wide experience, it can take a toll. In writing about the pope's representatives, Lamberto de Echeverría asks: "Has sufficient thought been given to what it means to a normal person to be uprooted from his own country to spend his life going from one country to another? To be deprived of genuine friendship in an area where relations are liable to be tainted by selfishness and ambition? To have to live in a very enclosed community and be deprived of freedom, knowing that information which is passed on can have a decisive influence on his future?"[12]

Promotion within the diplomatic service is principally through seniority unless a person messes up. "You are one year as an addetto, an attaché," explains an official in the Secretariat of State, "then six years as a secretary (three as second class, three as first class), and six years as uditore (three as second class, three as first class). Then generally there is a decision made whether they are going to promote someone to counselor or not. The major cutoff is whether you become a nuncio or not. If you are made a counselor, that would mean that eventually you would be made a nuncio." They and other diocesan priests in the curia also automatically become monsignors after five years of service.

"If you do a good job, you will be made a bishop by age 50," explains an Italian well connected in the Vatican. "If you are in the Secretariat of State, you will get a nunciature. Then you will go to a better one. Then [a few are] brought back to work in the curia." For a person to be promoted, "he has to become known as someone who does a good job, prepares a good speech for his cardinal, writes a good memo that goes to the pope." In other words, the man has to come to the attention of high-level Vatican officials.

Working for a key official, like the secretary of state or the two officials under him, the undersecretary and the sostituto, also makes a difference. "They speak very much of the widows of Benelli [the sostituto under Paul VI]," reports an Italian with decades of experience working in the Vatican. These are "all the people who served as close collaborators of Benelli [in the Secretariat of State] when they were young. Now every one of them has a good post. The widows are Rigali [archbishop of St. Louis], Re [sostituto], Rovida [the nuncio in Bern], and the last widow was Cacciavillan. So when Cacciavillan got the post of nuncio in the States, they told me, now all the widows have been taken care of."

The training and international experience of these diplomats make them very influential when they return to the Vatican. Having worked in different countries and cultures, they have direct knowledge of local churches and their countries. Having worked in the nunciatures, they are better able to interpret information that comes to Rome from the nunciatures. By moving around they have also made numerous friends and contacts in local churches, the Vatican diplomatic service, the Secretariat of State, and the curia. This informal network of friends and contacts, which begins at the academy, is an essential source of information that is necessary to get things done in the Vatican. "If you want to know all the rumors or what is going on," explains an Italian priest, "get in touch with two or three of them when they are together. You will learn a lot, because that is their life." "You get three or four priests gathered together and they are criticizing other people," says Archbishop Paul Marcinkus, who compared the Vatican to a village of washerwomen. "When you're in an enclosed place like this there's nothing else to do, nowhere to go, nothing else to talk about."[13]

For Italians, these contacts go back to seminary days. "It helps if he went to one of the right colleges," explains an Italian priest well connected in the Vatican. "For the Italians it would be the Lombardo, Capranica, and the Seminario Romano. They look out for one another. It is both the friends you made while you were in college and then the alumni who also help you advance. And if you have a difficulty, they rally around." Advancement can even be helped by the region of Italy an official originally came from. "They speak very much in the Vatican of the Mafia Emiliana," explains an Italian who has worked for decades in the curia. "At the time of Pius XII, they had as cardinals Amleto Cicognani, the secretary of state, and his brother Gaetano." Also coming from this area of Italy over the years have been Cardinals Agostino Casaroli, Pio Laghi, Silvio Oddi, Egano Righi-Lambertini, Opilio Rossi, Camillo Ruini, Aurelio Sabattani, Achille Silvestrini, Dino Staffa, Antonio Samorè, and Giovanni Nasalli-Rocca di Corneliano, as well as Archbishop Luigi Poggi, Bishop Dino Monduzzi, and Msgr. Claudio Celli.

The importance of personal and family relations in Italy leads to nepotism and cronyism in the Vatican. "This political situation, where you brought in your cronies, that was just a fact of life" in Italy, comments an American working in Rome since the early 1960s. "It is also a fact of life in the Vatican. You see people in the smallest jobs and in the highest jobs, and they are related to this person or that, or they are from the same neighborhood."

Hiring relatives is especially prevalent among lay employees in the curia and in Vatican City. "I used to think that was awful," reports another American with many years of experience working in the Vatican. "In America you are not supposed to hire people from your family. Here it would be an insult if you didn't. Jobs are passed along. In a way it works. They know the job better than anybody else. They know everybody. You are not getting somebody you don't know anything about. They probably could get another job somewhere, but they wouldn't be as happy. Because here, it is like working in a family." "The advantage of hiring your relatives," explains another American, "is that they will not cheat you too badly." The Venezuelan Cardinal Castillo, as head of Vatican City and the Administration of the Patrimony of the Holy See (APSA), fought this trend in lay employment and made enemies among the Italians.

For priests seeking employment or promotion, it is less likely to be a relative than a friend or a patron who makes a difference in getting a job or promotion. "When you need a secretary of a council," an Italian will say, "here is somebody from my neighborhood whom I can trust, he is one of my boys," according to an American with long experience in Rome. "That aspect of Italian social fabric is very characteristic of the Vatican." Hence the importance of the Mafia Emiliana and school ties.

Other people in the Roman curia, especially non-Italians, do not have the training, experience, or network of contacts of those who studied in the academy. Most non-academy priests were recruited through their bishops, their religious superiors, or the rectors of their national colleges in Rome to work in the curia on either a permanent or temporary basis. Others are recommended by their Roman university teachers who are consultors to various Vatican congregations. Often they are recruited for their linguistic skills and for some specialty they have (such as canon law, liturgy, ecumenism, theology, or seminary administration).

Some bishops' conferences, like the German conference, make it a practice of placing their people in various curial offices so they can look out for their interests. Most, like the Americans, are more passive and only respond to requests from Rome for personnel. Curial officials frequently complain that bishops sometimes refuse to let their best men go to Rome. Some bishops have even gotten rid of failed seminary teachers by sending them to Rome, where they wreaked havoc on the church universal. Sometimes it is up to the dicastery staff person to find his own replacement from his country or language before he can return home.

Most members of the curia claim that they were recruited for their positions, but long-time observers of the curia say that this is only partially true. Some students in Rome actively seek positions in the curia. "You kind of look around to the different Vatican offices and cardinal's offices, with your ear to the ground," explains an American priest who has observed the Vatican for years. Making friends with someone in the office and doing volunteer work helps bring one to the attention of the superiors.

"There's a certain breed that make themselves known and want to get over there," comments another American priest in Rome. "Many times, they've studied in Rome. They enjoy Rome. They speak Italian well and they see this as their place. They bring themselves to the notice of someone in Rome or their own bishops. The bishops are always getting requests to send somebody over. So if somebody will volunteer, fine, send him over. It doesn't mean we get the best people though. It's harder and harder to find priests who want to spend their life working in a curial office, even though it may mean you can eventually go up the ladder."

"There is a problem recruiting people for the Vatican," agrees the superior of a religious order in Rome. "People don't want to work there. They would rather work in their bishops' conferences." According to curial officials, it is especially difficult to recruit Americans and Germans, who would experience a lower standard of living in Rome than in their own countries. Candidates from the Third World, on the other hand, experience Rome as a move up. The increase in Third World priests in the curia "is good and bad," says an official in the curia. "Some of them never want to go home again" because they become accustomed to a better life style or because they lose touch with their local church.

For highly trained specialists, the recruiting process can be more targeted. For example, if the Council for Interreligious Dialogue is looking for an English-speaking Catholic theologian specializing in Islam, the pool of candidates is not large. The council staff would already know most of the possible candidates because they would be participating in interreligious dialogues. Often these specialists are working in academia or a church institution where they are needed. They would have to be persuaded to leave their current work and come to Rome to work in the curia. Since priests with specialized academic training are often members of religious orders with schools, prefects and presidents ask religious superiors in Rome if they have priests with the needed qualifications.

"Father Michael Glynn had to retire, so in anticipation of his retirement, we looked around the world to see who would have experience in the areas he had," explains Archbishop Foley, president of the Council for Social Communications. "His areas of responsibility were dealing with UNDA, the international Catholic communications organization for radio and television. He also dealt with English-speaking Africa, Asia, and Oceania. One of our consultors, Father Pat Casaroli, was familiar with the Asian scene and was active in OCIC and UNDA." After clearance with the Secretariat of State and his own religious superiors, Father Casaroli was hired.

Sometimes positions remain vacant because a willing person with the proper qualifications cannot be found. "Not everybody wants to come and work in the Vatican," explains a council secretary. "And not everybody who wants to come and work in the Vatican is what we want. We don't need activists here. Here people have to be able to stand back and reflect and try to understand. On the other hand, we don't want pure academics."

Once a candidate is found, there is no "civil service" exam to measure a person's qualifications for his or her position in the Vatican. "There is no centralized screening and no testing for competence whether in language or in their knowledge of church policy or law or things like that," explains an

American canonist. Information is gathered informally by asking the candidate's college rector, his fellow nationals in the curia, and his bishop.

The appointment process begins when the president or prefect of an office tries to fill a vacancy. He can ask bishops, nuncios, his own staff, or others for suggestions, but ultimately he nominates a person for the job. The personnel office in APSA determines the proper salary according to a set of formal criteria (position, academic degrees, length of service, and so forth). The nomination is then screened by the Secretariat of State and the Congregation for the Doctrine of the Faith, which checks its computer to see if the person's name is on file for having said or written anything contrary to church teaching. This clearance is needed for any employees involved in the preparation of documents, including typists. The person's bishop and the nuncio in his country would be asked if they have any negative information on the candidate.

Normally there is not a problem. "We would say no if the person is not competent, if there are doctrinal problems, or if even innocently there is some reason why the appointment of this particular individual might be offensive to a nation," explains an official in the Secretariat of State. "It depends on the office. If it is someone who is going to be an official at a minor level, the requirements are less strenuous than for someone who is going to be secretary, undersecretary, or prefect."

Since the Secretariat of State must approve hirings, it can impose someone on a reluctant prefect. An official in a highly technical field complains that "we have had the problem of asking for someone and having the Secretariat of State say no, and then have them offer us someone who is incompetent." This is especially a problem in positions that require trained lay personnel.

"The hiring will be done by someone quite remote from the office," explains an American monsignor, "who will say, 'We think so and so; we know the father of so and so.' Or 'so and so is well-educated, a doctor of something or another.' That is just dumb for us. That has gone on three or four times since I've been here. That is an Italian weakness. That weakness has unfortunately turned away one or two potentially very good non-Italian employees, and that is truly tragic, because the Italians are keeping it for their own plaything. That makes me very angry, I get cross when I get into that area because people are making decisions about hiring who know nothing about the job, absolutely nothing about the job! It's the weakness of the church."

Although the individual's bishop is consulted, the conference of bishops is not necessarily contacted. "We're never consulted here on any appointments to the Holy See as a conference of bishops," explains an official of the National

Conference of Catholic Bishops. "We're never asked, although a couple of years ago Cardinal Casaroli agreed that the conference would always be asked. It's never been implemented." Sometimes even the normal procedures are not followed. As this official commented, "In some instances that I'm aware of, people went over without even a consultation with the nuncio. It was just a deal, a done deal, between a congregation and the man's bishop."

Members of the staff are hired for a trial period of at least one year but not more than two years. During this period they can be fired for any reason. At the end of the trial period, the superior requests that the person be hired definitively and another review takes place. Once a person is definitively hired, as in Italy, it is almost impossible to fire him or her from the Vatican. The only example of a person being fired (after having been definitively hired) that I heard of was a woman who married a priest. One observer thought she would not have been fired "if she had not made a big deal of it."

Once in the Vatican, the various national groups or religious orders develop their own networks. Members of national groups or religious orders working in different dicasteries are likely to interact on an informal basis and exchange information. Some, like the Americans, even live together. Curial officials are more likely to help and share information with other nationals or members of their order than with outsiders.

Various groups have been considered powerful insiders during different pontificates. At one time the French were strong, but their numbers have declined with the decline in French vocations. The Jesuits were very influential during the pontificate of Pius XII but less so during later papacies. They continue to provide consultors or staff to various offices, especially Vatican Radio. Dominicans, Franciscans, Oblates, Claretians, and Salesians are also present in the curia in significant numbers. Today, Polish officials are referred to as the Polish Mafia because of their influence in the curia and their back-door access to the pope. Opus Dei, an organization of clergy and laity, is also said to be influential and to have members in every office, but because of their secretiveness this cannot be verified.[14]

Internal Culture of the Curia

Within the curia there are people with different views and attitudes. According to one American canonist, who has frequently visited the curia:

> Some people there are really dedicated Christians who really try to do a good job and are concerned about the welfare of the church. Some people

are like any bureaucrats who are deeply entrenched in their own little world and can't see beyond that and are going to make everything fit their own categories. Other people with a very broad vision are really concerned that what they are doing have a positive impact. There is clearly a distinct line between those who are really committed to implementing the Second Vatican Council and the current direction of the church, and people who think that "it's all going to hell in a hand basket and we've got to tighten this thing up and pull back." There's real tension within the staff on that.

Despite these differences and differences in cultural backgrounds, members of the curia speak of an overall atmosphere that permeates the Roman curia. It is sometimes referred to as "Romanità," which is not easily defined. Part of it comes from the Vatican's location. Rome was the capital of an ancient empire and then the seat of the popes through the centuries. "The ancient ruins are all around you," comments an American canonist. "It's the sense that this is the center and the rest of the world is the periphery, which is the language you will find in *Pastor Bonus,* the constitution on the Roman curia."

It is not only ancient Rome, but modern Italy that affects attitudes in the curia. In Italy, no one is surprised when the phones do not work, when the country is paralyzed by a strike, when the mail takes weeks to be delivered, or when the bureaucratic red tape makes it difficult to get anything done. "Italians are used to things not working," explains an American living in Rome. Another American working in a congregation comments: "Not only is it Italian, but it is Southern Italian. Efficiency is not a priority in this city. The *bella figura*—how you do things—is more important than what you get accomplished." Beauty *(bella)* is more important than speed, quantity, or efficiency. A craftsman judges himself by the beauty of his work, not by the amount he accomplishes. Nor is it simply the beauty of the finished product, but the way in which he does it. A good job allows an Italian to be an artist and a performer.

When I was preparing to leave Rome, I threw my books and belongings in some old boxes and went to the community mail room to get some tape and have them weighed. When the mail clerk saw the boxes he shook his head in horror. He proceeded to repack them, wrap the boxes in brown paper, and bind them with twine. Not only were they wrapped as perfectly as any Christmas present, but his every move was like a dramatic ballet. That this took extra time to accomplish was a minor consideration. They arrived in the States in perfect condition.

If a job does not allow for artistic performance, it is not an important part of an Italian's life. The job provides income and security but not necessarily fulfillment, which is found in other aspects of life. Employment mobility is not great. If an Italian is unhappy in his work and in a position of authority, he is likely to turn into a bureaucratic tyrant.

At the same time, there is a great admiration for the Italians' ability to respond flexibly to a crisis. "Italians rise to the occasion," explains an American in the curia. "They are the best improvisers in the world. They fake it and they have a lot of imagination." "The Italians have a kind of a genius for improvisation," agrees a French Canadian. "They can organize things very fast, and they don't worry too much about details."

Many Americans working in the curia grow to an appreciation of the Italian approach. Those who do not become frustrated or return to the States. "Frankly, I would much rather work for an Italian because they are more human," reports an Italian American in the curia. "They recognize that you can't work all the time. If there is a day off, I want a celebration. The Italians move from one celebration to the next. Yet they get their work done. When it gets tough, they get it done."

When John XXIII was asked, "How many people work in the Vatican?" his frequently quoted response was, "About half." Most of the negative comments about the Italian work ethic are directed at the nonprofessional staff. Most observers of the curia report that priests and laity at the professional level are overwhelmed with work. In many offices there is the feeling that they carry the burdens of the entire church and world as their responsibility. "We're understaffed and overworked," complains a Vatican official. "We've got rotten schedules, but this is for the service of mother church. That's the way I look at it."

"I think that John XXIII was very unjust in that famous joke," said Cardinal Gagnon, who interviewed people working in the curia as part of an internal study. "I was impressed by the amount of work and the generosity of the personnel of the Holy See. I found that the priests were working very hard and that they were taking work home. I would say about 90 percent work very hard with love for the church. Then 10 percent will profit by their work, take the glory, and take things easy." An Italian priest well connected to the curia notes that "some of them, mainly the secretaries, stay there all day really. They put in a long day. Humanly speaking, it is a very austere life. They don't have too many things. But they have the sense that they are influencing the decisions in the church. It gives them a sense of fulfillment too."

There is also a very different sense of time in the Vatican, where they talk of thinking in centuries. "In the United States, we tend to think in very short terms," explains an American monsignor with fifteen years' experience working in the Vatican. "If this is a problem, fix it. We are very pragmatic as a people. So we get it done. It doesn't matter if we have to do it a different way three months from now. That is not important, the problem is getting the paper off the desk or getting the decision made." In the Vatican, all the ramifications and philosophical underpinnings of the solution must be considered. The decisions must last for centuries. As a result, they see no problem in taking ten or twenty years to decide whether girls can be altar servers. Meanwhile a generation of American girls grows up angry at the church because they cannot serve Mass.

There is a joke circulating in the curia about finding a newborn baby in the Congregation for the Doctrine of the Faith. Cardinal Ratzinger was scandalized, thinking that it might belong to one of the priests, but a monsignor told him, "Surely it is not by us. In this office nothing is completed in nine months." Another official agreed, "A child is a very fine thing, it is the fruit of love. Therefore, it is surely not by us."

"In the Vatican, there is always tomorrow," explains an American priest trying to adapt to Vatican ways. "There is nothing urgent." He agrees that "sometimes it is best to just let it run for a little while. A lot of times things work out for themselves." On the other hand, at other times everything is urgent. "It is a mass of contradictions because they do have this attitude, 'Oh, there is always tomorrow,' but then when things get fired up, there is no tomorrow because of the urgency involved with things. The rush to get things done is always a difficulty in the office because you can't be precise when you rush to get things done."

The Vatican work schedule is not helpful in the view of many Americans and non-Italians. The Vatican has a 36-hour, six-day work week, with the offices opening between 8:00 and 8:30 A.M. and closing between 1:00 and 1:30 P.M. Lay Italians with second jobs (or a private business on the side) like these hours, but the six-day work week means that priests who do parish work on Sunday have no day off. On Tuesdays and Thursdays, employees are supposed to come back and work from 4:00 P.M. to 7:00 P.M. How many do so is uncertain. Laywomen especially find the 4-to-7 work period hard on their families. Many would like to see the Vatican move to a 9-to-5 schedule for a five-day week, but others strongly oppose it. Vatican employees also have about 20 holidays a year plus 30 days of vacation.

While the "job" may not be all-important for many Italians, personal relationships, friendships, and family are very important. "Through all of its social and political life, Italy has been under invasion or divided into all these little dukedoms," explains an American who worked for years in the Vatican. "You rely primarily on your family or the people from your hometown or people with whom you have some sort of a deep social connection."

Establishing personal relationships is the key to getting anything done in Italy and in the Vatican. "If I were starting all over again," comments one American priest returning to the States after years of working in Rome,

> I would be careful right from the beginning, even though it would cost me, to make special efforts to find contacts and then to take time to be very personal. Everything over here is personal. It is very, very personal. It used to drive me crazy that what you could do with a phone call in the United States you could only do with three phone calls to set up a personal visit and then with three or four personal visits.
>
> They don't do things the way we do things. You just can't call up a stranger and say, "My name is so-and-so, I am from [office deleted]. I understand that you know something about this and I would like to be able to pick your brains." They would talk to you, they would be polite, but you would get nowhere.
>
> What you need to do is find out whom do you know who knows this person. Get that person to call and say, "Look, I have a friend who is a priest and he is interested in such and such and I wonder if I could introduce you to him." When the person says yes, the next thing is you get introduced to that person and see him. They regard our approach as crass and offensive and they don't react to it very well.

"If they don't care about you, just forget about what you asked them," explains one American woman who had trouble at first getting the Vatican lay staff to do anything. "You will get there and find out that it wasn't done." After she developed personal relations with them, things changed. "They will do anything you want once they know you trust them and you become part of the clan."

Career and promotion are also very important in the curia. If an Italian cleric is not promoted, everyone in his family and village will want to know why. Careerism is not solely an Italian disease. "Careerism is one of the main sicknesses in the curia," reports an Italian whose service in the Vatican goes back to the time of Pius XII. "Once a person has been in a position, you can't remove him. You have to give him another place of honor or responsibility. If someone was worried about his career, I would send him to the poorest mission with a one-way ticket."

Careerism and ambition among clerics are universally condemned in the

Vatican, but everyone admits they are there. "Every seminarian wants to become a bishop," comments a congregation official.

> Multiply that by a factor of ten and you have got the Vatican. I can think of four or five people in my congregation who only want to run their office as well as possible. I can think of another four or five who are headed up. You can see that they are making the right moves. They are getting to know the right people, they are saying the right things. So it is career diplomacy—I do what I need to do to get promoted rather than what I need to do to do the right thing. That is another part of the Romanità.

But not everyone can be promoted. "How many people actually go up the ladder?" asks an American with years of contact with the curia. "There are only so many positions at the top and there are hundreds of priests working in the curia." Priests who do not advance in their careers are still reluctant to leave the Vatican. "Many of these people have nowhere else to go," explains an Englishman. "Their whole life has been here. So where do they go? How do they make a living? There is a certain status working for the Vatican that they would lose if they left."

The price of unfulfilled ambition is high. Priests involved in spiritual direction find much anger and frustration among the curia's priests who have not advanced. By the time they recognize that they are never going to be a bishop, it is too late to return to their dioceses, with which they feel out of touch.

"It's unhealthy, it's a political place," reports a monsignor who came to the curia in his mid-60s and has contact with priests retired from the curia.

> I don't think that a young man should ever come here. I'm quite happy to be here, but at 24 I would be ambitious and feeling that I was going to have to save the church. It isn't just purely personal glory. But it's amazing how quickly you get to be 65, and nothing has happened. I see these poor old souls. There's a bitterness there. I have no idea what their spiritual life is like. It must be awful. You can sense an unhappy kind of atmosphere, frustration, and resentful of the person next door who has perhaps done more or accomplished more. They aspired and worked hard at it, and didn't succeed. They're unhappy. And that is so sad.

Although many practice clerical ambition, only one former curial official actually defends it. "Ambitious people are not the problem that some other people think that they are," explains this pragmatic American, who had twelve years' experience in the Vatican and many more observing it from the outside.

The ambitious people that I knew during those twelve years did a good job for the church. Because they were ambitious, they were not going to make any mistakes. They were going to have a good record so that they could get up in the system. Fine. In the process they did a good job. What good are paper movers? What you want is people who are competent, people who can be movers of things, pushers, somewhat aggressive for their causes. If they are somewhat ambitious, so much the better. They are going to do their job as well as they possibly can to get ahead, and in the process they do the job well.

Making a big mistake can be deadly for one's career in the Vatican. "If a man handled his particular area poorly because of lack of information, lack of judgment, or lack of asking sufficient advice," a council official comments, he could be in trouble. "Those are bad mistakes that should hinder his promotion." A mistake can also involve offending somebody at a higher level so that he prevents you from getting promoted.

Fear of making mistakes makes Vatican officials naturally conservative rather than risk-takers. "Nobody wants to do something the first time," complains a Spaniard in the Secretariat of State. An Italian priest with many contacts in the curia comments that "if you have a cardinal prefect who doesn't know too much and a secretary who is hoping for a red hat and so doesn't want to do anything wrong, then things will not move at all." "I will not make a difficult decision" is a common attitude, according to a congregation official, "because if I make a difficult decision, either this side or that side is going to be offended. I don't want to offend either side, because if I do, I will not become cardinal. Therefore I will either push off the decision on somebody else to make, or I will never quite get around to making it."

A number of people quoted the British expression about not blotting your copy book. "If there is a small black spot, you are finished," explains an Italian. One congregation consultor articulated the five "don'ts" for surviving in the curia:

Don't think.
If you think, don't speak.
If you think, and if you speak, don't write.
If you think, and if you speak, and if you write, don't sign your name.
If you think, and if you speak, and if you write, and if you sign your
   name, don't be surprised.

Surviving a mistake depends on whether you have friends in high places to protect you. "If you don't have a cardinal protector, you cannot survive," explains an Italian in the curia. "If you make a mistake and have a good supporter, you can survive." With the right support at the top, a man can even be a petty tyrant if he has a reputation for loyalty and for getting things done. Such a career strategy is totally dependent on the continued influence of his cardinal protector. If the protector falls or dies, the tyrant's career is over because he has made too many enemies in the curia.

Loyalty to the pope and to church teaching is a sine qua non of working in the Vatican. "You don't explain the curia if you don't refer to loyalty," comments a former council secretary. "It is something certainly special that you don't find in the diocesan level. It is a deep motivation and great gratification. People are happy to do this kind of service to the church. I don't want to idealize everything, but you're working for Jesus Christ who is working through the pope." This spiritual motivation is very important for priests, religious, and laypeople in the curia.

This loyalty is shown by support for papal and curial statements. According to a priest with years of contact with the curia, "Any public statements you make would hew to the line of what the church has said about this. You know what you're expected to say about it, even though deep down you may think otherwise. When an encyclical comes out, you're expected to get behind it and say that this is a very much needed statement and it just shows how the church is close to things, close to people. You say well, the Holy Father is always right. You never knock a congregation."

Loyalty means never criticizing a papal decision. "You might thoroughly disagree but you do not criticize this in public," explains a German who worked in the curia. "It would be disloyal if I did that. When these things happen on a very high level, I said, well I accept every decision that the Holy Father is going to make and I accept it in silence." Journalists notice this reticence. "If you are covering the White House or Congress, you always have two parties," comments an American journalist with years of experience covering the Vatican. "One party is always willing to tell you stuff about the other. Here this doesn't happen. Even people who may be enemies in the Vatican are not willing to air these differences to journalists."

Anyone who has worked in the Vatican very long absorbs the proper curial attitudes and style. "You learn how to act in the manner that befits a Vatican personality," explains an American priest. "You learn this by experience, by watching the way these other people act and how they perform. And not only in public but also in these intimate gatherings. If you have been in Rome awhile, some of it's bound to rub off on you. If you come back to the States for a visit, people will notice and say, 'Oh brother, he's defending everything, he's not going to criticize anything.'"

As an Italian with decades of experience in the Vatican explains, "It is a court. No one wants to appear as against a proposal of the pope." In this court, the closer you are to the throne the more important you are. Becoming a bishop or cardinal is like entering the nobility or the royal family, and it is for life. Great deference is given to titles and hierarchy. There is "also a kind of submissiveness that is oily at times," comments an Italian American working in the curia, "a servility almost, practically a sycophancy." Even the Italian language lends itself to this by its use of "Lei" when addressing superiors and "tu" for friends and inferiors. It is a style and language that go back to a time of nobles and serfs when the ruler's merest whim was law. In such a context, disagreeing with a superior is considered unseemly.

Americans, Canadians, Australians, and younger Europeans find this attitude difficult to accept. "In the States, I am about as conservative as they get," reports an American sister dressed in full habit. "Here I feel like an activist. Something comes up, but 'Well, the cardinal said . . .' Then I say, 'Well, then, he ought to hear something.' I said a couple of strong things to him. I have said it to the bishop secretary as well. If something happens that I don't think is right, I go to them and say something. What I get a charge out of is that some people in the office, when anything is going on that bothers them, come and tell me because they know that if it bothers me, I will do something."

In this papal court, there is a style of communicating that is courteous, subtle, and nuanced, where reading between the lines is sometimes more important than the actual words. "The line between diplomacy and duplicity is a very thin one at times here," says a consultor to a Vatican congregation. "Politics pervades everything everywhere." Thus an inferior would never tell his boss that he is wrong, but rather that in these particular circumstances the superior would want to do it differently. Good superiors act the same way with those under them. "The bottom line is don't ever let them lose face," reports an American who has learned how to get things done in the Vatican. "Tell them that they are right all the time. Everybody likes to be complimented on their work. But you can't embarrass them."

This way of communicating confuses the uninitiated, especially Americans who prefer plain speech that in the Vatican court would be considered boorish and impolite. Often this diplomatic method of communicating is used to impose a decision without appearing authoritarian. The recipient is supposed to understand the message while at the same time the sender can deny having imposed his will. According to an American who works for the Vatican, "It is a subtle way to communicate a preference without being accused of dictating it. If something is raised explicitly, everyone looks around as if to say this is the first we have heard of it." Normally, no one raises the question because they understand the code.

"Once we got a very ambiguous message from the Vatican," reports an Italian American working in an institution in Rome. "Everyone capitulated under this thing except for an Australian who asked, 'Well, exactly what does that mean?' He wanted to have it spelled out. No one else wanted to raise that question because it sounded like (and in fact) they were trying to dictate something, but would never want to be quoted as having done that."

Ambiguity is often not challenged by the recipient because, "if you start raising questions," reports the same American priest, "you wonder, will you do more harm than good by forcing the issue. Is it better to leave something vague so that the people could put different interpretations on it? That would give more freedom than if we ask for an explicit, rigorous definition. I began to question my own infallible American way of saying, 'Let's talk this thing out and get this thing clear.'"

Ambiguity also allows different officials in the Vatican to give different interpretations to Vatican statements. This happens especially when there are internal disagreements that are papered over with ambiguous language. Vatican observers, including the press and bishops, must develop the ability to read between the lines of Vatican documents. In trying to understand a text, they are guided by different officials who might stress different sentences as key for understanding the total text. That the press sometimes gets it wrong or reads more into a text than is there is not surprising.

In the Vatican, tradition, precedent, and law are very important. The idea of law in Rome is quite different from that in the United States. In the United States, laws are highly detailed and are changed constantly to adapt to changing conditions and changing values in a democratic society. Roman law is less detailed and prizes stability. It does not matter so much that the law might not be observed as long as the law upholds the proper principles. Proper authorities can grant exceptions to the law in special cases. Even if a law is no longer valid, there is no hurry to remove it from the code.

Americans in Rome insist that the best way to understand church law is to watch the way Italians observe traffic laws. Immediately following the enactment of a law requiring crash helmets for motorcycle riders, the police gave out hundreds of tickets. Within a couple of weeks things were back to normal except that a bored policeman might stop a pretty girl on a motorcycle, but he would never give her a ticket.

"Here we promulgate laws and they observe them abroad," explains a former Vatican secretary. "The Code of Canon Law and all the guidelines, they are very important. But then you adapt, that's the Italian way, the Roman way, of doing things. It's Mediterranean and very human." Thus while in the United States pastors were being reprimanded for having altar girls, a Roman parish close to St. Peter's had altar girls for years before they were "legal." And when the pope visited suburban parishes, both boys and girls were dressed in albs and serving his masses before this was permitted.

"The Italian is very open to the personal aspects of a problem," reports an American who worked in the Vatican after Vatican II.

> Cardinal Ottaviani was an expert in civil and canon law. When he was prefect of the Holy Office he could come out with very definite decrees on marriages. But if you got a couple in front of Cardinal Ottaviani, the case became different, he would find some sort of solution. That is very Italian. The law, yes, but these are two people. But it would be horrible if he would write that in an article or write that into the law of the church. The Code of Canon Law is the code of ideals, that is why they have dispensation built into it, which we don't in English and American common law where you either do it or you don't or the law is changed. The code remains the basic thing, the ideal, and you have room for built-in exceptions.

With this view of law and tradition, it is hard to get things changed in the Vatican. "There is a lot of frustration obviously because the Italian mentality is that they don't want to change," says an Italian American in the curia. Even the pope has a hard time changing things, he explains.

> One of the Swiss guards was complaining that they have to be a corporal to get married. He wanted to get married and they said, "You can't get married, you are not a corporal." "Well," he said, "I feel that I have a right to be married if I am in love and ask for the sacrament." He brought the matter right to the pope, and the pope said, "Let him get married." "But Holiness, we will have to give him an apartment." The pope said, "Well, that doesn't matter." "But only corporals get apartments." "That doesn't matter," he said, "he is to be married and given an apartment. And that is the end of it."

They really don't want to change anything, so what do they do? The following week he was made a corporal. So nothing changed. The Holy

Father threw his hands up and said, "You try to change something . . ." But that would have set a precedent and that whole structure would have caved in and they would have had to deal with the next one. What is the solution? Make him a corporal. The Italians love that. Everyone got their way, and we haven't changed anything, and the principle is maintained.

Respect for proper legal procedures is also a way of protecting rights in the church. Thus if a bishop does not follow proper canonical procedures when closing a parish or taking away the faculties of a priest, the Congregation for the Clergy can overrule him. Likewise, if a diocesan tribunal fails to notify the defendant in an annulment case, the Roman Rota will reverse the annulment and insist that the process be redone.

Because of the importance of church law, the Vatican is filled with canon lawyers, especially in the congregations. The most common advanced degree for Vatican priests is in canon law, not theology. "Canon lawyers have an outlook that is different from people who are working in the field of pastoral theology, dogmatic theology, or history," comments a German who worked in the Vatican. While Italians might be flexible in their observance of the law, many Vatican canon lawyers have a tendency to "go by the book, let us say, whereas people with another kind of training or other experience would judge cases by individual merits." Canon lawyers trained in the United States tend to take a more pastoral approach to law, favoring changes and adaptations where those trained in Rome are more strict and static. The worst lawyers in the Vatican are often non-Italians who adopt a Roman strictness toward law without the Italian flexibility toward individual cases.

Sometimes this lack of pastoral sensitivity results from an absence of any pastoral experience. "Many people in the curia have never been in pastoral care," complains a former Vatican official from Germany. "They are living in a world of their own. That is a danger for all priests who work exclusively in administrative bodies. Some entered into this kind of career immediately after ordination and have never done any active priestly work. A number of them on Sundays go to parishes, but there are also some who never do anything. These people are out of touch with pastoral reality." For this reason, some people propose that priests should be rotated out of the Vatican every five or six years and be sent back to their countries to work in parishes.

The material rewards for working in the curia are not great. No one is getting rich in the Roman curia. While Vatican service may be a stepping stone to becoming a bishop, it does not open the door to alternative employment in business or law as would service in civil governments. Employment in the

Vatican might even harm a person's academic career in some universities. The spiritual rewards of working for the Vatican, the sense of being at the center of the church, the belief that this work is God's work—all these are crucial to an understanding of the people who work in the Vatican and how the Vatican gets so much out of its personnel.

"I ended up with a love-hate relationship with the Vatican," reports an American in the curia getting ready to leave Rome. "A tremendous respect for a lot of people who are dedicated, while at the same time knowing more than I want to know about the more sordid side of life. It exists in civil society. I would like to believe that it does not exist in the church, but I know better. I have always known better, and now I know even better."

Arrogance, ambition, careerism, cronyism, legalism, and politics are all alive and well in the Vatican. It is a slow-moving bureaucracy where it is difficult to get things done, especially any change in policy. On the other hand, one also finds humor, courtesy, hospitality to visitors, and a dedication to the service of the church and the Holy Father.

In *Pastor Bonus,* the apostolic constitution on the Roman curia, John Paul II articulated the theology of this ecclesial service whereby those in the curia are to labor "with the intent of truly serving and of following and imitating the *diaconia* [service] of Christ himself."[15] The curia "draws its existence and competence from the pastor of the universal church."[16] Since the pope is the Servant of the Servants of God, as the servant of Peter's successor, the Roman curia "looks only to help the whole church and its bishops."

In the curia, primacy is to be given to supporting the pope's ministry of unity in the church.

> This unity is in the first place the *unity of faith,* governed and constituted by the sacred deposit of faith of which Peter's successor is the chief guardian and protector and through which indeed he receives his highest responsibility, that of strengthening his brothers. The unity is likewise the *unity of discipline,* the general discipline of the church, which consists in a system of norms and patterns of behavior, gives shape to the fundamental structure of the church, safeguards the means of salvation and their correct administration, together with the ordered structure of the people of God.[17]

This ideal of ecclesial service and unity inspires those working in the Vatican. Unhappily, one person's idea of necessary unity can be another's experience of stifling uniformity. A vision of serving the universal church can slip into an attitude of arrogance that "we are in charge of the whole world, and you better know it," comments an American canonist who frequently visited the Vatican. "We are the pope's family, this is top of the line." Papal service cannot be performed without papal power, and yet the goal is always service. "You always have to find your way through both the fantasies of omnipotence and the fantasies of total powerlessness," admits a European in the curia. "You have moments of both."

Vatican personnel have a sense of history and tradition that goes back for centuries. Policy is based on philosophical and theological principles, on the deposit of faith, not on public opinion polls or whim. Decisions that might affect the church for centuries should not be made hastily. Change for the sake of change is ridiculed. This conservatism can go beyond an intelligent respect for tradition to a fear of any change. Rather than learning from history that things always change, history can be used as an excuse for not changing. "The old buildings, the things hanging on the walls set the tone," an American canonist explains. "Everything is five hundred years old. You can't help but catch the tradition. There is something in the air where you tend to know more about 1756 than you would know about, and even care about, 2056. The tradition is heavy. It wouldn't be a place where you would expect to find innovative, forward-looking, creative people. I don't know whether anyone could ever break out of it. It's an atmosphere you get."

The Vatican is a place of contradictions: steeped in history but trying to control the present; filled with people dedicated to the service of the pope and the church, who also suffer the temptations of ambition and power; a bureaucracy with all the trappings of a princely court. That the Vatican never matches its ideals should not be surprising or scandalous; the church has always been a human institution with more sinners than saints.

The people in the curia are the pope's helpers in guiding and governing the universal church. The attitudes, the style, and the abilities of these Vatican officials help determine what the Vatican does and does not do. The pope needs the service of competent people from a variety of backgrounds and nations who will loyally serve him in his ministry to the church. Not surprisingly, those who disagree with his policies often disagree with his choice of helpers. But even his most loyal supporters in the curia wish it were easier to recruit larger numbers of competent people. The inability to remove incompetent officials is also a constant complaint.

One reform that would increase the power and flexibility of the pope in dealing with the curia would be to stop making bishops of prefects, presidents, secretaries, nuncios, and other officials. Once a man is a bishop, he is part of the college of bishops and can no longer simply be sent back to his diocese or his order. Unless the pope wants to dump him on a local church by making him a diocesan bishop, he is stuck with him and has to find him work. This reform would reverse the mistake made by John XXIII in making bishops of all high Vatican officials. A parallel reform would be to stop making cardinals of prefects and presidents. This would eliminate the embarrassing situation of having a pope surrounded by curial cardinals who did not support his election.

Reform of the personnel system in the Vatican is desperately needed if it is to reflect the collegial character of the church and respond to changing needs. Nuncios, dicastery secretaries, prefects, and presidents do not need to be bishops, archbishops, or cardinals. Not making curial officials bishops and cardinals would do much to reduce ambition in the curia and encourage officials to return to their local churches after serving in the Vatican. More important, it would remove Vatican officials from the college of bishops so that they are clearly staff to the pope and not part of the magisterium.

These reforms could be executed incrementally by simply not ordaining as bishops any future Vatican officials. In addition, a new title for high Vatican officials could be created, "cardinal pro tem," so that during the life of the pope they would have the same dignity as a regular cardinal, but they would not be bishops or have the right to vote in a conclave.

Despite the complaints, everyone agrees that the Vatican is better run and more efficient than the Italian bureaucracy. The Vatican has better people today than it did in many past centuries. The pope is well served by his people, who are recruited and trained to serve his will. They are loyal, they are for the most part hard working, and they normally do not embarrass him by making egregious mistakes. Without them the Vatican would be a museum rather than a vital force in the church and the world. Through all these people the pope must exercise his ministry, and to do that he must learn how to direct and control them.

~ 7

Papal Leadership

PRESIDING OVER THE Vatican's extensive bureaucracy is the pope, who must supervise and control the people who work in the congregations, councils, and other offices. To accomplish his goals, he must somehow influence and direct this bureaucracy so that his interests and policies are given a priority in the Vatican. His job is made easier by the theology and culture of the curia, which sees itself in service to whoever is the reigning pope. On the other hand, like any large bureaucracy it has people who are pressing their own agendas, and these people are not easily removed or changed.

How successful the pope is in directing the curia depends on his abilities and experience. Most popes (except John Paul I and II) in this century had some experience working in the Vatican before becoming popes. Most (except Pius XII) also were diocesan bishops before being elected. Different experiences and different personalities have resulted in popes with different administrative styles.

The pope also has many other things to do with his time besides directing the bureaucracy: traveling around the world, meeting with people from outside the curia, writing, and speaking. He needs help in running the curia. One of the most important tools he has for controlling the curia and making his influence felt throughout the church and the world is the Secretariat of State.

The Secretariat of State, housed in the Apostolic Palace, is one of the least understood and yet one of the most important offices in the curia. Most Americans naturally presume that the Vatican secretary of state is equivalent to the U.S. secretary of state and that the Vatican Secretariat of State is the same as the U.S. State Department. In fact, the Vatican secretary of state, Cardinal Angelo Sodano, is closer to being a prime minister than a foreign minister, and the Vatican Secretariat of State is like a combination of the U.S. State Department and the White House staff. It coordinates the work of other Vatican offices and handles any issue that does not fall into some other office's jurisdiction.

Because of its role in the Vatican, not everyone in the curia likes the Secretariat of State. As a former Vatican official describes it, "The Secretariat of State is the organ between the pope and all the others. There are a number in the secretariat who consider themselves to be in a class above all the others. That is an attitude that is not accepted easily by all the others. But you can't generalize. A number of people there are very simple in their approach, gentle, and pastorally open minded. There are also a number of them, perhaps too great a number, who want to become nuncios and consider themselves to be two notches above the others. That is human."

There are two sections in the Secretariat of State: one for general affairs and the other for relations with states. Both are housed on the third floor of the Apostolic Palace, the same floor as the papal apartments. The two sections are sometimes referred to as dealing with ordinary affairs (first section) and extraordinary affairs (second section). This terminology led to a story, perhaps true, about a priest who brought to Msgr. Domenico Tardini, then the head of the second section, a report about a bishop who was having an affair with a woman. Monsignor Tardini told the priest to give it to Msgr. Giovanni Battista Montini, then head of the first section, "because it is only an ordinary affair."

The first section for general affairs acts as the pope's secretariat for any document or correspondence going to and from the pope, whether it comes from inside or outside the Roman curia. The first section also acts as a coordinating body for the curia as the White House staff does for the U.S. executive branch.

"Coordination comes with the fact that if the prefect has to present something to the Holy Father," explains an official in the Secretariat of State, "he will frequently do it through the secretary of state, because the pope does not have time to receive everyone." Before it goes to the pope, the first section can send the document to another dicastery for comments or ask the prefect to consult with another dicastery head. And since responses from the pope come through the first section, it knows what the pope is telling people. Thus the sostituto (substitute), Archbishop Giovanni Battista Re, who heads the first section, acts as the pope's chief of staff.

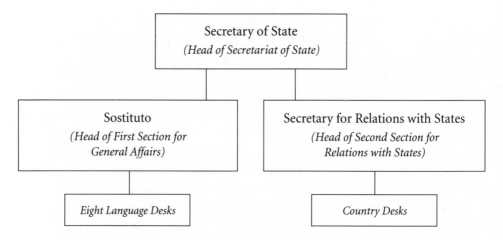

ORGANIZATION OF THE SECRETARIAT OF STATE

The first section is organized into eight language desks: English, French, German, Italian, Latin, Portuguese, Spanish, and Polish (added during this papacy). As an official in the Secretariat of State describes it, "Everything going in to the pope and out from the pope goes through the language desks: preparation of documents, translations of documents, correspondence. Every document, from the simplest letter—a letter to a woman dying of cancer—to an encyclical, and everything in between goes through the desks."

Although Italian is the working language of the curia, native speakers are needed to process correspondence in many languages. A majority of Catholics in the world are Spanish-speaking, but most of the world uses English in international communications. The English desk, currently headed by an American, includes about twelve priests from Canada, Britain, Ireland, South Africa, and India. A former head of the English desk, Justin Rigali, is now archbishop of St. Louis. The English desk covers Great Britain and its former colonies (including more than twenty countries in Africa). "Everything from Iraq to San Francisco (except Vietnam, Laos, and Cambodia)," reports an official in the Secretariat of State. Scandinavia, most of the Middle East, many countries in Eastern Europe, and most international organizations also use English in communications.

Mail addressed to the pope is processed by the Secretariat of State. "Thousands of letters come in from heads of state, bishops, priests, lay people, and crackpots," an official explains. "Some are organized letter campaigns when a parish is being closed or complaints about bishops. More letters come from the developed world because of higher literacy and money to send letters." "Americans are very enthusiastic in writing letters," reports an Italian in the Secretariat of State. "They write very much to the Holy Father."

Letters come asking for prayers, for apostolic blessings, for jobs, for money, for an audience, or for some other favor. Some writers complain about something in their parish, diocese, or country. Others complain about or praise some action of the Holy See. Some are seeking information. Some are sending donations. The Secretariat of State has established procedures for processing the most common types of letters.

What happens to a letter addressed to the pope depends on what it is about and whom it is from. The letters from personal friends would go directly to the pope's personal secretary. Letters from cardinals get high priority, going either to the pope or to the secretary of state. At least some requests for prayers are collected by the pope's personal secretaries and given to him. "I take note of the intentions which come to me from persons throughout the world," says the pope. "I keep them in my chapel on the prie-dieu."[1] The note on his prie-dieu lists a dozen or so names and a brief description of their needs. On any given day it may contain the name of someone asking for prayers for a father with cancer, a husband without a job, a young mother with a tumor, or a boy in a coma after a biking accident.

People writing to the pope are often referred somewhere else as the more appropriate place for their inquiry. If people are writing about a local problem, "generally they are told to talk to their pastor," explains an official in the Secretariat of State. "If that isn't good enough, talk to the bishop and, only as a last resort, talk to the apostolic nuncio." Other mail is passed on to the appropriate Vatican offices for a response.

Most of the mail that stays in the Secretariat of State would be processed in the first section where it is summarized by a priest on the language desk, who also suggests a response. If superiors approve the response, it is written by someone on the language desk and personally signed by the assessore, Msgr. Leonardo Sandri, the second in command under the sostituto. "Generally, unless the person is a very frequent writer or he is obviously really off the wall, they answer the letters," an official reports. "I would say that 75 percent of the time the response is just to acknowledge that the letter is received."

If the letter is from a government official, it would be sent on to the second section for relations with states. "If the question is at all related to a political issue, then it would go to the second section," explains an official. "For instance, the letters that protested that the Holy See maintained diplomatic relations with Haiti, those all came to the second section." The second section of the Secretariat of State is the foreign ministry of the Holy See. It is headed by the secretary for relations with states, Archbishop Jean-Louis Tauran, a Frenchman, who is equivalent to a foreign minister.

"The second section follows the whole world," explains a member of the staff. "However, there are only thirty-eight of us [including typists and technicians]. Everyone has more than he can handle." The staff is organized by country desks, a pattern similar to that in foreign offices around the world, but since the staff is small, one person normally is responsible for a number of countries. One, for example, deals with Eastern Europe, while another deals with the countries of the former Soviet Union. Not all the desks are so logically divided. One official, for example, has Angola and Cuba. Another has the Sudan, the Horn of Africa, and Greece. The mix of responsibilities changes as personnel change, depending on the language skills and background of the people going and coming.

It is an oversimplification to think that the first section of the Secretariat of State deals with religious and pastoral issues while the second deals with political and diplomatic areas. For the Holy See, important political issues are often intertwined with religious issues. The country desks in the second section follow not only church-state relations but also the internal life of the church in their countries. As a result, there is some overlap between the concerns of the language desks in the first section and the country desks in the second section.

Priests in the first section usually draft letters or speeches (even to government officials) because they are working in their native language whereas in the second section they often are not. The two sections frequently work together on communications with governments, with the first section drafting correspondence based on input from the second section. "Anything that is written that might have some political sensitivity is always seen by the second section," reports another official. "So there is a continual consultation back and forth. Even a telegram to a head of state for the national day has to be seen by someone in the second section who says it is all right. Generally it is fine, but maybe the second section would know something."

Even a congratulatory letter to a bishop on the major anniversary of his ordination as a bishop would be checked by the second section. According to one writer, usually "it is kind of innocent, although sometimes, I write, 'The bishop did a good job,' and he didn't do a good job, and then it will come back" with that scratched out. Sometimes the second section will suggest changes, "maybe say, 'you should change this' or perhaps 'this should be a little more forceful,' or perhaps, 'let's tone this down.' That is a continual process, that is part of the normal consultation back and forth."

The second section normally deals with major international issues. "Let's say the Holy Father wants to make an appeal about Bosnia," explains an official. "Nine times out of ten that would be written in the second section rather than the first." Papal speeches to the diplomatic corps are also written in the second section. Documents addressed to international organizations could be written in either section. On the other hand, letters of credentials to new ambassadors are written in the first section.

"Particularly on the issue of correspondence, it is not hard and fast," an official reports. "You have many issues where the competency is not clear." Sometimes the staffs simply work it out among themselves. Another official comments, "There is a tremendous amount of cooperation in that regard, in that they work together on any number of questions. I can think of times when talks were being prepared and over the phone saying, 'Why don't you develop this idea, it would be helpful.'"

The confusion between the two sections is accentuated by responsibilities that have been assigned to the sections over history. As one official describes it:

> It may be that a question, even one that was dealt with many years ago, started in a certain section for a certain reason. All the archives are in that section and therefore that section continues to treat it.
>
> A good example would be honorary doctorates from universities chartered by the Congregation for Catholic Education. The nihil obstat [no objection] comes from the section for relations with states. The [university writes the congregation and the] congregation asks for an opinion, which is binding, from the section on relations with the states.

Likewise, since in the past the Holy See had to negotiate with many governments over the appointment of bishops, this matter was handled in the second section, which negotiated the concordat or treaty governing the appointment of bishops and other church-state issues. It also dealt with the pastoral governance of these dioceses, so their bishops would see the second section on their "ad limina" visits, visits to Rome that bishops must make every five years. The second section still handles appointments in former Soviet bloc countries. Even with other countries, the nuncio sends to the second section a copy of the terna and the report that he sends to the Congregation for Bishops. The same is true of the nuncio's report on meetings of episcopal conferences.

The second section also has an office (one priest), which predates the Council for the Laity, for watching over international organizations of Catholic laity. Another office follows ecumenical issues, especially those that have political aspects. On the other hand, the first section has offices for topic areas like Vatican personnel, Vatican finances (including Peter's Pence), theology, canon law, sacraments, and the press; these offices are primarily staffed by Italians.

To confuse things further, the first section also has the protocol office that deals with ambassadors from states with diplomatic relations with the Holy See. For example, they might want to discuss plans for a papal visit to their country or a visit of their head of state to the Vatican.[2] The first section is also responsible for supervising the Holy See's diplomatic corps. Thus the second section for relations with states deals with the appointment of bishops (something of great pastoral importance), while the first section for general affairs deals with ambassadors and nuncios (something of great political and diplomatic importance).

Despite the confusion, over time Vatican dicasteries learn which section they deal with for what business. Because bishops and even Vatican officials are sometimes confused, they often simply write to the secretary of state and let him pass the question on to the appropriate office. If the sender wants to keep everyone happy, he sends copies to each section.

While this overlapping between the two sections appears to be redundant and confusing, it has some advantages for the pope. The two sections can provide him with different perspectives on an issue so that he does not become too dependent on one office. Each section protects him from becoming the captive of the other. The pope can have one section check the information and recommendations of the other. They also provide him with two arms to choose from to execute his commands.

Top Officials in the Secretariat of State

After the pope, the secretary of state is the number two person in the Vatican, with an office on the second floor of the Apostolic Palace. He meets three days a week from 9:30 to 10:45 A.M. with the heads of the two sections of the Secretariat of State to coordinate the work of the curia and the work of the pope. "He might have two or three appointments after that," explains an official who works closely with Cardinal Sodano. He meets with many civil and religious dignitaries who come to visit the pope or himself. "Any time he is not receiving people he would be working at his desk, not only the office hours but also other times as well. He really has no free time at all. The only time that you could conceivably construe as free would be Sunday afternoon."

Practically all the secretaries in this century have been Italians from the diplomatic service of the Holy See, Cardinal Jean Villot (1969–1979) being the striking exception. "It was a shock, the nomination of Villot," recalls French Cardinal Paul Poupard, "because he was French and from a diocese." Many secretaries of state served first as secretary of state for relations with states before being promoted. Because of their backgrounds, most of them have focused more on diplomatic affairs than on internal church issues, especially in times of world turmoil.

Agostino Casaroli, for example, while secretary for relations with states was the architect of Paul VI's *Ostpolitik,* an attempt to establish a dialogue with Eastern European governments in the 1970s in the hope of improving the situation of the church. Many thought the new Polish pope would put aside Casaroli since the Polish bishops were suspicious of Casaroli's strategy. But his loyalty and expertise impressed John Paul, who made Casaroli his secretary of state and a cardinal in 1979 and used him in his efforts to help the church in Eastern Europe. However, the pope used Casaroli mostly in dealing with governments, but not very much in dealing with local churches. For example, on papal trips he would not be consulted on the issues touching local churches. Sometimes the sostituto did not even keep him informed on these issues.

When Cardinal Casaroli retired in 1990, Vatican insiders were sure that Cardinal Eduardo Martinez Somalo would succeed him. But John Paul chose Archbishop Angelo Sodano, perhaps having been convinced by those who argued that a non-Italian pope needed an Italian secretary of state. Peter Hebblethwaite considered him "the most limited secretary of state of the twentieth century."[3] John Paul, on the other hand, was impressed by Archbishop Sodano's handling of church-state issues while he was nuncio in Chile (1978–1988) during the Pinochet regime. As nuncio he discouraged confrontation with the government and oversaw the appointment of conservative bishops. The pope brought him back to Rome and made him secretary for relations with states. Cardinal Martinez, also a career diplomat, had been sostituto and was prefect of the Congregation for Divine Worship at the time of Cardinal Casaroli's retirement.

After the secretary of state, the most influential official is the sostituto (substitute) who presides over the section on general affairs of the Secretariat of State. In this position he acts as chief of staff to the pope, to some degree controlling whom the pope meets and what documents he sees. "He is the clearing house or the bottleneck," reports an American priest, "depending on how you want to look at it." "Anything of importance goes up" to the pope, according to Cardinal Edward Cassidy, a former sostituto. "Some things need to be discussed, other things simply the Holy Father may wish to see. If he signs them, indicating that he has seen them, then it is up to you to go ahead."

Although only an archbishop, the sostituto is more influential than most cardinals. "The key person in the administration is always the substitute," agrees an Italian priest who knows the Vatican well. "If you have a good substitute, things really get moved along and there is much more coordination, much more communication among the various dicasteries."

For example, if the pope wants to issue a document on the family, he might have the sostituto bring together officials from Doctrine of the Faith, the Family, Christian Unity, Justice and Peace, and the Laity to discuss it. "There are many questions that cross the normal boundaries" of dicasteries, explains Cardinal Cassidy. "Sometimes you can deal with it through correspondence between the two offices, but the Holy Father might think that it is a good idea to have them come together to discuss. So the Secretariat of State would suggest that to the congregations concerned."

Some complain that power in the curia is excessively centralized in the sostituto. Every appointment, every document, goes through him. "There is very little delegation of power," complains one Vatican official. "Now that does not mean that everything is under control, because when you want to check everything, very often you finish not checking at all." The same official recalls that Archbishop Giovanni Benelli as sostituto gave him instructions contradicting written instructions he had received earlier. When he pointed this out to Archbishop Benelli, the response was, "Oh really? I had not noticed." "When you have to sign everything," the official notes, "you cannot give much importance to everything. There is also the danger that you put everything on the same level."

This detailed review of documents is exemplified by an incident recalled by John Long, who as an official in the Christian unity office was involved in an ecumenical dialogue with the Coptic church. Although Arabic was their first language, the text was in English. The Copts were suspicious of any attempt to improve the English style of the text because they feared the changes would be substantive. Paul VI got the text for his approval while the meeting was still going on, and Archbishop Benelli telephoned to propose changes in the text. Father Long, who was on the other end of the telephone, recalls:

> After about the third time, I recognized that these were purely stylistic changes, there was nothing of substance. I said to Benelli, "Who is with the pope working over this text?" Benelli said, "Monsignor Rigali [an American who headed the English desk in the first section]." So I explained the situation, I said, "Would you tell Monsignor Rigali to only notice questions of substance and not to pay any attention to style."

Benelli started to laugh, and said, "I understand." Justin [Rigali] was perfectly right. His reactions were exactly the same as mine, but we had been through this and it wasn't worth it. They [the Copts] would think that any little suggestion coming up meant that we were changing substance.

Since he is busy dealing with governments, the secretary for relations with states does not normally challenge the position of the sostituto except in political and diplomatic matters. The one person who is in a position to challenge the sostituto is the pope's private secretary, who has constant contact with the pope. In many pontificates, the pope's personal secretary has functioned as a back door to the pope that bypasses the Secretariat of State. Under the best of circumstances there is a creative tension between the two officials, but in some pontificates they have been at each other's throats.

The current personal secretary, Msgr. Stanislaw Dziwisz, is one of the most powerful secretaries in recent times, but others, like Msgr. Loris Capovilla under John XXIII and Msgr. Pasquale Macchi under Paul VI, have also had significant roles. "There are no rules for private secretaries," explains a Vatican official. "He gets all the papers that go to the pope. Does the pope see them? People will say, 'Upstairs says . . .' or 'The apartment wants . . .' But is that the pope or the secretary? Has the Holy Father actually seen this?" Another Vatican official complains, "He just gives orders and nobody has the courage to ask the pope, 'Did you say that or not?'" But it would be foolish to think that any secretary who acted counter to the pope's views on important issues would last very long.

Archbishop Giovanni Benelli, under Paul VI, was the most powerful sostituto (1966–1977) in recent memory. Many felt he was even more powerful than Cardinal Villot, the secretary of state. "Villot would see the pope several times, maybe on big policy," explains an American who dealt with him. "But Benelli would see the pope every morning and he would get things to do, and he would carry them out in the pope's name." Benelli would telephone people, say he was speaking for the pope, and tell them what to do, and then he would ride herd on people to make sure they did it. He would review and change documents that came up from the congregations and offices.

Americans compare Archbishop Benelli to H. R. Haldemann. He was an aggressive, authoritarian, workaholic master of detail who was devoted to his boss and his policies. He was not afraid to play "bad guy" to Paul VI's "good guy." "He was determined to put Vatican II through," comments an official in the Secretariat of State, "and he was Paul VI's man to get this thing moving. It was a very, very satisfying time." But many in the curia grew to both hate and fear him. "If you got a note from Benelli to come and see him, my Lord, you just about wet your pants because this was like going to the throne of God." On the other hand, Vatican officials knew that if Archbishop Benelli was on their side, things would happen.

Walter Abbott recalls that when he was in the Secretariat for Christian Unity they had arranged for an audience with the pope for the Italian bishops and their Protestant counterparts who had been in charge of the ecumenical translation of the Bible into Italian. At the last minute, the audience was canceled. "This is impossible," Father Abbott told Bishop Cascante Torrella, the council vice president (the president was out of town). "These people are beginning to arrive in the city. Already several have phoned me that they are here. This is incredible, this is an emergency." The vice president called Archbishop Benelli to find out what had happened. The archbishop checked and called back to say that the Papal Household said that the pope had already done this a year ago and they did not want to waste the pope's time. "We had done the same thing with the French" the year before, Father Abbott recalls, "but now it was the Italians' turn." After this was explained to Archbishop Benelli, "he told Bishop Torrella, 'Hold on, I will go to the pope and explain it and fix it up.' He came back in a minute or two and said, 'It is OK, we go ahead with it.' He went right into the pope and came right back to the phone."

"He was a strong man and he corrected many abuses," reports Cardinal Edouard Gagnon. "This is why he had such opposition from the other cardinals in the curia. For example, if a cardinal needed his TV set repaired, he would call the engineer-in-chief of Radio Vatican and he would have to come. Benelli stopped a lot of those things."

"He was called not 'His Excellency,' but 'His Efficiency,'" recalls an Italian priest. "At the same time, he was such a warm personality. The only one who knew each employee in the Vatican. Each birthday, he would go personally to greet them. Very efficient, very tough, but very warm."

The Benelli years (1966–1977) are seen as the glory years of the first section of the Secretariat of State, when even the Congregation for the Doctrine of the Faith took a second place. But because he had made so many enemies, Archbishop Benelli was shipped off to Florence and never had a chance to become secretary of state or pope. His successors tried not to make so many enemies, and as a result, all have become cardinals in the curia. Nor were his successors able to keep up his level of work and attention to detail. "If you have extraordinary persons like Paul VI or Benelli, who were hard workers, who were working day and night and giving more importance to the control of the documents in preparation on behalf of the Holy See," explains an Italian with decades of experience working in the Vatican, "then perhaps you can have control. But that doesn't exist anymore."

Archbishop Benelli's successor, Archbishop Giuseppe Caprio (1977–1979) proved less effective and less organized, but he did not make enemies. Into this power vacuum stepped the pope's secretary, Monsignor Dziwisz. Archbishop Caprio was promoted to cardinal and placed in charge of the Administration of the Patrimony of the Apostolic See (APSA) and then the Prefecture for the Economic Affairs of the Holy See until his retirement in 1990. This prefecture was an ineffective backwater until his successor, Cardinal Edmund Szoka, modernized it.

Eduardo Martinez Somalo (1979–1988) followed Archbishop Caprio and restored order to the first section, but he never achieved the power that Archbishop Benelli had. "Martinez was able through close friendship with the secretary of the pope to manage the secretary a little bit," explains an official. "Sometimes in this very friendly way following him, but also many times changing his mind." Martinez was made cardinal prefect of the Congregation for Divine Worship and later prefect of the Congregation for Institutes of Consecrated Life.

After Cardinal Martinez, Archbishop Edward Cassidy (1988–1989) was appointed sostituto by John Paul in an attempt to bring a different style into the Secretariat of State. It was under Archbishop Cassidy that the first personal computers entered the Secretariat of State. His style was so different that it clashed with the internal culture of the curia. Many inside the Secretariat of State did not like his style because "he was delegating power, it was terrible," explains a Vatican official. "It was the end of the curia. So they did not like his method," which would reduce the role of the Secretariat of State.

"They would keep losing dossiers," reports another person on familiar terms with the curia, "so that he would not know what was going on. He would be bypassed." Archbishop Cassidy had his defenders in the Vatican, however. "Cassidy was great as sostituto," says one official. "He believed in delegation, he knew how to be an executive. The Italians didn't like that. He made people take responsibility." They did not want to be responsible for making a wrong decision.

"Cassidy is a marvelous man, a saintly man," says an Italian with high-level contacts in the Vatican. "Cassidy is such a gentleman, such a nice man. But he didn't care about this infighting. He had been always outside. He didn't know the workings of the Secretariat of State and of the palace. It was the moment when the other section became very powerful. Sodano was in the second section, and things were taken away from the first and going directly to the pope."

Archbishop Cassidy's style also clashed with that of the pope. A Vatican observer reports that Archbishop Cassidy would try to cheer up the pope by telling him jokes. "He did not understand the pope." On the other hand, "Cassidy told it like it is to the pope," comments an American who had dealings with a number of substitutes. "Dziwisz didn't like that because the pope was beginning to worry about things. Cassidy, like most Anglo-Saxons, would say, 'Holy Father, here's the situation in this country, here are the options that are available to you. What do you want me to do? What decisions do you want me to convey?' That was just unacceptable and they got him out after thirteen months because he troubled the pope with reality. They just wanted somebody who would not be bringing those issues forward in that way."

Cassidy was made cardinal president of the Council for Promoting Christian Unity, where his style has gone over very well with Catholics and non-Catholics in the ecumenical movement. Cardinal Cassidy's successor, Archbishop Giovanni Battista Re, understands the curia's ways, but he is not forceful enough to be another Archbishop Benelli. Documents from dicasteries are treated more gently than they were under Archbishop Benelli, with fewer changes made by the sostituto. The crucial review of documents is now back in the Congregation for the Doctrine of the Faith, as it was under Pius XII, not in the Secretariat of State. If a document is approved by the congregation, it will not have much trouble in State unless it poses a political problem. Archbishop Re is careful not to make enemies and is especially deferential to the pope's secretary. The office of sostituto has continued to decline under him, and the power of the pope's secretary and the Congregation for the Doctrine of the Faith has continued to grow. It has gotten to the point that when any important issue comes up, Archbishop Re will say, "Let's ask Dziwisz." Archbishop Re is also "so concerned about detail and controlling everything that he can't do the important things," says an official in the Secretariat of State.

Msgr. Stanislaw Dziwisz is the most powerful personal secretary in recent times. He has been with the pope since his days in Krakow. He knows the views and needs of the pope very well, and the pope trusts him completely. Because he is so close to the pope, Vatican officials, including the secretary of state and the sostituto, defer to him. Whereas in Paul VI's time the sostituto, Archbishop Benelli, arranged most meetings between the pope and Vatican officials, today the pope's secretary is just as likely to arrange them. Cardinals wanting to see the pope might go through either the sostituto or the secretary, whereas in Archbishop Benelli's time no one would dare go around him. But even in Benelli's time, Pasquale Macchi, Paul VI's personal secretary, could at times successfully challenge him.

"Those who want special favors" go to Monsignor Dziwisz, reports an Italian priest. "They see that through the normal channels they don't get it." For example, Opus Dei and the Legionaries of Christ wanted to have ecclesiastical universities in Rome. They claimed that the other universities were not sufficiently orthodox. All the other universities were opposed to them, as was the Congregation for Education. "So they go not to the Secretariat of State, they go to Monsignor Dziwisz. In the end, they are approved by papal decree and the congregation is told to sign."

Curial cardinals say that they can see the pope whenever they ask, but most indicate a reluctance to impose themselves on him frequently. Some cardinals appear to have difficulty getting in to see the pope. Cardinal Gagnon reports that every time he would see Paul VI in an audience, the pope would say, "Why don't you come and see me?" "But they never let me approach him personally," complains the cardinal. "Two or three times he asked me because he had certain missions to give me. But they always kept me away. The official channels with the present pope are the same. But there are unofficial channels, and I have lunch or supper with him, but on a very irregular basis." Cardinal Gagnon came to know Wojtyla at Vatican II and through Archbishop Andrzej Deskur, a close friend of the pope, kept in contact with him before he became pope.

While Archbishop Benelli played the role of Mr. Fix-It under Paul VI, Monsignor Dziwisz plays that role today. For example, after the pope decided to hold a concert in the Vatican in 1994 to honor the victims of the Holocaust, Bishop Dino Monduzzi, prefect of the Papal Household, continued to throw up obstacles in the way of the concert. Monsignor Dziwisz was the real force behind making the concert happen, and in response to requests from the Jewish sponsors, he would get the pope to intervene periodically to remove obstacles.

Monsignor Dziwisz's power as secretary is enhanced by the style of the pope. John Paul is a very social person who likes to have people at his private Mass in the morning, and to meet with people over meals. It is the secretary who usually arranges these invitations. Pius XII ate alone, and Paul VI ate with his personal secretaries. The few times Paul did have guests for dinner, it was purely social. For John Paul, meals are working occasions.

While Paul VI spent most of his time going over documents and reports from the curia, John Paul learns verbally, through interaction with other people. As a result, it is extremely important who gets in to see him, and Monsignor Dziwisz is the gatekeeper. He is influential in deciding "who has more or less access to the pope," explains an Italian priest well informed on the workings of the Vatican. "This one every time. This one never. This cardinal, if he comes to Rome, can at once be received. The other has to wait or is told, 'It is impossible to find time.'"

Many complain that Monsignor Dziwisz gives special access to conservative Catholic organizations. Monsignor Dziwisz has "never met a conservative movement that he didn't fall in love with," complains one official with the National Conference of Catholic Bishops. "Therefore Opus Dei, the Neo-Catechumenate, Communione e Liberazione, Legionaries of Christ—these people have great access." But as an Italian Vatican official points out, it is probable "that the secretary is choosing very well, choosing really the people the pope likes just because they are the same nature."

A third official involved in scheduling the pope is the prefect of the Papal Household, Bishop Dino Monduzzi, who handles both public and private audiences with the pope. The public audience is held on Wednesdays in Paul VI Hall, which seats 7,700 for those given free tickets by the Papal Household. "We can squeeze 15,000 into the hall with the seats out," reports a Vatican official, "but it overwhelms the air-conditioning and the rest rooms." In the heavy tourist season, a second audience might be held in St. Peter's Basilica, which can hold another 7,000 to 8,000 people. St. Peter's Square, which can hold 150,000 people, is another option in good weather. For an audience in the square, as many as 28,000 places might be available in the enclosed sections toward the front for those with tickets.

John Paul often goes down the center aisle greeting people in the audience. The first section on the right is reserved for the sick and suffering, many in wheelchairs or on crutches. On the left is a VIP section for celebrities and special guests. The media went wild when Brigitte Bardot and the pope shook hands in 1995. Other special guests could be less famous: people dying of cancer, newly married couples, and married couples and priests celebrating major anniversaries. Paul VI used to be given the names and stories of each person in the front row and would spend more time with them and not move around the hall the way John Paul does.

Private audiences are held by special arrangements for smaller groups, for example, government officials, religious dignitaries, or a special group visiting Rome, like an organization of Catholic professionals. When some person or group requests a special audience, the Papal Household will check them out with the local nuncio, the Council for Promoting Christian Unity (if they are

Protestants or Jews), and the Secretariat of State. The Secretariat of State would decide whether and when a government official has an audience with the pope, but the Papal Household would handle the logistics of the meeting. During his first seventeen years in office, John Paul had 730 private audiences with heads of state or prime ministers.[4]

The prefect of the Papal Household has more discretion over audiences with nongovernment visitors. After the election of John Paul I, a young cardinal asked for a private audience for himself and his visiting compatriots but was told by the prefect that the pope was too busy. "Maybe next time," he was told. The next time this cardinal came to Rome he was elected John Paul II. Not surprisingly, most Polish groups make their arrangements for visiting the pope through Monsignor Dziwisz rather than through Bishop Monduzzi. Many groups "go up the back stairs," bypassing the Papal Household.

The Papal Household arranges a private audience for the members of a Vatican congregation or council in Rome for a plenary meeting. Likewise, members of a religious chapter or other Catholic organization meeting in Rome would normally meet with the pope as a group, as would the bishops from a country making their ad limina visit. John Paul II also enjoys meeting with youth groups, so they get audiences. In the past, some clerics secretly took money in exchange for arranging private audiences. After one group left, John XXIII shook his head and wondered out loud about the dollars that changed hands to get them in to see him. More recently, a senior Italian cardinal told the chaplain of an association of ophthalmologists that his group could have an audience if it paid for insulating a hospital in Russia. The cardinal would not get the money, but one of his favorite charities would. The chaplain refused and the group did not get an audience. Such shenanigans are the exception.

Papal Management

John Paul begins a typical day in Rome around 5:30 A.M. "By 6:00 or 6:10, he is in his chapel [praying] until 7:00, which is the usual time for the celebration of his Mass," according to Joaquin Navarro-Valls, the Vatican press officer. "After Mass he meets just for a moment with the people attending the Mass. He often has people for breakfast, either a bishop who has concelebrated with him or some other person." The pope's secretary is the one who controls access to his private Mass and meals, which are "what you Americans call a working breakfast, working lunch, working dinner."

He is normally at his desk by 8:30. "Until 11:00 in the morning," Dr.

Navarro-Valls continues, "he usually takes a couple of hours, sometimes more than that, for reading and writing, for example, reading dossiers that come usually from the Secretariat of State." This is the time when he writes the speeches, homilies, and documents that are not written for him by others. The pope has a computer but normally writes in longhand, although after he dislocated his shoulder he began to dictate to a secretary. He usually writes in Polish, which the Secretariat of State then translates into Latin, Italian, and other languages. The pope also has two multilingual priest secretaries who work under Monsignor Dziwisz. The English-speaking secretary is from Vietnam.

"The way the Holy Father's day is set up," explains an official in the Secretariat of State, there is "nothing that involves the outside world before 11 o'clock." At 11 A.M. begin the audiences, which can go until around 1 o'clock. Normally the pope does not hold audiences after lunch. Wednesday is the day for the weekly public audience in Paul VI Hall. Private audiences are held during the rest of the week, except on Tuesday, which is a "free" day, and on Sundays when he is visiting a Rome parish. On his "free" day the pope often holds interdicasterial meetings "on various topics on which the Holy Father wants to hear people from different dicasteries." At noon he recites the Angelus, which is broadcast over Vatican Radio.

On Tuesdays and on days when audiences do not go on until lunch, he often meets with a group of people at around 12:30 to discuss a particular issue. Sometimes this is an interdicasterial group from two or more curial offices. The prefects always come, but the meeting might also include the secretary, undersecretary, and some staff from a particular dicastery. Sometimes there are people from outside the curia. Often these people are invited to continue the discussions over a working dinner at 1:30 P.M., which following the Italian custom is the main meal of the day. A working dinner could last until 3:00 P.M. The papal apartments on the third floor have a small dining room that can seat ten, but there is a larger one for fifteen people on the second floor. Those who have been invited say that the pope is a gracious host who enjoys his food, including a glass of wine with dinner.

"He is an excellent host," reports Clarence Gallagher, rector of the Oriental Institute, who has had dinner with the pope a number of times. "I have dined at embassies here in Rome and I have rarely met anyone who is such a good host at dinner. He gets everyone to speak. He leads the discussion. He's got a good sense of humor. He listens. Even the youngest people, everyone has been impressed by this aspect. He has the most warm, really welcoming personality. Very different from the public image I had of him. One of our young professors said, 'This is not the pope we see on television.' He is very warm and very unassuming. He doesn't want any bowing and scraping."

There is usually someone with him for dinner. For example, he will always have a dinner with a group of bishops visiting every five years for their ad limina. If there is a synod going on, various participants in the synod will dine with him over the course of the month-long meeting. They will normally be grouped by language—for example, all the guests at one dinner will be English-speaking—so that everyone can follow the conversation.

After the midday dinner the pope will often take a 20-minute nap, and then he is back at work "going through the papers, the dossier, the appointment of bishops," explains Dr. Navarro-Valls. "Unfortunately, in view of the amount of work, everything must pass through him." He usually takes 30 minutes and goes up to a small terrace that was constructed for Paul VI. "It is not very large but he can walk there," says Dr. Navarro-Valls. "Usually he prays part of the rosary on that occasion while he is walking there and finishes part of the breviary. That is roughly between 5:15 and 5:45."

At 6:30 he meets with his top curial officials. On Monday and Thursday he normally meets with Cardinal Sodano, the secretary of state. On Tuesday he meets with Archbishop Re, the sostituto, to discuss curia business; on Wednesday with Archbishop Tauran, the secretary for relations with states, to discuss international affairs; on Friday with Cardinal Joseph Ratzinger, prefect of the Congregation for the Doctrine of the Faith, to discuss the work of his congregation; and on Saturday with Cardinal Bernardin Gantin, prefect of the Congregation for Bishops, to decide the appointment of bishops. He also meets with Cardinal Jozef Tomko once a month to appoint bishops in the mission dioceses. These regularly scheduled meetings do not rule out the possibility of additional meetings with these officials at other times during the week.

Supper is at 7:30, and again guests are invited. Beginning around 8:45 the pope takes time to do some reading other than dossiers and documents until he goes to bed between 11:00 and 11:40 P.M. For example, before going to Lithuania he read some Lithuanian history and literature. He also practiced giving his speeches in Lithuanian, Estonian, and Latvian at this time.

Although he does not have much time for outside reading, the pope has a wide range of interests, including anthropology, theology, philosophy, geography, history, ecology, and poetry. He can read Polish, Russian, German, French, English, Spanish, Italian, and Portuguese. When he is traveling he often has six or seven books next to his seat on the airplane that he reads. His other time for reading is when he is on vacation in August at Castel Gandolfo. But the Vatican generates most of his reading material, including news clippings from a worldwide range of newspapers provided to him by the Secretariat of State and the Vatican press office. The Vatican also subscribes to about a dozen wire services including AP, Agence France Presse, Reuters, Tass, and CNS. Although the Secretariat of State prepares an Italian summary of the news, "the great advantage for the pope is that he can read the originals, not just translations," explains Dr. Navarro-Valls. From the United States he would see clippings from the *New York Times, Washington Post, Los Angeles Times, Time, Newsweek,* and *America.*

Besides saying the breviary and praying for an hour before Mass in the morning, the pope makes frequent visits during the day to a small chapel in his apartment. Before going to bed, he takes time in the chapel to examine his day. During the day when "he is working or studying dossiers or something like that," says Dr. Navarro-Valls, "it is very difficult to say whether he is working or whether he is praying."

The pope cannot write all the letters, speeches, and documents that come out in his name. At first John Paul II tried to write many of his documents, and even now he usually writes his homilies. But many papal documents are written in the curia, especially in the Secretariat of State. "This is an old tradition in the Secretariat of State," explains a Vatican official, "they are able little by little to enter into the mentality of the pope and become good ghost writers. I don't think that the poor man really has good writers among his collaborators, but they are good ghost writers in the sense that they are faithful to his mentality." This is often done through having the pope quote himself: "If I quote you, I am certain that I am more or less interpreting your mind."

Sometimes John Paul II will add meditative or theological material at the beginning and end of a document or speech without changing the middle. This leads to long documents with changes in style. "He wants five pages" for a speech, complain his collaborators, "but then he will add so much that at the end there are seven, eight, nine, ten pages or so. That means more than half an hour when they are beyond eight pages." Sometimes, especially in longer documents, it is possible to see the changes in style from one section to another and to figure out which sections were actually written by the pope.

Different popes have different styles of working. Paul VI traveled only a few times outside Rome, while his twentieth-century predecessors rarely left Rome. During his first seventeen years, John Paul traveled 620,000 miles. In his 68 trips outside Italy he spent 448 days visiting 540 cities, giving 2,023 speeches and homilies in 112 countries.[5] Another 122 trips within Italy involved 844 speeches and homilies in 184 days. This adds up to 10 percent of his time being spent outside Rome and away from the office. In addition, these trips require extensive preparation, which takes additional time away from "traditional" papal work. "John Paul wishes to preach the Gospel to the world and not to remain in the Vatican with the documents," explains an Italian priest who works in the Vatican.

Paul VI spent a great amount of time going over dossiers and other documents from the Vatican. "With Paul VI they were bringing to him big suitcases filled with documents in the evening," reports an Italian who has worked for decades in the curia. "The pope would check everything until one or two o'clock in the morning, and next morning they would receive again the pile of dossiers with annotations approving or disapproving or asking for new documentation about the case and so on."

John Paul I, with no experience in the Vatican, was overwhelmed when the curia expected him to keep up a similar regimen. He told Cardinal Villot that he did not want to receive a pile of documents every night: "This is not the role of the pope," he told him. "Take your responsibility as cardinal secretary of state and decide these things." John Paul I only wanted to sign those things that he had time to ponder and understand, and he only wanted to make the speeches that he himself wrote. Whether such a strategy would have proved successful over the long run is uncertain, but John Paul I did not live long enough to find out.

Nor does John Paul II work like Paul VI, although he has more energy and better health than John Paul I. At first the curia officials brought him the same number of dossiers as they had given to Paul, but they quickly learned to be more selective in what they brought him. "This pope does not like the ordinary government," comments a Vatican official who has watched a number of popes. "He loves to meet people, to be a preacher, to teach the people, to travel, to stimulate the local churches, to meet with youth. He is more a pastor than a governor or president. Paul VI was more working at his desk. I don't think John Paul loves working at his desk except for writing his own things." As a result, John Paul does not closely review the documents that are being developed in congregations. This means that the changes made by the Secretariat of State or the Congregation for the Doctrine of the Faith often determine the final shape of the document.

John Paul prefers to learn from conversations with people rather than from dossiers. "He loves to discuss things with the people," explains a Vatican official. "I don't think that he will follow very much the opinion of the other people around the table, but certainly he asks the right questions and he learns quite a lot. Even if he doesn't agree with everything, he wants to know what the opinion of the people is. Generally he is influenced by that way of being informed. He doesn't express his opinion in those meetings. He just asks questions. He makes some remarks, but never a real confrontation. It is rather difficult to know what he really thinks until he has decided."

When the pope wanted to learn more about the theology of the Orthodox church, in 1993 he invited a half-dozen professors from the Oriental Institute and the Gregorian University to give him a private seminar before and during lunch on Tuesdays. His secretary joked that "for a group of students, you need one professor. But for a pope, you need a group of professors." The professors found him a very knowledgeable and bright student with a photographic memory. "His knowledge of Eastern theology is remarkable," reports Father Gallagher, rector of the Oriental Institute. "He has read a lot of Russian theologians. He is a man who is really thoughtful, who is really doing his homework, who really wants union in the church." Among the topics covered in the seminars were the "Filioque" controversy, the Orthodox view of redemption, creation, liberty, and the church (especially the issue of papal primacy), and Orthodox theologians like Sergiei Bulgakov.

The major complaint of the curia against John Paul is that he does not take their work seriously. "They agree with the pope on most things," explains a Vatican official. "But perhaps many of them do not like the pope because he does not appreciate very much their work or does not give much importance to them." Under Paul VI, the head of each dicastery would meet with the pope once a month. The only dicastery heads who regularly meet with John Paul are the prefects of the Congregation for the Doctrine of the Faith, the Congregation for Bishops, and the Congregation for the Evangelization of Peoples. The last two must see him regularly because of episcopal appointments. Other dicastery heads see him only when he asks to see them or they request an audience.

As a result, Pope John Paul has been accused of being a bad manager. It would be more accurate to say that he pays attention to those areas that interest him and leaves the rest to the Vatican bureaucrats after having set the general policy direction. For example, for the International Year of the Family, he showed superb management skills in organizing all the organs of the Vatican to promote his views in the church and in the international arena. He also pays close attention to the work of the Congregation for Bishops, the Council for Promoting Christian Unity, the Congregation for the Doctrine of the Faith, and the Council for Justice and Peace, but gives less attention to the congregations for Divine Worship, Clergy, Consecrated Life, and Catholic Education. These congregations pretty much run themselves following the general direction he has set. For example, in the area of liturgy, John Paul's only major initiative has been the reintroduction of the Tridentine Mass—the Mass as it was before the reforms of Vatican II—under certain circumstances.

John Paul also gets things done without worrying about going through proper channels. "This pope really values people who can get things done," a Vatican official reports. "This pope is more concerned about personal qualities of thinking and leadership than the person's title or position, that this one is head of this dicastery or that one." Thus he uses Cardinal Roger Etchegaray, the president of the Council for Justice and Peace, as a roving goodwill ambassador to visit places like Bosnia, China, Cuba, and Vietnam even though he is not a member of the Secretariat of State. Not being an official diplomat helps in certain circumstances because Cardinal Etchegaray can make "unofficial" visits more easily. Whenever the pope sends someone on a special mission, he usually meets with him before and after the trip.

The pope also calls in the heads of different dicasteries to discuss what to do about a specific problem like the accord with Israel, the Cairo conference on population and development, or the strife in Bosnia or Rwanda. By inviting the heads of various dicasteries (Justice and Peace, Christian Unity, Interreligious Dialogue, Migrants, Oriental Churches, Secretariat of State, and so forth) to the meeting, he gets different perspectives on complex issues. He sometimes invites people who though not the head of a relevant dicastery still have experience that would be helpful. For example, in a discussion of the Middle East, Cardinal Pio Laghi would be invited because he was apostolic delegate to Jerusalem.

"The pope simply opens" the discussion, explains Cardinal Jozef Tomko, prefect of the Congregation for the Evangelization of Peoples. "He puts the questions, but [they are] very general. Everybody is prepared on the topic, but somebody who is very important for the topic, this man speaks. Then everybody speaks. It goes all around. Now, if they have one man who is in charge of being a reporter [presenter], he has a right to reply and then some more discussion. The pope is an extremely attentive listener. He doesn't interrupt. The discussion continues also during the meal. It is simply like a familial meeting, which is the best one. Everybody is really relaxed."

The pope likes strong, forceful characters like himself. The cardinals who are most influential in his papacy are strong personalities who argue their positions forcefully and know how to get things done: Cardinals Castillo, Tomko, Sodano, Ratzinger, and Schotte. Some say that Cassidy's problem as sostituto was that he would describe the pros and cons of various options rather than proposing a solution. When the pope wants something done, he will frequently turn to strong people who are sure of their opinions.

Most of the presidents and prefects I interviewed did not recall receiving specific instructions from the pope when they got their job. They met individually with the pope soon after their appointments, but he did not give them any detailed instructions on what to do. "It is presumed," explains Cardinal Cassidy, "that by the time you are appointed to a job like this [president of the Council for Promoting Christian Unity] you must know what you should be doing." With some officials the pope had a general discussion about the work of the dicastery, especially if it was an area he is interested in.

"He spoke of his ideas to do with this congregation," recalls Cardinal Ratzinger when John Paul first asked him to be prefect of the Congregation for the Doctrine of the Faith,

> not about bureaucratic details, because he cannot know what is here, but about the sacred contents, about the ideas of his pontificate, about the doctrinal aspect. I did not know what are here the rules and mechanism, but I could see what was his intention in selecting me for this position.
>
> When he was archbishop in Krakow, he had seen some of my books, especially *Introduction to Christianity,* and he felt I could collaborate with him in this time to help promote on the one hand sound theological development and a good contact with theologians in the world. This is one of his preoccupations, to have positive relations between the magisterium of the pope and the magisterium of the theologians. [The cardinal laughed at this point, recognizing that his own media image in this area is not positive.] And so to be in a real fraternal dialogue. And on the other hand, in these difficult times to see what are the essential points to defend.
>
> So it was a dialogue [between us] about the contents of the faith, the theological development at this time, and the essential points of his pontificate. It was not discussion about how to do it.

A president or prefect can always ask for an appointment to talk to the pope, but they appear to be reluctant to impose on his limited time except when necessary. Much of their contact with the pope is in writing through the Secretariat of State. They also pay close attention to speeches and statements by the pope that touch on responsibilities of their dicastery. They frequently quote the pope in their speeches and documents as a way of bolstering their arguments, supporting his policies, and showing their loyalty. At the same time, since they have input on these papal statements, sometimes they are quoting their own words as spoken by the pope.

At the beginning of his pontificate, John Paul met with the prefect and secretary of each dicastery as a way of getting to know what they did. Sometimes the undersecretary and other top staff in the dicastery were invited as well. Usually the meeting lasted an hour and continued over a working lunch. The pope has continued to meet with dicastery officials, but normally this does not happen more than once or twice a year. Whenever it does happen it is the high point of the year for the officials, and everyone speaks highly of the experience of meeting with the pope. Each official reports on his work in the office, and there is a "very easy discussion of those things with the Holy Father," explains Cardinal Cassidy. "You don't read out a paper necessarily. If it's a question on which you want to have a particular input, then you might have a paper prepared. Otherwise you simply discuss the general problem or particular questions with which you are dealing."

John Paul uses these meetings plus lunch as a way of finding out what is going on and directing the curia. "Once he called us for such a lunch when I was beginning my first year," reports a cardinal. "With the secretary and undersecretary, we prepared seven points that we wanted to discuss with him on our work. We got it all typed out and kept in our pocket. I said to them, 'If I forget one point, you raise it.' So we sat down and the Holy Father said, 'Well, let's see how the work is going.' He raised one point on his own and we discussed that point exhaustively. Then he raised another point, and we discussed it. And he raised a third one until he cleared five of the seven points in our pocket." The topics might cover anything within the competence of the dicastery, including documents under development.

At subsequent meetings, the cardinal and his staff prepared two pages reporting to the pope what they had done and what they were planning to do in the next three months to a year. "Without tying the Holy Father to one point," the cardinal explains, "we see where he has more interest. In that way we see whether he approves of a line we are following. If he does not approve, which is very rare, and we think it is important, we argue it then to try to get him to approve. We want his approval because if he doesn't approve, we don't do it. It never happened that he would disapprove, but we would obviously see where he has more interest and in the same way we also share with him where we think our interest should be. That is the way we do it. However, he leaves very much to our discretion."

The pope takes an active part in leading these discussions. "He will ask a question, usually a very pointed question that gives direction to your discussion," explains an undersecretary. The pope does not normally direct the curia with a heavy hand. "He won't say, 'You have to do this. You have to do that,'" reports one secretary. "He is more kind because he knows that our preoccupation is to know his mind and to go in his mind," comments another secretary. The dicastery superiors are very sensitive to what the pope brings up, what he responds to, where he places emphases, and what questions he asks. "It is more of a general impression," explains a secretary. They will pick up on what was important to the pope and follow through on it. During the discussions he might simply say, "'Yes, yes, it will be good to go in this way,'" reports a secretary.

Some cardinals have received specific instructions from the pope. For example, the pope asked Cardinal Gagnon to look into sex education texts used in the United States. "People in the United States whom he knew personally had brought in a lot of documentation and had spoken to him about it," explains Cardinal Gagnon. "And when I came back in 1983, the first thing he asked from me was that. He himself gave me a lot of books." The decision to allow more use of the Tridentine Mass also came directly from the pope. John Paul also told Cardinal Silvio Oddi, prefect of the Congregation for the Clergy, to encourage clerical dress by priests.

Because he wishes to emphasize his papal role as teacher, John Paul gives special attention to doctrinal issues and the work of the Congregation for the Doctrine of the Faith. He meets with Cardinal Ratzinger at least once a week on Friday. The topic of these Friday meetings is the work of the congregation, especially the monthly meetings of its members (called the Feria Quarta for Wednesday, the day it meets) and the meetings of its consultors. The issues discussed can involve a wide variety of "disciplinary problems or doctrinal problems," reports Cardinal Ratzinger.

> The problem of the admission of Anglicans to ordination, problems of the reintegration of priests who were dispensed and returned. Or it can be only a review of the central problems of the moment. Or also proposals, what are the next points to discuss, to study? Or also concrete problems, positions—the preparation of a document, first or second reading of a document or final presentation of a document. Or what to do about publications in some theological areas, and so forth.
>
> The Holy Father receives the documentation [from the meeting of the congregation] and can see the arguments, and I explain what was the discussions of the cardinals and what are the proposals of the cardinals. So this [Friday meeting] is essentially centered about what was in the Feria Quarta and can give also the occasion for the Holy Father to say, "But I have another idea."

At the Friday meetings between Cardinal Ratzinger and the pope, specific decisions are made about the work of the congregation. At other times, the cardinal, the pope, and other experts meet to have more general discussions before lunch. "It begins with one-and-a-half hours of free discussion and after this it continues in a working lunch," says Cardinal Ratzinger.

It can be for three hours, and always with the participants of different specializations. Here we are more free [than at the Friday meetings]. The Holy Father joins the arguments. We have time simply to discuss an idea and to prepare decisions, without the need to make decisions. These discussions in the working lunches can be most interesting.

As I said in relating about the results of the Feria Quarta, often the Holy Father says, "I will reflect a little about this. This is also a problem." This is important because the Holy Father especially with working lunches prepares also our work. So when we come with the result of the Feria Quarta, this is not an absolutely new thing that he must decide now in one minute. He knows the development. This is very important that the Holy Father know not only in the last moment when decisions are made, but he can accompany and guide the development of the ideas.

The pope, because of his background as an academic and his vision of himself as a teacher, enjoys working on doctrinal issues much more than on the canonical issues dealt with by many other congregations. In addition, since the Congregation for the Doctrine of the Faith must review and approve every other dicastery's documents with any doctrinal content, the pope is able by working with Cardinal Ratzinger to keep an eye on the documents of the other dicasteries.

The relationship between John Paul and Cardinal Ratzinger is much debated by Vatican officials and Vatican observers. Some critics see Cardinal Ratzinger as the "Grand Inquisitor" who is trying to suppress all dissent. As evidence, they note that the pope gave a more nuanced critique of liberation theology after the cardinal's congregation gave a more negative response to it. Others claim that Cardinal Ratzinger restrains the pope from issuing infallible declarations and from coming down even more strongly on dissident theologians. One thing is clear: they have great respect for each other and are loyal to each other. As a result, as far as doctrinal issues are concerned, Cardinal Ratzinger is the number two man in the Vatican after the pope himself.

The pope also meets about five times a year with all the cardinal presidents and prefects in a cabinet-like meeting in the evening, from 5:00 to 8:00 P.M. Originally archbishop presidents were also invited to these meetings, but *Pastor Bonus* limited attendance to cardinals. Thus Archbishop John Foley, president of the Council for Social Communications, and Archbishop

Giovanni Cheli, president of the Council for Pastoral Care of Migrants and Travelers, do not attend.

The agenda and discussions at the meetings are secret. Usually the topics are broad because they have to be relevant to a large number of dicasteries. "Generally they would discuss particular problems that need more study or need input from different dicasteries," explains an official in the Secretariat of State.

> For instance, about a year ago the Doctrine of the Faith published a document about communio [the church as a communion]. Before publication that was discussed by the dicastery heads. The whole situation in the Balkans was once the topic of a meeting. Topics where the input from different prefects would be helpful.
>
> If it is a question specifically related to two or three congregations, then they will probably have a meeting by themselves. For instance the question of pedophilia in the States, that was a committee of Clergy, Seminaries, Secretariat of State, and some of the judicial people. That is a topic that is more limited in scope. [For a meeting of presidents and prefects] we are talking about something where the church might take a position on a universal level, and something that is not necessarily cut-and-dried where there are not clear precedents.

The presidents and prefects have also discussed the preparation for different synods, the preparation of the Holy Year, the preparation for the international year of the family, or the need for an encyclical on a particular topic. Other topics have included Protestant sects in Latin America and relations between the Oriental Catholic churches and the Orthodox. "Whatever the Holy Father thinks is something that everybody should know about and should be able to give some opinion about," explains Cardinal Cassidy.

The usual procedure is that one or two cardinals, whose dicasteries would normally be responsible for the topic, make a presentation and then the others give five-minute responses in order of seniority. These meetings have received mixed reviews from the cardinals. Some believe that they help in coordinating the curia, others feel that the structure of the meeting (speaking in order of seniority) inhibits the free flow of discussion.

Through the centuries the popes have found a variety of structures through which to exercise their ministry to the church. Today's curial structures are working surprisingly well considering the limited size and expertise of the staff and the increased centralization that has occurred in the Catholic church over the last hundred years. Different popes have directed the curia in different ways. For the most part, the Roman curia is doing pretty much what the pope wants it to do. It allows him to focus on areas of interest while delegating other areas to his subordinates. The curia has its human limitations, but it would be difficult to find a work force of similar size anywhere else in the world that is more dedicated to its work and its leader. People in the Vatican admit that the curia needs to be improved, with better staff, less careerism, and more coordination. More comprehensive reform proposals come from people who have a radically different view of the papacy than those who now work in the curia.

A radical reform of the curia would require a different vision of the papacy, one that allowed for more freedom and autonomy by local churches and episcopal conferences. If fewer matters needed Roman approval, the curia could be a smaller operation. As the papacy is currently envisioned, it needs numerous offices and employees, and that means it needs money. Besides running the curia, the pope has to find the money to pay for it.

~ 8

Vatican Finances

WITHOUT MONEY, the pope would not be able to exercise his ministry. Money is needed for salaries, supplies, utilities, building maintenance, and all the other things necessary to run a bureaucracy. It is also needed to help poor local churches and other charities of the pope. On the other hand, papal finances have been the cause of scandal in the church for centuries. The extravagant life styles of Renaissance popes and cardinals, the financing of the construction of St. Peter's through the sale of indulgences, and more recently the Vatican bank scandals have all shocked the faithful as well as those outside the church. Rumors of hidden wealth, of money laundering, and of Vatican ownership of major corporations periodically appear in the press. There have also been reports of million-dollar deficits and major losses through bad investments. The Vatican tradition of secrecy has done nothing to quiet these rumors—in fact it has tended to feed them. How wealthy is the Vatican? Where does its money come from and where does it go? Only recently has the Vatican begun to be forthcoming with partial answers to these questions.

When Peter needed to pay the temple tax, Jesus worked a miracle for him (Matthew 17:27), and ever since popes have prayed for miracles to make ends meet. Like any bishop, the bishop of Rome needs money to support his ministry.[1] When it was a poor, persecuted minority, the church's needs were met by using people's homes as churches and by collecting food and clothing for the needy. The clergy were either fed and housed by the faithful or they supported themselves, like St. Paul, who made tents.

After the Edict of Milan (313), the wealth of the popes grew. "There were gifts from the emperors and the faithful (4th century), taxes from lands or monasteries placed under papal protection (9th century), feudal dues, Peter's Pence (11th century), and the various fees connected with benefices, which rapidly multiplied until they reached their maximum in the 14th and 15th centuries," reports the historian and canonist Ignazio Gordon.[2] The first papal financial officer was simply the person responsible for the strongbox. As time went on, administrative organs, including the Apostolic Camera, were developed to deal with papal property, income, and expenses. At one time this included a network of tax and rent collectors covering all of Europe. As these sources of income dried up in the sixteenth and seventeenth centuries, so did the duties of the Apostolic Camera.

Revenues from the papal states were also a source of income, but the expense of defending and governing these states was also high. The end of the papal states in 1870 meant the loss of tax revenues and income from church properties confiscated by the new Italian government. The pope gave up his claim to the papal states in 1929 when he agreed to the Lateran Treaty. In exchange, Italy agreed to subsidize the Italian Catholic church and give the pope $91.7 million as an indemnity for the papal states. Some of this indemnity was immediately used for construction within Vatican City—the train station and an office building for Vatican City. The rest was invested as the patrimony or endowment of the Holy See.

Not surprisingly, given the complexity of the papacy, papal finances are also complex. Some of this complexity is of recent origin and well grounded in intelligent financial administration. For example, there are separate budgets and accounts for the diocese of Rome, the Vatican City State, the Vatican bank, the Roman curia, Peter's Pence, St. Peter's Basilica, Lateran University, Gesu Bambino Hospital, and a dozen autonomous operations.[3] The divisions are not airtight. Most of them use the financial services of the Vatican bank and the Administration of the Patrimony of the Holy See (APSA), and the Vatican City State provides many services (telephone, mail, and so forth) to them for a fee. Keeping the finances of these entities substantially separate and distinct is essential for sound financial accounting and planning. It is also necessary to keep track of the income and expenses of different projects because church law requires that money donated for one purpose (for example, the missions) not be spent for any other purpose (like cleaning St. Peter's).

On the other hand, since the Vatican has only made public the finances of the administrations of the Holy See, this partial disclosure leaves people wondering what is in the other accounts.[4] The situation is also confusing because entities like the Vatican bank, the Administration of the Patrimony of the Holy See (APSA), the Vatican City State, and the Congregation for the Evangelization of Peoples have their own investments that they manage themselves. For example, APSA, Vatican City, and the Congregation for the Evangelization of Peoples own rental apartments in Rome.

The finances of each Vatican entity are complex, and their interrelationships make the financial situation even more complex. Only since the early 1990s has the Vatican been attempting to keep its books in a professional fashion. Since the finances of some of these entities are kept secret from the others, no one even within the Vatican completely understands the finances of all these entities and their interrelationship. This is especially true because most prelates at the very top have no training in finances and have trouble understanding financial reports if they ever look at them. Despite these problems, the administration of papal finances has improved immensely in recent years as a result of papal initiatives and pressure from Catholics in Germany and the United States who threatened not to contribute unless the situation improved.

In a move aimed at improving financial accountability and reducing the Vatican deficit, the finances of the diocese of Rome became independent of the Vatican in 1988. Some Romans referred to this as "robbing Peter to pay Paul." Although the finances of the diocese are not public, it was reported in 1988 that without the Vatican subsidy, the diocese of Rome faced a $5 million deficit. Fewer than 15 to 20 percent of Catholics in Rome attend church weekly, and they have not traditionally given much in the collection because they knew the government subsidized the Italian church as a result of the 1929 Lateran Treaty. The government subsidy to the Italian church paid priests' salaries and other expenses. The physical maintenance of the old historic churches in Rome was also the responsibility of the Italian government.

The government subsidy did not cover all costs, however. The expansion of Rome into the suburbs has meant the building of sixty-five new churches in recent years, with another forty still needed. In addition, John Paul II has added to the budget by encouraging diocesan programs to help drug addicts, abandoned children, illegal immigrants, and the homeless.

Separating Vatican and diocesan finances prepared the church for changes in government financing of church activities. In 1990, Italian church finances changed dramatically with the end of direct government subsidies to the church. The last direct payment to the Italian bishops from the government amounted to about $290 million in 1988. In its place was established a system of voluntary tax deductions and credits. Italians can deduct up to 2 million lire from their taxable income for donations to the church. (During 1994, the value of the dollar fluctuated between 1,525 and 1,700 lire and closed the year at around 1,630 lire.) In addition, in a checkoff system similar to that used in the United States to fund presidential election campaigns, Italian taxpayers can designate 0.8 percent of their income tax payments for the Catholic church, for other churches in Italy, or for state programs.

The Italian bishops feared and the Italian politicians hoped that the church would get much less money under the new system than under the old. They expected that only churchgoers would use the checkoff to designate 0.8 percent of their taxes for the church. In fact, 42 percent of Italian taxpayers chose the church in the checkoff system its first year (1991), garnering about $650 million for the Italian church. Another 44 percent made no choice at all, leaving only 14 percent who chose an institution other than the Catholic church.[5] The results were even better in subsequent years as more people used the checkoff to support the church.[6] Perhaps the best explanation for this comes from a Communist who announced he was designating the church on his tax form because he had more confidence that his money would be used well by the Catholic church than by the Italian government.

The diocese of Rome no longer needs a subsidy from the Vatican; in fact the Italian church is able to help others. "The reform of the clergy compensation system is producing significant results," reported John Paul II in 1994, "and, thanks to the generosity of the national community as a whole, the Italian bishops have been able significantly to aid the missions and to meet the needs of churches in difficulty, both in Europe and on other continents."[7]

The Vatican Bank

Before looking at the finances of Vatican City and the Holy See, it is useful first to examine the operations of the Istituto per le Opere di Religione (Institute for the Works of Religion), more commonly known as the IOR or the Vatican bank. Because of recent scandals, Vatican officials are very touchy when it comes to the Vatican bank. For example, Cardinal Edmund Szoka, the internal auditor of the Vatican, repeatedly points out that his prefecture has no authority over the IOR and he has nothing to do with it. Vatican officials assert that although the bank is in Vatican City, it is not part of the Holy See. Such talk, however, is misleading. The IOR is the pope's bank since, in a sense, he is the one and only stockholder. He owns it, he controls it.

The IOR was founded in 1887 to help manage church finances after the fall of the papal states. It provided the Vatican with a financial institution that was independent of Fascist Italy both before and during World War II. Its depositors are primarily Vatican employees, Vatican agencies, religious orders, dioceses, Catholic charities, and other church organizations. In the past, numerous lay Italians friendly with the church also used its facilities, but recent reforms reportedly restrict the bank's use to charitable purposes and Vatican employees.

As a result of reforms instituted in 1989, a supervisory council consisting of five financial experts with banking experience from around the world was appointed to oversee the bank and appoint its first lay director general. The first director chosen had extensive experience in Italian banking before his selection. The council members are appointed by a commission of five cardinals, who in turn are appointed by the pope. The council of experts is responsible for supervising the activities of the bank, while the commission of cardinals is responsible for making sure the bank observes its statutes. The president or chairman of the commission of cardinals, Cardinal Rosalio José Castillo Lara, says that the bank is run by the lay director and he only spends a couple of hours each week supervising the bank. Cardinal John O'Connor of New York is a member of the cardinals' commission, and Thomas M. Macioce, a New York businessman and member of the board of directors of Manufacturers Hanover Corp., was appointed to the first supervisory council.

The cardinals' commission only deals with "the most important things," explains Cardinal Castillo. This would include the bank's "relationship with the public opinion and its relations with the dicasteries of the Roman curia. Then the balance sheet and the budget are more or less approved by us. And we approve also the destination of the net income."

The IOR has been accused of everything from helping rich Italians avoid taxes to laundering money for the Mafia[8] and for people who wanted to pay bribes to Italian politicians. Its involvement with the 1982 collapse of the Banco Ambrosiano has been widely reported.[9] Although the Vatican denied any wrongdoing, in 1984 the bank paid $244 million to the Banco Ambrosiano creditors in exchange for their dropping any further claims against the Vatican. Archbishop Paul Marcinkus, head of the bank from 1971 to 1989, opposed this payment but was overruled by Cardinal Agostino Casaroli, the secretary of state, and the pope. The bank affair was complicating the Holy See's relations with Italy at the time it was renegotiating the concordat. The pope and the cardinal also may have been influenced by a confidential report on the affair prepared by three outside banking experts commissioned by the pope.

While no one believes that Archbishop Marcinkus personally profited from his tenure as head of the Vatican bank, many think that he was naive in trusting Roberto Calvi, the chairman of the Banco Ambrosiano. To give Calvi time to straighten out his financial affairs, Archbishop Marcinkus gave him letters of patronage asserting the IOR's backing for his activities in the Banco Ambrosiano. The archbishop thought he was protecting the Vatican by requiring Calvi to give him a letter freeing the IOR of any responsibility, but some considered this fraud since only the letters of patronage were given to Calvi's creditors. Eventually thirty-three people were convicted in the $1.2 billion collapse of the bank, including the chairman of the Olivetti company. Roberto Calvi was found hanging from Blackfriars Bridge in London after the bank's collapse. As a Vatican official, Archbishop Marcinkus had diplomatic immunity and could not be charged under Italian law.

Archbishop Marcinkus had no training in business, let alone the complexities of international banking. He thought he was following a practice common in Italian banking, and Italian banking practices are shadier than the Italian banking community would like to admit. This was partly a result of the over-regulation of the banking industry by the government, especially in the area of currency exportation during the 1960s and 1970s. In addition, at the time Archbishop Marcinkus was holding down two other full-time jobs: he was head of Vatican City and the organizer of John Paul's foreign trips. Thus he was unable to give the bank the attention it deserved, and he was probably poorly advised by his subordinates. Despite his lack of financial experience, the IOR made a lot of money under Archbishop Marcinkus, perhaps as much as a billion dollars according to his defenders. As a result, the IOR did not have to borrow or take money from its depositors to pay the $244 million to the Banco Ambrosiano creditors. On the other hand, this hit significantly reduced the bank's assets and future income.

Although the average Italian lay worker in the Vatican liked Marcinkus, some influential Italians opposed him because they considered the Vatican City State and the Vatican finances their private turf. "The biggest mistake he made in his life was that he was the first American who climbed so high in the Vatican," said a European official in the Vatican. "Nobody can forgive him for that." Other non-Italians, Cardinal Szoka and Cardinal Castillo, have also come under attack when they stepped into the area of Vatican finances.

Today the Vatican bank is working to clean up its image. In 1994, for the first time in its history, the bank was audited by an outside firm, Price Waterhouse. And in 1993, when a witness in a government bribery case said that he laundered $50 million at the Vatican bank, Cardinal Castillo immediately promised full cooperation with the Italian authorities. He turned over the bank's records on the matter through diplomatic channels. Bank officials say that a man representing Montedison, an Italian chemical company, claimed to be sending the money abroad for charitable purposes. Instead the money was used for bribes to Italian politicians. The Italian prelate who accepted the money no longer works in the Vatican bank.

Although he was willing to cooperate with Italian authorities, Cardinal Castillo believes that the Vatican is the object of a conspiracy. "Here in Italy there is a big Masonic influence in some banks and in some newspapers," says the cardinal, "and they attack very harshly the Holy See in everything and the IOR."

Cardinal Castillo has begun making information public about the bank, and more may become available after the audit is completed. In a June 1994 interview Cardinal Castillo told me that the Vatican bank had deposits of about 7,000 billion lire, which would be about $4 billion. He said that the bank's net income for the year was 70 billion lire ($40 million).[10] "Most of the profit comes to the Holy Father to help the churches that are in need," reports the cardinal. "There are many churches in the Third World and now many in the East Europe. The Holy Father needs money for so many things now: Rwanda or Mozambique and the others. All of that is for charitable works. Some part, a little part, is contributed to the maintenance of the Roman curia." It is unclear how much working capital the bank has beyond its deposits. Some estimates have been as high as $1 billion before the $244 million payment to the creditors of Banco Ambrosiano.

The purpose of the bank is not simply to make money. It also provides banking services (checking and savings accounts, currency exchange, and so on) to dioceses, religious orders, Vatican offices, charities, and other religious institutions. For example, keeping money in the Vatican bank protects Catholic institutions from having their money confiscated or frozen by unfriendly governments. The banking services are especially important for institutions with multinational sources of income and ministries in many countries. If a missionary order wishes to transfer money from the United States to its African members, it can do so by keeping the money in a dollar-denominated account in the Vatican bank and only converting it to the African currency when needed.

These religious institutions, especially the Italian ones, sometimes got the Vatican bank into trouble by using their accounts to help Italian benefactors avoid government regulations in transferring their money out of Italy. Since there are hundreds of orders and religious institutions with deposits in the bank, this abuse is difficult for the bank to police, although it might notice a large sum transferred by a small order and ask questions.

Sometimes the Vatican bank is deliberately used to avoid national restrictions on the transfer of church funds. For example, the Holy See opposed economic sanctions against Poland after the imposition of martial law in 1981 and continued to funnel money to the Polish church and Solidarity through the Vatican bank. Likewise, the Holy See opposes the economic embargo against Cuba. Funds from the United States can be sent to the Cuban church through the Vatican bank, thus circumventing U.S. laws.

Auditing and Budgeting

Although he has no jurisdiction over the Vatican bank, accounting practices in the rest of the Vatican improved tremendously after the appointment in 1990 of Cardinal Edmund Szoka of Detroit as the president of the Prefecture for the Economic Affairs of the Holy See. The prefecture acts as the internal auditor of the Vatican. It does not handle any money or investments but exercises oversight and gives direction for the financial management of all entities linked to the Holy See except the Vatican bank and Peter's Pence. It examines and audits the accounting records of these entities, reviews their financial statements and budgets, and recommends the approval or disapproval of these budgets and financial statements to the pope.

Although the prefecture was responsible for auditing the financial statements of the Holy See beginning in 1987, the prefecture did not have any computers, nor did the Vatican have a unified chart of accounts applicable to all entities, when Cardinal Szoka arrived in 1990. There were only three full-time accountants, who were helped by seven outside accountants from a major accounting firm. The audit and consolidated financial statements were not completed until about sixteen months after the close of the fiscal year.

Great progress has been made under Cardinal Szoka. The office was computerized (thanks to $450,000 given by American Catholic foundations)[11] and additional internal auditors were hired (mostly young people because the Vatican pay scale is not competitive for experienced professionals). Now detailed consolidated financial statements for the Holy See are completed five months after the close of the fiscal year, which ends December 31. A group of outside experts reviews the audit before it is given at the end of June to a council of fifteen cardinals responsible for overseeing the finances of the Holy See. This council, which includes Cardinal O'Connor of New York and Cardinal Roger Mahony of Los Angeles as members, has been an important force in pushing for reform of Vatican finances. After getting a handle on the finances of the Holy See, the prefecture began in 1995 the first audit of the Vatican City State, a job that will take two years.

The other principal financial office in the Vatican is the Administration of the Patrimony of the Holy See (APSA), headed from 1989 to 1995 by Cardinal Rosalio José Castillo Lara, who also pushed to improve the financial administration of the Holy See. With American Catholic foundations paying the bill ($160,000), Cardinal Castillo had an Arthur Andersen management team examine APSA's operations and make recommendations for improving them. His personality and Cardinal Szoka's have clashed, which is unfortunate since united they could have accomplished more. The new head of APSA is Archbishop Lorenzo Antonetti, who most recently was nuncio to France but had been secretary in APSA and has a reputation for knowing what he is doing.

APSA is divided into two sections: ordinary and extraordinary. The extraordinary section manages the Holy See's cash and investments, including its patrimony and pension fund. This section also manages the cash and investments of Vatican dicasteries, such as the Congregation for the Evangelization of Peoples, which have their own funds. The ordinary section acts as the accounting and business office of the Holy See. It handles the administration of personnel, payroll, pensions, legal affairs, and the rental and maintenance of apartments owned by the Holy See. Some of these services, like payroll, are handled not just for the Holy See but for other entities like the Vatican City State.

A major cost for both the Vatican City State and the Holy See is salaries. The Vatican City State employs about 1,300 people (mostly Italian and lay) and the Holy See employs another 2,483 (719 clergy, 261 religious men, 110 religious women, 1,115 laymen, and 278 laywomen as of 1994). Vatican employees, like any others, complain about their salaries, but around 2,000 lay people apply for the few jobs open each year in the Vatican City State, and hardly anyone ever quits.

"Only two people [quit] in three years," reports Cardinal Castillo. "We would like to dismiss some people, but this is not easy in Italy and in the Vatican. I would like to have the situation like in America where we are more free" (to dismiss people who are not efficient). Vatican officials are afraid of the bad publicity and labor problems that would come from firing someone in the Vatican. Many Vatican employees are members of an employee association, and although Vatican officials publicly say that it is not a union, privately they admit that it acts like a union. Although Vatican officials meet with the association's officers, they say that this is for communications, not negotiations. Despite the church's social teaching, Vatican officials have a difficult time understanding why people working for the pope would want a union.

The pay for those at the lower end of the Vatican salary scale is better than the salary paid to comparable workers in Italy. The pay for those at the higher end of the scale, however, is not as good as the salary received by comparable managers and professionals in Italy. This reflects a clear bias in the Vatican toward paying a living wage to the lowest-skilled workers rather than rewarding skills and merit. The Vatican pay and personnel policies are more paternalistic than market-sensitive. Some high Vatican officials say they would like to raise salaries for lay professionals and managers if the Vatican could find the money, but they fear that all Vatican employees would demand a similar raise.

In 1994, the lowest salary was about 1.5 million lire a month while the top salary would be around 2.5 to 3 million lire. The monthly salary is misleading since Vatican employees are paid for 13 months each year. Cardinals receive about 53 million lire a year (about $32,900 at the end of 1994).[12] Cardinals get free housing but must pay utilities and living expenses, including any personal staff. "I get twice as much as I did in Detroit," reports Cardinal Szoka, "but fewer expenses are covered. In Detroit room and board were covered just like for any parish priest. I would not be able to cover my costs if I did not have other sources of income."

The actual pay other employees receive is based on a complex formula that considers the number of dependents, length of service to the Vatican, and a 10-level salary scale based on one's job in the Vatican. There is an annual indemnity paid to those who come from outside Italy to work at the Vatican (to allow them to visit home). There is no provision for merit increases. To get a raise, an employee has to move up a category, which some can do after gaining experience or additional training. An automatic raise is also given with every two years of service, which means that sometimes a senior porter is paid more than top officials in an office. Cardinal Edouard Gagnon reports that in 1983, "the porter at the committee on the family earned about twice what I earned [as the new archbishop president]. He was a layman so it was all right, and he had worked for thirty years."

Recently, the Vatican has started paying new porters and cleaners according to the Italian pay scale that is set through national negotiations between their unions and the Italian employers' association. This has simplified labor relations for the Vatican and allowed it to pay the same rates as are paid in Italy, which are lower than would be paid under the Vatican pay scale.

Before 1985, clergy and religious were paid less than laity on the grounds that they did not have a family. Now the same formula is applied to all equally, except that priests and religious are not paid overtime as laypersons are. Religious, because of their vow of poverty, normally turn their pay over to their community and live in one of the community's houses in Rome. As a result, their temporal well-being is dependent on the overall financial health of their community rather than their personal salary.

Diocesan priests do not take a vow of poverty or live in a community. They pay for their housing and living expenses out of their salaries. "Diocesan priests make great sacrifices to work here unless they have other sources of income," comments an American religious working in the Vatican. "Half their salary might go to rent plus electricity, which is very expensive. If they have a car, they have payments and gas. They need Mass stipends, and some teach to supplement their income." A diocesan priest would not receive any bonus for dependents unless he had an elderly parent who was dependent on him. It is especially priests from First World countries like the United States and Germany who feel the pinch. The U.S. bishops provide Villa Stritch as a place where American priests working in the Vatican can live at subsidized rates. If they were in a parish in the United States, they would get free room and board.

In addition to salaries, Vatican employees have some significant benefits. Most important, their salaries are exempt from the Italian income tax, and there is no Vatican income tax (although Americans have to pay U.S. income taxes at the rates set for Americans working abroad). Thus even the Vatican porters and cleaners under Italian contracts are doing significantly better than their non-Vatican colleagues because they pay no taxes.

Women employees can receive up to six months of maternity leave at full salary and another six months at half pay. Employees, their dependents, and retirees also receive 100 percent health coverage (about 9,000 persons are covered). The Vatican has a small clinic with general practitioners present every day and different medical specialists on different days. "If you have something beyond what they can handle, you are referred to specialists outside the Vatican," explains an American employee. "You have to go to the doctor they refer you to." Although most Americans in Rome have little confidence in Italian doctors, this person feels that "it is great coverage."

Employees also receive a pension and severance pay. There is withholding for pension (5 percent), for health insurance (2 percent), and for severance pay (1.5 percent), but the benefits are worth more than the cost to the employee. For example, the Vatican contributes three times as much to the pension fund as does an employee. The pension liability of the Vatican is of special concern since the pension program was set up without doing a proper actuarial study of Vatican employees to establish the potential cost to the Vatican. Only in 1993 was a separate pension fund established to cover future retirees. Pensions of current retirees are carried on the books as a liability, which for the Holy See alone amounts to 262 billion lire.[13]

An unusual fringe benefit for employees is access to Vatican stores, where food, liquor, tobacco, clothing, consumer electronics, and gasoline can be bought at prices lower than in Italy. For example, gasoline prices are 30 percent lower than in Italy, and cigarettes are 40 percent less than in Italy, where they can cost $3 a pack. These stores are mobbed by employees and anyone else who can sneak in. Because of complaints from the Italian government, the sale of gasoline and tobacco is rationed since Vatican employees were reselling the items at a profit in Italy.

Finally, some employees also rent apartments owned by the Vatican at prices below those charged by most landlords.[14] These apartments are so popular that there was a waiting list of about 500 Vatican employees in 1994, and the Vatican was looking to buy another 160 apartments to accommodate its employees. Some who have been on the waiting list for years complain about preferential treatment for people with friends in high places. Clearly a new cardinal or archbishop coming to work in the Vatican does not have to wait in line.

Because salaries are a major expense and it is almost impossible to fire anyone, Vatican regulations make it difficult to hire new people. Each Vatican office has a "tabella organica" that sets the number of positions with specified rank and salary levels. No permanent employee can be hired unless his position is on the list. A new employee is hired on a trial basis lasting one to two years, during which he can be dismissed for any reason. Some people are also hired under short-term contracts for particular projects, but when the work is done or the contract expires, they are let go. When offices submit their budgets each year, their staffing levels cannot exceed their set limit, which is reviewed every five years by a commission in the Secretariat of State. Because of the computerization of offices, these reviews have recently tended to reduce the number of typists, replacing them with professional staff who are more expensive.

The Budget of Vatican City

The Vatican City State budget, separated from the Holy See's in 1982, includes the Vatican museum and the departments of technical services, economic services, and health services. Also included in the Vatican City budget are the papal villa (Castel Gandolfo) and the Vatican Observatory. The budget of the Governatorato is about $130 million a year and pays the salaries of 1,300 Vatican employees.[15] Although the Vatican City budget is not made public, it reportedly makes money (about $5 million) because of its various sources of income, and about half its profits are used to help finance the Holy See.

The museum (which actually is a series of museums and galleries) has 250 employees and is expensive to maintain. It is self-supporting through charges to visitors (in 1994 it took in about 27 billion lire from admission fees from 2.6 million visitors),[16] rental of cassette guides, and the sale of reproductions, books, and other items in its gift shops. The museum even makes a little profit for the Vatican.

Major restorations and other projects are financed through fund raising or contracts with other museums. A 1992 fund-raising dinner by museum patrons in Los Angeles included former President Ronald Reagan, Jimmy Stewart, Bob Hope, and Ricardo Montalban. The biggest gift came from the Nippon Television Network (NTV) which financed the cleaning of the frescoes in the Sistine Chapel, a project that took thirteen years.

The Vatican museum has also loaned works of art to other museums in arrangements that have profited the Vatican museum financially. It received $580,000 from the Metropolitan Museum in New York to restore works before their visit to New York. Royalties on reproductions and other income from this 237-piece exhibit eventually brought the Vatican museum about $2 million for restoration of art works in the Vatican. In 1995 the Franklin Mint began offering reproductions of a Vatican museum 12-piece porcelain Nativity collection at $135 a piece. The Vatican Library received $4 million for reproduction royalties from Belser Verlag, a German publisher, that it used to build a new wing.[17] In 1995, the library signed a licensing deal allowing companies to market products inspired by its collection that will bring in $5 million annually. And just in time for Christmas 1995, Turner Publications in Atlanta began selling a $395 Bible with hundreds of full-color illustrations from the Vatican Urbino Bible. Like museums and galleries all over the world, those at the Vatican have learned how to market themselves.

Not infrequently there are calls to sell the art collection either to finance the Vatican or to give the money to the poor. The Vatican response has been that it holds these works in trust for humanity and cannot sell them. In keeping with this philosophy, the Vatican Library is working with IBM to optically scan its collection and make it available on the Internet. The Vatican does not even bother to estimate the value of its works of art in its financial statement. The art along with the Vatican buildings is listed under assets at a token value of one lira each (less than a penny). In addition, since much of the art is an essential part of the Italian cultural heritage, selling it to collectors or museums outside Italy would be very controversial. When the Vatican first started lending works of art to museums outside Italy, anticlerical Italian politicians charged that this was the first step toward selling works that should belong to

Italy. Because of this outcry, the Italian government stopped Italian church organizations from sending their art on tour, although it could not stop the Vatican. The Vatican museum will continue to look for ways to raise money, but the sale of the art will not occur in the foreseeable future.

The buildings, equipment, streets, and grounds of the Vatican are maintained by the department of technical services, which employs about 380 people including plumbers, electricians, and carpenters. "Our budget for the year in the technical office," reports Cardinal Castillo, "is no less than $40 million." These expenses are similar to those for a college campus except that the maintenance costs are higher because the buildings have historic and artistic value that cannot be ignored when doing repairs and renovations. For example, cracks appeared in the walls of the Sistine Chapel soon after it was built because of its position on a geologically delicate area of the Vatican Hill. Although it appears stable today, "an accidental variation of consistency due to sewer seepage, or modification of the water table due to faulty construction repairs, must always be watched."[18]

Even the "newer" buildings, constructed early in this century, are old and not very functional for modern office use. "This building is very expensive to heat, tall ceilings and huge staircases that just suck out the heat whenever a door is opened," complains an employee in one of the buildings in Piazza San Calisto. "All these wooden windows and marble are expensive to maintain. If something is wrong with the window, you have to get a carpenter to fix it." Because of the age of the buildings and the high cost of electricity, hardly any Vatican offices have air conditioning. "Parts of the building are like an oven in the summer." During August, most of the Vatican, like most of Italy, is shut down for vacation.

The technical services department has engineers and architects who review construction and renovation projects that may be done by the department or contracted out. After St. John Lateran was bombed, this office dealt with the repair of the pope's cathedral. In 1994, Cardinal Castillo received a proposal for renovating the Apostolic Palace where the Secretariat of State has its offices and where the pope lives and works. In the summer of 1995 the facade outside the pope's apartment was repaired. "Every year we are restoring the facade," he said.

Besides the repair and maintenance of the buildings and grounds, Vatican City also pays for firefighters, postal clerks, over 100 security guards, and other employees as well as paying for electricity, water, and natural gas bought from Italy. The cost of some of these items, like postal clerks, is covered by charging the Roman curia and others for the services. Cardinal Castillo has been looking for every source of revenue that he can find. For example, in the past the Vatican allowed religious orders based in Rome to have packages sent from outside Italy to the Vatican where they would be picked up, thus avoiding the Italian tariffs and bureaucracy. This used to be a free service, but now the Vatican charges a tariff. The cardinal has even increased the charges to photographers and film crews who want to take pictures within the Vatican.

While these fees raise a little money for the Vatican, more significant revenues come from sales in its supermarket, gasoline station, clothing store, and electronics stores, which are heavily used by Vatican employees. To use the stores, one must have a pass that is given to Vatican employees and buyers for religious orders in Rome. Passes are frequently borrowed by friends, or those with passes simply buy things for their friends. Although the prices are usually lower than in Italy, the stores make significant profits because the items are not subject to Italian tariffs or taxes. Especially profitable are items highly taxed in Italy like gasoline, liquor, and tobacco. As a result of a study funded by American Catholic foundations, which included the first survey of customer preferences, the stores have become more efficient and more consumer-friendly. They now have better hours, scanners at the checkout counters, and more products that the customers want, such as meat.

Other big money makers for Vatican City are the sale of coins and stamps to collectors. The postal service also makes a small profit, as does the telephone service that charges other Vatican offices for their calls.

Finally, the Vatican City State and APSA also own about 2,400 apartments that are rented to Vatican employees and others and thus provide income to the Vatican. Some apartments were rented to nonemployees in the past, but now when space becomes free, the Vatican makes it available to employees. For Vatican employees, the rents are below market value. The Congregation for the Evangelization of Peoples also owns apartments, but they are rented as an investment to make money.

Financial Statements of the Holy See

The "Consolidated Financial Statements of the Holy See," as distinct from the finances of the Vatican City, IOR, and autonomous agencies, includes those entities that directly help the pope in the government of the church: the Secretariat of State, nine congregations, eleven councils, three tribunals, Papal Household, office for liturgical celebrations, Libreria Editrice Vaticana (Vatican bookstore/publisher), Tipografia Poliglotta (Vatican press), Vatican Radio, *L'Osservatore Romano*, the Vatican Archives, and the Vatican Library.

At the end of 1994, the audit listed 1,483 billion lire in assets and 732 billion in liabilities in the "Consolidated Financial Statements of the Holy See." Included in the assets are 410 billion lire in cash, 479 billion in stocks and bonds, 29 billion in gold, and 470 billion in fixed assets (mostly investment real estate, since institutional real estate is listed at one lira). Included in the liabilities are 269 billion lire in deposits and current accounts held for other Vatican entities, 95 billion for employees' severance indemnities, and 262 billion as the present value of pensions payable to retired employees. There are 750 billion lire in net assets.

Few of the Holy See's operations have much income, and only the Libreria and the Tipografia make a small profit (and the press's profit disappears if sales to other Vatican entities are subtracted). The Holy See's income comes primarily from investments and donations.

For twenty-three years, from 1970 to 1992, the budget of the Holy See was in the red, peaking in 1991 with a deficit of about $87.5 million. The Vatican asserts that to a great extent, these deficits "were due to the ever increasing expenses for new offices created by the Holy See in response to the decrees of the Second Vatican Council."[19] Although clearly the Holy See was having financial difficulties, the true financial situation of the entire Vatican during this period is still unclear because the Vatican has not been as forthcoming with information about the profits from the Vatican City State and the IOR.

In addition, during this period various accounting changes took place that significantly increased the Holy See's deficit. For example, in 1989 the cost of the papal embassies was moved from the Vatican City State budget to the Holy See budget because "they are considered necessary services for the universal church."[20] Similarly, before 1985, Vatican Radio was part of the Vatican City State budget. It was moved into the Holy See budget because it was seen as part of the pastoral ministry of the pope. Vatican Radio has a large staff (406 people, half journalists or announcers, with significant overtime costs) and a large deficit (30.5 billion lire in 1994). As a result, moving it from the Vatican City State budget to the Holy See's budget allowed the Vatican City State to be in the black and pushed the Holy See further into the red.

The senior staff and most of the priests in Vatican Radio are Jesuits. It broadcasts around 40,000 frequency hours in 37 languages each year but takes no advertising. The broadcasts include music, news, papal events, and devotional programs. In Italy Vatican Radio has an AM and an FM station, but outside Italy its broadcasts are shortwave. Its classical music programs are among the best in Italy, but its news coverage of the Vatican is usually behind other media because it cannot report rumors but only official statements and interviews. Its coverage of the Third World, however, is extraordinary by commercial media standards. Before the fall of the Iron Curtain, the persecuted church highly valued Vatican Radio's broadcasts in many languages to Eastern Europe. Vatican budget cutters look at Vatican Radio the way congressional Republicans look at National Public Radio, but so far the pope has protected his radio from draconian cuts. Whether it could raise money through advertising on its Italian stations or fund raising would be worth looking into. It is currently investigating the possibility of broadcasting on the Internet.

L'Osservatore Romano has been compared to Pravda in the pre-perestroika days of the Kremlin. Its dull format is filled with papal speeches, Vatican documents, and approved commentary. As a documentary service it is an invaluable research tool, but for the average reader it is a cure for insomnia. There is a daily Italian edition, weekly editions in Spanish, English, French, German, Italian, and Portuguese, and a monthly edition in Polish. The paper takes practically no advertising, and it lost 5.5 million lire in 1994. Expenses have been reduced by modernizing the production process. As late as 1991, it was still using lead type. One printing press was so old it was given to a museum after it was replaced. Sales from subscriptions and newsstands cover about half the costs of the publication, but total sales have been steadily declining from 5.5 million copies in 1991 to 4.9 million in 1994. Unless the decline in sales stops, the paper's financial problems will grow.

The dicasteries in the Roman curia have little revenue (about 3 billion lire a year). Having been burned by selling indulgences in the sixteenth century, the Holy See avoids any practice smacking of simony. There is a small administrative fee for processing a papal blessing, but the Apostolic Almonry gives the money to the poor. Some dicasteries charge fees for various bureaucratic services, but most do not amount to more than $30 each although a few are in the $200 to $300 range. Dioceses and religious institutes are charged for permission to alienate property. Since this fee is a percentage of the amount alienated, it goes up with the amount. Some fees, like court fees for marriage cases before the Rota, are lower for dioceses from poor countries. There is no charge for processing laicization petitions, even though the process is time-consuming, because officials feared it would look as if a laicization could be bought.

As mentioned earlier, the biggest expense for the Roman curia is personnel (about 74 billion lire).[21] Another 27 billion is spent on papal embassies, 3.7 billion on utilities (which includes office cleaning), 3.9 billion on maintenance and repair, and 15 billion on general and administrative expenses. Not surprisingly, the major items in the last category are travel, mail and telecommunications, publishing and printing, and consulting (legal, technical, and so on).

The budgetary process in the Vatican is similar to that in most bureaucracies. Individual offices prepare their budgets on the basis of the previous year's experience and instructions they receive from above. "Throughout the attempt is to cut expenses," reports one Vatican official. "If there is an increase, then it has to be justified. Some things, even though they are overboard so to speak, will still be allowed because the Holy Father wants it, because this has to be done, or whatever. In the past, they have sent out notices that the budgets will all be a percentage lower, a certain percentage cut. Cut where you think best. Those instructions would come generally from the council of cardinals."

The curia budgets are reviewed first by APSA and then by the Prefecture for the Economic Affairs of the Holy See, which gets them by August 1. "In general, we operate on a pretty lean budget, but you always look for ways of cutting costs," explains Cardinal Szoka. At the beginning of November the budgets are reviewed by the council of cardinals overseeing the finances of the Holy See; then they go to the pope through the Secretariat of State.

Although it is difficult to put together the budgets of the 49 entities that make up the budget of the Holy See, the prefecture reports that for the most part "costs can be foreseen and budgeted with reasonable accuracy."[22] On the other hand, "It is virtually impossible for us to determine with any accuracy our income for the coming year. The reason is that most of our income is from sources that are beyond our control." These uncontrollable sources include donations and gains from financial activities that "depend on market forces, which as you know, are difficult to predict and can swing back and forth during the year."

With little income from its activities, the Roman curia must be supported by gifts and revenue from investments. As mentioned earlier, the Holy See received $91.7 million in exchange for the papal states in 1929. If all of this money had been invested in the New York Stock Exchange in a representative set of stocks, the principal would have been worth almost $1.6 billion in 1993.[23] That is 1.7 times greater than if the original investment had merely grown at the rate of inflation, not counting dividends that would have been paid out. In fact, the popes spent a chunk of this money on new buildings in the Vatican and only the remainder became the endowment or patrimony of the Holy See.

The current value of Vatican investments is unclear. The Vatican City and IOR financial statements are not public. And the consolidated financial statements of the Holy See list stocks at purchase price, not market value.[24] In addition, the value of the Holy See's real estate investments has not been updated in a manner acceptable to the auditors. As a result, the real worth of the stocks and real estate of the Holy See is undervalued in financial statements.

Little is known about the Vatican's investments early in this century, but it appears to have done fairly well by speculating in currency and gold during the depression and the Second World War.[25] After the war, the Vatican invested heavily in certain Italian industries in the hopes of rebuilding the country and keeping it free of Communist control. Paul VI began removing the Vatican from direct ownership and control of Italian companies, limiting ownership to no more than 6 percent and spreading its investments in stocks and bonds. He believed that the church got too much bad publicity because of the activities of these companies. Under Paul, the investments were still predominantly Italian. More recently Vatican investments have become more international.

The Vatican has traditionally been a fairly professional and aggressive currency trader in the management of its cash. Giorgio Stoppa, the lay Italian delegate, heads the second section of APSA and has the authority to buy and sell currency. "He is especially capable and moves very quickly in the area of currency transactions," reports Msgr. Robert Devine, a Canadian investment consultant in APSA. "You don't have time for consultations and things like that. You just move. He's very good at that."

The Holy See protects itself from being trapped with too many lire in a declining market by keeping some of its cash (including short-term bills and notes) in other currencies. At the end of 1994, for example, only 30 percent of its cash (valued at 410 billion lire) was in lire, while 45 percent was in dollars. The rest was in other currencies, especially Japanese yen, U.K. pounds, and German marks. Since the Holy See's budget is in lire and most of its bills are paid in lire, which way the lira goes can have a tremendous impact on its bottom line.

For example, in 1992, the fall of the lira after Italian and German monetary authorities failed to keep it within the European Monetary System resulted in a foreign exchange windfall of 50 billion lire for the Vatican. An international currency exchange firm, which examined the 1992 financial statement of the Holy See for me, called the Vatican strategy "commendable" and the windfall "extraordinary." But in 1994, a falling dollar and other factors resulted in a 24 billion lire loss to the Holy See because of exchange fluctuations.

Until recently, the Holy See's investment strategy (as opposed to its cash management) has been extremely conservative. When the Vatican bought stock or real estate, it tended to hold on to the investment for decades. When the first audit was being done, some investments had been purchased so long ago and the records were so poorly kept that no one knew what had been paid for them.

For example, until the early 1990s the Vatican held on to gold it had bought as early as the 1930s, partly in the belief that all states must hold gold and partly as a hedge against currency fluctuation when most of the Vatican's money and investments were in lire. The gold was held at the Federal Reserve Bank of New York. The problem with gold is that it produces no income. In the early 1990s, at the urging of Cardinal Szoka and others, the Vatican began selling its gold and buying other investments. In January 1992 it held 235,765 ounces of gold valued at $83 million. By the end of the year this was down to 139,302 ounces, and by the end of 1993 it was down to 47,772 ounces.[26]

The timing of the gold sales is much debated in the Vatican, with Monday morning quarterbacks claiming that Cardinal Szoka pushed for a quick sale when the market was down. There is no question that the Vatican could have done better if it had not sold 40 percent of its gold holdings during 1992. Russia and Middle Eastern countries were selling gold at the same time, which brought down the price. In addition, there was a gold rally in 1993, sparked by George Soros buying a stake in Newmont Mining, when gold climbed 23 percent from its lows at the end of 1992. The Vatican continued to sell gold in 1993 when prices improved. In 1994 it held on to the remainder of its gold and lost $384,000 because of price declines, giving support to those who wanted to sell.

Although the timing of the gold sales was not perfect, the Vatican appears to have not done badly. "The delegate here is very clever about the sale of gold," reports Monsignor Devine. "He sells futures only in it. We got a very good average price. He deserves lots of credit for that. I wouldn't have done it that way. I would have just dumped it and gotten the money working."

Whether selling gold makes sense depends on where the Holy See invests the proceeds. The investment strategy of the Vatican has become more professional under Cardinal Castillo, who brought in Msgr. Robert Devine as a consultant to the second section of APSA which manages the Holy See's portfolio. As a layman, Monsignor Devine had owned a successful investment firm in Canada, which he sold to Merrill Lynch before entering the seminary. "Because of the size of the account and the fact that we are in the Vatican," reports Monsignor Devine, "we attract excellent advisers in the form of investment bankers and stockbrokers. Anyone of any size in the business would like to have an account with the Vatican. As a result of this, we can pick brains from across the world and get very good investment advice. And so we meet with fair success." In purchasing stocks and bonds, he says, "we deal with all the major investment houses in the world, Merrill Lynch in the States, Barclays

Bank in London, Nomura in Japan. People who underwrite and distribute securities."

The Vatican follows an internationally diversified investment policy for its portfolio of stocks and bonds, valued at 495 billion lire at the end of 1994. A third of its bonds and stocks were in lire, while 30 percent were in dollars (in 1988, 50 percent of the portfolio was in the Milan stock exchange and only 20 percent in the New York Stock Exchange).[27] The Vatican also had bonds in German marks, Swiss francs, and other currencies in 1994. Monsignor Devine would like to see even fewer investments in Italy. "There are too many things owned in Italy by the church in real estate and churches and all sorts of other things," he comments. "Any extra dollar that can be taken out of Italy for investment should be taken out of Italy."

Surprisingly, given John Paul's interest in Eastern Europe, the Holy See has no investments there. "We have stayed away because we can't get a handle on investing in Eastern Europe," explains Monsignor Devine. "The nature of the patrimony carries with it a great trust. So, we cannot speculate. We cannot move in and say, let's take a chance on this. So we'll probably miss all sorts of good buying opportunities because of that. We don't take chances. Buy only proven companies and industries that are sound." For the same reasons, investments in developing countries are limited. "We have participation in the emerging world, in Latin America, Mexico, and Asia," he reports. "But the majority certainly are in the established world, where the investment can be identified clearly and where there's a history."

The Vatican avoids some investments. "We cannot buy into drug companies that are producing birth control devices," explains Monsignor Devine. "We're very much aware of the moral teachings of the church, which we apply in our investments." When newspapers reported that a company was negotiating to sell engines to China for military use, Monsignor Devine took notice. "If this comes about, that company becomes a candidate for sale of course."

The portfolio is predominantly bonds (375 billion lire) as opposed to stocks (120 billion lire), although the stock figures are somewhat misleading since they are listed at purchase price. "We stay liquid," explains Monsignor Devine. "There's criticism of that mix, and frankly, I'm critical of it. I think we should have a larger equity position. For the past 40 months, the stock markets of the world have gone almost steadily up [the interview was on May 31, 1994]. We should have had a stronger equity position. I was screaming that and preaching that, but things move slowly here." On the other hand, the Vatican's conservative strategy of investing in gold and bonds reduced its losses from the October 1987 crash of the stock market.[28]

"We manage our own funds here," he continued. "We have to keep on top of all markets," using Blumbergs and other sources of financial information. "We're a little short of sophisticated staff here for that. The cost is prohibitive. We can't compete with the leading investment houses for personnel. So it makes it really difficult. The people who are managing at the moment are Italians, many of whom have been here for a number of years. They are very good people, very hard-working, and very devoted to the church, the Vatican. But there is generally a lack of professionalism." The Vatican salary structure makes it difficult for APSA to pay competitive salaries for professional staff. The IOR, on the other hand, does not have to observe the Vatican salary scale.

APSA has a committee of outside consultants that offer their services free. Members have included the presidents of Merrill Lynch, Barclays Bank, Allied Signal, and others from Italian, French, and Swiss financial institutions and businesses. They meet twice a year to review what APSA has done and make recommendations. Since some of these firms do business with the Vatican, one wonders about the potential for conflict of interest. No one else outside APSA appears to review its investment program, so it is impossible to tell how its results compare with various financial indices. The council of cardinals responsible for overseeing the finances of the Holy See has had enough trouble dealing with budgets and audits, and has not yet looked at investments. The net revenues from stocks, bonds, and currency fluctuations were 90 billion lire in 1993 and 31 billion lire in 1994. The decline in income was caused primarily by the swing from 30 billion lire in currency exchange profits in 1993 to 24 billion in losses in 1994.

The Holy See also has real estate investments around the world that were valued on the books at about 781 million lire at the end of 1994. The outside auditors could not verify this number because independent appraisals were not available.[29] This was the only qualification the auditors gave in their opinion that the financial report of the Holy See followed appropriate accounting principles. The prefecture believes that the current value of the real estate is much higher than that listed. Buildings in Italy, for example, are estimated to be worth 1,150 billion lire and those abroad approximately 700 billion lire. The net revenues in 1994 from all the Holy See's real estate investments amounted to 19 billion lire.

Included in the assets of the Holy See are funds dedicated for particular uses because of the will of the donor or other reasons. For example, the Congregation for the Evangelization of Peoples, once known as the Congregation for the Propagation of the Faith (Propaganda Fide), has an endowment and a staff that administers it. At the end of 1994, the congregation had 93 billion lire in securities, 11 billion lire in cash, and an unknown amount of investment property (the Congregation for the Oriental Churches also has an endowment, but a much smaller one). Propaganda's revenues (26 billion lire in 1993 including non-endowment sources) are used to support its activities, including a college in Rome that houses seminarians from mission countries.[30]

The revenues from the Roman curia and the investment income are not enough to finance the Holy See; donations are also needed. Beginning in 1990, dioceses were required to contribute to the support of the Holy See under the new Code of Canon Law (canon 1271). Just as parishes contribute to the support of diocesan chanceries, dioceses were asked to contribute to the support of the Roman curia. No amount was mandated, but one suggestion was that dioceses give an amount equal to what they contribute to their national episcopal conference. This formula gets more money from rich countries than poor, since rich countries tend to have better financed episcopal conferences. For the United States this contribution would amount to about 17 cents per Catholic. Religious communities of men and women are asked to contribute as well. The Vatican also seeks support from foundations and other sources. In 1994, the Holy See received 24 billion lire from dioceses and 2 billion from religious orders. Another 75 billion lire came from "institutions, foundations, associations, and other entities."

This last source has jumped 73 billion lire in two years. It is not clear from the audit where this money is coming from, but it has kept the Holy See out of the red. Some of this increase may be due to a 1993 accounting change that places gifts from foundations here rather than in Peter's Pence. For example, the Knights of Columbus give the pope about $2 million a year that used to be credited to Peter's Pence. "Other entities" may also include some profits from the Vatican City State and the Vatican bank.

Separate from the budget of the Holy See is the money that comes to the pope from the *Obolo,* known in English as Peter's Pence. The name dates back to ninth-century England, when King Alfred the Great collected a penny tax from each landowner for the pope. Today, Peter's Pence refers to money given to the pope to be used at his discretion. Most of it comes from an annual collection taken up in dioceses around the world, but it also includes money sent directly to the pope in Rome. For example, in 1992, 3,000 Americans mailed unsolicited donations directly to the pope. When letters come with these donations, a selection of them is sent to the pope, but the negative letters are screened out. Sometimes people even hand the pope cash during audiences. "I don't recall a single occasion when the pope has kept the money [for himself]," reports a Vatican official. "And he receives a lot of money in cash."

The pope used to just pass it to anyone in his entourage, but not all of it reached the Peter's Pence office. Now he gives it to his secretary, who hands it to a special security person.

In 1992 Peter's Pence brought in $67 million, of which about $47 million came through dioceses, $11 million from donations sent directly to the Holy See, $3 million from foundations, and $6 million from religious orders. The United States contributed the most with $23 million, followed by Germany with $9.5 million, Italy with $8 million, France with $3 million, and Spain with $2.5 million. The top ten countries contribute 78 percent of the total. Although most of the money comes from the First World, some very large donations come from individuals in the Third World. "Rich people have so much money there," explains a Vatican official, "and sometimes their consciences bother them."

In the years before 1993 when the Holy See was in the red, money from Peter's Pence was often used to cover the deficit. Cardinal John Krol of Philadelphia complained publicly that Peter's Pence was not meant to finance the Roman curia but to allow the pope to support spiritual and charitable works around the world. By redefining Peter's Pence in 1993 to not include gifts from foundations and religious congregations, the Vatican has quietly and permanently redirected some money from Peter's Pence to the support of the Holy See. This accounting change will make future revenues from Peter's Pence look lower than they would have under the older accounting rules.

There is no public report on what the pope does with the money from Peter's Pence, the one source of his money that comes directly from the faithful. The faithful do not seem to mind since the revenue continues to climb, from $27.5 million in 1983 to $67 million in 1993. In the two years it dropped, 1984 and 1990, the first appears to be the result of an accounting change. The second drop appears to be the result of bishops taking money from Peter's Pence to pay their contribution to the support of the Holy See under canon 1271, something they were not supposed to do.[31]

Vatican officials say that most of Peter's Pence today goes to help the church in poor countries. "When the bishops from the poor countries come to see the pope, we are scared to death," explains one Vatican official, "because, at the end of the visit, all of our accounts are empty. Very often we will receive a telephone call from his apartment at 10 o'clock: 'Before 12 o'clock I need ten envelopes with $50,000 each, or $20,000 each.' He is very, very generous. Also when he visits poor countries, we have to make sure that our foreign accounts have plenty of money because everything is used [as gifts] by the pope."

It is not just Third World countries that are helped. When the pope received a £4 to 5 million gift from England, an English bishop asked if some of it could go to the English College in Rome. A Vatican official passed on the request with a recommendation to give 5 or 10 percent to the college. The answer came from the pope, "No, this is too little, at least one half," much to the surprise and delight of the English College.

The pope also gives money through the Council Cor Unum to alleviate suffering from natural or man-made disasters. This money is not usually from Peter's Pence, but from money specifically given to the pope to aid disaster areas. In 1994, for example, the pope gave $5 million to help victims of disasters. Almost a fifth went to help orphans and refugees in and around Rwanda, and about $436,000 went to help people in the former Yugoslavia. Cor Unum works together with other Catholic agencies like Caritas and Catholic Relief Services that contribute hundreds of millions of dollars in disaster relief. Coordination of these agencies is accomplished through communication and voluntary agreements rather than through Roman mandates.

Papal finances are better managed today than they have been for many years. This resulted from John Paul's decision to bring in Cardinal Szoka to head up the Prefecture for the Economic Affairs of the Holy See and Cardinal Castillo to head up APSA, Vatican City, and the Vatican bank. John Paul also approved the reorganization of the Vatican bank, which has given it more professional leadership and supervision. Improved financial procedures and reporting practices have been put into place, and these reforms made by Cardinals Szoka and Castillo will be difficult to reverse. "It's very difficult to get anything done in the Vatican because you're dealing with an ancient public service," comments Monsignor Devine. "But if you do accomplish anything, you can be confident no one will touch it for at least 400 years. There are very few jobs that offer that kind of satisfaction."

The management of Vatican finances still has many areas that are in need of improvement, as the two cardinals would be the first to admit. With the financial support of American Catholic foundations, they have had professional management consultants examine parts of their operations and make recommendations. These foundations have made it clear that they will not fund studies that go nowhere—they want to see results. Cardinal Szoka fully implemented the recommendations for his prefecture, as did Cardinal Castillo for the study of the supermarket in Vatican City.

But reorganization plans, such as the one for APSA, or technological improvements that threaten jobs are difficult to implement. In an extreme example of sensitivity to anything that threatens jobs, the Vatican press office decided to delay online distribution of press bulletins until two hours after "hard copy" had been given to the Vatican press corps. The press office was concerned that too speedy delivery directly to news organizations would short-circuit some reporters working in the press room, perhaps threatening their jobs.[32] And these were not even Vatican employees!

Given the clerical nature of church governance and the lack of training of clerics in finances, the most critical financial problem for the pope is to find cardinals with the ability and the willingness to manage Vatican finances. Cardinal Castillo, for example, was holding down three major financial positions until June 1995: chairman of the commission of cardinals overseeing the Vatican bank, president of the Vatican City State, and president of APSA. Any one of these could have been a full-time job. Although lay financial experts can be hired, someone must understand finances at least enough to hire the right people to do the job. Popes will continue to need cardinals capable of overseeing professional financial managers and willing to push financial reforms on a reluctant bureaucracy. Cardinals Szoka and Castillo have done this, but a system that depends on individuals in key positions is inherently unstable.

There is also a need for more coordination among the Vatican agencies dealing with finances. "Too many people in the Vatican are playing banker," complained one Vatican official. APSA, the IOR, the Congregation for the Evangelization of Peoples, and the Secretariat of State all seem to have money that they manage. Centralizing the finances could result in more professional management, but it could also put everything at risk under one set of managers. At a minimum there should be more communication among the financial offices. For example, the Vatican bank, APSA, and the Congregation for the Evangelization of Peoples are all involved in investments, yet the personnel of these organizations are not sharing information or helping each other. One might be selling stock in a company at the same time that the other is buying. Likewise, APSA and the Congregation for the Evangelization of Peoples are both managing rental properties in Rome.

Better coordination requires less secrecy. The pope will always need the ability to keep confidential the sources and destination of some of his funds as long as there are political regimes antagonistic to the church. But communication among Vatican offices is essential to better coordination. For example, the pope is giving millions of dollars from Peter's Pence to Third World bishops, but there is no coordination between him and the mission societies under the Congregation for the Evangelization of Peoples that gave about $113 million to help the Third World missions in 1994 (another $8 million was distributed to Oriental churches by the Congregation for the Oriental Churches). These organizations have a formal process for distributing their money. For example, the Society for the Propagation of the Faith gives each diocese $25,000 to $60,000 a year as an ordinary subsidy. Dioceses can also request extraordinary grants that are reviewed by Propagation's staff and voted on by an assembly of about 100 national directors. "Last year we had roughly one-third the amount that was needed," reports Msgr. Bernard Prince, general secretary of the Propagation of the Faith. "So we don't accept all the projects and we don't fund them totally."

Keeping financial information secret invites speculation, rumors, and distrust. The review of the Holy See's finances by outside auditors and the distribution of the audit to all the bishops of the world have begun to restore confidence in the Vatican's financial management. Distribution of the audits of the Vatican City State and the Vatican bank would further this process of confidence building. Some argue that outside auditors are not needed and that the Prefecture for the Economic Affairs of the Holy See can do the job itself. But the credibility of the prefecture, which under Cardinal Szoka is high, is very dependent on who is the prefect. Outside auditors provide a check on Vatican officials and ensure that the reports will be believed by the public.

Besides building confidence, greater disclosure would also benefit the pope and other church officials, who have little financial expertise, by allowing more Catholic business and financial experts to review the work of the Vatican financial personnel. For example, if the results of the Vatican investment portfolio were published, they could be compared with international mutual funds and financial indices. If the Vatican personnel are doing better than average, they should be congratulated. If not, questions should be asked.

Finally, there remains the question of just how good a financial manager the Vatican should be. One Vatican official joked that the Vatican museum was becoming the Vatican boutique because of the numerous gift and souvenir shops located there. On the other hand, the Vatican bookstore is tucked away in an unobtrusive corner of St. Peter's Square, with very limited floor space. With a better location, more floor space, and merchandise attractive to tourists and pilgrims, the bookstore would make a lot more money. But would this give the impression that the money changers had taken over the temple court?

Some, even within the Vatican, would argue that the Vatican bank is no longer needed and that commercial banks can provide the same services to the Vatican and to other religious institutions. Some believe the investments of the Vatican, especially the pension fund, should be managed by outside firms rather than by Vatican personnel. Some critics would prefer a poor papacy without stores and investments, which would be totally dependent on the free offerings of the faithful. Such Franciscan poverty would result in a one-time distribution of the assets to the poor, but afterward the Vatican and the poor churches it helps would be dependent on contributions each year from the richer countries of North America and Western Europe. In addition, the Vatican has contractual and moral obligations to its employees for salaries, health care, and pensions. The Vatican must have a pension fund and other reserves to meet these obligations.

The "Consolidated Financial Statements of the Holy See" reports net assets of 750 billion lire at the end of 1994, or about $460 million. Because of undervalued real estate and the listing of stocks at cost, the real market value of these assets is probably much higher. One can only speculate what the figures would look like with the inclusion of the Vatican City and Vatican bank net assets. Perhaps they would add another $500 million to $1 billion. In 1994, thirty-two American colleges and universities had endowments larger than the net assets of the Holy See.[33]

As long as the papacy lasts, popes will need money for salaries, buildings (churches, housing, and offices), and other expenses as well as for their charities. Money has to be raised and spent. It is not something that popes like to give much attention to, but when financial problems do occur, the pope feels them.

~ 9

Outside the Vatican

A POPE'S WORST NIGHTMARE is a bishop, like Archbishop Marcel Lefebvre, who cuts himself loose from the college of bishops and goes into schism. Just as scary are dissident theologians, like Martin Luther, whose ideas can fracture the unity of the church for centuries. If these are not enough to make the pope lose his sleep, there are always secular rulers like Henry IV of Germany, Henry VIII of England, Napoleon, Hitler, or Stalin who can make life excruciatingly difficult for the church. On the other hand, bishops, theologians, and secular rulers who are supportive of papal initiatives are a special blessing. Any occupant of the chair of Peter cannot ignore the world outside the Vatican. An essential part of the papal ministry is encouraging and supporting friends while trying to limit the damage from loose cannons and enemies.

The Roman curia and the Holy See's representatives around the world are essential tools of the pope for dealing with the world outside the Vatican. Papal representatives to local governments and churches are called nuncios. They are accepted and accredited as ambassadors by practically every country in the world except China and Vietnam. In many Catholic countries the nuncio is automatically the dean of the diplomatic corps. The nuncios represent the Holy See, not the Vatican City State. Vatican officials argue that under international law and tradition, the pope as head of the Catholic church would have the right to nuncios even if he did not rule the Vatican City State.[1]

Nuncios, who are archbishops, are the eyes and ears of the Holy See in a country. They are almost always from the Vatican diplomatic service and graduates of the Pontifical Ecclesiastical Academy. Most of the papal representatives are still Italian, although the percentage of Italians has dropped from 76 percent in 1967 to 60 percent in 1990.[2] Usually they have about twenty-five to thirty years' experience in nunciatures around the world before their first appointment as a nuncio to a small country. Those who make it to the major capitals either have done a good job or have powerful friends in the Vatican. To fill a vacancy at a nunciature, the secretary of state presents a list of three names to the pope after they have been examined by the Commission for Personnel in the Secretariat of State, which is headed by the sostituto and includes the secretary and undersecretary of state for relations with states, the delegate for papal representatives, and the secretaries from the congregations for Bishops and for the Evangelization of Peoples.

Before going to a new country, the nuncio receives detailed instructions from the Secretariat of State and from the other dicasteries of the Roman curia "because every congregation is following the church in the various countries," explains Msgr. Claudio Celli, undersecretary for relations with states. "So when the nuncio is leaving we give to him a dossier in which every congregation is reminding him of the problems that are pending in that country or some main questions that he must follow attentively." These issues would deal with the state, with the bishops' conference, or with individual bishops.

With no interest in trade or military alliances, the Vatican focuses its diplomatic efforts with states on the good of the local church (especially its religious freedom) and the foreign policy goals of the Holy See, which center on human rights, economic justice, and peace. But most of the nuncios' work is with local churches, not local governments. In dealing with local churches, the nuncios play an extremely important role in fostering union with the Holy See, especially through the appointment of bishops.

Selection of Bishops

In the first centuries of the church, the local bishop was chosen by and from the people. In the ideal, the people of the community gathered in the cathedral where they prayed and selected a holy and talented man to lead them. In practice, irreconcilable factions supporting opposing candidates could clash, sometimes violently splitting the community. Hired thugs, demagogues, local powerful families, and outright bribery could sway an illiterate populace that had little experience in democratic processes.

As time went on, the selection process evolved to include the clergy, the people, and the provincial bishops. Pope Leo I (440–461) described the ideal by saying that no one could be a bishop unless he was elected by the clergy, accepted by his people, and consecrated by the bishops of his province. The clergy knew the candidates better than the populace and were less likely to resolve their disputes by recourse to arms. Most important, they would have to work closely with the bishop once he was elected. Often the electors were limited to a portion of the clergy, for example, the canons of the cathedral.

At the same time, since he was to be the bishop of the community, he had to be acceptable to the people. The clergy's candidate would be presented to the people, who would normally indicate their approval by cheering. If they booed, the clergy might have to try again. To become a bishop, the candidate had to be consecrated by the bishops of his province under the leadership of the metropolitan archbishop. If he was unacceptable because of heresy or immorality or some other fault, the bishops could refuse to ordain him. Once consecrated, the bishop would usually notify the bishop of Rome with whom he wished to maintain communion. After the Byzantine empire lost control of the West, the pope often became the judge between rival candidates claiming the same see.

This process provided a good system of checks and balances until the episcopacy became not only a religious office but an important economic and political office coveted by secular leaders who intervened to get their candidates made bishops. Especially during periods of crisis and disorder, local rulers would step in and force their candidates into the episcopal offices. Thus in 1016, Fulbert of Chartres writes, "How can one speak of election where a person is imposed by the prince, so that neither clergy nor people, let alone the bishops, can envisage any other candidates?"[3]

In 1073 Gregory VII was elected as a reforming pope. His goal was to root out moral abuses in the church and free it from political control. His view of the papacy included its absolute supremacy over temporal and spiritual leaders with the right to depose them. He legislated various church reforms (against clerical marriage and simony) and was fairly successful in imposing those reforms in France and Germany. He claimed the right to supervise episcopal elections and to judge disputed elections. He also removed corrupt bishops and replaced them with men more sympathetic to his agenda of reform.

Where Gregory VII got into trouble was over lay investiture of bishops, which brought him into conflict with Henry IV of Germany. When Henry appointed his own bishops in Germany and Italy, Gregory took him to task. Henry responded by convening a synod of German bishops that voted to depose the pope in 1076. Pope Gregory excommunicated Henry, suspended him as king, and released his subjects from obedience to him. Henry was forced to ask forgiveness from the pope and to do penance at Canossa, but seven years later the king got even by occupying Rome and installing an anti-pope. Pope Gregory fled Rome and died in exile.

Through the centuries, control over the appointment of bishops went back and forth between church and civil leaders. Kings wanted to appoint as bishops men from noble families who would use the church's wealth and power to support the king politically and militarily. These bishops were often more interested in money, politics, and pleasure than in their flock. When the cathedral chapter was free to elect the bishop, church politics could also be ugly and divisive. Factions would divide the chapter, and this sometimes resulted in lengthy vacancies. Because of conflicts within the chapter or conflicts with the king, the local church often turned to the papacy for arbitration or help.

Usually popes were better at picking bishops than kings, but corrupt popes sold benefices or exchanged them for military or political support for the papal states. The sale of benefices was a major source of revenue for the Avignon papacy. And at the time of Spanish expansion into the Americas and Asia, the popes gave the Spanish crown extensive power over the church in colonial territories in exchange for support of its missionary efforts. But whether reformed or corrupt, the papacy usually saw the desirability of having the greatest possible role in the appointment of bishops and worked to have the filling of bishoprics reserved to the Holy See. After a heated debate, the Council of Trent in 1563 mandated that the chapter would send the names of candidates to Rome, but that the pope would appoint the bishop.[4] Despite Trent, secular rulers were not willing to give up their role in the selection of bishops. Absolute monarchs from the sixteenth to eighteenth centuries demanded the right to nominate or approve nominees.

When the thirteen American colonies gained their independence from England, the papal nuncio in Paris approached the American ambassador, Benjamin Franklin, to see about the establishment of a diocese. When Ambassador Franklin asked the Continental Congress for instructions, he was told not to have any discussions with the nuncio because this was a purely religious matter outside the jurisdiction of the government. Happily surprised by this response, the Vatican approved the clergy's election of John Carroll as the first bishop of Baltimore. Carroll was from a prominent Maryland family that supported the revolution. His cousin, Charles Carroll of Carrollton, signed the Declaration of Independence. Ambassador Franklin, despite his instructions, put in a good word with the nuncio for Father Carroll, who was a close friend. They had traveled together to Canada in a failed attempt to get the Canadians to join the rebellion. When Franklin fell ill on the return trip, Father Carroll had nursed him.

It was only with the fall of the Catholic monarchies that the church began to gain a similar independence from political control in Europe and Latin America. Since the church was usually on the losing side of these revolutions, the new secular authorities often stripped the church of its property and institutions. Restrictions on the appointment of bishops continued for some time because of the fear that bishops would use their moral and political influence with the people against the government. In most cases, the only remnant of state involvement today is the right of some governments to be notified before the announcement of the appointment of a new bishop. But in China and Vietnam, bishops still cannot be appointed without government approval. Describing the situation in Vietnam, Msgr. Claudio Celli, undersecretary for relations with states, said in an interview on April 15, 1994: "Before presenting the candidate to the Holy Father for appointment, we must request the approval of the government. Some days ago the ambassador came to tell me that the government was not agreeable about the candidate. We can do nothing. In a country like Vietnam, you can appoint a bishop, but this man cannot be ordained because every activity of the church is under government control and [requires] the permission of the government. The secret police are following things very attentively."

From the end of the nineteenth century, a principal goal of Vatican diplomacy was to establish the independence of the pope in the appointment of bishops. In negotiating concordats, governments were asked to give up any role in the appointment of bishops. As the principle of religious freedom became more widely accepted, the papacy was increasingly successful in getting its way except under Fascist and Communist regimes. Since the local church and bishops were normally not involved in these diplomatic negotiations, little concern was given to the rights of the local church in the selection of bishops. Thus papal nuncios rather than the local church nominated candidates for appointment by the pope, and the role of the local church became purely consultative. The 1917 Code of Canon Law made this explicit by stating that the pope appoints Latin-rite bishops and that rights of chapters or others in the process are merely a concession.

Latin-rite bishops are thus appointed by the pope, and they normally stay in office until they die or reach seventy-five years of age.[5] According to canon law, a bishop must be a Catholic single male, at least thirty-five years of age, and an ordained priest for at least five years. For the appointment of an

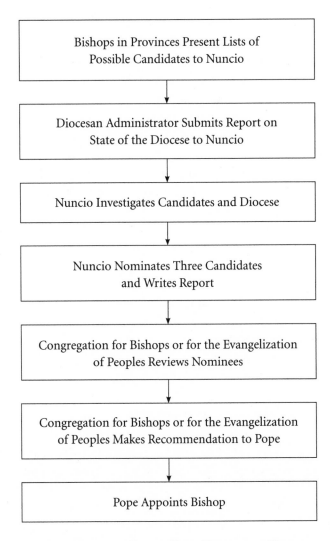

Bishops in Provinces Present Lists of Possible Candidates to Nuncio
Diocesan Administrator Submits Report on State of the Diocese to Nuncio
Nuncio Investigates Candidates and Diocese
Nuncio Nominates Three Candidates and Writes Report
Congregation for Bishops or for the Evangelization of Peoples Reviews Nominees
Congregation for Bishops or for the Evangelization of Peoples Makes Recommendation to Pope
Pope Appoints Bishop

APPOINTMENT OF LATIN RITE DIOCESAN BISHOPS

auxiliary bishop to help a diocesan bishop, the diocesan bishop prepares a terna (a list of three names)[6] and sends it to the nuncio.[7] The nuncio does his investigation and sends the three names on to Rome with his recommendation. For a diocesan bishop, the three names are prepared by the papal nuncio and sent to Rome with his recommendation. The nuncio and the bishop can consult people individually about the candidates, but any public discussion of the candidates is strictly forbidden. Campaigns supporting candidates are forbidden and usually counterproductive. For the appointment of a diocesan bishop, both the nuncio and the retiring bishop (or the temporary administrator if the see is vacant) write a report on the condition of the diocese and the type of bishop needed. They can publicly consult the clergy and people in drawing up their reports, but they rarely do so.

The report and recommendation of the nuncio are crucial. He is responsible for making sure that the priest will be a good bishop and loyal to the pope. To get information about a priest for the terna, the nuncio sends a confidential questionnaire on each candidate to twenty or thirty people who know him. Most of the questions deal with the physical, intellectual, moral, spiritual, social, and priestly characteristics that one would hope for in a bishop. The question on leadership qualities indicates the desire for a pastor with "a fatherly spirit . . . the ability to lead others, to dialogue, to stimulate and receive cooperation . . . to direct and engage in team work; appreciation for the role and the collaboration of religious and laity (both men and women) and for a just share of responsibilities." Not only pastoral skills are sought, but also "a spirit of ecumenism" and "the promotion and defense of human rights."

The questions on orthodoxy and church discipline are crucial. A priest supporting the ordination of women, optional priestly celibacy, or birth control will not be made a bishop. Some critics feel that the Vatican's emphasis on appointing people loyal to Rome has resulted in bishops who are out of touch with their priests and people. Father Andrew Greeley has been most outspoken in his criticism: "With unrelenting consistency in recent years, the Vatican has appointed to the American hierarchy men who are mean-spirited careerists— inept, incompetent, insensitive bureaucrats who are utterly indifferent to their clergy and laity."[8]

In Rome, three Vatican congregations and a council are involved in the selection of new bishops. The Council of Cardinals and Bishops (formerly the Congregation for Relations with States) handles appointments in countries where there is, or was recently, a history of government involvement in the appointment of bishops (mostly in Eastern Europe and the old Soviet Union).[9] The Congregation for the Evangelization of Peoples deals with appointments in mission countries, which include about 970 dioceses or 37 percent of the sees in the world, mostly in Africa and Asia. The Congregation for the Oriental Churches handles elections or appointments in the Oriental churches. These would include Greek or Byzantine churches in union with Rome, such as the Ukrainian and Melkite churches. Finally, the Congregation for Bishops handles all other appointments, that is, those for most of the Latin-rite churches in the Americas and Europe.

The process of selecting bishops for the Oriental churches in their ancient territories (mostly in the Middle East and Eastern Europe) is very different from that for selecting bishops for the Latin rite. The selection of Oriental bishops reflects the more ancient tradition involving local synods. The customs of the various Oriental churches differ. In some churches, a synod of bishops elects a bishop who is then confirmed by the pope. In some cases, it is debated whether the pope has the right to reject the person chosen by the synod. Some synods make the selection from a list of candidates already approved by the pope. Or the synod may present a list of three candidates from whom the pope makes his selection. In the diaspora (for example, in North and South America), the Oriental bishops are usually nominated by the nuncio. In all these cases, the local nuncio carries out an investigation and sends the information to the Congregation for the Oriental Churches, which then advises the pope on the selection. About fifteen episcopal selections are processed each year by the congregation. The work of the congregation is done by the staff and the prefect since the members of the congregation never meet. Some have complained that Rome pushes candidates who oppose the ordination of married men, a practice still permitted in some Oriental churches. Despite Rome's attempts to increase the role of the pope in the selection of Oriental bishops, the process still involves the local churches more than does the process for selecting Latin-rite bishops.

In the Latin church, the process for selecting bishops by the congregations for Bishops and for the Evangelization of Peoples is basically the same, with minor differences.[10] Approximately 51 appointments are processed each year by the Congregation for the Evangelization of Peoples and about 135 by the Congregation for Bishops.[11] A staff person reads the nuncio's report and the entire dossier. "Most of the nuncios are pretty good," said one official. "Nobody is fully objective. But that is taken into consideration." The staff person makes sure that the dossier is complete and that the candidates are viable. If there are any problems, he brings them to the attention of superiors. For example, if there is insufficient information about the candidate's orthodoxy, the nuncio would receive a letter from the prefect asking for more information.

As part of the process, the candidates' names are sent to the Secretariat of State, the Congregation for the Doctrine of the Faith, and Congregation for the Clergy to see if they have any information on them in their files. If the candidate is a religious, the Congregation for Institutes of Consecrated Life would also be asked. Likewise, if he had been a seminary professor or rector, the Congregation for Catholic Education would be asked. These dicasteries would check their files to see if the priest is mentioned. If they have reports that he is a troublemaker or disloyal to the Holy See, his candidacy would be in difficulty.

After the staff person has completed his work and made his recommendation, the appointment is discussed in a staff meeting attended by the prefect, the secretary, and the undersecretary. A staff person has no power, noted one official, "but he does have an awful lot of influence due to the nature of his job and the fact that his superiors cannot be expected to study the whole issue as thoroughly as that person has to."

If everything is in order and the cardinal prefect approves, the appointment process moves forward to the congregation. The nuncio's report plus other documents that the staff considers relevant are bound together in a book and given to each member of the congregation in Rome before the ordinary meeting. Normally this book is about an inch thick. Before the members meet, the same book is sent to the pope by way of the Secretariat of State. The documents are usually not sent to members of the congregation outside Rome, although Cardinal O'Connor receives these documents in New York and telephones in his vote.

Before the appointment goes to the congregation, a cardinal (called a ponente or relator) is chosen by the undersecretary of the congregation. The relator must be capable of reading the language of the correspondence and documents that are made available to him. After reviewing the full dossier, the relator, who is usually a curial cardinal, presents a summary to the other members. As Cardinal John O'Connor describes it, the relator "synthesizes, analyzes, and presents the entire picture" to the rest of the congregation. "The relator also gives his own opinion, his own choice in the terna," another cardinal reports. He might say, "'I think that this man is better for this and this and this reason. And the second one, maybe in the future.'"

Any member of the congregation can be the relator, but some of the members are very busy with other work as prefects of their congregations. "They know [I am busy] and they are kind with me [understanding] that I cannot take them," explains Cardinal Jozef Tomko, a member of the Congregation for Bishops but also prefect of the Congregation for the Evangelization of Peoples. "But sometimes, they give me such things because they say, 'You have this experience.'"

In 1995, the Congregation for Bishops had 37 members, appointed by the pope for five-year renewable terms—31 cardinals and 6 archbishops. Twenty-four of the cardinals are permanently stationed in Rome as part of the Vatican curia. Ex officio members of the congregation include the secretary of state (Angelo Sodano) and prefects of the congregations for the Doctrine of the

Faith (Joseph Ratzinger), for the Clergy (José Sánchez), and for Catholic Education (Pio Laghi). The Congregation for the Evangelization of Peoples has 62 members (47 cardinals and 15 bishops), 21 of whom are cardinals in Rome.

The Congregation for Bishops meets in ordinary sessions about nineteen times a year, or about twice a month from October to June. The meetings, on Thursdays, begin at 9:30 A.M. in the Vatican Apostolic Palace and go for three or four hours. The relator gives his report and the members of the congregation discuss the appointment under the chairmanship of the prefect, Cardinal Bernardin Gantin. The secretary and undersecretary of the congregation are the only staff present. "Generally it is twenty, twenty-five members" present at meetings of the Congregation for Bishops, reports an official. "Sometimes a few less, sometimes a few more." Most members living outside Rome do not attend unless they happen to be in Rome on other business. The Congregation for the Evangelization of Peoples meets about nine times a year, or about once every three to four weeks from October to June. Attendance by members from outside Rome is even lower because so many are from distant and poor dioceses in Africa and Asia.

When outside members "are interested in some particular dossier that is going to be presented," they may make an effort to come "because they are advised in advance what is going to be discussed and they are free to come," according to an official in the Congregation for Bishops. "I try to get there when an American appointment is under consideration," explains Cardinal O'Connor. As a result, he reports attending meetings that consider from 75 to 80 percent of the American appointments. But with only a few weeks' advance notice of the agenda, attending is difficult especially for members living a great distance from Rome. Most American members living outside Rome rarely attend. Cardinal Terence Cooke of New York never attended because he did not understand Italian, the language used in the meetings. Cardinal Humberto Medeiros of Boston attended once or twice a year when he was in Rome for other business. Archbishop Joseph Bernardin did the same when he was a member from 1973 to 1978.

Since the vast majority of those discussing the candidates are from the curia, a Roman perspective comes into play. A candidate who has studied in Rome has an advantage with these cardinals. More than a third of the U.S. bishops and about half of the archbishops have studied in Rome.[12] As early as 1880, a "Roman education was seen as guaranteeing loyalty to Rome."[13] As a student, the candidate would have imbibed Roman culture and tradition, and would have been exposed to the universal church. More important than where he studied would be his views on doctrine, morals, and church discipline, since John Paul considers these elements extremely important in the appointment of bishops.

After the members of the congregation discuss the appointment, they vote. "All of this is recorded and presented to the pope at the end, including the way each person votes," explains a Vatican official. Very often (some estimate 80 to 90 percent of the time) they follow the recommendation of the nuncio. This would especially be true if his views coincided with those of the local hierarchy. But sometimes the congregation recommends the nuncio's second or third choice. Sometimes it rejects the terna altogether and tells the nuncio to present a new one. "Yes, some are sent back," said a Vatican official. "This reflects the pope's concern about the choices."[14]

When Archbishop Jean Jadot was apostolic delegate to the United States from 1973 to 1980, his recommendations at the beginning of his term were usually approved, but toward the end more were rejected. "Some in Rome," reported an official, "thought that some of the bishops appointed during his years in Washington were not completely faithful to the teaching of the church. They spoke poorly of him because they thought some of the appointments . . . [like] Hunthausen and Gerety, were considered to be Jadot's mistakes." Once he was transferred to Rome, Archbishop Jadot was not consulted concerning appointments to the U.S. hierarchy. He is the only papal representative to the United States who was not made a cardinal.

The final step in the appointment process is the weekly Saturday audience between the prefect of the Congregation for Bishops and the pope. The staff prepares a three- to five-page memo on the appointment, which is sent to the pope before the audience. The report gives the background for the appointment, the recommendation of the nuncio, and the votes of each member of the congregation. The prefect summarizes the discussions of the congregation, gives his recommendation, and reports any dissenting opinions and votes.

Popes recognize that the appointment of bishops is extremely important. An official who had been in the Vatican since 1977 reported that John Paul "takes a deep and personal interest in the appointment of bishops, especially to the larger sees. It is a major theme on his agenda."[15] The pope's travels give him personal knowledge of some dioceses and their needs. He also gets to know the bishops during these visits and during their ad limina visits to Rome. In addition, he meets with papal nuncios when they visit Rome.[16]

On the other hand, John Paul appoints almost 200 bishops a year. With many other things to do and with only a limited amount of time, he must depend on the congregation's recommendations for most of these appointments. If all of his advisers agree, the decision is normally easy. If the congregation is divided or if the local bishops disagree with the nuncio, the pope has to choose whom he will follow. Cardinal O'Connor reports that the "overwhelming percentage of the congregation's recommendations are accepted by the pope." If the pope consistently did not like the nominees, he would replace the people on the congregation.

Most important is the general orientation and direction that the pope gives to the congregation, the nuncio, and the bishops. For example, Paul VI and the prefect of the Congregation of Bishops told Archbishop Jadot to appoint pastoral bishops in the United States, which had a reputation for having bishops who were corporate managers and not pastors. He also looked for priests who were respected by their peers since this was a time of conflict between bishops and priests.

John Paul II has other priorities. In a 1983 address to American bishops in Rome for their ad limina visit, he stressed unity and fidelity to the magisterium when speaking about the appointment of bishops. He said that the bishops should look for "priests who have already proven themselves as *teachers of the faith as it is proclaimed by the magisterium of the church,* and who, in the words of St. Paul's pastoral advice to Titus, 'hold fast to the authentic message.'"

He told the bishops,

> It is important for the episcopal candidate, as for the bishop himself, to be *a sign of the unity of the universal church* . . . Never is the unity of the local church stronger and more secure, never is the ministry of the local bishop more effective than when the local church under the pastoral leadership of the local bishop proclaims in word and deed the universal faith, when it is open in charity to all the needs of the universal church and when it embraces faithfully the church's universal discipline.[17]

The pope has been very successful in finding bishops who reflect his views on women's ordination, clerical celibacy, and birth control. In the United States, he has been successful in finding bishops who also share his social justice agenda. In other parts of the world, like Latin America, traditional theological views often go hand in hand with conservative political views. As a result, although these bishops reflect the pope's views on the church, they are less enthusiastic about social justice and human rights. In addition, by stressing fidelity to the pope over sensitivity to local concerns, the Vatican's choices of bishops have in many cases alienated the local church from Rome rather than fostered unity. In Austria, the Netherlands, Switzerland, Germany, and other countries there have been loud public protests from priests and the people over the appointment of some bishops. In Germany and Austria a petition was circulated that gathered millions of signatures protesting Vatican policy.

Under the current system, the pope is getting bishops who support his policies, but he is not getting bishops capable of winning over their people. European and American theologians and canonists have objected to the highly centralized character of the current appointment process. A system needs to be devised that gives greater influence to local bishops and local churches. For example, the priests' council (or chapter) of a vacant see and the bishops of the province or region should be allowed to comment on the nuncio's terna. This could be a first step toward the day when these bodies would actually draw up the terna. If Rome cannot trust the priests' council of a diocese or the bishops of a province, then the state of the church is in serious trouble.

After appointing a bishop, the Vatican keeps in touch with him through the nuncio in his country, who is the normal channel of communication between the Vatican and the local bishops. The Vatican sends scores of documents and letters through the nuncios to episcopal conferences every year. These conferences then copy and distribute the documents among their members. Individual bishops also correspond with the Vatican on specific issues; sometimes this is done through the nuncio and sometimes directly with a dicastery. Normally, a dicastery keeps the nuncio informed of its dealings with a local church.

Bishops and the Vatican

Every bishop in the world must also come to Rome every five years to see the pope. This is referred to as an "ad limina" visit, short for *ad limina apostolorum* (to the thresholds of the apostles), because the visiting bishop must pray at the tombs of the Apostles Peter and Paul.[18] This ad limina visit is an important opportunity for the pope and the Roman curia to interact with bishops from around the world. A bishop normally comes to Rome with the other bishops of his episcopal conference, but large conferences visit in regional groups rather than all at once.

Before the visit each bishop and his staff fill out a detailed questionnaire on the state of his diocese.[19] This quinquennial report is divided into thirteen sections asking for information on (1) the pastoral and administrative organization of the diocese, (2) the general religious situation, (3) the economic situation of the diocese, (4) liturgical and sacramental practice, (5) the clergy, (6) religious and secular institutes, (7) cooperation with the missions, (8) seminaries and universities, (9) Catholic education, (10) the life and apostolic action of the laity, (11) ecumenism, (12) social assistance, and (13) other pastoral questions. In addition, the report asks for statistical data on advisory councils, the tribunal, publications, the clergy, and educational institutions. The report goes to the Congregation for Bishops, which distributes pertinent parts to other dicasteries. For example, the material on schools and seminaries would go to the Congregation for Catholic Education.

Each bishop visiting Rome meets with the pope for 15 minutes. The meeting is of important spiritual significance to most bishops and is the high point of their visit, but it is of little practical value, given the shortness of the meeting. Early in his pontificate, John Paul II asked bishops to point out on a map the location of their dioceses. He then asked them about the number of priests and other information that was already in their report. This colloquy was not very satisfying for the bishops, and a few simply took the initiative and brought up the one or two points they wanted to make with the pope. Later in his pontificate, when a papal commission was examining religious life in the United States, the pope asked each American bishop how he was getting along with the religious in his diocese. The pope was surprised by the positive response from the bishops since he had heard many negative reports about American women religious. Sometimes the pope has something very specific to say to a bishop. For example, Pope Paul VI told Archbishop James Casey of Denver during his ad limina visit to tell his auxiliary, Bishop George Evans, to stop publicly supporting the ordination of women. John Paul II told one Ukrainian bishop to get a haircut.

John Paul II also shares a meal with small groups of bishops from the same country where a more informal exchange can take place over an hour and a half to two hours. "There were no topics barred," says one American archbishop. "We didn't get organized to have prepared topics, they just came up casually. The Holy Father is open to discussing any topic." John Paul is a gracious host and attentive listener, but he also pounded on the table for emphasis when the question of women's ordination came up at one lunch.

The pope is the center of attention at these gatherings, but "he made sure that every person spoke," says Archbishop Francis Hurley of Anchorage in describing the lunch he attended in 1983. As they sat down, the pope identified each bishop by the name of his diocese. Then, the archbishop recalls,

We went through an unstructured conversation.

The pope said, "I have learned two new words: undocumented and unchurched." So we talked about that and pointed out that unchurched in the U.S. does not mean atheistic. We were able to point out to him that atheism is not a major force in the U.S. in a formal way.

We talked about the poor, what do we do about the poor. I said, "One of the things is to work cooperatively with government, because we do not have the funds ourselves." I gave a quick reference to my experience. He wanted to know about working with the government.[20]

During the ad limina visit, the pope gives at least one major speech to the bishops that provides a good indication of his views on the church in their nation. When the American bishops asked the pope what he thought of the American church, the pope responded, "Read my ad limina talks." In his talks to the American bishops, Paul VI (and later John Paul II) discouraged the use of general absolution and insisted that first confession take place before first communion. Paul VI repeated a statement he had made to other bishops of the world: "The faithful would be rightly shocked that obvious abuses are tolerated by those who have received the charge of the episcopate, which stands for, since the earliest days of the church, vigilance and unity." He congratulated them on their pro-life work and their support of natural family planning.

In his addresses to the American hierarchy, John Paul II has stressed fidelity to doctrine and church discipline.[21] Quoting John XXIII, he said that the great concern of Vatican II and "my own deepest hope" was "that the sacred deposit of Christian doctrine should be more effectively guarded and taught." His second hope was "for the preservation of the great discipline of the church." He went on to say it was his "ardent desire today that a new emphasis on the importance of doctrine and discipline will be the postconciliar contribution of your seminaries." Specifically, the pope wanted the bishops to proclaim "the indissolubility of marriage . . . the incompatibility of premarital sex and homosexual activity with God's plan . . . the unpopular truth that artificial birth control is against God's law" and "the rights of the unborn, the weak, the handicapped, the poor and the aged." The bishop must also explain the church's teaching on the exclusion of women from priestly ordination and "give proof of his pastoral ability and leadership by withdrawing all support from individuals or groups who in the name of progress or compassion, or for other alleged reason, promote the ordination of women to the priesthood." The pope has also commended the bishops for their concern for the needy through their social service agencies.

The bishops also visit curial offices during their ad limina visit. If there is a large number of bishops, as when the U.S. bishops come, they will divide up the dicasteries with bishops going as a group to those in which they have more interest. Some offices make an effort to review the quinquennial reports before the bishops come so that they can respond to them. Before visiting the dicasteries, some bishops' conferences send written questions to indicate the areas they are interested in discussing. Most offices give presentations on their work by the prefect, the secretary, or a staff person. If the official does not know the language of the visitors, a congregation staff person or one of the visiting bishops translates. Some Americans have complained that these "show and tell" presentations leave little time for questions or input from the visiting bishops as they run from office to office. In some offices, bishops feel that if they raise questions they will be noted down as troublemakers, but in other offices a good interchange can occur. For the dicasteries, these are time-consuming events. Some staff members feel the visits are a distraction from their real work, while other staff see the visits as opportunities to get the bishops interested in the issues of concern to the dicastery.

Individual bishops also visit those dicasteries with which they have pending business to find out where the congregation stands. For a bishop, the key curia offices are the Congregation for Bishops (if he wants an auxiliary, wants his diocese divided, or wants to be promoted), the Congregation for the Doctrine of the Faith (if he or someone in his diocese has written or said anything controversial), the Congregation for Catholic Education (if he has a seminary), the Congregation for the Clergy (if an appeal has been made on the bishop's decision to close a parish or suspend a priest), the Congregation for Consecrated Life (if he has a dispute with a religious community), and the Roman Rota (if his tribunal gets overruled frequently on the granting of annulments). For missionary bishops, the Congregation for the Evangelization of Peoples is important for diocesan business and as a source of money. Other offices (dealing with refugees, ecumenism, justice, family, or laity) might be visited because of the particular interests of the bishop or the issues of his diocese.

Some bishops approach these congregations because they are required by canon law to get their permission before doing certain things. For example, if a U.S. bishop wants to alienate church property valued at more than $3 million, he needs the approval of the Congregation for the Clergy.[22] Likewise, if he is trying to help a resigned priest get laicized so he can get married, this would have to be done by the Congregation for Divine Worship and the Discipline of the Sacraments.

Some bishops come to the attention of these dicasteries because of complaints from priests, religious, or laity in their diocese. American bishops have sometimes been the targets of organized letter writing campaigns that tend to be orchestrated by conservative groups. Some dicasteries do not respond to letters complaining about bishops, especially if they result from an organized campaign. Other prefects believe that anyone who writes should receive a response. The response usually encourages the writers to talk to their pastor or bishop and try to settle the dispute in a charitable fashion. The dicastery will sometimes write the bishop asking for his side of the story. In some cases the dicastery overrules the bishop. For example, the Congregation for the Doctrine of the Faith has told individual bishops to withdraw their imprimatur from catechetical texts it questions. This happened in 1984 with *Christ Among Us,* an adult education text that had sold 1.6 million copies in the United States. In 1995, the congregation demanded the withdrawal of the imprimatur for an AIDS prevention booklet in Scotland.[23]

Decisions overruling a bishop can be very embarrassing and controversial since they often involve contentious public disputes between the bishop and a priest or a parish. For example, the Congregation for the Clergy overruled Cardinal Joseph Bernardin because, it said, he did not follow proper canonical procedures in consulting his priests' council before closing a parish in Chicago. Bishop Donald Wuerl of Pittsburgh was supported by the Congregation for the Clergy when he suspended a priest accused of sexual abuse, but he and the congregation were overruled on appeal to the Apostolic Signatura, the highest church court. Both Cardinal Bernardin and Bishop Wuerl appealed these decisions to the Signatura, and in 1995 the Signatura reversed itself and upheld Bishop Wuerl.[24]

Over the centuries, canon law has developed to protect priests and nondiocesan institutions (like religious communities, hospitals, and schools) from the arbitrary actions of local bishops. This is the church's way of protecting rights of individuals and independent institutions by insisting on due process and the rule of law. Some laws also attempt to protect the patrimony of the diocese from a foolish or dishonest bishop. The laws and procedures are complex and sometimes unique to the church. For example, before he can borrow large amounts of money, or sell or give away valuable church property, the bishop must have the approval of his finance council and his consultors. If a bishop violates the law, Rome can overrule him.

Typically the Vatican does not overrule a bishop on the substance of the case (whether the parish should or should not be closed) but on procedural grounds. Not infrequently, a bishop is not thinking about the danger of an appeal to Rome when he starts a process and does not get good canonical advice. Since the other parties in the dispute often do not know canon law, they fail to appeal or their appeal is rejected because it has not been properly argued. But an adversary backed by a good canon lawyer can tie up a bishop in appeals for years. If the bishop is reversed, he can start the process again. If he follows proper procedure he will probably get his way, but the dispute can take years to resolve.

The ultimate sanction against a bishop is to remove him from his diocese. Such removals are extremely rare. The Vatican will do everything possible to get a bishop to resign voluntarily and quietly rather than publicly remove him. If a bishop is caught in a public moral scandal, he normally resigns. Thus when it became public that Bishop Eamon Casey of Ireland had fathered a child, he resigned, as did Bishop Hansjorg Vogel of Switzerland when he got a woman pregnant in 1995. Likewise, Archbishop Eugene Marino of Atlanta resigned in 1990 and Archbishop Robert Sánchez of Santa Fe resigned in 1993 after it became public that they had been sexually involved with women. Bishop Robert Tracy of Baton Rouge also resigned after being arrested for drunk driving in 1974, but in 1985, when Archbishop John Roach of Minneapolis and St. Paul was arrested on the same charge, he continued in office after dealing with his problem.

Differences between a bishop and the pope over doctrine and church discipline are more complicated. Very few bishops have resigned in protest over papal teaching. Auxiliary Bishop James Shannon of Minneapolis and St. Paul, who objected to *Humanae Vitae,* resigned shortly after the encyclical was issued. In 1995 Bishop Jacques Gaillot of Evreux, France, refused to resign when pressured by the Vatican. He was removed from office after he publicly supported a married clergy, advocated the use of condoms to prevent AIDS, and expressed willingness to bless homosexual unions. He also questioned the church's opposition to RU-486 (a pill to induce abortions) and to the French bishops' support of nuclear deterrence. The Vatican said, "Unfortunately, the prelate has not shown himself to be qualified to exercise the ministry of unity which is the first task of a bishop." Bishop Gaillot was a popular champion of the poor, the homeless, AIDS patients, and other marginal groups in France, and he frequently expressed his views on television. He had often criticized the French government for doing so little for these groups. His removal caused a furor in France, where even some bishops questioned the Vatican's action.

The Vatican took on Bishop Gaillot because he publicly broke ranks on so many issues and because he was out of step with his fellow French bishops. Other bishops who have opposed Vatican policy have usually limited themselves to one issue—birth control, clerical celibacy, or excluding divorced Catholics from Communion. In 1993 three German bishops, including the president of the German bishops' conference, announced that Catholics in unapproved second marriages could receive Communion if they in good conscience thought their first marriage was invalid even though no church courts had annulled the marriage. A year later, they backed down under pressure from the Congregation for the Doctrine of the Faith.[25] Normally bishops disagreeing with the Vatican do it with more diplomacy and less publicity. For example, they will acknowledge that many theologians and lay people disagree with the magisterium on an issue and will say that the church's position needs to be "reexamined" or "discussed." By using such code words they avoid a direct confrontation with the pope and do not alienate their fellow bishops. The Vatican may pressure these bishops to conform, but it could not remove them without causing tremendous disruptions in the church and risking schism.

If a bishop formally breaks with the pope and his brother bishops, it is called a schism.[26] This is a very serious situation because a bishop does not lose his power to ordain priests and bishops even if he breaks with the pope and the college of bishops. When Archbishop Marcel Lefebvre refused to accept the reforms of Vatican II, many conservative French Catholic priests and laity followed him. He soon had his own seminary and about 25,000 followers around the world. Since he was already retired from his mission diocese, Paul VI could not remove him from office but he did suspend him from ministry in 1976, a suspension Lefebvre ignored. Numerous attempts were made to negotiate with Archbishop Lefebvre even when he was contemptuous of the pope and the Vatican. All efforts by John Paul II to appease him failed. By ordaining bishops in 1988 without the approval of the pope, he started a schismatic church and automatically incurred excommunication.[27] These bishops have allowed his schismatic church to continue to ordain priests and bishops after his death in 1991. In the case of Bishop Gaillot, it is uncertain how many liberal French Catholics would have followed him into schism because his conscience prevented him from breaking irrevocably with the church. Between 15,000 and 20,000 people came to his final Mass as bishop of Evreux.

Relations with Theologians

While bishops can avoid problems with the Vatican by using vague language or simply avoiding certain topics, this is more difficult for theologians. As teachers and writers, they are supposed to be clear and precise in expressing their views. Nor can they claim to be misquoted when it is their writings under question. The Vatican is concerned about the views of theologians because their teaching and writings can have a wide impact on the church. Many of them teach future priests, catechists, teachers, and pastoral ministers. Some write for a wide general audience. If their views are out of sync with the Vatican's, there will be theological confusion in the church. The Vatican sees its role as protecting doctrinal unity even if this means disciplining or silencing theologians.

The relations between theologians and the papacy have not always been antagonistic. Often the papacy protected theologians and universities from interference by local bishops and secular authorities. The granting of a papal charter to a university gave it a degree of autonomy and independence. During their early history, universities and theologians felt safer under papal authority than under local kings and bishops. For the most part, the theological community policed itself through debate, peer review, or the internal procedures of the university. The printing press and the Protestant Reformation changed this as the Vatican became more concerned about suppressing heresy wherever it was found. Even so, it was local inquisitions and not Rome that did most of the investigating and the suppressing of heretics.

During the Reformation, when a nation or territory went Protestant, the local universities also became Protestant. In the nineteenth century a new situation developed in Germany where the schools and universities had both Protestant and Catholic departments of theology. Having Catholic theologians appointed by a Protestant or secular state presented a serious problem for both the church and theologians. In 1848 the German bishops ruled that no one could teach the Catholic religion in a state school without a "missio canonica" or canonical mission from the local bishop. After much negotiation with the government, this system was incorporated into concordats between the Holy See and the German government. The purpose of the canonical mission was "to protect the church's teaching office and the freedom of theology from the hostile interference of civil states and secular political control."[28] Although its original purpose was to protect the church and theologians from secular interference, the missio canonica is now used to control theologians. If they teach views contrary to those of the Vatican, their missio can be withdrawn, as happened in 1979 with Hans Küng who challenged papal infallibility. He continued to teach at the University of Tübingen, but as a professor of ecumenical theology, not Catholic theology.

In 1931 similar regulations were applied to pontifical universities chartered by the Holy See, where the university chancellor would grant the authorization to teach (missio canonica). More recently, the 1983 Code of Canon Law (canon 812) has tried to extend these procedures to all Catholic universities by requiring that theologians have a "mandatum docendi," a mandate to teach, from their local bishop. This gradual but persistent attempt to tighten control over

Catholic theologians reflects the Vatican's view that theologians are to serve, not to challenge, the magisterium, a view that is running head on into contemporary understanding of academic freedom. In the United States, the implementation of canon 812 is still under study. The most likely outcome would allow the local bishop to declare (after a due process procedure) that a specific theologian is not teaching Catholic doctrine, but the academic institution would not be required to fire the teacher. Civil lawyers are warning bishops that if they get involved in hiring and promotion decisions, they are bound to be sued. Some also fear that hierarchical intrusions into academic life may put at risk government funding of Catholic universities and colleges.

The Vatican congregations that deal most directly with theologians are the Congregation for the Doctrine of the Faith, the Congregation for Catholic Education, and the Congregation for Consecrated Life (if the theologian is a religious). For example, for a person to be appointed dean or president or to be promoted to full professor (or tenured) in an ecclesiastical faculty chartered by the Holy See, the Congregation for Catholic Education must give its approval by granting a "nihil obstat" (no objection). The congregation routinely refers the names to the Congregation for the Doctrine of the Faith, which checks its files for anything that would be suspicious. The chancellor of the school and the local papal nuncio would also be asked for an opinion. There are only about a half dozen pontifical faculties in the United States. All of them, except the Catholic University of America, are seminaries, and at CUA the bishops on the board of trustees grant the nihil obstat in the name of the Holy See.

"It is impossible, simply impossible to study all those professors" for whom the nihil obstat is requested, explains Cardinal Joseph Ratzinger, prefect of the Congregation for the Doctrine of the Faith. Of the hundreds of names processed each year, about ten or twenty are turned down.[29] "The general rule is we follow the views of the chancellor and the nuncio," says the cardinal. "Only if the two are in hesitation or if the person is known with publications, we study it. But generally the position of the nuncio and the chancellor is decisive." If the congregations are not satisfied, they can demand that the teacher respond in writing to their questions. This process can go on interminably with requests for more clarifications. Ultimately if they are not satisfied, the Congregation for Catholic Education denies approval of the promotion or simply does not respond. In either case the person cannot be promoted.

In discussing the nihil obstat, "it is important to distinguish between teaching in the name of the church and theological research," explains Cardinal Ratzinger.[30]

Theological research must be responsible and, if it will be theological, it must be oriented in the faith. But [it] has more freedom than when I am teaching in the name of the church and my disciples think that this is a teacher from whom they can learn the faith of the church and the theology of the church. So the nihil obstat presupposes that he, in his teaching, will mediate really the faith of the church and give the possibility to learn what is the faith of the church. We cannot give the nihil obstat if we can see from the publications that he has a quite other thinking and that he is not willing, or perhaps also with his conscience is not able, to teach doctrine in conformity with the faith of the church.

Most theologians would acknowledge the right of the Vatican and bishops to admonish and even condemn the ideas and writings of a wayward theologian. But to silence theologians or fire them crosses the line into an authoritarian response that violates academic freedom and is ineffective in the long run by making a martyr of the theologian. Many do not see themselves as church officials teaching "in the name of the church" but as professors by reason of their training and competence. They argue that separating teaching from research is an artificial distinction since good teachers also do research. They believe that a theologian, after accurately and respectfully explaining the views of the pope and bishops, should be able to evaluate them and give his or her own views, especially when it is noninfallible teaching.

Since positions condemned by the hierarchy in the past have later been accepted in the church, theologians argue that greater freedom for discussion and research is essential. Vatican II encouraged this thinking by reversing earlier positions of the Roman magisterium. It "rehabilitated many theologians who had suffered under severe restrictions with regard to their ability to teach and publish," wrote Avery Dulles. "The names of John Courtney Murray, Pierre Teilhard de Chardin, Henri de Lubac, and Yves Congar, all under a cloud of suspicion in the 1950s, suddenly became surrounded with a bright halo of enthusiasm. By its actual practice of revision, the council implicitly taught the legitimacy and even the value of dissent. In effect the council said that the ordinary magisterium of the Roman Pontiff had fallen into error and had unjustly harmed the careers of loyal and able scholars."[31]

Vatican action is not simply against fringe theologians. According to the *National Catholic Reporter*, Michael Buckley and David Hollenbach were not promoted to full professor at their ecclesiastical faculties because the nihil obstat was not granted.[32] Father Buckley is so highly thought of by his peers that he was elected president of the Catholic Theological Society of America.

He has written a number of statements for bishops and was staff to the NCCB Committee on Doctrine. He was even a principal author of an extensive papal statement. Father Hollenbach was so well thought of by the U.S. bishops that he had had a major role in drafting their pastoral letter on the economy. Both ultimately left their ecclesiastical faculties to teach at Boston College, where the nihil obstat is not required. They were quickly made full professors.

In 1983, German-speaking theologians issued the "Cologne Declaration," which eventually was signed by more than 500 theologians. The declaration expresses their distress that many qualified theologians are being denied ecclesiastical permission to teach: "This represents a serious and dangerous interference in the free exercise of scholarly research and teaching, and in the pursuit of theological understanding through dialogue, principles which Vatican II repeatedly emphasized. The power to withhold official permission to teach is being abused; it has become an instrument to discipline theologians . . . Roman intervention in granting or denying permission to teach without consulting the local church risks undermining established and approved areas of juridical procedure."[33] Rome did not change its procedures as a result of this declaration, but it did add the names of the signers to its files.

In addition to reviewing faculty appointments and promotions at ecclesiastical faculties, the Congregation for the Doctrine of the Faith also examines the writings of theologians brought to its attention by bishops, nuncios, or other theologians. Greater attention is given to those theologians who become popular in the mass media and whose books are read by a wide audience. The Vatican also focuses on theologians who deal with certain topics: sexual ethics, birth control, abortion, clerical celibacy, divorce and remarriage, papal authority, episcopal authority, the resurrection, and the divinity of Christ. Liberation theologians in Latin America and Africa have received attention because of their writings on church authority and on class conflict. Asian theologians, writing on the relation between Christianity and Asian religions, have been investigated as well. The Vatican is also concerned about feminist theologians writing on sexuality, patriarchy in the church, and women priests. The content of the theological arguments in these disputes is beyond the scope of this book, but it is important to examine the procedures used by the Vatican and the response to these procedures by the theological community.

If questions are raised about the writings of a theologian, the Congregation for the Doctrine of the Faith opens a file on the theologian that would contain complaint letters, newspaper clippings, and writings by the theologian. "I get many letters from the United States," reports Cardinal Ratzinger, "not only from bishops but from Catholic lay people as well. The United States and

France are the two countries we hear from the most." Although many believe that the letter writers are predominantly conservative, Cardinal Ratzinger says that he thinks "the letters provide us with a reflection of typical Catholics. They are people who are preoccupied with the thought that the Catholic church would remain the Catholic church."[34]

Following procedures published in 1971, the staff and superiors of the congregation meet on Saturday to study the complaint.[35] "If the opinion subjected to examination clearly and certainly contains an error in faith and if at the same time, as a result of its diffusion, proximate harm is threatened for the faithful or already exists, the staff can stipulate that the matter proceed in an extraordinary manner, namely, that the ordinary or ordinaries concerned should be informed at once about the matter and the author should be invited through his own ordinary to correct the error."[36] The ordinary for a diocesan priest or lay person is the local bishop; the ordinary for a religious is the religious's superior.

If the situation is neither pressing nor clear, the congregation follows the "regular procedure." It may or may not notify the author's ordinary, who may or may not notify the person under investigation. The staff designates two experts to examine the theologian's writing and give their opinions on its orthodoxy. The staff also makes a report on the case. Meanwhile, an outside consultant is appointed as a reporter or spokesperson for the author. The reporter reviews the experts' opinions and the staff report and defends the author when the matter is discussed at a meeting of the consultors of the congregation. He may not consult the author who, at this point, may not even know the investigation is taking place. According to the procedures of the congregation, "The task of the reporter for the author is: to point out, in the spirit of truth, the positive aspects of the doctrine of the author and his merits; to cooperate for the correct interpretation of the genuine meaning of the opinions of the said author in their general and their theological context; to respond to the observations of the other reporters and consultors; to express a judgment on the influence of the author's opinions."[37]

The congregation's consultors receive copies of the experts' opinions and other material on the case before their meeting, which is presided over by the secretary of the congregation. After hearing from the reporter for the author, each consultor gives his opinion on the matter under examination. The reporter for the author is then given a chance to respond. After the matter has been discussed, the reporter for the author leaves the room and the consultors give their definitive opinions. The opinions of the experts, the report "for the author," and the views of the consultors are given to the cardinals before an ordinary meeting of the congregation presided over by the prefect. The prefect "sets forth the issue itself, and declares his mind on it; the others follow in order." The prefect communicates the opinions and decision of the congregation to the pope.

If "false and dangerous opinions are found, that is announced to the author's ordinary . . . The propositions which have been declared to be considered false or dangerous are made known to the author himself so that within a month of available time he can transmit his written response."[38] This notification may be the first time that the theologian or his ordinary learns that he has been under investigation. The congregation defends the secrecy of the process by saying that, if the complaints are unfounded, the file can be quietly closed and stored without harming the theologian's reputation. The congregation may also invite the author to Rome to discuss the issues. The author's response and a summary of any discussions that took place are presented to an ordinary session of the congregation so that it can decide the matter. Its decision is submitted to the pope for his approval and then communicated to the theologian's ordinary.

According to Cardinal Ratzinger, the regular procedure described above has been used only five or six times in fifteen years. Normally matters are taken care of through informal procedures and requests for clarifications. Some of the more controversial cases have gone through the whole process: in 1978, Jacques Pohier, O.P., of France;[39] in 1979, Hans Küng of Germany;[40] in 1979, Edward Schillebeeckx, O.P., of the Netherlands;[41] in 1985, Leonardo Boff, O.F.M., of Brazil;[42] in 1986, Charles Curran of the United States;[43] and in 1988, Luis Maria Bermejo, S.J., of India.[44] A Canadian theologian was also under investigation, but he died before the process was completed.

Those who have been subjected to the process object that it is flawed. They say that the accusations brought against the accused are sometimes vague; there is a failure to distinguish between dogma and theological opinion; only experts agreeing with the Vatican are consulted; the reporter for the author is not chosen by the author; and the theologian is not notified of an investigation until after the congregation has concluded that errors are present. "From the very beginning I have pointed out some serious deficiencies in the justice of their process," said Father Curran in 1986. "I have never been told who my accusers are. I have been given no opportunity for counsel. The congregation itself has performed the roles of both accuser and judge."[45]

"The procedures of the Congregation for the Doctrine of the Faith used in investigations of theologians' views fail to honor fundamental human rights and the safeguards regarded in our countries [U.S. and Canada] as absolutely necessary to protect these human rights," reported the Catholic Theological Society of America in 1990.[46] The International Theological Commission, an advisory body to the Congregation for the Doctrine of the Faith, recommended in 1976 that before an official examination of a theologian's writings is initiated, there should be personal conversation as well as inquiries and responses by mail between the theologian and the competent authority. If such a flexible response fails to resolve the question, the congregation should reach out to a broad spectrum of theological opinion before deciding on its next move.[47]

Not everyone considers informality a good thing. Father Schillebeeckx was investigated three times from 1968 to 1984 by the Congregation for the Doctrine of the Faith, but survived by making minor changes in subsequent editions of his books. He reports that under Cardinal Ratzinger the process became more informal rather than the previous formal reading of prepared criticisms and defenses, followed by question-and-answer sessions. The cardinal's approach "in my opinion is worse," said Father Schillebeeckx. "Everything is according to his will."[48]

Father Bernard Häring, a moral theologian, said that his honor was offended more when the congregation was examining his works than during the four times he was brought to court during the Nazi rule in Germany. "The processes of Hitler were more dangerous, but they were not an offense to my honor, while those of the Holy Office were a grave offense," he said.[49] Leonardo Boff complained that the exercise of doctrinal power "is cruel and without pity." He wrote that "it forgets nothing, pardons nothing, covers everything," and that the result is "the boxing in of intelligent theology."[50]

Father Küng has been most acerbic in his criticism of the procedures. "The Inquisition is once again in full swing," he writes. "It has been especially active against North American moral theologians, Central European dogmaticists, and Latin American or African liberation theologians."[51] "Cardinal Ratzinger is afraid," he asserts. "And just like Dostoyevsky's grand inquisitor, he fears nothing more than freedom."[52]

If a theologian's writings are found to be unorthodox and he or she refuses to recant, there are a number of options open to the Vatican. If the writer is a priest or religious, his bishop or religious superior can be told to intervene by silencing the theologian or removing him from his position. In 1978, Father Pohier's Dominican superiors told him that he could no longer teach or preside at public liturgies. In 1985, Father Boff was informed by his Franciscan superiors that he was to observe a year of silence. In 1995, Brazilian Sister Ivone Gebara was ordered to an Augustinian convent in Brussels for study "to correct her theological imprecisions." During what her supporters called a two-year "forced exile," she was not allowed to express herself publicly. Matthew Fox, O.P., was dismissed by his Dominican superiors in 1992 when he refused to return to Chicago from California where he had founded the Institute in Culture and Creation Spirituality, which had a witch on its staff. If the theologian works at a seminary, he or she can be fired. In 1995, Mercy Sister Carmel McEnroy was dismissed from St. Meinrad School of Theology in Indiana for signing a statement supporting the ordination of women.

If the theologian is a priest or a religious, the Vatican prefers to deal with the theologian's ordinary (bishop or religious superior) rather than with his or her academic institution, which may have regulations covering due process and academic freedom. The Vatican hopes that the theologian's ordinary can persuade or pressure him or her into cooperating and conforming. Ultimately the ordinary can order the theologian to stop teaching and writing and to do something else. This strategy turns a complicated theological dispute into a simple matter of obedience to legitimate superiors. One reason the Vatican had such a difficult time dealing with Father Curran, the American moral theologian, was that his bishop in Rochester refused to cooperate and the Vatican had to work through the academic structures of the Catholic University of America, where Father Curran eventually lost his right to teach theology. A more authoritarian bishop could simply have ordered him to move from teaching theology in Washington to being a pastor in Rochester. Likewise, Gustavo Gutiérrez, the father of liberation theology, was protected by the Peruvian bishops despite Cardinal Ratzinger's complaints against him in 1983.

The result of this Vatican strategy has been that theologians who are religious and priests have tended to move out of controversial theological areas. For example, the creative theological writing today on sexual ethics is being done by lay theologians, like Professor Lisa Cahill at Boston College, who cannot be controlled by the Vatican unless they are teaching at a seminary or pontifical university.[53]

Because of the doctrinal congregation's record of silencing or condemning theologians (Henri de Lubac, Pierre Teilhard de Chardin, Yves Congar, John Courtney Murray) who were later rehabilitated and honored by the church, I asked Cardinal Ratzinger if he ever worried about doing that. "Every day we make an examination of conscience if we are doing good or not," he responded. "But finally only our Lord can judge."

Rather than silencing dissent, the Vatican's actions have tended to stir the fires. Father Dulles proved to be prophetic when he wrote in 1976, "Any attempt by the hierarchy to settle disputed questions by unilateral decrees will inevitably be met by dissent or even protest on the part of some."[54] The congregation's actions against theologians have stimulated organized protests by theologians in Germany, France, Italy, the United States, and other countries. Cardinal Ratzinger's reaction to the statements and petitions from these groups has as much to do with their style as their content:

> The [1989] declaration of the French theologians was made in a good way because they did not go to the media. They sent it to me in my position as president of the International Theological Commission. I found it very good because it can be that the theologians have very good questions and they were searching for a real dialogue . . .
>
> The [1988] declaration of Cologne was different. It was insulting. It was in a bad manner, bad style, not respectful of the persons. Essentially there was more disciplinary than doctrinal contents. It was against the nomination of bishops by the pope. I do not remember all the other things. There were also some theological points, but not so specified and not so formulated that there was an invitation to a real dialogue.
>
> Also in America there were different things. There was a declaration in favor of Father Curran. And there was another declaration[55] about our [1990] document about theologians and theology[56] . . . I remember one paper was respectful and was also really argumentations and part of a dialogue. I think it shows real intention to clarify, to understand better, to have a real dialogue. This could be a normal thing in the church. But if there are insults, this is not so good a thing.

An American priest no longer working in the Vatican believes that conflict between theologians and the Congregation for the Doctrine of the Faith is inevitable:

> The Vatican as a bureaucracy has no intention of being inspirational, they have no intention of leading or pushing back the frontiers. The whole bureaucracy exists to hold things together. When it comes to faith questions that means specifically orthodoxy.
>
> I don't like the way that the CDF operates, but I can't expect them to promote theological investigation. I would like them to allow theological investigation, but their purpose is to defend not to promote. If you start with that image, it lowers your expectations.

Cardinal Ratzinger agrees that a certain tension between theologians and the congregation is inevitable:

We have to promote but also to defend the faith of the church and to indicate also with authority, "This is the faith of the church and if you will be a Catholic theologian you must observe this and this."

The theologian is responsible to research, to deepen the reflection, to make experiments [to find out] what is possible and what could be compatible with the faith, how can faith be in dialogue with the modern vision of the world. So for the theologian [with] this scientific method, it is quite difficult to accept an instance of someone saying, "But you cannot do this." No. Because essentially he will see what is possible, and he will follow only arguments and the evidence of reason. If one comes and says, "No," this cannot seem reasonable, this is difficult to accept for a theologian.

On the other hand, even if we will be open, and we must be open, it is natural that from our responsibilities it follows that we are prudent. And we say, "But here you are in a street that can't be finished and has a bad conclusion."

So I think that there are natural structural difficulties and, as we said in our document [on the vocation of the theologian],[57] that can be a positive and fruitful thing if we accept and tolerate the contrasts and the tension. Certain tension, a vital tension, can be a sign of vitality and can stimulate the one and the other.

Given this, I do not think we can simply eliminate the tensions. It would be unrealistic to think that we can be without tension, and a simple peace perhaps would not be good, to have a peace without tensions. But given this, we must do all possible for mutual understanding.

In 1989, the Congregation for the Doctrine of the Faith increased the pressure on theologians by requiring that newly appointed rectors, presidents, and professors of theology and philosophy at seminaries and Catholic universities take an oath of fidelity as well as make a profession of faith. The oath and profession of faith are also required of new pastors. This action was taken without any consultation with the theological community or with episcopal conferences and came as a surprise even to other offices in the curia.

From ancient times, a profession of faith was common before baptism and ordination. The Council of Trent greatly expanded the practice in response to the Reformation. Beginning in 1910, all priests and seminary teachers were also required to take an oath against Modernism, as condemned by Pius X in 1907. The oath was dropped in 1967, and only a profession of faith that included the Nicene Creed was required. Canon 833 of the 1983 Code of Canon Law extended the profession of faith to Catholic universities and colleges. U.S. Catholic colleges and universities, however, have interpreted the canon as not applicable to them.[58]

The 1989 profession of faith was revised to include, in addition to the Nicene Creed, the following statement: "I also firmly embrace and hold each and everything that is definitively proposed by the same church concerning the doctrine of faith or morals. What is more, I adhere with religious *obsequium* of will and intellect to the doctrine which either the Roman pontiff or the college of bishops enunciate when they exercise the authentic magisterium even if they proclaim those doctrines in an act that is not definitive."[59] Father Umberto Betti, a consultor to the congregation, opined on Vatican Radio that the profession of faith included the teaching of *Humanae Vitae* on birth control.[60] The oath promises to undertake one's office "with great care and fidelity," to "preserve the whole deposit of faith," and to "pass it on and explain it faithfully." The oath also states, "With Christian obedience I will follow what is expressed by the sacred shepherds as authentic [official] doctors and teachers of faith or stated by them as rulers of the church."

The immediate reaction in the theological community to the profession of faith and oath was "a deep and profound disquiet."[61] In the American academic community, the oath of fidelity reminded people of the loyalty oaths of the McCarthy period. In time, the requirement was either ignored by schools or nuanced away by creative canon lawyers around the world. Canonists pointed out that the Congregation for the Doctrine of the Faith had not originally followed proper canonical procedures in mandating the oath. In addition, the meaning of some of the words in the profession and oath was not clear: "embrace and hold," "definitively proposed," and "obsequium," which has been variously translated as loyalty, respect, or submission.[62] By applying their own interpretation to the words, many were able to take the oath and make the profession without violating their consciences.

At the same time, all of these Vatican actions were seen by the theological community to reflect what John Coleman refers to as Catholic fundamentalism. Rather than appealing to the Bible like Protestant fundamentalism, it "appeals to a literal, ahistorical, and nonhermeneutical reading of papal and curial pronouncements as a sure bulwark against the tides of relativism, the claims of science, and other inroads of modernity." Theologians had traditionally taught that there is a "hierarchy of truths," that is, some papal teachings have more authority than others. Father Coleman writes:

> Against the authentic Catholic tradition, papal fundamentalism forgets that there is a hierarchy of truths even among defined doctrines and that,

traditionally, different "theological notes" of certitude were attached to assess the varying authoritativeness of magisterial pronouncements (ranging from formally defined to solidly probable as a safe, if reformable, guide). It also turns discipline into dogma. "Creeping infallibilism," which makes all statements of the pope and the curia equivalently infallible, is substituted for the genuine Catholic doctrine of papal and episcopal infallibility. It proposes a "solum magisterium" litmus-test of orthodoxy in place of a traditional Catholic sense of balanced and multiple sources of authority (scripture, magisterium, human experience, "sensus fidelium").[63]

The relationship between theologians and the papacy is worse today than at any time since the Reformation. The number of theologians investigated, silenced, or removed from office is at an all-time high, even exceeding the numbers during the Modernist crisis at the beginning of this century. The rhetoric used by theologians in response to Vatican actions has been bitter and biting. The chasm between the two appears to be getting wider, not narrower. A breach between the intellectual and administrative leaders of an organization is, of course, a recipe for disaster. If this breach continues into the next century, the church will be incapable of creatively responding to new needs and new opportunities, instead repeating old formulas that do not address new questions and ideas. If the papacy continues to lose its credibility in the intellectual community, schism could be the disastrous consequence.

The Vatican's concern with faith and morals is not confined to playing watchdog to theologians. The papacy is a bully pulpit from which to preach to the world. John Paul II, a former university professor, has emphasized his teaching ministry by issuing 12 encyclicals, 8 apostolic exhortations, 8 apostolic constitutions, and 30 apostolic letters in seventeen years.[64] His use of television and his travels have taken his message to millions of people all over the world. His most successful initiative has been *The Catechism for the Catholic Church*, written by a papal commission, which is a best seller in many languages. This catechism will be a guidepost for orthodoxy into the next century. John Paul's teaching has been strong and firm. Without personally invoking papal infallibility, he has written that certain teachings are "definitively" taught by the church. In 1995, the Congregation for the Doctrine of the Faith issued a short statement declaring that the teaching against women priests is based on Scripture, part of the deposit of faith, and infallibly taught by the college of bishops through history. Theologians immediately pointed out that the statement of the congregation is not infallible.

The effect of papal teaching is mixed. John Paul has published best sellers, and crowds come out to cheer him wherever he goes. His encyclicals and some of his other statements get wide but brief publicity in the press, while other statements are ignored.[65] Public opinion polls show 86 percent of American Catholics giving the pope a favorable rating, but 73 percent said the pope's position on an issue makes no difference to them.[66] The pope has not been successful in convincing people on issues like birth control, premarital sex, divorce, clerical celibacy, and women priests. Sixty-two percent of American Catholics say that local church officials reflect their views better than the pope does. As Peter Hebblethwaite said, "They like the singer but not the song." In addition, much of his writing is impenetrable prose to most readers. Even some of his Vatican supporters think that he and the Vatican issue too many statements and statements that are too long.

At the heart of the Vatican's failure to convince is the belief that the word of a teacher must be accepted simply because of his authority and not because of his arguments. Americans familiar with progressive education methods find such thinking incomprehensible, but for older Europeans raised in more traditional educational systems, such thinking is normal. An American priest in Rome explains the Italian educational system:

> It is an educational process based on the authority and the wisdom of the teacher. It is called the *cattedradico metodo,* the chair method would be the literal translation. It means that the professor sits in a classroom. I have observed classes in Italy and Spain and been amazed by it. They are heavily lecture oriented. The only questions asked by students are for clarifying the notes that they are taking. There are never questions for contrast or to object. Or to say, "Well in our economics course we heard this, how does this square with what you are talking about in history?" Never, never, never, never. The only questions are "What was that person's name, what was that date again? Would you repeat the definition that you just gave?"
>
> The lectures are very good. They are well prepared. In the exams, the students have to come up and disgorge this. The exams are urbane conversations that are thinly veiled attacks and repulses where the teacher will say, "Well what about the Napoleonic invasion of Italy?" The student will go back into his memory bank and think, "Ah, file 'Napoleon,' subfile 'Invasion of Italy.'" Then he drags out his little oral essay that he has prepared.
>
> The students are very verbal and know very well the material. What

they don't do, because it is not part of the education, they don't link what they have heard, what they are disgorging, to their lives. Because it really doesn't matter. They may believe it or not believe it, but that doesn't matter, what they do is get it ready to give back for examinations. So they are not interested in questioning for the real meaning of this because that is not part of this closed system.

The Vatican is a product itself of that kind of education and is part of the culture out of which that came. Therefore, when the pope speaks ex cathedra and when the congregations speak and give their statements, they are speaking like a professor in Italy does. The people are expected to listen to it the way a student in Italy does, which is understand it, be able to give it back, always say the right thing, always hold on to those principles, but not necessarily apply it to their lives. And that is what Italians do. That is why they are perfectly at ease with the pope coming out with all these statements, they would never think of questioning it. They wouldn't dissent. Dissent isn't done. You don't dissent from your professor, you don't dissent from the pope. But does it necessarily apply to your life? Well no, not necessarily.

That is a little bit of a caricature, but not really. Down deep, that is a key to the relation of the magisterium to the rest of the world. It is the reason the Vatican can't stand what happens in the States, where you have all these people dissenting, because it is not done. You don't do that, that is not the way you handle a teacher. The way you handle a teacher is to always repeat what he said, which is beautiful and integral and all the rest, and then you live your life. Hopefully there is some little spillover, but that is not the key thing. You always hold on to these beautiful first principles and you never question them, and you never obtrude yourself into them with a discordant note, and then everything is fine. Of course, human life is filled with difficulties and people are weak. So the very people in the Vatican who hold up a hard, hard line of the theory, if you went to confession to them, you would probably find them perfectly pastorally understanding.

This method of teaching is still alive and well in the Roman universities. One bright American student taking a course in Hegel took the initiative to read an essay by Hegel referred to in a class lecture. After reading it, he had some questions about what the professor had said in class. When he explained this to the professor, the professor asked, "Why are you reading Hegel?" The student presumed he had expressed himself poorly in Italian and began explaining again. The professor interrupted him, saying, "Why are you reading Hegel? I will explain to you what Hegel means." Many Vatican watchers point to the 1968 student protests in Europe as the turning point in the theology of Joseph Ratzinger, who was then a German professor. According to this theory, the shock of being challenged by protesting students was so traumatic that it turned him into a conservative.[67]

One practical effect of the papal and Vatican statements declaring matters "definitively taught" or even "infallible" is to tie the hands of John Paul's successors. His successors would not want to make the papacy look foolish by reversing teachings that a recent pope had insisted on so strongly.

Civil Society

Since the church's teachings touch on areas of population control, human rights, justice, and peace, the pope's words have an impact on the world of politics.[68] John Paul II's teachings have challenged government laws and programs that he considers contrary to human rights and morality. His opposition to Communism and his support of Solidarity in Poland were essential to the demise of the Soviet empire.[69] For this alone he will go down in history as the most important world figure in the second half of this century. The pope has also focused public attention on the victims of war, especially civilians and refugees in Africa, the Middle East, the former Yugoslavia, and East Timor. On the Balkans alone, the pope personally made 123 written or spoken appeals for peace in less than five years.[70]

For the pope, human rights include the right to life of unborn children, which has put him in direct conflict with those favoring abortion. Before the 1994 UN conference on population and development in Cairo, the pope orchestrated a full court press against abortion involving the Vatican diplomatic service, the Roman curia, and bishops around the world. Before the conference, all the ambassadors to the Holy See in Rome were called in to have the Vatican's position explained to them by the Secretariat of State. The pope also wrote every head of state. Each office in the Roman curia was told to emphasize family issues since 1994 was also the international year of the family. Many dicasteries issued statements on family issues, and the pope wrote a letter to families. Bishops' conferences around the world were asked to pressure their governments to oppose pro-abortion language in the Cairo document. Nuncios also worked at developing alliances with Muslim and Catholic countries that opposed abortion.

Early in 1994, U.S. Ambassador Raymond Flynn notified the U.S. State Department that the Clinton administration was heading toward a serious confrontation with the Holy See. Ambassador Flynn, a professional politician, was especially concerned about the negative political fallout among Catholic voters from a conflict that pitted the president against the pope. This warning was ignored by the State Department, which considers Flynn a political hack and did not see the Holy See as an opponent worth serious consideration. Unnamed high-ranking officials in the State Department were quoted by the press as saying that Flynn's post was "highly ceremonial."

"I've got to try to get the staff in the United States to understand that Bill Clinton, the president of the United States, wants to have a good working relationship with the pope and the Catholic church," explained Ambassador Flynn in a March 30, 1994, interview. "He doesn't need these ideologues coming forward, advancing their own agenda. And that's basically what we have. I'm sure the pope is not going to change his position on abortion, and Bill Clinton is not going to change his position on abortion. While I agree more with the Holy Father than I do with the president on that particular issue, my job is to make sure that there can be this difference in opinion . . . so that there is a level of respect for each other's point of view."

When Archbishop Jean-Louis Tauran, the Vatican secretary for relations with states, was sent to Washington to confer with the State Department, he was told that the U.S. secretary of state was too busy to meet with him. When he visited the assistant secretary for population, Timothy Worth, he saw a glass bowl filled with condoms prominently displayed in his office. Although President Clinton during his June 1994 visit with the pope indicated a desire for accommodation, there was no follow-up by the White House or the State Department. White House press officers accompanying the president to Rome even told reporters that some of Clinton's conciliatory statements to the press after the papal meeting were not administration policy. In addition, the Holy See's delegation was treated with contempt when it made its presentation at preliminary UN committee meetings in New York.

When the conference started in Cairo in September 1994, the Vatican's position had hardened and it used every obstructionist tactic available under the UN rules.[71] The other delegates had expected the pro-abortion language to pass easily now that the U.S. delegation was no longer controlled by a Republican administration. By playing hardball, the Vatican angered many delegates, but it eventually got their attention. By the time the U.S. delegates finally signaled their willingness to compromise, the Vatican did not believe or trust them. In addition, the Vatican delegation had to check back with Rome for instructions. As a result, the confrontation went on for days during the conference.

While the positions of the United States and the Vatican on abortion continued to differ at the 1995 UN conference on women in Peking, it was Chinese ineptitude and harassment that made the headlines. The U.S. delegation, having been burned once, was more professional and diplomatic in dealing with the Holy See. In addition, the pope's support for equal access to education, equal employment and pay for women, and his appointment of Mary Ann Glendon, a Harvard law professor, to head the Vatican delegation undercut accusations that the church was simply anti-woman. The Vatican's support for the equality of women put it in opposition to many Muslim countries at Peking.

The conflict with Communism in Eastern Europe and the conflict with the United States at the Cairo conference show in a dramatic way how the pope can marshal his resources to push his positions on the world stage. Helping the pope in these conflicts is a moral vision uncompromised by concern over public opinion, media reaction, or the next election. He cannot always get his way, but he does not fear taking on world opinion or the most powerful nations in the world. He is not afraid to take on an issue even if he will lose, because he sees it as an opportunity to proclaim the truth to the world. Failures are evident, as shown in 1995 by the inability of the pope and the Vatican to deliver the vote in Ireland against divorce and in Poland against a "reformed" Communist president. Nor has the Holy See yet been successful in getting international support for a comprehensive nuclear test ban treaty or an end to the production and use of land mines, but it continues to press for these at international meetings.

When confronted by an adversary willing to use violence and persecution, the Vatican is in an especially weak position. The Vatican can denounce the government for its persecution, but this might make matters worse. "It can be done," explains Msgr. Claudio Celli, undersecretary for relations with states, "but the local church is always asking us to be quiet because for them later on the situation is more difficult. The government itself knows very well how the press is working today. One day the minister for religion in Vietnam was telling me, 'Yes you can shout, you can denounce us to the press. How long do you think the press will continue to talk about this problem? One day, two days? But if you do that, this man will never enter Vietnam again.' What can you do? Nothing."

Despite the Vatican's numerous statements, the press and the world community usually ignore the situation in East Timor, where the Indonesian government and army have suppressed the rights of the local people for independence and religious freedom. Speaking out on human rights abuses is not easy, and sometimes the Vatican is criticized for not speaking out. "It depends on the place," explains Monsignor Celli.

> Where we have a certain standing it is easier. For example in China, we prefer to leave some shouting to other people because now [April 15, 1995] we are trying to deal with the government to see if we can solve some problems. It is a problem of conscience. Sometimes it is difficult to choose.
>
> In some other regions like France, in the States, in Europe, it is easier to talk, nothing happens against [the church]. But in countries where you are a very small minority, where the local authorities are not much respectful of certain rights, you can disappear.
>
> Certainly the Holy See must also follow the indications of the local episcopal conference. This is not an easy decision, I tell you frankly.

In some cases the Vatican quietly encourages the bishops' conferences in the United States and Europe to speak out on human rights issues when the Vatican itself cannot. These conferences are told to say that they are speaking on their own initiative and not at the request of the Vatican or the suffering local church.

In pushing his political and international agenda, the pope has a trained diplomatic service and the Roman curia to argue his case. At the Cairo conference, for example, the staff of the Secretariat of State, the Council on Justice and Peace, and the Council on the Family were important in preparing supportive documentation and in arguing the Vatican case. The Secretariat of State and its nunciatures around the world are also tremendously helpful. Nuncios gather information and report back to the Secretariat of State and the other dicasteries. They also speak for the pope to local governments and local churches. As professional diplomats who know their business, they are given high grades by their secular counterparts because of their training, experience, and extensive contacts in the country. While most embassies have few contacts outside government circles, nunciatures through contacts with the local church have sources of information unavailable to most embassies many times their size. The newsgathering potential of these contacts would be the envy of CNN or the CIA. This is one reason governments find it valuable to have embassies to the Holy See.

"If you want to know what's going on in Mozambique" or other countries, Ambassador Flynn reports, "there's any one of a thousand Catholic workers that are in there administering to the poor, out in the villages, out in the boondocks, out in the grassroots, and they report back to the Vatican. I can have conversations with the Vatican, and the Vatican can tell me what's going on there or in Libya." The Vatican has also been secretly used to convey messages to governments that the United States has poor relations with, such as Iraq, Iran, and Libya. The nuncio in Iran visited the American captives at the U.S. embassy, and the nuncio in Iraq helped in getting two American prisoners released in 1995.

Ambassadors and their staffs praise the quality of the officials in the Secretariat of State. "With the Vatican Secretariat of State, you get to deal with people who are truly world class at their skill," says Cameron Hume, deputy chief of station at the U.S. embassy to the Holy See. "It is efficient. You go in and you have a conversation, and it is always factually based, meaningful, frank, diplomatic dialogue. I never found any problems going in and talking about anything and having an entirely open and professional discussion. They are highly trained and disciplined as diplomats. So one can go in and have a meaningful conversation as one can in London or Paris." Another reason the Vatican diplomats do well is that they are focused. "In the Vatican, as small as it is, they have a good idea what their policies are, what their interests are. In lots of other places in the world, either the diplomatic service doesn't work well or the government is a mess."

In addition to using their embassies to the Holy See to collect information, governments lobby the Vatican with their positions on international issues and try to influence Vatican positions. The United States encouraged the Holy See to establish diplomatic relations with Israel. It defended its policies in the cold war, the Vietnam War, Eastern Europe, the Persian Gulf, Somalia, and Bosnia. The Reagan administration, for example, lobbied to keep confidential a negative report on its anti-missile strategy by the Pontifical Academy of Science.[72] All U.S. ambassadors deny ever being involved in church issues like the appointment of bishops.

Liberal critics in Western democratic countries assert that the nunciatures are anachronisms that are unnecessary in countries where freedom of religion is respected and where the local bishops can speak to their government on behalf of the church. Many liberal critics also see the nuncios as curial spies on the local church. They believe that the leadership of the episcopal conferences should represent the local churches to Rome without the nuncio's interference. In less democratic countries and in Third World countries where Catholics are few, the presence of the nuncio is usually welcomed by the local church. It reminds the regime that the outside world is watching how it treats Catholics. Although a number of women's groups after the Cairo and Peking conferences called for eliminating the permanent observer status of the Holy See at the

United Nations, many world leaders, including President Clinton and Secretary General Boutros Boutros-Ghali, support the status quo especially because the Vatican has from the beginning been a strong supporter of the UN.

Bishops, theologians, and government officials will always be of deep concern to the Vatican. The Vatican recognizes that these elites can have a tremendous impact on the life of the church. The papacy wants to support bishops who are under attack by their governments. Because of its concern for unity within the college of bishops, the Vatican also admonishes bishops who stray outside its norms. Through gaining control of the appointment of bishops, the Vatican has successfully constructed a college that is very deferential to the pope. Whether these bishops will be able to keep the faithful in union with the magisterium remains to be seen. With the growth of mass education and communications, theologians and their ideas will have an increasingly large impact on the life of the church. As a result, they will be of continuing interest to the Vatican. Finally, as the world becomes smaller through technology and communications, the pope will continue to have a role on the world stage as he speaks prophetically to the world community for human rights, justice, and peace.

~ 10

Toward the Next Millennium

FOR ALMOST TWO THOUSAND YEARS Christianity has faced numerous challenges from persecution to state support, from poverty to prosperity, from Neo-Platonism to Marxism, from paganism to atheism, from feudalism to capitalism, from the Black Plague to AIDS, from the crossbow to the H-bomb, from the printing press to the Internet, from religious wars to ecumenism. In the next millennium, Christianity will face further challenges. What these will be is as hard to predict as the future: global warming or a new ice age, world government or decentralized chaos, growing prosperity or shortages of energy and natural resources, biotech miracles or disastrous plagues, space travel or decaying infrastructures, extraterrestrial intelligent life or an empty universe, direct democracy or government by terror, a new spiritual awakening or an agnostic materialism.

Whatever the future, Christian leaders will be called upon to face it with faith, hope, and love, although judging from history they are just as likely to face it with ignorance, fear, and sin. History also tells us that a key player in this future will undoubtedly be the Vatican, although, as in the past, external forces or internal corruption could marginalize the papacy.

Responding to Modernity

The immediate future includes the need for the Vatican to continue to respond to modernity. The papacy and the church were hostile toward many of the economic, political, intellectual, and cultural developments of the nineteenth century. In the face of rapid and frightening changes, the church came to be understood as a sign and stronghold of what was eternally valid and unchangeable. Socialism, the secular state, and the influence of the Enlightenment were seen as threats to religion and the church's position in society.

The church's failure to respond adequately to economic developments in the nineteenth century spawned anticlericalism among the European working classes, which is only now beginning to fade. In the United States anticlericalism rarely existed because the Catholic clergy were on the side of immigrants, workers, and labor unions against a WASP establishment. Pope Leo XIII (1878–1903) responded to the industrial revolution with his social encyclicals, trying to find an alternative to unbridled capitalism and state socialism. The church still lost millions of working-class people because it lacked practical pastoral and social programs that could reach them. Centuries of ministry to peasants and nobles in an agricultural society did not prepare the church to deal with urban laborers and the middle class.

Although the church is still critical of any policies that appear tainted with Marxism (for example, violent revolution and class warfare), today it is very sympathetic to the rights of workers and the needs of the poor. Thus local bishops, like local politicians, frequently decry the closing of local factories because they see the impact on workers and the community. Third World bishops object to IMF policies that impose fiscal restraint on government services to the poor and eliminate price controls. Bishops do not have absolute faith in the workings of the free market, free trade, or government deregulation, and they challenge policies that have a negative effect on workers and the poor. Whether these policies make economic sense in the long run is irrelevant to them since their people live in the short run. Displaced workers and the poor, they would argue, should be helped by governments through job training and jobs programs.

This sympathy for workers and the poor may cause increasing conflict with a middle class that values economic efficiency and feels exploited by government taxes and labor unions. In the future, the church as an international organization will also be confronted by conflicting constituencies in a world economy. A factory that moves from the United States to Mexico means jobs in Mexico and laid off workers in the United States. In their economic pastoral letter, the U.S. bishops parted company with American labor unions on the question of Third World imports because the bishops would not sacrifice the needs of workers in developing nations to protect the jobs of American workers. For the same reason the U.S. bishops had difficulty responding to NAFTA.

The growing numbers of Third World bishops in the church, and of Third World clergy in the Vatican, will undoubtedly result in further challenges to the economic interests of the First World.

Political change also challenged the church. The papacy's response to the political developments of the nineteenth century was colored by its experience under the French Revolution, Napoleon, and the Italian revolution. Secular European governments in the nineteenth century were often antagonistic toward the church, expropriating schools and property. The experience of the U.S. church was very different because the Catholic clergy supported the American revolution, and the Catholic church prospered under religious freedom and the separation of church and state. As secular European democracies began to respect religious freedom and church autonomy, the church became more open to democracy. In the twentieth century, Fascist and Communist regimes attacked the church, but with papal leadership the church survived and triumphed.

Today the papacy is a staunch defender of democracy and human rights, and the church does well in democratic societies where freedom of religion is respected. Policies that concern families (birth control, abortion, and divorce) and schools (teaching religion and sex education) are still areas of church-state conflict, but the struggles take place within a democratic framework. In the postwar era, German, Italian, and Latin American Catholics often worked within Christian democratic parties, whose platforms were influenced by Catholic social teaching. The recent political corruption and ineptitude of these parties has encouraged some European bishops to imitate their U.S. colleagues in keeping all political parties at arm's length. But many in the Vatican hope the Christian democratic parties can be reformed and revived.

From the very beginning, the papacy has also been a strong supporter of the United Nations, despite its problems, as the best hope for peace. In his second trip outside Italy, Paul VI spoke before the UN in 1965 and pleaded, "No more war!" John Paul II has addressed the UN in 1979 and 1995, reinforcing the church's commitment to international peace and justice. As the head of the world's largest multinational institution, the papacy with its diplomatic corps is in a position to be a moral superpower in international affairs. How the papacy will concretely exercise this commitment in the next century will vary in response to changing world events, but it will certainly continue to be a player on the world stage.

The end of colonialism also called for a response from the church and the papacy. Although the American revolution freed the church in the United States, the fall of the Spanish and Portuguese colonies in the nineteenth century caused chaos in the Latin American church, which had been closely aligned with the colonial powers. In some countries it took decades to reestablish church institutions and leadership as the papacy worked for church independence from political interference. The postwar end of French and British colonialism also forced the Vatican to deal with new regimes and to find local leadership for churches in Asia and Africa. The result is a more colorful and less European college of bishops. The college of cardinals and the Vatican bureaucracy have also become increasingly multinational, reflecting the new reality of the church. Thus the Catholic church has become truly universal and no longer simply European. During the next century, the church will undoubtedly see a pope from outside Europe.

Because of the growing numbers of African Catholics, many in the Vatican look to the Third World as the future of the church. But most of the conversions are occurring among followers of native African religions. Catholicism has failed to make significant inroads among Muslims, Hindus, or Buddhists in Asia or Africa. Rather than representing the future, the African experience may be a repeat of the past, that is, the conversion of European and Latin American tribes to Christianity from their primitive native religions. Already there is a growing desire among African elites for greater inculturation of Christianity in ways currently unacceptable to the Vatican. There is not much support in African culture for a celibate clergy, canon law, or the doctrinal distinctions developed through centuries of debates by European theologians.

The decline of priestly and religious vocations in the developed world and their growth in Africa and parts of Asia will have further consequences as the Vatican bureaucracy becomes more dependent on Third World clergy. Whether the high vocation rate will continue as these countries modernize is an open question (there are already signs of a decline in modernized sections of India like New Delhi). As Africa and Asia become more modernized, the church will face many of the same problems that it has in the Americas and Europe. Because of the widespread impact of American culture, trends in America will spread around the world. American and Western culture is already flooding though Eastern Europe, dashing John Paul's hopes that Eastern Europe would re-evangelize the West.

The expansion of literacy and education during the last two centuries has challenged the position of the church officials in society and culture. The clergy are no longer the only or the best educated people in the community. Beginning in the Enlightenment, intellectuals broke free of church control and developed philosophies at odds with church teaching. The development of the physical and social sciences in the nineteenth and twentieth centuries challenged the supremacy of philosophy and theology. Secular universities and state schools created cultural elites who were often without religious affiliations. These opinion leaders challenged clerical supremacy in the world of ideas and culture. No longer is the word of church leaders unquestioned because of the authority of their office; they have to convince people with their arguments or the compelling power of their witness. Meanwhile, through the mass media, culture was being commercialized, becoming a tool of advertising as well as a product for sale through the entertainment industry. For the first time since the conversion of the barbarians, Western culture is no longer Christian, let alone Catholic. The Christian message is now countercultural and has to compete for time, attention, and acceptance in a pluralistic environment.

The initial papal response to this intellectual and cultural transformation was antagonistic and critical. Slowly the papacy acknowledged what was good in modern culture and tried to use it in the service of the gospel. The physical sciences were the first to be accepted, with the Vatican Observatory and the Pontifical Academy of Science leading the way. The conflict between science and religion has become less of a problem as philosophers of science and theologians have conducted a fruitful dialogue. At the same time, the damage done by the scientific and technological manipulation of humans and the environment has made people more sympathetic to the church's view that science must be guided by moral principles. Environmentalists are beginning to see religious leaders as their natural allies rather than their enemies.

Classical theology was ill prepared to respond to the scientific, philosophical, and cultural changes of modernity. Its static view of culture contained normative and universalistic presuppositions that were no longer acceptable to modern scholars. The hierarchy and classical theologians lashed out at any challenge to their systems, whether from outside or inside the church. The Vatican-led persecution of Catholic Modernists, who tried to adapt Christianity to modernity at the turn of the century, severely damaged the church's ability to respond intelligently to the times. Only in 1943 were biblical scholars officially set free by Pius XII to use linguistic, literary, and historical tools to transcend false problems and to open the Bible to new and richer insights. Church historians were also allowed to examine the history of the church with all its warts. The Vatican Archives, with 75 kilometers of documents, and the Vatican Library, with 150,000 manuscripts and 2 million books, were opened to scholars with some restrictions. Biblical and historical studies eventually had an impact on systematic theology and ethics as theologians became aware of the historicity of the dogma and practices of the church. These developments frightened church leaders, who clung to neoscholasticism in the face of the relativism of twentieth-century philosophies.

At the Second Vatican Council, great strides were made in updating the church's response to the modern world especially in the areas of liturgy, collegiality, ecumenism, religious liberty, social teaching, pastoral practice, and the role of the laity. The Vatican continues to defend the perennial value of ethical principles and their supremacy in human activity in the face of moral relativism. The Vatican's countercultural critique of sexual promiscuity, consumerism, and secularism has recently received a more sympathetic hearing as people recognize that moral relativism has done much damage in the twentieth century. But the philosophical conflict still exists between the traditional approach based on unchanging principles and a modern approach acknowledging historical changes that include the development of doctrine.[1] Even when doctrinal developments in the past are acknowledged, the possibility of contemporary developments is frightening to an institution that prizes stability, tradition, and magisterial authority. Intellectually this is the most challenging issue facing the church today.

Like its earlier attacks against Modernists, the Vatican's current strategy against dissident theologians is proving counterproductive and is alienating the very intellectuals the church needs to respond to a changing world. The conflict between the Vatican and the theological community has become intense. The issues of women's ordination, married priests, remarriage after divorce, and birth control have become litmus tests of orthodoxy and loyalty. If theologians question the Vatican's positions on these issues, they cannot teach in seminaries or ecclesiastical faculties. Yet insisting that people not ask questions is an ineffective response to an intellectual challenge. Such questioning is part of the dialectical process by which humanity seeks for better understanding of the truth. In frustration, theologians are expressing their differences with the Vatican with more force and anger. As occurred during the Modernist crisis, Vatican officials and theologians are defining themselves by their opposition to each other rather than by what they share together.[2]

This alienation from the hierarchy includes not only professional theologians but also many canon lawyers, chancery officials, priests, sisters, educators, marriage counselors, youth leaders, and lay pastoral leaders. What these elites, many of whom work for the church, have in common is a feeling that they are not being listened to by the leadership, which insists that its views be accepted on faith without question. This continuing conflict does not portend well for the church, which needs its intellectual and administrative leaders to work together to confront the challenges of the next millennium.

The magisterium's failure to convince significant numbers of the clergy or the faithful of its teaching on birth control, divorce, sexual ethics, and a male celibate priesthood has undermined its credibility on other issues. Magisterial statements on these issues are being greeted with a hermeneutic of suspicion or are simply ignored by the faithful. Not surprisingly, this alienation from the hierarchy and the Vatican tends to increase among educated Catholics exposed to contemporary theology. What is remarkable is that alienation among lay Catholics often increases as they become more active in their parishes as volunteer liturgical ministers, religious educators, or social ministers.

The growing alienation of educated Catholic women from the church is especially critical for the future since women traditionally filled the churches in Europe and Latin America and were more deferential than men to clerical influence. More important, they are the ones most involved in passing the faith on to the next generation, both as mothers to their children and as teachers to young students. A ten-minute homily by a priest once a week cannot compete with what children learn from their mothers and from religious education programs. That women religious and women educators feel more alienated than other women is of special concern, since their influence on the future is greater. Women, not the clergy, are determining the faith of the next generation. If large numbers of women become anticlerical, their children will too. The likelihood of the children of these women becoming sisters or priests is slim.

Increased education and a desire to play a greater role in society and the church have changed women's attitudes toward the church. Feminism has helped women become conscious of how they were exploited and kept subservient. While some in the Vatican consider feminism an American aberration, John Paul in 1995 took it seriously by issuing a letter on women.[3] He acknowledged the positive aspects of feminism and put the church behind the struggle for equal educational, political, and employment opportunities for women. Drawing the line at artificial birth control, abortion, and women priests, he adopted much of the mainline feminist agenda while still singing the praises of motherhood in the family. Whether an all-male hierarchy will be able to satisfy women with such a platform in the long run is unlikely. The Vatican's attempt to silence the debate over women's ordination has only succeeded in angering more women. If the church loses educated women in the twenty-first century the way it lost European working-class males in the nineteenth century, it will be in serious trouble. The church has already seen a drastic decline in the number of women willing to be sisters in the First World. The shortage of religious women is having a serious financial and spiritual impact on the church's educational and social service programs.

While these alienated Catholics might be labeled "liberal," there is another group of politically and socially conservative middle-class Catholics who are alienated from the hierarchy because of its teaching on social justice. They believe that the hierarchy should stay out of economic and political discussions. As Catholics move from working-class and peasant backgrounds into the better-educated middle class, the hierarchy loses their unswerving allegiance. Neither liberal nor conservative middle-class Catholics will accept church teaching simply on the word of the hierarchy. Nor do they encourage their children, who because of birth control are fewer in number, to become priests or religious. Whether the church will lose the educated elite is uncertain, but as education continues to spread worldwide, the Vatican's job will become more difficult unless it finds a new style of leadership acceptable to the educated middle class.

Until recently, this division has not led to open conflict between church officials and the laity; rather, the teachings of the former are simply ignored. Lay Catholics dissatisfied with their pastor go parish shopping until they find a priest who is pastorally sympathetic to their concerns. As a result of this mobility, Catholic parishes are becoming based less on geography and more on ideology and culture. Some geographical parishes keep their people by offering liturgies geared to different types of parishioners: family masses for parents and children, masses for senior citizens, youth masses, Spanish masses, and masses for young single adults. The sermons and music are adapted to the spiritual and cultural tastes of each group. If Catholics fail to find a Catholic parish that meets their needs, they look elsewhere, as is happening with some Hispanic Catholics in the United States.

More recently, organized dissent has moved beyond the theological community with large-scale petition drives netting millions of signatures in Germany, Austria, Belgium, and Italy. If this movement spreads, internal church conflict and anticlericalism will increase unless church leaders find a way of responding positively to the issues. There is always a danger of a schism on the left matching Archbishop Lefebvre's schism on the right, although such a threat is not imminent. The more likely response will be the withdrawal from active participation by Catholic elites alienated from the hierarchy or by ordinary Catholics upset by bickering within the church.

The next millennium will require a new style of leadership, which is only now beginning to develop in the Catholic church, to deal with an educated populace used to asking questions and exercising freedom. It is a style that American Catholic leaders are more comfortable with than their European and Latin American colleagues. Having functioned in an isolated and homogeneous environment, many European and Latin American bishops (like Russian Orthodox bishops) have a cartel vision of Christianity. They object to other churches coming into their territory. They fear a free market where individuals are approached by different churches and allowed to choose.

Some American religious leaders, having prospered in a pluralistic environment, recognize that people can no longer be commanded in the church but must be persuaded. The new leadership must be comfortable with mass communications, a variety of views, group discussions, dialogue, and consensus building in a setting of diversity. Many in the Vatican are uncomfortable with a dialogic leadership style because it gives the impression that truth can change and that the magisterium does not know what it is doing. But without a change in leadership styles, the church will face serious problems in the years to come.

Although ecumenism has made great strides in the last forty years, as the Christian churches move into the next millennium we may see not greater union among the churches but growing denominational irrelevance. People are picking the local church that fulfills their personal spiritual needs and their need for community without much concern for its connections to a wider communion of churches. This is already common among American Protestants and is becoming more common among Catholics, especially those in mixed marriages who feel comfortable attending the churches of both spouses. As denominational loyalty declines, some churches will seek the lowest common denominator to attract members, while others will accentuate their uniqueness so that they stand out from the competition in the religious marketplace. The next century may see a realignment of churches that will have little to do with the doctrinal divisions of the Reformation and more to do with marketing and media strategies.

Many in the Vatican, including John Paul, believe that more authoritative statements will accentuate Catholic identity and make the church more attractive in the religious confusion. Some Vatican officials believe that the church would be better off without dissident Catholics, who simply sow confusion. A smaller, more faithful church, even a remnant, is the future they see for the church. While some Protestant sects have prided themselves on being a small remnant, the Catholic church has traditionally striven to be a big tent enclosing divergent nations, cultures, spiritualities, devotional practices, and theologies. The current Vatican strategy of accentuating differences is going in the opposite direction, toward a more centralized, uniform, and doctrinaire church. It is beyond the scope of this book to analyze the theological validity of this approach, but there is little evidence that it will appeal to an educated middle class that will be an ever larger part of the population in the future.

Institutional Reform

The Vatican as an institution has evolved over the centuries in response to the needs and opportunities of the times. Throughout history, the Vatican has borrowed structures and procedures from secular society. From the Roman empire it took Roman law as a model for canon law, and the procedures of the Roman senate as a model for ecumenical councils. The papal court and bureaucracy often mimicked their secular counterparts in Constantinople or Paris. The Vatican has responded to changes in technology through the centuries, using parchment, the printing press, radio, photocopy machines, and computers. The operations of the Vatican were transformed in this century by modern means of communication including airmail, telephone, fax machines, and jet planes, which allow church leaders to interact as never before. The Vatican will continue to evolve in ways that could make it look very different from what it is today.[4]

Although the Vatican has responded more slowly to technological change than Western governments and businesses, the next century will see a paperless Vatican at the center of a church connected by computers and telecommunications. At the end of 1995, the Vatican opened its home page at http://www.vatican.va. on the World Wide Web. Plans are under way to make information from various dicasteries available to Web browsers, including news bulletins, encyclicals and other documents, in-house news reports, reference material, information about the Vatican museums, and news from Vatican Radio.[5] The Vatican may attempt to use modern technology to increase centralization and to micro-manage local churches. Imposing such uniformity could strangle local initiative so that the church would lose out to other religious and secular organizations competing for hearts and souls. The result would be greater Vatican control over a smaller church. On the other hand, the Vatican will probably find it impossible to control the flow of information and ideas as communications technology allows more people to have access to a variety of views. For example, Bishop Jacques Gaillot no longer has a diocese, but he now has a Web site (http://www.partenia.fr).

Alternatively, the Vatican could become a centralized clearinghouse, a forum for discussing ideas and programs coming from local churches that could be shared and evaluated by other local churches. This would require a loosening of control by the Vatican, where the pope would be seen as a facilitator of communication and a consensus builder rather than a monarch who knows what is best for everyone. Under this model, experimentation would be encouraged, and episcopal conferences would be allowed to make more decisions responding to local situations without having them reviewed in detail by Rome. Such decentralization has risks because experimentation and local initiatives mean that mistakes will be made, and local churches and episcopal conferences could develop policies that are at odds with one another. But local churches could also correct their mistakes and learn from them. Mistakes can be made by a centralized bureaucracy as well, and these mistakes cause greater damage because their impact is wider.

No organizational structure is perfect; each has its strengths and weaknesses. Structures are simply the ways in which people, resources, and technologies are organized to accomplish certain goals in a given environment. When the goals, environment, personnel, resources, or technologies of an organization change, then the organization needs to adapt its structures and procedures accordingly. New goals from Vatican II (ecumenism, collegiality, liturgical reform, incultu-ration, social justice, and peace), new technologies (computers, telecommuni-cations, and air travel), and new personnel (a Polish pope and other non-Italians) as well as a new environment (modernity and postmodernity) have had an impact over the last thirty years on the way the Vatican operates.

Although the organizational structure of the Vatican has been tinkered with since Vatican II, it has not truly been reformed.[6] As would be expected in an ancient institution where tradition is important, the changes have been incre-mental rather than radical: the creation of new offices, a modest revision of the Code of Canon Law, the gradual internationalization of the curia, and the use of technology to do more efficiently what was done in the past. When new institutions were created, like episcopal conferences and the synod of bishops, they were heavily circumscribed with controls lest they get out of hand.

More incremental change is to be expected, but radical reform is unlikely. Incremental rather than radical change is probably a good idea in an institution like the Vatican, but the incremental change needs to be directed by a vision of what the church should look like in the next millennium. The reform of the curia could be based on a more decentralized vision of the universal church as a communion of churches.[7] This would not be a decision to abandon the papacy as an institution, since the ministry of promoting and sustaining unity in the communion of churches is a specific characteristic of the Petrine office. In addition, in a world daily growing smaller and more interconnected, new and important tasks that were never dreamed of will have to be undertaken by the papacy for the unity and global effectiveness of the church.

Seeing the church as a communion of churches would encourage limiting membership in the college of bishops and college of cardinals to those who head local churches. This would affect the makeup of ecumenical councils, synods of bishops, consistories, and conclaves since members of the Roman curia and the papal diplomatic corps would no longer be made bishops or cardinals. Such a reform would strengthen the college of bishops in its relations with the Vatican curia. The college could be further strengthened by having an ecumenical council at least once every twenty-five years so that each generation of bishops could share experiences, reflect on the state of the church, and take actions necessary to respond to a rapidly changing cultural and religious environment. The role of the synod of bishops could also be enhanced by reducing secrecy and encouraging honest debate, and local bishops and the synod could be given a greater role in overseeing the curia.

Seeing the church as a communion of local churches means that reform of church structures would be guided by the principle of subsidiarity, which holds that those things that can be done in society or the church at a lower level should be done at that level rather than at a higher level. How to implement the principle of subsidiarity in practice by dividing up responsibilities among the various levels of the church (parishes, dioceses, episcopal conferences, Vatican agencies, and the papacy) is not clear and needs a thorough discussion within the church.[8] Local churches could be given more freedom by reducing the restrictions on episcopal conferences so that they can respond to the pastoral needs of their countries. This would encourage inculturation and experimentation to respond to local situations. Local churches could also be given a greater role in choosing their bishops, for example, by allowing the priests' council of a vacant see and the bishops of the province to comment on the terna submitted by the nuncio or to submit the terna themselves. Greater local autonomy would also make union with Protestant and Orthodox churches easier.

To respond to the needs of a communion of churches, the curia might be reorganized on geographical lines rather than the current mix of geography, issues, and constituencies. There could be five offices, one for each continent (Africa, Asia, Europe, North America, and Latin America), that would handle the appointment of bishops and relations with the local churches in each region. A curia organized by geographical regions might more easily implement the principle of subsidiarity in the church. Such a structure is likely to be more sensitive to the need to inculturate Christianity in local contexts, with less concern for uniformity around the world. Under this model, there could be interdicasterial committees to coordinate policy toward seminaries, clergy, laity, religious, liturgy, doctrine, and finances in different regions of the world. But the institutional thrust would be toward inculturation rather than uniformity. Some offices could be maintained or created to deal with international concerns like ecumenism, peace, and inter-church assistance and cooperation.

Some will see these suggestions as revolutionary; others will consider them minor tinkering. I would argue that they are incremental changes, in line with those begun by Vatican II, that will better enable the church to face the challenges of today and tomorrow.

These changes in the Vatican would have to be matched by greater collaboration between the clergy and the laity on the local and national level, not only in consultation but also in decision making where possible. Karl Rahner believed that the church of the future would everywhere be a diaspora-church, a minority church in a secular, non-Christian culture and society with no cultural or governmental props to support it.[9] Many in the Vatican agree and have adopted a siege mentality in response. Rahner, on the other hand, felt that the real effectiveness of the church's mission and message in the world will depend on the assent of faith freely given by individuals and the commitment of its members from below. Parishes, he believed, will have to become living communities involved in determining their ecclesial life style and selecting their officials, while maintaining a unity of faith with a diversity of emphasis on the various aspects of their Christian and ecclesial life. Greater collaboration and co-responsibility in local churches are essential for the church to survive and accomplish its mission in the decades to come.

An institution that is heading toward its two thousandth anniversary is remarkable simply because of its age. The papacy, aided by the Vatican curia, has the potential to be a leading force in Christianity and in the world during the next millennium. John Paul II is well aware of this and is preparing to put his personal stamp on the millennial celebrations. His actions and those of his successors will help shape the Catholic contribution to politics, religion, and culture in the next millennium. The Vatican curia will continue to play an important role in supporting the papal ministry within the college of bishops, but that role will undoubtedly change in response to different needs in different times.

Whether the papacy can reform itself remains to be seen. Self-perpetuating bodies that are independent of external control rarely reform themselves unless their very survival is at stake. The papacy has reformed itself in the past, although with much reluctance and not great speed.[10] The papal court returned to Rome from Avignon. The corruption of the Renaissance papacy was ended, and the papacy finally reconciled itself to the loss of the papal states so that it could devote itself to the service of the church and the world community. Pius XII and Paul VI internationalized the curia and the college of cardinals. John XXIII called an ecumenical council that began an ecclesial revolution by legitimizing ideas like collegiality, ecumenism, inculturation, and religious liberty. Paul VI brought the council to a successful conclusion and began its implementation but became disillusioned by the response to *Humanae Vitae.* John Paul II uses the media and his travels to project the papacy in a new way that has captured the attention of millions around the world. He has also supported the reform of Vatican finances.

While some have accused John Paul II of rolling back the reforms of Vatican II, it would be more accurate to say that progress in institutional reform has simply stopped, and those proposing more changes or raising questions have come under Vatican scrutiny. That the postconciliar period of reform has reached a plateau should not be surprising. Large institutions do not like change, and they normally change only when forced to do so by their external environment. The environment is sending signals to the Vatican in the form of public opinion polls, petition drives, dissident theologians, the decline in vocations, anticlericalism among women, and a desire by local churches for more autonomy. Raising the walls in fear against such signs of the times is one response. Taking the initiative through dialogue would be a response based on faith in the God of history, hope in power of the Spirit, and love of Christ's people. Liberals and conservatives can legitimately disagree on how the papacy and the church should be structured to meet the needs of the next millennium. Unhappily, these disagreements are often antagonistic and divisive rather than constructive and respectful. In dealing with its internal disagreements the church should be a model to the wider community so that people will say, "See how they love one another" rather than "See how they fight one another."

Church history teaches that there are periods of progress when the church responds with intelligence, reason, and responsibility to new situations. Periods of decline have also marked the church, when individual and group biases blinded people to reality, hindered good judgment, and limited true freedom.[11] Although this is true of any organization or community, what marks the church is its openness to redemption which can repair and renew Christians as individuals and as a community. Despite their weakness and sinfulness, Christians have faith in the word of God that shows them the way, Christians have hope based on Christ's victory over sin and death and his promise of the Spirit, and Christians have love that impels them to forgiveness and companionship at the Lord's table. The future of the church and the papacy must be based on such faith, hope, and love.

Notes

Introduction

1. James D. Thompson, *Organizations in Action* (New York: McGraw-Hill, 1967).

1. Papal Roles

1. The pope's role as patriarch of the West, for all practical purposes, has been submerged by his role as head of the universal church. In a reunion with the Orthodox churches, a distinction between the role of the pope as patriarch of the West and his role as head of the college of bishops could be important since the patriarch of Constantinople is the patriarch of the East. There is also the possibility of creating additional patriarchs in the West as a way of decentralizing power in the church. See James H. Provost, "Structuring the Church as a Communio," *Jurist,* 36 (1976): 236–238.

2. For a description of how U.S. dioceses are organized, see my book *Archbishop: Inside the Power Structure of the American Catholic Church* (San Francisco: Harper & Row, 1989).

3. Paul VI, *Vicariae Potestatis in Urbe,* January 8, 1977, *Canon Law Digest,* 8: 254–266. See also Thomas Donlan, O.P., "Pope Gives His Diocese New Laws," NC News [later renamed CNS], January 11, 1977.

4. "Rome's Catholics Gone Astray, Study Shows," *National Catholic Reporter,* May 26, 1995, p. 6.

5. John Thavis, "Pope Says Rome Church Must Turn Attention to Suffering People," CNS, October 5, 1992.

6. John Paul II, "Address to Extraordinary Consistory," *L'Osservatore Romano: Weekly Edition in English,* June 22, 1994, p. 6. By October 1995 this number had risen to 237 of the 331 parishes; Cindy Wooden, "Vatican Trots Out the Stats on Pope's 17th Year in Office," CNS, October 16, 1995.

7. Tad Szulc, *Pope John Paul II* (New York: Scribner, 1995), pp. 207–208.

8. Cindy Wooden, "Pope Answers Kids' Questions Patiently at Roman Parish," CNS, March 14, 1994.

9. John Thavis, "Pope Seems to Enjoy Role as Bishop of Rome in Weekly Parish Visits," NC News, March 4, 1985.

10. Wooden, "Stats on Pope's 17th Year."

11. A number of offices and agencies housed in the Vatican under the pope seem narrowly focused on Italian issues; they have little to do with the pope's role as head of the universal church and only make sense when he is seen as the bishop of Rome or primate of Italy: for example, the Pontifical Commission for Sacred Archeology, the Cardinals' Commission for Pontifical Sanctuaries of Pompeii, Loreto, and Bari. The pope even owns two of the best hospitals in Italy, Gesu Bambino Hospital and San Giovanni Rotondo, the latter given to him by Padre Pio. The diocese of Rome or the Italian bishops' conference could appropriately take over these responsibilities.

12. John Paul II, "Address to Extraordinary Consistory," *L'Osservatore Romano: Weekly Edition in English,* June 22, 1994, p. 6.

13. Greg Erlandson, "The Pope Takes on Rome's Politicians," CNS, February 24, 1989.

14. Peter Nichols, "Daily Life in the Vatican," in *The Vatican* (New York: Vendome Press; Dublin: Gill & Macmillan, 1980), p. 107.

15. *L'Attività della Santa Sede 1994* (Vatican City: Libreria Editrice Vaticana, 1995), p. 1609.

16. The other cardinals on the commission in 1995 do not play an active role in the city. In 1995, Cardinal Antonio Innocenti turned 80. Cardinal Andrzej Maria Deskur, a personal friend of the pope, has been in poor health for many years. Cardinal Jozef Tomko is prefect of the Congregation for the Evangelization of Peoples, one of the busiest offices in the curia. Cardinal Alfonso López Trujillo is president of the Council on the Family.

17. John Thavis, "No Butts About It: At the Vatican, Smoking's No Sin," CNS, May 20, 1994.

18. John Thavis, "From Fires to Stray Bees: A Busy Spring for the Vatican Firemen," CNS, May 24, 1991.

19. Kenneth Doyle, "Why Is Agca Being Tried in Italy for Crime Committed at Vatican?" CNS, July 21, 1981.

20. Odilio Engels, "Council, II. History," in Karl Rahner, S.J., et al., eds., *Sacramentum Mundi* (New York: Herder and Herder, 1968), vol. 2, p. 10.

2. The College of Bishops

1. Some of the material on regional councils and episcopal conferences has been adapted from my book *A Flock of Shepherds: The National Conference of Catholic Bishops* (Kansas City, Mo.: Sheed & Ward, 1992), pp. 20–21, 28–30 (reprinted by permission of Sheed & Ward).

2. Brian E. Daley, "Structures of Charity: Bishops' Gatherings and the See of Rome in the Early Church," in Thomas J. Reese, S.J., ed., *Episcopal Conferences: Historical, Canonical, and Theological Studies* (Washington, D.C.: Georgetown University Press, 1989), p. 29.

3. Daley, "Structures of Charity," pp. 25–58; Hermann-Josef Sieben, S.J., "Episcopal Conferences in Light of Particular Councils During the First Millennium," in Hervé Legrand, Julio Manzanares, and Antonio García y García, eds., *The Nature and Future of Episcopal Conferences* (Washington, D.C.: Catholic University of America Press, 1988), pp. 30–56.

4. Odilio Engels, "Council, II. History," in Karl Rahner, S.J., et al., eds., *Sacramentum Mundi* (New York: Herder and Herder, 1968), vol. 2, p. 13.

5. James H. Provost, "Title II: Groupings of Particular Churches," in James A. Coriden, Thomas J. Green, and Donald E. Heintschel, eds., *The Code of Canon Law: A Text and Commentary* (New York: Paulist Press, 1985), p. 356–357.

6. Joseph A. Komonchak, "Introduction," in Thomas J. Reese, S.J., ed., *Episcopal Con-*

ferences: Historical, Canonical, and Theological Studies (Washington, D.C.: Georgetown University Press, 1989), p. 2.

7. This debate, which is still going on, is too complex and extensive for treatment here. See the articles by Joseph A. Komonchak, Avery Dulles, S.J., Ladislas Orsy, S.J., Michael A. Fahey, S.J., and James H. Provost in Reese, ed., *Episcopal Conferences.*

8. "Decree on the Bishops' Pastoral Office in the Church," in Walter M. Abbott, S.J., ed., *The Documents of Vatican II* (New York: America Press, 1966), pp. 425–426.

9. Thomas J. Green, "The Normative Role of Episcopal Conferences in the 1983 Code," in Reese, ed., *Episcopal Conferences,* p. 143.

10. Ibid., p. 139.

11. "Review" (recognitio) has a technical meaning when applied to general decrees of councils and conferences. It implies a less significant Roman intervention than the papal approval (approbatio) required for a program of seminary studies or a conference catechism.

12. Provost, "Title II," p. 362.

13. Reese, *Flock of Shepherds,* pp. 353–357.

14. Ibid., pp. 225–268.

15. For a brief history of the councils, see Engels, "Council," pp. 9–18, and F. Dvornik, "Councils, General (Ecumenical), History of," *New Catholic Encyclopedia* (New York: McGraw-Hill, 1967), vol. 4, pp. 373–377.

16. Engels, "Council," p. 12.

17. See Hubert Jedin, "Conciliarism," in Rahner et al., eds., *Sacramentum Mundi,* vol. 1, pp. 401–403; and B. Tierney, "Conciliarism (History of)," *New Catholic Encyclopedia,* vol. 4, pp. 109–111.

18. Dvornik, "Councils," pp. 374–375.

19. Ibid., p. 377.

20. Xavier Rynne, *Vatican Council II,* 2 vols. (New York: Farrar, Straus & Giroux, 1968).

21. Avery Dulles, S.J., "The Theologian and the Magisterium," *Proceedings of the Catholic Theological Society of America,* 31 (1976): 240, as cited in Richard A. McCormick, S.J., *The Critical Calling: Reflections on Moral Dilemmas since Vatican II* (Washington, D.C.: Georgetown University Press, 1989), p. 33.

3. The Synod of Bishops

1. For a report on the Vatican II discussions on the synod, see Robert Trisco, "The Synod of Bishops and the Second Vatican Council," *American Ecclesiastical Review,* 157 (July–December 1967): 145–160.

2. Rene Lauretin, "Synod and Curia," in Peter Huizing and Knut Walf, eds., *The Roman Curia and the Communion of Churches, Concilium,* 127 (1979): 91–103.

3. The term "synod" was once applied to any gathering (local, regional, national, or ecumenical) called to discuss and sometimes resolve church issues. In this sense it was synonymous with "council." Patriarchal and other synods are still common in the Eastern Catholic churches. The 1983 Code of Canon Law permits diocesan and national synods, but the latter are extremely rare while the former are not numerous.

4. Paul VI, *motu proprio Apostolica Sollicitudo,* September 15, 1965, *Canon Law Digest,* 6: 388–393.

5. John Paul II, "Address to the Council of the General Secretariat of the Synod of Bishops," April 30, 1983, *L'Osservatore Romano: Weekly Edition in English,* May 23, 1983, p. 5.

6. In 1983, John Paul II indicated that he preferred documents from the synod that

would have not only moral authority but juridical authority binding on the whole church, but no such synod document has yet been issued. Sister Mary Ann Walsh, "Pope Willing to Make Synod Binding, Archbishop Tomko Reports," CNS, September 30, 1983.

7. The organization and structure of the synod are described in the *motu proprio Apostolica Sollicitudo* (September 15, 1965) by Paul VI and the *Ordo Synodi Episcoporum Celebrandae*, recognitus et auctus (August 20, 1971). See "*Motu Proprio Apostolica Sollicitudo* [and] *Ordo Synodi Episcoporum Celebrandae*, recognitus et auctus," an unofficial English text by the general secretariat of the synod of bishops (Vatican City: photocopy, undated).

8. On the recommendation of episcopal conferences and the Council of the General Secretariat, the frequency of synods was changed after the 1971 synod from every two years to every three years. John G. Johnson, "The Synod of Bishops: An Analysis of Its Legal Development" (J.C.D. diss., Catholic University of America, 1986), p. 113 (also published as *Canon Law Studies*, vol. 480). The 1974 synod overwhelmingly supported this move; see Johnson, "The Synod of Bishops," p. 132. The pattern of meeting every three years was followed except for the synod on the laity, which was postponed a year to 1987 to make more room for the extraordinary synod in 1985. The 1994 synod was the first to occur four years after its predecessor, the 1990 synod.

9. The number of episcopal members elected depends on the size of the bishops' conference: one for national conferences with 25 members or less; two for conferences with between 26 and 50 members; three for conferences with between 51 and 100 members; and four for those with over 100 members. Conferences with membership just below the borderline between categories (like Poland and Zaire) have been known to try to get additional auxiliary bishops appointed before the election takes place.

10. See my book *A Flock of Shepherds: The National Conference of Catholic Bishops* (Kansas City, Mo.: Sheed & Ward, 1992), pp. 70–72.

11. Normally papal approval of elections to the synod is not a problem, but when the Brazilian episcopal conference elected a retired bishop there was a dispute over the validity of the election since retired bishops cannot vote or be elected to an office in a conference. Ultimately he was accepted more out of deference to the Brazilian conference than to canon law.

12. Jan Schotte, C.I.C.M., "The World Synod of Bishops: Media Event or Pastoral Powerhouse?" *CLSA Proceedings*, 50th Annual Convention (October 10–13, 1988): 66. According to Schotte, the percentages from the Third World at the synods are as follows: 1971: 52 percent; 1974: 54 percent; 1977: 56 percent; 1980: 56 percent; 1983: 57 percent; 1987: 57 percent.

13. Some commentators believe the 1969 extraordinary synod was called because some of the conferences of bishops were out of harmony with the pope on *Humanae Vitae*. There is also evidence that an extraordinary rather than an ordinary synod was called in 1969 simply as an experiment to see how it would work. Johnson, "The Synod of Bishops," p. 50.

14. There is some confusion over the classification of the 1980 Dutch synod and the 1980 Ukrainian synod. I treat the first as a special synod of the synod of bishops and the second as an extraordinary synod of the Ukrainian church. The latter was extraordinary because it was called by the pope (mainly to nominate a coadjutor to the major archbishop of the Ukrainian church) rather than by the major archbishop of the Ukrainian church. For a discussion of whether or not these were "special" synods, see Johnson, "The Synod of Bishops," p. 215; Jan Schotte, C.I.C.M., "The Synod of Bishops: A Permanent Yet Adaptable Church Institution," *Studia Canonica*, 26 (1992): 299–300, which gives Schotte's explanation of why the Dutch synod was called "particular"; and James H. Provost, "Part II: The Hierarchical Constitution of the Church," in James A. Coriden, Thomas J. Green, and Donald E. Heintschel, eds., *The Code of Canon Law: A Text and Commentary* (New York:

Paulist Press, 1985), p. 285. The secretariat of the synod of bishops lists the Dutch synod but not the Ukrainian synod as a special synod. General Secretariat of the Synod of Bishops, "Summary of the Synod Assemblies to Date," distributed as part of "Information Kit" (Vatican City: General Secretariat of the Synod of Bishops, photocopy [1994]). For a discussion of the Ukrainian synod, see Johnson, "The Synod of Bishops," pp. 210–214; Peter Hebblethwaite, *The Papal Year* (London: Geoffrey Chapman, 1981), pp. 60–63.

15. Johnson, "The Synod of Bishops," pp. 194–210; Peter Hebblethwaite, *Synod Extraordinary* (New York: Doubleday, 1986), pp. 38–49; Hebblethwaite, *The Papal Year*, pp. 54–59.

16. Philip J. Rosato, "The Church of United Europe: Reflections on the Recent Special Synod," *America*, 166 (January 11, 1992): 4–7. Also see Schotte, "The Synod of Bishops," pp. 300–304, for a description of the procedures followed at the synod for Europe.

17. See my articles "The Synod on the Church in Africa," *America*, 170 (May 14, 1994): 3–6, and "The African Synod: You Had to Be There," *America*, 170 (June 4, 1994): 8–9.

18. The bishops are asked to keep in mind the following criteria when making a recommendation: "(a) that the topic have a universal character, that is, a reference and application to the whole church; (b) that the topic have a contemporary character and urgency, in a positive sense, that is, having the capability of exciting new energies and movement in the church toward growth; (c) that the topic have a pastoral focus and application as well as a firm doctrinal basis; (d) that the topic have a feasibility; in other words, that it have the potential actually to be accomplished." General Secretariat of the Synod of Bishops, "Preparation for a Synod Assembly," distributed as part of "Information Kit" (Vatican City, photocopy [1994]).

19. It is not called the council of the synod but the Council of the General Secretariat of the Synod of Bishops because Vatican canonists argue that the synod has no permanent existence whereas the secretariat is a permanent organ. In practice the distinction has made little difference. The first Council for the General Secretariat of the Synod of Bishops was elected by the 1969 extraordinary synod through a mail ballot after the members had gone home. Before the 1969 extraordinary synod, the pope appointed an interim commission to review suggestions sent in by delegates and to draft a schema.

20. At the end of the 1985 extraordinary synod a dispute arose when officials planned to have the synod elect a new council to replace the one elected at the last ordinary synod. The officials argued that each new synod, whether ordinary or extraordinary, must elect a new council. The problem was that the old council had already begun preparation for the next ordinary synod. It was impossible for the extraordinary synod to simply reelect the old council members because some of them (like Cardinals Evaristo Arns, Joseph Bernardin, and Carlo Martini) were not members of the current synod since it was an extraordinary synod with conference presidents instead of elected members. Surprisingly, the pope had not appointed these men to the extraordinary synod. Liberal critics saw a conservative plot in this move since some of the old council members were considered more liberal. Ultimately, the pope intervened to keep the old council.

21. A person needs an absolute majority (more than half) to be elected to the council on the first vote. A relative majority (more than anyone else) is sufficient on the second ballot.

22. My interview of Cardinal (then Archbishop) Jan Schotte took place at the Canon Law Society of America (CLSA) meeting in Baltimore, Maryland, October 12, 1988. All quotations from Schotte come from this interview unless otherwise noted.

23. For example, to the first council in 1972 Paul VI appointed Cardinal Maurice Roy, president of the Council for the Laity and the Commission on Justice and Peace. Since one of the topics of the preceding synod had been "justice in the world," Roy's appointment was probably looking backward rather than forward to the next synod on evangelization. Paul VI also appointed Cardinal Pericle Felici, president of the Apostolic Signatura, to the

council in 1978. Felici, a canon lawyer critical of making marriage annulments easy, may have been appointed in anticipation of the synod on the family to be held in 1980.

24. The topics chosen by the pope for the 1971, 1974, 1980, and 1983 synods were from the three recommended by the Council of the General Secretariat of the Synod of Bishops. The council did not recommend a topic for 1977 but sent to the pope the suggestions from the conferences.

25. The 1987 synod had been on the laity, but many religious were not very eager to have a synod about religious life. Although the pope wanted to have a synod on religious eventually, he may have felt it would be better to deal with priestly formation before a synod on religious. After a synod on the laity and then another on the formation of priests, it became inevitable that the next synod would be on religious.

26. A series of volumes in Italian gives the most exhaustive documentation and history of the synods: Giovanni Caprile, S.J., *Il Sinodo dei Vescovi* (Rome: La Civiltà Cattolica, 1968–1990). For the best English history of the synods from 1967 to 1983, see Johnson, "The Synod of Bishops."

27. Francis X. Murphy, C.SS.R., and Gary MacEoin, *Synod '67: A New Sound in Rome* (Milwaukee: Bruce, 1968); Johnson, "The Synod of Bishops," pp. 5–42.

28. Francis X. Murphy, C.SS.R., "The Roman Synod of Bishops, 1971," *American Ecclesiastical Review,* 10 (1971): 74–83; Johnson, "The Synod of Bishops," pp. 77–109.

29. Johnson, "The Synod of Bishops," pp. 110–138.

30. Ibid., pp. 139–158.

31. See my articles "Report from the Synod," *America,* 143 (October 11, 1980), "The Close of the Synod," *America,* 143 (November 8, 1980), and "Report on the Synod," *America,* 143 (December 20, 1980); see also Jan Grootaers and Joseph A. Selling, *The 1980 Synod of Bishops "On the Role of the Family": An Exposition of the Events and an Analysis of Its Text* (Leuven: University Press, 1983); Johnson, "The Synod of Bishops," pp. 159–184; Hebblethwaite, *The Papal Year,* pp. 100–109.

32. Johnson, "The Synod of Bishops," pp. 217–239.

33. Ibid., pp. 43–76.

34. See my articles "Extraordinary Synod," *America,* 153 (December 14, 1985), and "Synod Relaunches Vatican II," *America,* 153 (December 21, 1985); see also Giuseppe Alberigo and James H. Provost, eds., *Synod 1985: An Evaluation, Concilium,* 188 (1986); Richard Cowden-Guido, *John Paul II and the Battle for Vatican II* (Manassas, Va.: Trinity Communications, 1986); Hebblethwaite, *Synod Extraordinary;* Francis X. Murphy, C.SS.R., "The Politique of the Synod," *America,* 154 (January 25, 1986): 49–51; Xavier Rynne, *John Paul's Extraordinary Synod: A Collegial Achievement* (Wilmington, Del.: Michael Glazier, 1986).

35. John Paul's words were:

"in some way to relive that extraordinary atmosphere which characterized the ecumenical council, through mutual participation in the sufferings and the joys, the struggles and the hopes, that pertain to the Body of Christ in the various regions of the world;

to exchange and examine experiences and information concerning the application of the council, both at the universal and the local level of the church;

to promote the further study of ways of incorporating Vatican II into the life of the church, and this in the light of new needs as well." *L'Osservatore Romano,* January 27, 1985.

36. Although "lineamenta" is a plural noun in Latin, since it refers to a document it may take singular verbs and pronouns in English.

37. Hebblethwaite, *Synod Extraordinary,* p. 49.

38. In 1974 there were 98 responses; in 1977, 86 replies; in 1980, 68 replies.

39. Jan P. Schotte, "Conferenza Stampa per la Presentazione dell'Instrumentum Laboris

per la IX Assemblea Generale Ordinaria de Sinodo dei Vescovi" (Vatican City: Bollettino Sala Stampa della Santa Sede, June 20, 1994), p. 4. According to Johnson, there were 76 responses from episcopal conferences in 1971, 72 in 1974, 86 in 1977, 79 in 1980, and 42 in 1983. Johnson, "The Synod of Bishops."

40. John G. Johnson, "Subsidiarity and the Synod of Bishops," *Jurist*, 50 (1990): 450.

41. If there is more than one topic, more than one relator and secretary are appointed, as occurred in 1967, 1969, 1971, and 1974. For a list of relators and secretaries, see Johnson, "The Synod of Bishops," pp. 13, 53, 83, 118, 147–148, 168, 224.

42. John Thavis, "Making a Splash at the Synod: The Case for Women Cardinals," CNS, October 14, 1994.

43. Beginning with the 1991 European synod, representatives from non-Catholic Christian communities were referred to as "fraternal delegates" and allowed to participate fully except for voting. The Synod on Lebanon in 1995 had Orthodox, Protestant, and Muslim fraternal delegates. John Thavis, "Muslim, Christian Synod Delegates Agree Lebanon Needs Unity," CNS, November 29, 1995.

44. At the beginning of the 1971, 1974, and 1977 synods an appointed bishop also presented a "panorama," or report on the state of the church around the world. This practice was dropped in 1980 because so few bishops' conferences sent in material for the presentation. In 1983 it was restored as a means of reporting on the implementation of the 1980 synod on the pastoral care of families.

45. The 1971 synod on justice and priesthood was the first to allow observers (laypersons and priests) to address the synod.

46. The president has little discretion in controlling debate or deciding who can speak. He can propose ending discussion of a topic, a proposal the assembly can decide by a majority vote. He can also try to persuade members of different groups to agree to a few speaking in the name of all according to different opinions. If during the synod issues need further study, the president can with the approval of the pope form various study commissions, although this appears to have been done rarely. Unless the pope decides otherwise, these commissions have twelve members, eight elected by the synod and four appointed by the pope.

47. "Certain Explanations on the Order of the Synod of Bishops," in "*Ordo Synodi*," p. 23. The rules state that those speaking for conferences will speak according to precedence, but one participant's recollection is that the order of speakers is determined by when they submit their requests to speak. "*Ordo Synodi*," article 35, p. 19.

48. "Certain Explanations," pp. 23–24.

49. Johnson, "The Synod of Bishops," p. 175n80.

50. Schotte, "The World Synod of Bishops," p. 58.

51. Originally the relator was chosen at the beginning of the discussions, but the bishops asked that he be selected at the end because they wanted to get to know one another before they selected one of their group to be their spokesperson. However, one participant reports that for practical reasons the group relator is still chosen at the beginning so that he can take notes on the discussions in the group from the beginning.

52. Some observers believe that the synod would take a more activist role if the small groups were arranged by topics rather than by language groups. A committee devoted to a particular topic would attract those bishops most interested in that issue. The language groups deal with everything and thus do not deal with anything in detail. On the other hand, it would be difficult for synod committees to work without a common language or simultaneous translations.

53. Johnson, "The Synod of Bishops," p. 175n80.

54. Ibid., p. 158.

55. Before 1980, the members of the commission to write the message to the people of God were appointed by the president. From 1980 on they were elected.

56. Grootaers and Selling, *The 1980 Synod of Bishops,* pp. 303–304, as quoted by Johnson, "The Synod of Bishops," p. 179.

57. Sister Mary Ann Walsh, "Pope Willing to Make Synod Binding, Archbishop Tomko Reports," CNS, September 30, 1983.

58. Likewise, the 1991 European synod also produced a document even though its meeting lasted only two weeks.

59. Grootaers and Selling, *The 1980 Synod of Bishops,* pp. 337–338, as quoted by Johnson, "The Synod of Bishops," p. 179.

60. Murphy, "The Roman Synod of Bishops, 1971," p. 75.

61. A special synod committee decides, subject to the approval of the president, what information will be provided to the press. On the committee are the general secretary, the president of the Pontifical Council for Social Communications, and two synodal delegates appointed by the president of the synod.

62. Attempts to limit press access to official channels have failed. Members from different countries often meet with the press from their countries. Originally unofficial press conferences were forbidden, but various tactics were used to get around this prohibition. For example, the British delegates would not hold press conferences, but they would invite selected members of the press to afternoon tea.

63. Originally it was forbidden to release the full text of synod speeches. Many bishops, including most of the Americans, ignored this restriction or deleted a small amount of text so that technically it was no longer a full text.

64. James H. Provost, "Structuring the Church as a Communio," *Jurist,* 36 (1976): 240.

65. Ibid.

4. The College of Cardinals

1. See Stephan Kuttner, "Cardinalis: The History of a Canonical Concept," *Traditio,* 3 (1945): 129–214; K. F. Morrison, "Cardinal, I (History of)," in *New Catholic Encyclopedia,* vol. 3, pp. 104–105; John F. Broderick, S.J., "The Sacred College of Cardinals, Size and Geographical Composition (1099–1986)," *Archivum Historiae Pontificiae,* 25 (1987): 7–71.

2. In ancient times a man was ordained for a particular church and normally stayed there for the rest of his life. He had a "title" to this position and was called a titular priest. A priest who moved to another assignment was incardinated in that assignment and was a cardinal priest. He was attached to that post, as a door is attached by a hinge or "cardo" to a door post. The root of the word "cardinal" *(cardo)* was later reinterpreted to mean that cardinals were hinges holding the church together.

3. In determining precedence at court and liturgical ceremonies, the cardinal bishops outrank the cardinal priests and deacons, and the cardinal priests outrank the cardinal deacons. Within each order, precedence is determined by date of appointment.

4. Since many of these men appear to have received minor orders (for example, tonsure), they were technically clerics and not laymen, although today one becomes a cleric only be being ordained a deacon.

5. Broderick, "Sacred College," p. 20.

6. Morrison, "Cardinal," p. 105.

7. The consistory also performed a judicial function until the thirteenth century when this function was given to a new body, the "Auditorium," which later evolved into the current apostolic tribunals.

8. Petrus Canisius van Lierde and A. Giraud, *What Is a Cardinal?* (New York: Hawthorn, 1964), p. 95.

9. Ibid.

10. B. Tierney, "Capitulations," in *New Catholic Encyclopedia,* vol. 3, p. 90; Lierde and Giraud, *What Is a Cardinal?* pp. 48–49.

11. Paul VI held a secret consistory in 1964 to discuss ecumenical relations, especially with the Orthodox church.

12. John Paul II, "Pope John Paul II Opens College of Cardinals Meeting," *Origins,* 9 (November 15, 1979): 356.

13. Ibid., p. 357.

14. John Paul II, "Current Questions That Concern the Vatican," *Origins,* 12 (December 9, 1982): 414.

15. John Paul II, "Address to Consistory" (November 26, 1994), *Origins,* 24 (December 8, 1994): 448.

16. Canon 353, §3. This terminology is new, so it is not surprising that the distinction between consulting the cardinals in an ordinary versus an extraordinary consistory is not clear. It appears that the code was left vague so that the pope could consult the cardinals in whatever way he wanted.

17. Vatican officials confused matters by originally using the term "general assembly" or "plenary assembly" of the cardinals to describe early meetings called by John Paul, implying that they were not consistories. This may have been John Paul's way of avoiding the ceremonies and procedures of traditional consistories. The 1979 meeting of cardinals was referred to as an "extraordinary meeting" by the pope. The 1982 meeting was called a "plenary assembly" and a "convention" by the pope and a "plenary assembly" by a communiqué issued on the final day. The 1985 meeting was referred to as a "general assembly" or "plenary assembly" of the cardinals. In 1991 the Vatican called that year's meeting an extraordinary consistory and began referring to the earlier meetings as extraordinary consistories, the term I will use to describe them. See also Jerry Filteau, "When Cardinals Meet to Advise, It's a Consistory," CNS, June 22, 1988; James H. Provost, "Part II: The Hierarchical Constitution of the Church," in James A. Coriden, Thomas J. Green, and Donald E. Heintschel, eds., *The Code of Canon Law: A Text and Commentary* (New York: Paulist Press, 1985), p. 290.

18. "Communiqué: College of Cardinals Meeting Ends," *Origins,* 9 (November 22, 1979): 371–372.

19. "Communiqué on the Cardinals' Meeting," *Origins,* 12 (December 9, 1982): 416–418.

20. See Peter Hebblethwaite, *Synod Extraordinary* (New York: Doubleday, 1986), pp. 93–106; "Communiqué" on finances of Holy See and Vatican City [November 23, 1985], *L'Osservatore Romano: Weekly Edition in English,* December 2, 1985, p. 7; "On File," *Origins,* 15 (December 5, 1985): 410.

21. "Communiqué Following the College of Cardinals' Meeting," *Origins,* 20 (April 25, 1991): 745, 747–748.

22. Peter Hebblethwaite, "Pope discusses millennium with cardinals," *National Catholic Reporter,* July 1, 1994, p. 17.

23. There were 122 cardinals present at the first extraordinary consistory in 1979; 97 in 1982; 122 in 1985; 112 in 1991; 114 in 1994.

24. *L'Osservatore Romano: Weekly Edition in English,* June 22, 1994, pp. 6–7.

25. Francis Arinze, "The Challenge of New Religious Movements," *Origins,* 20 (April 25, 1991): 748–753; Jozef Tomko, "On Relativizing Christ: Sects and the Church," *Origins,* 20 (April 25, 1991): 753–754.

26. Joseph Ratzinger, "Doctrinal Document on Threats to Life Proposed," *Origins*, 20 (April 25, 1991): 755–759.

27. Patrick Granfield, "Papal Resignation," *Jurist*, 38 (1978): 118–131. Pius XII reportedly planned to resign if he was arrested and removed from the Vatican by the Nazis. John Thavis, "Pius XII Prepared to Resign if Arrested by the Nazis, Says Official," NC News, January 28, 1988.

28. Peter Hebblethwaite, *Paul VI: The First Modern Pope* (New York: Paulist Press, 1993), pp. 691–692.

29. Despite church teaching that extraordinary means need not be used to keep alive a dying patient, who will have the courage to unplug the life support systems of a pope? More important, who will have the credibility within the church to do this without having their judgment or motives questioned? It would be prudent for the pope to write a living will to indicate his desires and who has the authority to make such a decision if he is unconscious. The best choice would be a family member or old friend whose love and loyalty to the pope would be unquestioned but who could also make a tough decision.

30. The resignation of an insane pope could be problematic because under canon law a person has to be of sound mind when he resigns an office or his resignation is not valid. Nor is a resignation induced through fear or fraud considered valid under canon law.

31. Some medieval theologians and canonists argued that a heretical pope would be spiritually dead or outside the church, and therefore out of office. How this would be done is uncertain. Who can judge the pope? How could this be done without causing a schism? In any case, the definition of papal infallibility at Vatican I has made it more difficult to use heresy as grounds for removing a pope.

32. The camerlengo (Cardinal Eduardo Martinez Somalo) tells the vicar of Rome (Cardinal Camillo Ruini) of the pope's death and the vicar then informs the people of Rome. Meanwhile the prefect of the papal household tells the dean (Cardinal Bernardin Gantin) of the college of cardinals, who informs the rest of the college, the ambassadors accredited to the Holy See, and the heads of nations. Although this is the formal procedure, most people will hear of the death of the pope through Vatican Radio and other news media.

33. These rumors were investigated and put to rest by John Cornwell, *A Thief in the Night: The Mysterious Death of Pope John Paul I* (New York: Simon and Schuster, 1989).

34. John Paul II, *Universi Dominici Gregis*, February 22, 1996, *Origins*, 25 (March 7, 1996): 617–630. This supersedes Paul VI, "*Romano Pontifici Eligendo*" (October 1, 1975), *L'Osservatore Romano: Weekly Edition in English*, November 20, 1975, pp. 1–7. Only the second part of *Romano Pontifici Eligendo* is printed in *Origins*, 5 (November 27, 1975): 360–367. I will use the English translation in *L'Osservatore Romano* and *Origins*, which is the same. For a different English translation, see *Canon Law Digest*, 8: 133–169.

35. While the pope is alive, the camerlengo has the authority to act for the pope in certain areas when the pope is away from Rome. With John Paul traveling as much as he does, this could have been an important job, but modern communications technology has allowed the pope to be in continuous contact with the Roman curia. As a result, major decisions are referred to the pope or wait for his return.

36. The dean of the college of cardinals is elected by and from the cardinals who possess a title to a suburbicarian church. These are the cardinal bishops, excluding the oriental patriarchs. See canon 352.

37. Zsolt Aradi, *The Popes: The History of How They Are Chosen, Elected, and Crowned* (London: MacMillan, 1956), pp. 66–67; Valérie Pirie, *The Triple Crown: An Account of the Papal Conclaves from the Fifteenth Century to the Present Day* (London: Sidgwick & Jackson, 1935; Wilmington, N.C.: Consortium Books, [1976?]), pp. 157–159.

38. Richard McBrien, "Pope's health puts church in end-of-regime mode," *National Catholic Reporter*, October 14, 1994, pp. 19–20; J. N. D. Kelly, *The Oxford Dictionary of Popes* (New York: Oxford University Press, 1986), p. 56.

39. Kelly, *Oxford Dictionary of Popes*, pp. 13–15.

40. Ibid., pp. 32–33. See also Aradi, *Popes*, pp. 62–63.

41. Kelly, *Oxford Dictionary of Popes*, pp. 60–62.

42. Ibid., pp. 119–120. See also Aradi, *Popes*, p. 63.

43. Broderick, "Sacred College," p. 14.

44. Despite the prestige of their office, only a handful of the approximately 2,900 cardinals have been called saints: Peter Damian (1007–1072), Bonaventure (1217–1274), John Fisher (1469–1535), Charles Borromeo (1538–1584), Robert Bellarmine (1542–1621), Gregory Barbarigo (1626–1697), and Giovanni Maria Tomasi (1649–1713).

45. Lierde and Giraud, *What Is a Cardinal?* p. 69.

46. Constructing a list of cardinalitial sees is inherently risky because the makeup of the college has changed so much in this century. But sees that might expect to have cardinal archbishops today include: Armagh, Barcelona, Berlin, Bogota, Bologna, Boston, Bombay, Brasilia, Budapest, Buenos Aires, Caracas, Chicago, Cologne, Cordoba, Detroit, Dublin, Florence, Genoa, Krakow, Lima, Lisbon, Los Angeles, Lyon, Madrid, Mechelen-Brussel, Manila, Marseilles, Mexico City, Milan, Munich, Naples, New York, Palermo, Paris, Philadelphia, Prague, Quebec, Quito, Rennes, Rio de Janeiro, San Juan (Puerto Rico), Santiago in Chile, Santo Domingo, São Paulo, São Salvador da Bahia, Sydney, Toledo, Turin, Utrecht, Venice, Vienna, Washington, Westminster (London), Warsaw, Zagreb. In the United States, St. Louis and Baltimore have sometimes had cardinals. In Canada, the red hat could go to Montreal, Toronto, or Quebec, but probably not to all three at once. In Africa, it is too early to determine which sees will be cardinalitial, but cardinals have resided in Algeria, Angola, Benin, Burkina Faso, Cameroon, Ethiopia, Ivory Coast, Kenya, Madagascar, Mauritius, Mozambique, Nigeria, Samoa, Senegal, Seville, South Africa, Tanzania, and Zaire. In Asia, the cardinals have been from China (and Hong Kong), Korea, Lebanon, Pakistan, Japan, Thailand, the Philippines, and Vietnam.

47. Since canon law invalidated a ballot cast by an elector for himself, electors signed their ballots so that if someone received just two-thirds, his ballot could be checked to make sure he did not vote for himself. By requiring a two-thirds majority plus one, Pius XII did away with the need to sign ballots or check the winners. John Paul II does not seem to be concerned about this problem.

48. Aradi, *Popes*, pp. 64–66.

49. For a list giving the lengths of the conclaves since Gregory X's Constitution of 1274 to 1978, see Raimondo Manzini, "Papal Elections," in *The Vatican* (New York: Vendome Press; Dublin: Gill & MacMillan, 1980), pp. 183–188.

50. Pirie, *Triple Crown*, p. 294.

51. These are the secretary of the college of cardinals, the master of papal liturgical celebrations with two masters of ceremonies and two religious attached to the papal sacristy, an assistant to the cardinal dean, some religious priests to act as confessors in various languages, two doctors, and persons for preparing and serving meals and housekeeping.

52. John Paul II, *Universi Dominici Gregis*, no. 53.

53. Ibid., no. 52. Prior to the opening of the conclave, another ecclesiastic presents a similar meditation to the cardinals in the general congregation on the problems facing the church and the need for careful discernment in choosing the new pope.

54. Paul VI, *Romano Pontifici Eligendo*, no. 63.

55. Ibid., no. 64.

56. Peter Hebblethwaite, *The Year of Three Popes* (New York: Collins, 1978), p. 74; Hebblethwaite, *Paul VI*, pp. 327–328; Andrew M. Greeley, *The Making of the Popes 1978* (Kansas City, Mo.: Andrews & McMeel, 1979), p. 260. For more information on the 1963 conclave, see Giancarlo Zizola, *Quale Papa?* (Rome: Borla, 1977).

57. John Paul II, *Universi Dominici Gregis*, no. 66.

58. Hebblethwaite, *Year of Three Popes*, p. 81.

59. Pirie, *Triple Crown*, p. 49.

60. Ibid., pp. 94–95.

61. If during the tabulation of the votes the scrutineers discover two cards folded in such a way as to appear to be filled in by one elector, they are counted as one vote if they are for the same person. If they are for different persons, then neither vote is counted. A ballot with two names written on it is not counted.

62. John Paul II, *Universi Dominici Gregis*, no. 75.

63. Broderick, "Sacred College," p. 21.

64. Excellent statistics are available in Broderick, "Sacred College," pp. 46–47, 60, 62–63.

65. Giancarlo Zizola, *Il Conclave: Storia e segreti* (Rome: Newton Compton, 1993), p. 388.

66. For statistical purposes, the vicar of Rome is counted as a curial cardinal.

67. For Andrew Greeley's list of great electors at the 1978 conclaves, see Greeley, *Making of the Popes 1978*, pp. 118–121.

68. After the 1963 conclave, rumors circulated that Montini agreed to keep Cardinal Amleto Cicognani as his secretary of state in exchange for the support of curial cardinals. "The evidence counts against the tale," according to Hebblethwaite, *Paul VI*, p. 328.

69. Hebblethwaite, *Year of Three Popes*, pp. 83–84. Giancarlo Zizola and Andrew Greeley report that the Siri supporters remained with him on the second ballot and moved to Luciani on the third. Greeley, *Making of the Popes 1978*, pp. 152–153; Zizola, *Il Conclave*, p. 275. See also Francis X. Murphy, *The Papacy Today* (London: Weidenfeld & Nicolson, 1981), pp. 160–161.

70. Leo XIII was 67 years of age when elected; Pius X, 68; Benedict XV, 59; Pius XI, 64; Pius XII, 63; John XXIII, 76; Paul VI, 66; John Paul I, 65; and John Paul II, 58.

71. At the August 1978 conclave, there were 39 cardinals between the ages of 60 and 70. Greeley, *Making of the Popes 1978*, p. 136.

72. Joseph Gallagher, "24 Popes, Some Good, in Years Leading Up to First Millennium," *National Catholic Reporter*, March 17, 1995, p. 22.

73. Arthur Jones, "How Crime Writer Came to Probe Pope's Death," *National Catholic Reporter*, November 17, 1989, p. 19.

74. Peter Hebblethwaite, *The Next Pope* (San Francisco: HarperCollins, 1995), p. 31.

75. Prior to Pius XII, one has to go back to 1830 to find a curial cardinal who was never a diocesan bishop elected pope (Gregory XVI).

76. P. Rabikauskas, "Popes, Names of," in *New Catholic Encyclopedia*, vol. 11, pp. 576–577.

77. Aradi, *Popes*, p. 66.

78. Greeley, *Making of the Popes 1978*, p. 215.

79. Kelly, *Oxford Dictionary of Popes*, pp. 227–228.

80. Clement XI was not a bishop when elected in 1700. He had been a priest for less than a year, although he had been a cardinal for ten years.

81. Other popes who were deacons when elected include: Gregory the Great (590), Celestine III (1191–1198), Gelasius II (1118–1129), and Innocent III (1198–1216).

82. Pirie, *Triple Crown*, pp. 17–18.

83. Kelly, *Oxford Dictionary of Popes*, p. 200. There is a debate going on among canon lawyers and theologians on whether a person without orders can have jurisdiction. Those

who say yes point to the fact that non-ordained popes made decisions that were accepted by their successors. Alfonsus M. Stickler, "Votum," in Pontifical Council for the Interpretation of Legislative Texts, *Congragatio Plenaria diebus 20–29 Octobris 1981 habita* (Vatican City: Typis Polyglottis Vaticanis, 1991), pp. 49–65.

84. Kelly, *Oxford Dictionary of Popes*, p. 167.

85. Eight more popes are considered blessed.

86. Paul VI, March 24, 1973, address to Council of the Permanent Secretariat of the Synod of Bishops, *Origins*, 2 (April 12, 1973): 674.

87. See Hebblethwaite, *Next Pope*, pp. 68–69, for an account of Cardinal Giuseppe Siri's objections to adding noncardinal electors.

88. Hebblethwaite, *Year of Three Popes*, pp. 46 and 78.

89. Peter Huizing and Knut Walf, ed., *The Roman Curia and the Communion of Churches, Concilium*, 127 (1979): xiii; Hebblethwaite, *Next Pope*, p. 66.

5. The Roman Curia

1. For histories of the curia see Ignazio Gordon, "Curia: Historical Evolution," in *Sacramentum Mundi: An Encyclopedia of Theology* (New York: Herder & Herder, 1968–1970), vol. 2, pp. 49–52; Giuseppe Alberigo, "Serving the Communion of Churches," in Peter Huizing and Knut Walf, eds., *The Roman Curia and the Communion of Churches, Concilium*, 127 (1979): 12–33; Reginald L. Poole, *Lectures on the History of the Papal Chancery Down to the Time of Innocent III* (Cambridge: Cambridge University Press, 1915).

2. Poole, *Papal Chancery*, p. 14.

3. Gordon, "Curia," p. 50.

4. Ibid., p. 51.

5. There are 405 additional employees in Vatican Radio, 116 in Tipografia Poliglotta Vaticana, 20 in Libreria Editrice Vaticana, and 99 in *L'Osservatore Romano*.

6. *L'Attività della Santa Sede nel 1994* (Vatican City: Libreria Editrice Vaticana, 1995), pp. 1227–1228.

7. John Paul II, "Apostolic Constitution *Pastor Bonus*," in Ernest Caparros, Michel Thériault, and Jean Thorn, eds., *Code of Canon Law Annotated* (Montreal: Wilson & Lafleur, 1993), pp. 1166–1279. For an analysis of the constitution, see Piero Antonio Bonnet and Carlo Gullo, eds., *La Curia Romana nella Cost. Ap. "Pastor Bonus," Studi Giuridici*, vol. 21 (Vatican City: Libreria Editrice Vaticana, 1990); James H. Provost, "Pastor Bonus: Reflections on the Reorganization of the Roman Curia," *Jurist*, 48 (1988): 499–535; Joël-Benoît d'Onorio, *Le Pape et le Gouvernement de L'Église* (Paris: Fleurus-Tardy, 1992).

8. Not all curial decisions carry the same juridical authority. For an analysis of the juridical significance of different curial documents, see Francis G. Morrisey, O.M.I., "Papal and Curial Pronouncements: Their Canonical Significance in Light of the 1983 Code of Canon Law," *Jurist*, 50 (1990): 112–125.

9. The three tribunals also have jurisdiction over the universal church. The Congregation for Divine Worship and the Discipline of the Sacraments also handles certain marriage cases for all the churches.

10. "Religious" was included in the title of the Commission for Religious Relations with Jews to make clear that it did not deal with political relations with Israel, which come under the competency of the Secretariat of State.

11. Statistics on the size of congregations are based on the 1995 *Annuario Pontificio* (Vatican City: Libreria Editrice Vaticana, 1995).

12. John Paul II, *Pastor Bonus*, p. 1199. In the strict sense, only cardinals and bishops are

members of congregations. Even so, the Congregation for the Evangelization of Peoples has three religious priests, all superior generals of religious orders with large numbers of missionaries, who sit as members of the congregation during plenary meetings.

13. Ibid., p. 1201.

14. There is an unwritten rule, however, that former prefects of a congregation do not become members of their old congregation. It is felt that once a prefect leaves a congregation, he should not be involved in supervising the work of his successor. This leaves the new prefect and congregation free to discuss changes in policy and administration without having a defensive former prefect on the congregation. This rule does not apply to former secretaries of congregations, who after they are made cardinals are frequently appointed members of their former congregations.

15. John Paul II, *Pastor Bonus,* p. 1203.

16. John Paul II, "Apostolic Constitution *Divinus Perfectionis Magister* [January 25, 1983]," *Canon Law Digest,* 10: 257–273. For excellent treatments of the Congregation for the Causes of Saints, see Kenneth L. Woodward, *Making Saints* (New York: Simon & Schuster, 1990), and Lawrence S. Cunningham, "The Politics of Canonization," *The Christian Century,* 100 (May 11, 1983): 454–455.

17. Some councils have vice presidents, who are bishops and rank above the secretary and under the president. In 1994 there were vice presidents in the councils for the Laity and for Justice and Peace. In the past, there have also been vice presidents in the councils for Christian Unity, for the Family, Cor Unum, and for Social Communications. Often they do work similar to that of a secretary and sometimes (as in the case of Laity) replace the secretary. Sometimes the positions are honorific. Another title used infrequently is *segretario aggiunto,* who ranks above an undersecretary but below a secretary. In 1995 Charles Schleck, undersecretary of the Congregation for the Evangelization of Peoples, was made an archbishop and segretario aggiunto in the congregation. The previous two occupants of that position in the congregation had already been bishops when appointed and within a couple of years were made secretary of the congregation. Other dicasteries that have had this office include the Congregation for Divine Worship, the Council for Promoting Christian Unity, and the Council for Culture.

18. Exact numbers are difficult to obtain because the *Annuario Pontificio* only lists permanent employees who have been definitively hired after a trial period that can last up to two years. In addition, it does not list employees on short-term contracts or those paid by grants from outside sources. Nor does the *Annuario* list vacant positions. Despite these limitations, the *Annuario* gives a good indication of staff size, with nonlisted personnel not adding more than 10 percent.

19. The title "capo ufficio" is sometimes used for the head of an office in the Vatican, but some offices are headed by people who are not *capi* and some *capi* are not heads of offices. The title appears to have more to do with pay than power. Sometimes the title and pay are a way of rewarding someone for years of loyal service.

20. According to John Paul II, *Pastor Bonus,* p. 1237, the Apostolic Signatura adjudicates conflicts of competence between dicasteries, but no known case has been heard by the Signatura.

21. John Paul II, *Pastor Bonus,* p. 1217, makes the Congregation for the Doctrine of the Faith the gatekeeper on doctrine. *Pastor Bonus* also says the Council for the Interpretation of Texts is "at the service of the other Roman dicasteries to assist them to ensure that general executory decrees and instructions which they are going to publish are in conformity with the prescriptions of law" (p. 1249). The council staff believe this makes them the gatekeeper on canonical issues, but they do not have the political clout to do it.

6. Vatican Officials

1. The 1961 and 1970 figures are from Fiorello Cavalli, S.J., "Sviluppo dell'Internazionalizzazione nella Curia Romana," *La Civiltà Cattolica,* 121 (1970): 555–568. See also Joël-Benoît d'Onorio, *Le Pape et le Gouvernement de L'Église* (Paris: Fleurus-Tardy, 1992), pp. 529–537.

2. At my request, a staff person in each dicastery classified by nationality the names listed in the 1994 *Annuario Pontificio* (Vatican City: Libreria Editrice Vaticana, 1994). The *Annuario* does not list part-time staff or nonprofessional staff such as porters, messengers, and the like. Since Father Cavalli had access to internal Vatican records, his staff statistics are not exactly comparable to those in my study, but the difference would be slight. Anecdotal evidence indicates that the nunciature staffs are also becoming more internationalized.

3. Karl Rahner, S.J., "Structural Change in the Church," *Theological Investigations* (New York: Crossroad, 1981), vol. 20, p. 120.

4. Gregoire Pierre Agagianian XV had been patriarch of Cilicia for the Armenians and Marcello Mimmi had been archbishop of Naples.

5. John Thavis, "Roman Rumba: Doing the Vatican Shuffle," CNS, June 16, 1995.

6. A few officials have been allowed to remain dicastery heads for some years after their 75th birthday: Cardinal Angelini (79 in 1995, president of the Council for Pastoral Assistance to Health Care Workers) and Cardinal Willebrands (retired at 79 from the Council for Promoting Christian Unity). Cardinal Angelini runs the Council for Health Care Workers by raising his own funds. A new president will mean either reduced activity by the council or a financial drain on the Vatican treasury. Cardinal Willebrands was so expert in ecumenism and so highly respected by the church's dialogue partners that he was considered practically irreplaceable.

7. Some councils have vice presidents who are bishops and rank above the secretary and under the president. In 1994 there were vice presidents in the councils for the Laity and for Justice and Peace. They usually do work similar to that of a secretary and sometimes (as in Laity) replace the secretary, but sometimes the positions are honorific.

8. D'Onorio, *Le Pape,* p. 532. In 1978, 61 percent of the secretaries were Italian; in 1980, 54 percent; in 1991, 30 percent.

9. These figures are based on the 1994 *Annuario Pontificio.*

10. D'Onorio, *Le Pape,* p. 532. In 1978, 57 percent of the undersecretaries were Italian; in 1980, 47 percent; in 1991, 32 percent.

11. For a description of the role of women in the curia of the 1970s, see Emma Cavallaro, "Women in the Roman Curia," in Peter Huizing and Knut Walf, eds., *The Roman Curia and the Communion of Churches, Concilium,* 127 (1979): 52–55.

12. Lamberto de Echeverría, "The Pope's Representatives," in Huizing and Walf, eds., *The Roman Curia,* p. 63n13.

13. John Cornwell, *A Thief in the Night: The Mysterious Death of Pope John Paul I* (New York: Simon & Schuster, 1989), pp. 142–143.

14. Joaquin Navarro-Valls, director of the Vatican press office, is an open member of Opus Dei. John Paul is a strong supporter of Opus Dei, although Paul VI was cold toward them. One source said that when Paul objected to a member of Opus Dei being hired in a congregation, he was surprised to be told that there was one in the Secretariat of State.

15. John Paul II, "Apostolic Constitution *Pastor Bonus,*" in Ernest Caparros, Michel Thériault, and Jean Thorn, eds., *Code of Canon Law Annotated* (Montreal: Wilson & Lafleur, 1993), p. 1189.

16. Ibid., p. 1185.

17. Ibid., p. 1191. Italics in the original.

7. Papal Leadership

1. Cindy Wooden, "Praying for the World's Intentions: Pope Is a Priest Too," CNS, November 11, 1995.

2. John Paul II, "Apostolic Constitution *Pastor Bonus*," in Ernest Caparros, Michel Thériault, and Jean Thorn, eds., *Code of Canon Law Annotated* (Montreal: Wilson & Lafleur, 1993), p. 1213, states that the first section "deals with everything concerning the ambassadors of States to the Holy See."

3. Peter Hebblethwaite, *The Next Pope* (San Francisco: HarperCollins, 1995), p. 136.

4. Cindy Wooden, "Vatican Trots Out the Stats on Pope's 17th Year in Office," CNS, October 16, 1995.

5. Ibid.

8. Vatican Finances

1. For a treatment of diocesan finances in the United States, see my book *Archbishop: Inside the Power Structure of the American Catholic Church* (San Francisco: Harper & Row, 1989), chap. 5.

2. Ignazio Gordon, "Curia: Historical Evolution," in Karl Rahner, S.J., et al., eds., *Sacramentum Mundi: An Encyclopedia of Theology* (New York: Herder & Herder, 1968–1970), vol. 2, p. 51.

3. "In general, these autonomous entities do not have a deficit," according to Cardinal Edmund Szoka, "A Presentation to the National Conference of Catholic Bishops of the United States of America on the Financial Situation of the Holy See" (Washington, D.C., photocopy, November 12, 1991), p. 6. Some of these autonomous entities, like St. Peter's, have endowments, donations, fees, or other sources of income. If St. Peter's is used for a non-Vatican event, for example, a beatification or the ordination of priests, the sponsor would have to pay to cover the costs. The Lateran University is another autonomous entity. The Holy See pays for the salaries of the faculty, but the university has to cover other costs with tuition and other sources of income.

4. Financial figures for the Holy See are based on "Consolidated Financial Statements of the Holy See," an annual report by the Prefecture for the Economic Affairs of the Holy See sent to the bishops of the world. Copies for years 1992 (which includes figures for 1991), 1993, and 1994 were made available to me from various sources. Although this 40-page annual report is detailed, it is also very complex and in places unclear and is difficult to understand even for accountants. Other offices that disclose financial information publicly or to the bishops include the Council Cor Unum, the mission societies under the Congregation for the Evangelization of Peoples, and the Peter's Pence office. My figures for the Vatican bank and the Vatican City State are based on interviews or news reports.

5. Clyde Haberman, "Taxes Flow to the Church: Its Cup Runneth Over," *New York Times International*, June 14, 1991. The money is divided on the basis of the people who used the checkoff. Thus in 1991, the church got 75 percent of the money because 75 percent of the people who used the checkoff chose the church.

6. Giuseppe Brunetta, S.J., "Un Bilancio del Sostentamento Economico alla Chiesa Cattolica in Italia," *La Civiltà Cattolica* (1993): 265.

7. John Paul II, "Address to Extraordinary Consistory," *L'Osservatore Romano: Weekly Edition in English*, June 22, 1994, p. 6.

8. Philip Willan, "Mafia cash 'taken by Vatican banker,'" *Times* [of London], November 18, 1994, quotes testimony of Vincenzo Calcara, who said that as part of a Mafia delegation in 1981 he delivered 10 billion lire to bank officials. The Vatican bank also made it into the movie "Godfather III."

9. Charles Raw, *The Money Changers* (London: Harvill, HarperCollins, 1992); Rubert Cornwell, *God's Banker: An Account of the Life and Death of Roberto Calvi* (London: Gollancz, 1984).

10. "The IOR manages a patrimony of about $3 billion, with annual profit estimated at about $29 million," according to Antonio Gaspari, "The Reform of the Vatican Finances," *Catholic World Report*, February 1994, p. 38.

11. Funds from the Brencanda, Doty, Lewis, and DeRance foundations paid for a management study by Merrill Lynch as well as a network of seventeen computers and financial software including Micro Control by IMRS and Microsoft Excel and Word ("FADICA Annual Report 1991"). Luckily at the same time Cardinal Szoka found an American sister, who is an expert with computers, willing to work in the prefecture. Even after the new equipment was installed, she found the staff did not know that they could put stationery through the laser printers. She also found that Excel had been improperly installed in the network so that it could only be used by a few people at a time. Within a short time, she was showing them how to process a mailing in a few hours that in the past had taken a week.

12. According to the "Consolidated Financial Statements of the Holy See, Year 1994," 49 cardinals, 22 of whom are over 75 years of age, received 2,619 million lire in remunerations, or about 53 million lire (approximately $32,900) each in 1994. Cardinals do not receive a salary but a "plate" of 4 million lire a month, plus another 250,000 lire if they are working.

13. The pension liability of 262 billion lire in 1994 was the result of an upward adjustment of 50 billion lire that was made after an updated evaluation of pension liability. In 1993 there were 873 pensioners receiving a total of 18 billion lire annually. The number of pensioners and the amount were not reported in the 1994 audit.

14. The "Consolidated Financial Statements of the Holy See" states that "Buildings located in Rome are mostly let to Holy See employees at the same rents as prevail in Italy," but those interviewed say the rents are lower. For many years, rents in Rome were set by rent control laws that were widely ignored by most landlords except for the Vatican. The laws also made it very difficult to remove individuals or their heirs from an apartment. Although the controls have been loosened, the Vatican appears to be still following the old rules.

15. Figures on the Vatican City budget are based on interviews, especially with Cardinal Rosalio José Castillo Lara.

16. *L'Attività della Santa Sede 1994* (Vatican City: Libreria Editrice Vaticana, 1995), pp. 1616–1617.

17. John Thavis, "The Vatican Projects: Putting Images, Issues before the World," and "The Vatican Projects: Linking with Science, New Media," CNS, July 24, 1984. Sharon Tully, "The Vatican's Finances," *Fortune*, December 21, 1987, p. 31.

18. Dott. Ing. Massimo Stoppa, "Role of the 'Servizi Tecnici' in the Restoration of the Sistine Chapel" (Vatican City, press release, April 8, 1994), pp. 1–2.

19. Prefecture for Economic Affairs of the Holy See, "Consolidated Financial Statements of the Holy See," year 1993, p. i.

20. Szoka, "Financial Situation of the Holy See," p. 14.

21. This does not include Vatican Radio, *L'Osservatore Romano*, Libreria Editrice Vaticana, and Tipografia Poliglotta.

22. Prefecture for Economic Affairs of the Holy See, "Consolidated Budget of the Holy See, Year 1995," p. i.

23. "In 1929, the Holy See received Lit. 1.750.000.000 (according to the exchange rate at the time, US $91,714,270.74). This amount included Lit. 1.000.000.000 (US $52,408,154.70) in securities and Lit. 750.000.000 (US $39,306,116.06) in cash in foreign currencies." Szoka, "Financial Situation of the Holy See," p. 9. My thanks to Allen D. Manvel for estimating the current value of the settlement if it had been invested in the New York Stock Exchange. He reports that "between 1929 and 1993, the average price of common stocks on the New York Stock Exchange multiplied approximately 17 times (according to an index of 500 stocks, with 1941–1943 at 10, from 26 to 450). The calculated ratio is 17.3."

24. Until recently, reporting of investments at cost was acceptable in the United States for nonprofits like the church. Auditors are now demanding that nonprofits report investments at market value.

25. James Gollin, *Worldly Goods* (New York: Random House, 1971); Corrado Pallenberg, *Vatican Finances* (London: Peter Owen, 1971); Arthur Jones, "60 years of inept management, bad investments lead to Vatican deficit," *National Catholic Reporter*, March 11, 1988, pp. 1, 23.

26. Prefecture for Economic Affairs of the Holy See, "Consolidated Financial Statements of the Holy See," year 1992, p. 24, and year 1993, p. 25.

27. Robert Moynihan, "Rome's Money Managers: Who & How," *National Catholic Register*, March 18, 1988.

28. Tully, "The Vatican's Finances," p. 35.

29. In the 1994 balance sheet of the "Consolidated Financial Statements of the Holy See," land and buildings are listed at 453 billion lire with an additional 328 billion credited to net assets as voluntary reevaluations of properties.

30. The 1994 "Consolidated Financial Statements of the Holy See" did not include "Summary Statements of Operations of Consolidated Administrations," which was included in earlier years.

31. On May 21, 1993, the secretary of state announced further accounting changes for Peter's Pence. In the future, grants from foundations ($3 million in 1992) as well as part of the donations from religious institutes ($6.5 million) will no longer be credited to Peter's Pence. This will decrease the totals for Peter's Pence.

32. John Thavis, "Vatican's Online Revolution Produces Some Paradoxes," CNS, November 3, 1995.

33. "Fact File: 446 College and University Endowments," *Chronicle of Higher Education*, February 17, 1995, p. A25.

9. Outside the Vatican

1. Hyginus Eugene Cardinale, *Holy See and International Order* (Gerrards Cross: Colin Smythe, 1976); Robert A. Graham, *Vatican Diplomacy* (Princeton: Princeton University Press, 1959); Pio Laghi, "Statement on Establishment of Vatican-U.S. Relations," *Origins*, 13 (January 19, 1984): 530; Laghi, "The True Nature of Papal Diplomacy," *Origins*, 13 (May 3, 1984): 770–773.

2. Joël-Benoît d'Onorio, *Le Pape et le Gouvernement de L'Église* (Paris: Fleurus-Tardy, 1992), p. 535.

3. Jean Gaudemet, "Bishops: From Election to Nomination," *Concilium*, 137 (July 1980): 11.

4. Jean Bernhard, "The Election of Bishops at the Council of Trent," *Concilium*, 137 (July 1980): 24–30.

5. For a more extensive treatment of the process for appointing bishops, see my earlier books, *Archbishop: Inside the Power Structure of the American Catholic Church* (San Francisco: Harper & Row, 1989), chap. 1, and *A Flock of Shepherds: The National Conference of Catholic Bishops* (Kansas City, Mo.: Sheed & Ward, 1992), chap. 1.

6. Canon Law Society of America, *The Code of Canon Law, Latin-English Edition* (Washington, D.C.: Canon Law Society of America, 1983), uses "ternus" in the English translation rather than "terna," but this word has not caught on.

7. Fewer auxiliaries are appointed in mission countries where the nuncio, not the diocesan bishop, prepares the terna for auxiliary bishops.

8. Andrew Greeley, "Look Out for the Ambitious Clerics in Purple," *National Catholic Reporter*, September 9, 1995.

9. The Council of Cardinals and Bishops is made up of exactly the same cardinals as are on the Congregation for Bishops, except that the secretary of state is the chair and Archbishop Jean-Louis Tauran, the secretary for relations with states, acts as secretary. If the papacy continues to be free to appoint whomever it wants in Eastern Europe, these episcopal appointments will eventually be transferred to the jurisdiction of the Congregation for Bishops. The secretary for relations with states also sits in on meetings of the Congregation for Bishops when it considers the appointment of bishops in countries that have concordats with the Holy See, for example, Argentina, Venezuela, and Spain.

10. It differs "only in some marginal things, nothing substantial," reports Cardinal Jozef Tomko, prefect of the Congregation for the Evangelization of Peoples, who once was secretary of the Congregation for Bishops. "Before the nuncio starts asking for information about the terna, we must give him the green light. This is very important here because we can sometimes have here in our archives more materials than the nuncio has. It is in some ways only prudential caution to avoid work and then we can discover, 'Oh but we have something more here.'" Evangelization receives fewer questionnaires on the candidates than does Bishops. For apostolic vicariates officially under the responsibility of a religious order in missionary territories, the terna would be prepared by the superior general of the order and not the nuncio.

11. *L'Attività della Santa Sede 1994* (Vatican City: Libreria Editrice Vaticana, 1995), pp. 1047–1050, 1097–1114, 1122. I do not count the appointment of apostolic administrators.

12. Thomas J. Reese, S.J., "A Survey of the American Bishops," *America*, 149 (November 12, 1983): 286.

13. Gerald P. Fogarty, *The Vatican and the American Hierarchy from 1870–1965* (Stuttgart, Germany: Anton Hiersemann, 1982; Wilmington, Del.: Michael Glazier, 1985), p. 26.

14. John Thavis, "The Pope's Bishops: Consulting on the Selections," NC News, January 13, 1988.

15. John Thavis, "The Pope's Bishops: Shaping the World's Hierarchy in His Image," NC News, January 13, 1988.

16. Thavis, "The Pope's Bishops: Consulting on the Selections."

17. "Ad quosdam episcopos e Statibus Foederatis Americae Septemtrionalis occasione oblata ad Limina visitationis coram admissos" (September 5, 1983), *Acta Apostolicae Sedis*, 76: 103–104; italics in original.

18. For more information on ad limina visits of the U.S. bishops, see Thomas J. Reese, S.J., "Quinquennial Dialogue," *America*, 158 (April 30, 1988), and Reese, *Archbishop*, pp. 317–331.

19. Congregation for Bishops, "Quinquennial Report by Residential Bishops [1975]," *Canon Law Digest*, 9: 214–238; "Form for the Quinquennial Report" (Vatican City: Vatican Polyglot Press, 1981).

20. Reese, *Archbishop*, pp. 319–320.

21. For an analysis of the pope's ad limina addresses to the U.S. bishops, see Reese, "Quinquennial Dialogue," and Reese, *Archbishop,* pp. 317–331.

22. For more on the alienation of church property, see Reese, *Archbishop,* chap. 5, and Reese, *Flock of Shepherds,* pp. 255–257.

23. "Vatican Intervenes to Stop HIV Pack," *The Tablet* [of London], 249 (November 18, 1995): 1489; Clifford Longley, "The AIDS Dilemma," *The Tablet* [of London], 249 (November 18, 1995): 1468.

24. Ann Rogers-Melnick, "Vatican Alters Rules for Disciplining Priests," *Pittsburgh Post-Gazette,* October 13, 1995; Mike Aquilina, "Church High Court Upholds Bishop in Suspension of Priest," CNS, October 12, 1995.

25. Agostino Bono, "After Vatican Letter, German Bishops Reverse Communion Policy," CNS, October 14, 1994.

26. Three major schisms have occurred in the church: the East-West schism of 1054 between Roman Catholics and the Orthodox churches, the Western schism of 1378–1417, and the Anglican schism in the mid-sixteenth century. More recent schisms include the Old Catholic movement, which began in Germany in 1870 as a rejection of Vatican I. The Polish National Catholic Church in the United States was formed in 1897 as a result of administrative and property disputes between Polish immigrant parishes and non-Polish bishops. In 1976, retired Vietnamese Archbishop Pierre Martin Ngo Din Tuc of Hue ordained five bishops from a group of devotees to alleged apparitions of Mary at Palmar de Troya, Spain. Although he later reconciled with the church, his line of schismatic bishops has grown to 46 who, like Lefebvre, oppose the reforms of Vatican II. See Jerry Filteau, "Lefebvre Movement Could Join List of Modern Schismatic Groups," CNS, June 20, 1988.

27. The Vatican has preferred to turn a blind eye to the unauthorized ordinations of bishops in the Chinese patriotic church, where the bishops must operate under an oppressive regime.

28. James A. Coriden, "Book III: The Teaching Office of the Church," in James A. Coriden, Thomas J. Green, and Donald E. Heintschel, eds., *The Code of Canon Law: A Text and Commentary* (New York: Paulist Press, 1985), p. 572.

29. When I asked Cardinal Ratzinger how many theologians did not receive the nihil obstat, he said, "We have some hundreds of cases and perhaps 10 or 20 *Obstare* [negative responses]. I would not be too sure of the numbers, but it is a small number . . . I think in a year we have 500 or 600 [cases]." This number appears high and may include nihil obstats for people other than professors. He said that I could get the statistics from the congregation, but my letter requesting the data was not answered.

30. For more on Cardinal Ratzinger's views, see Joseph Ratzinger, "The Church and Theologians," *Origins,* 15 (May 8, 1986): 761–770.

31. Avery Dulles, S.J., "The Theologian and the Magisterium," *Proceedings of the Catholic Theological Society of America,* 31 (1976): 240, as cited in Richard A. McCormick, S.J., *The Critical Calling: Reflections on Moral Dilemmas since Vatican II* (Washington, D.C.: Georgetown University Press, 1989), p. 33.

32. Pamela Schaeffer, "Four Jesuits Denied Promotion by Rome," *National Catholic Reporter,* March 29, 1996, p. 5.

33. "The Cologne Declaration," *Commonweal* (February 24, 1989), p. 102; "The Cologne Declaration," *Origins,* 18 (March 2, 1989): 633–634.

34. Gerald M. Costello, "U.S. Catholics Loyal to Church and Pope, Cardinal Ratzinger Says," NC News, February 1, 1988.

35. Congregation for the Doctrine of the Faith, *Nova agendi ratio in doctrinarum examine* (January 15, 1971), *Canon Law Digest,* 7: 181–184; Jerome Hamer, "In Service of the Magis-

terium: The Evolution of a Congregation," *Jurist,* 37 (1977): 340–357; Leo O'Donovan, ed., *Cooperation Between Theologians and the Ecclesiastical Magisterium* (Washington, D.C.: Canon Law Society of America, 1982) [studies by Granfield and Provost explore existing procedures, especially those of the Congregation for the Doctrine of the Faith]; CLSA Task Force to Study Procedures of the Congregation for the Doctrine of the Faith, "Annual Report," *CLSA Proceedings,* 51st Annual Convention (October 9–12, 1989): 235–237.

36. Congregation for the Doctrine of the Faith, *Nova agendi,* pp. 181–182.

37. Ibid., p. 182.

38. Ibid.

39. John J. Conley, "The Vatican and Jacques Pohier," *America,* 142 (June 21, 1980): 520–522; Jean-Pierre Jossua, "Jacques Pohier: A Theologian Destroyed," in Hans Küng and Leonard Swidler, eds., *The Church in Anguish: Has the Vatican Betrayed Vatican II?* (San Francisco: Harper and Row, 1987), pp. 205–211.

40. Congregation for the Doctrine of the Faith, "Declaration on Some Major Points of the Theological Teaching of Hans Küng [December 15, 1979]," *Canon Law Digest,* 9: 752–757; John Jay Hughes, "Hans Küng and the Magisterium," *Theological Studies,* 41 (1980): 368–389; Hans Urs von Balthasar, "On the Withdrawal of Hans Küng's Authorization to Teach," *Communio: International Catholic Review,* 7 (1980): 90–93; Leonard Swidler, "A Continuous Controversy: Küng in Conflict," in Küng and Swidler, eds., *The Church in Anguish,* pp. 205–211.

41. Peter Hebblethwaite, *The New Inquisition?* (London: Collins, 1980); Ad Willems, "The Endless Case of Edward Schillebeeckx," in Küng and Swidler, eds., *The Church in Anguish,* pp. 212–222.

42. Harvey Cox, *The Silencing of Leonardo Boff* (Oak Park, Ill.: Meyer Stone Books, 1988); Dennis M. Doyle, "Communion Ecclesiology and the Silencing of Boff," *America,* 167 (September 12, 1992): 139–143; Leonardo Boff and Clodovis Boff, "Summons to Rome," in Küng and Swidler, eds., *The Church in Anguish,* pp. 223–234.

43. Charles E. Curran, *Faithful Dissent* (Kansas City, Mo.: Sheed & Ward, 1986), pp. 26–49; William W. May, ed., *Vatican Authority and American Catholic Dissent: The Curran Case and Its Consequences* (New York: Crossroads, 1987); Larry Witham, *Curran vs. Catholic University* (Riverdale, Md.: Edington-Rand, 1991); McCormick, *The Critical Calling,* esp. chap. 6, "L'Affaire Curran," pp. 111–130; Bernard Häring, "The Curran Case: Conflict between Rome and the Moral Theologian," in Küng and Swidler, eds., *The Church in Anguish,* pp. 235–250.

44. "Indian Theologians Criticize Vatican for Ban on Priest," CNS, February 17, 1988; "Indian Catholic Official Defends Vatican Ban of Theologian," CNS, March 24, 1988.

45. "Remarks of Charles E. Curran," March 11, 1986 (photocopy), p. 1.

46. Catholic Theological Society of America, "Do Not Extinguish the Spirit," *Origins,* 20 (December 27, 1990): 464; see also CLSA Task Force to Study Procedures of the Congregation for the Doctrine of the Faith, "Annual Report," *CLSA Proceedings,* 51st Annual Convention (October 9–12, 1989): 235–237.

47. O'Donovan, *Cooperation,* p. 148.

48. Agostino Bono, "Loyal Gadfly: Septuagenarian Theologian Still Raising Questions," CNS, July 9, 1993.

49. "Theologian Suggests Reforms to End Doctrinal Congregation 'Nightmare,'" NC News, April 18, 1989.

50. Rochelle Saidel, "Brazilian Theologian to Leave Franciscans, Priesthood," CNS, June 29, 1992.

51. Hans Küng, "Cardinal Ratzinger, Pope Wojtyla, and Fear at the Vatican," in Küng and Swidler, eds., *The Church in Anguish,* p. 68.

52. Ibid., p. 59.

53. For a fascinating look at the difficulties of doing moral theology today, see McCormick, *The Critical Calling,* esp. chap. 4, "The Chill Factor in Contemporary Moral Theology," pp. 71–94.

54. Dulles, "The Theologian and the Magisterium," p. 242.

55. It appears Cardinal Ratzinger is referring to CTSA, "Do Not Extinguish the Spirit," pp. 463–467.

56. Congregation for the Doctrine of the Faith, "Instruction on the Ecclesial Vocation of the Theologian" (May 24, 1990), *Origins,* 20 (July 5, 1990): 117, 119–126.

57. Ibid.

58. For the application of canons 812 and 833 to American colleges and universities, see Coriden, "Book III," pp. 575–576, 585–586; Ladislas Orsy, "Profession of Faith and the Oath of Fidelity," *America,* 160 (April 15, 1989): 345–347, 358.

59. Orsy, "Profession of Faith," pp. 345–346.

60. Greg Erlandson, "Vatican Releases New Fidelity Oath for Church Officials," CNS, March 2, 1989.

61. M. Theresa Moser et al., "Preliminary Report, Committee on Profession of Faith/Oath of Fidelity," College Theology Society (photocopy, November 18, 1989), p. 10. See also Thomas J. Reese, "Bishops and Theologians: A Report," *America,* 161 (July 1, 1989); James A. Coriden, "Inflating the Oath: The Rule Maker Breaks the Rules," *Commonweal* (September 8, 1989): 455–456.

62. Orsy, "Profession of Faith," pp. 345–346; Francis A. Sullivan, S.J., "Some Observations on the New Formula for the Profession of Faith," *Gregorianum,* 70 (1989): 549–558.

63. John A. Coleman, S.J., "Who Are the Catholic 'Fundamentalists'? A Look at Their Past, Their Politics, Their Power," *Commonweal* (January 27, 1989): 42.

64. Cindy Wooden, "Vatican Trots Out the Stats on Pope's 17th Year in Office," CNS, October 16, 1995. For an analysis of the juridical significance of different Vatican documents, see Francis G. Morrisey, O.M.I., "Papal and Curial Pronouncements: Their Canonical Significance in Light of the 1983 Code of Canon Law," *Jurist,* 50 (1990): 102–125.

65. For an extensive study of the media's coverage of the pope, see the four-part series by David Shaw in the *Los Angeles Times,* April 16–19, 1995.

66. "Special Report: Catholics Support Pope but Hold Independent Views," *CARA Report: Research on American Catholics and the U.S. Catholic Church,* 1 (Fall 1995): 4–6. This report gives an excellent summary of the surveys done before the pope's visit to the United States in 1995.

67. For an analysis of Ratzinger's theological evolution by a former student, see Hermann Häring, "Joseph Ratzinger's 'Nightmare Theology,'" in Küng and Swidler, eds., *The Church in Anguish,* pp. 75–90.

68. Eric O. Hanson, *The Catholic Church in World Politics* (Princeton, N.J.: Princeton University Press, 1987).

69. Tad Szulc, *John Paul II* (New York: Scribner, 1995); Carl Bernstein, "The Holy Alliance," *Time* (February 24, 1992): 28–35 (see *National Catholic Reporter,* February 28, 1992, for a response to this article).

70. Cindy Wooden, "War and Remembrance: Papal Appeals Keep Bosnia in Forefront," CNS, October 20, 1995.

71. From the beginning of the United Nations, its secretary general has granted nonvoting, permanent observer status to any state that belonged to one or more of the specialized international agencies. Although the Holy See participated in several UN agencies in the 1950s, it only appointed a permanent observer in 1964. The Holy See is a full member of four

such agencies: the Universal Postal Union, International Telecommunications Union, World Intellectual Property Organization, and International Atomic Energy Agency. The Holy See attends as a full voting member of UN international conferences because the invitation formula for such meetings used by the UN general assembly usually includes "all states" or "members of the UN or members of the specialized agencies." Tracy Early, "U.N. Official: Vatican's U.N. Status in Accord with Usual Practice," CNS, October 4, 1995.

72. Thomas J. Reese, S.J., "Three Years Later: U.S. Relations with the Holy See," *America*, 156 (January 17, 1987): 29–35.

10. Toward the Next Millennium

1. Bernard J. F. Lonergan, *Method in Theology* (Toronto: University of Toronto Press, 1990).

2. Lester R. Kurtz, *The Politics of Heresy: The Modernist Crisis in Roman Catholicism* (Berkeley: University of California Press, 1986).

3. John Paul II, "Letter to Women," *Origins*, 25 (July 27, 1995): 137, 139–143.

4. Although the definition of Vatican I concerning the plenitude of papal power is still in force, "The concrete forms in which this papal authority has been exercised have not only varied very greatly in the past, but in the future too can undergo such far-reaching transformations that so far as the average everyday impression of an individual Christian is concerned the directive power of the pope may be encountered in some new form in which it seems to retain only a slight connection with that authority which was once and for all defined in the First Vatican Council as permanently enduring." Karl Rahner, S.J., "Basic Observations on the Subject of Changeable and Unchangeable Factors in the Church," in *Theological Investigations* (New York: Seabury Press, 1976), vol. 14, p. 17.

5. John Thavis, "Vatican's Online Revolution Produces Some Paradoxes," CNS, November 3, 1995.

6. Peter Huizing and Knut Walf, eds., *The Roman Curia and the Communion of Churches, Concilium*, 127 (1979); James H. Provost, "Reform of the Roman Curia," in Giuseppe Alberigo and James Provost, eds., *Synod 1985: An evaluation, Concilium*, 188 (1986): 26–36; James H. Provost, "Pastor Bonus: Reflections on the Reorganization of the Roman Curia," *Jurist*, 48 (1988): 499–535.

7. James H. Provost, "Structuring the Church as a Communio," *Jurist*, 36 (1976): 191–245; see also James H. Provost, "Structuring the Church as Missio," *Jurist*, 39 (1979): 220–288.

8. Joseph A. Komonchak, "Subsidiarity in the Church: The State of the Question," *Jurist*, 48 (1988): 298–349.

9. Karl Rahner, S.J., "Structural Change in the Church of the Future," in *Theological Investigations* (New York: Seabury Press, 1976), vol. 20, pp. 128–129.

10. For efforts to reform the curia at the Council of Trent, see Robert Trisco, "Reforming the Roman Curia: Emperor Ferdinand I and the Council of Trent," in Guy Fitch Lytle, ed., *Reform and Authority in the Medieval and Reformation Church* (Washington, D.C.: Catholic University of America Press, 1981), pp. 143–333.

11. For a theology of history, see Lonergan, *Method in Theology*, pp. 175–234. See also Joseph A. Komonchak, "The Church," in Vernon Gregson, ed., *Desires of the Human Heart* (New York: Paulist Press, 1988), pp. 222–236; Bernard J. F. Lonergan, "Dialectic of Authority," in Frederick E. Crowe, S.J., ed., *A Third Collection: Papers by Bernard J. F. Lonergan, S.J.* (New York: Paulist Press, 1985), pp. 5–12.

Index

Bishops (*continued*)
  Congregation for the Evangelization of Peoples; Congregation for the Oriental Churches; Ecumenical councils; Episcopal conferences; Gaillot, Bishop Jacques; Synod of bishops
Boff, Leonardo, 254, 255
Boniface II, Pope, 78
Boniface III, Pope, 78
Borgia. *See* Callistus III
Bosnia, 179, 195, 226, 263, 267
Brazil, 46, 93, 97, 254, 255. *See also* Arns, Cardinal Evaristo; Latin America; Lorscheider, Cardinal Aloisio; Neves, Cardinal Lucas Moreira
Buckley, Michael, 251–252

Cacciavillan, Archbishop Agostino, 153
Cahill, Lisa, 256
Cairo Conference, 3, 4, 73, 195, 263–267. *See also* Abortion; Peking Conference
Callistus I, Pope, 79
Callistus III, Pope, 100
Calvi, Roberto, 207. *See also* Banco Ambrosiano; Vatican bank
Camerlengo, 76, 77, 82–83, 86–87, 294n35. *See also* Interregnum
Canada, 176, 221, 234, 254; cardinals from, 90, 91, 101. *See also* Gagnon, Cardinal Edouard
Canon law. *See* Code of Canon Law
Capitulations, 69. *See also* Election of popes
Capovilla, Loris, 183
Caprio, Cardinal Giuseppe, 185
Cardinals, as saints, 295n44
Cardinals, college of, 66–105, 301n12; early history, 66–69, 292n2; dean, 75, 77, 99, 294n36; appointments to, 80–81, 89–92; internationalization of, 89–92; sees of, 295n46. *See also* Consistories; Election of popes; Interregnum; United States cardinals
Carroll, Archbishop John, 233
Casaroli, Cardinal Agostino, 146, 154, 158, 181, 206
Casoria, Cardinal Giuseppe, 144, 145
Cassidy, Cardinal Edward, 130, 135–136, 145, 196–197, 200; as sostituto, 181–182, 185–186, 195
Castillo Lara, Cardinal Rosalio José, 97, 144, 195, 221, 226, 227; as head of Vatican City, 19, 21, 154, 215; as head of APSA, 154, 210, 221; as head of Vatican bank, 206–208
Catechesi Tradendae, 59
Catechism of the Catholic Church, 3, 60
Catholic Near East Welfare Association, 121, 125. *See also* Congregation for the Oriental Churches
Catholic Theological Society of America, 251, 255. *See also* United States theologians

Cé, Cardinal Marco, 14
CELAM, 93. *See also* Latin America
Celibacy, 3, 38, 261; theologians on, 26, 129, 252, 275; bishops on, 236, 237, 241, 247. *See also* Laicization
Celli, Claudio, 154, 231, 234, 265, 266
Charlemagne, Emperor, 17, 31
Cheli, Archbishop Giovanni, 144, 200
China, 3, 28, 195, 222, 230, 234, 266, 304n27
Christus Dominus, 42
Cicognani, Cardinal Amleto, 154
Clergy. *See* Priests
Code of Canon Law, 7, 112, 167–168; the 1917 Code, 31, 37, 74, 234; the 1983 Code, 32–33, 37, 68, 70–71, 103, 224, 249, 258; revision of, 32–33, 48, 71, 280. *See also* Council for the Interpretation of Legislative Texts; United States canon lawyers
Coleman, John, 259
College of bishops. *See* Bishops
College of cardinals. *See* Cardinals, college of
Cologne Declaration, 252, 257
Communione e Liberazione, 188
Communism, 28, 234, 272; John Paul II and, 2, 16, 89, 137, 263, 265; in Italy, 15–16, 102, 205, 220. *See also* China; Cuba; Eastern Europe; Poland; Russia; Soviet Union; Vietnam
Conciliarism, 36. *See also* Ecumenical councils
Conclaves. *See* Election of popes
Congregation for Bishops, 47, 72, 116, 122, 126, 243; members, 118–121, 238; role in appointment of bishops, 179, 191, 194, 236–240, 245. *See also* Council of Cardinals and Bishops
Congregation for Catholic Education, 126, 133, 143, 187; granting nihil obstat, 114, 179, 250; seminaries, 114, 116, 117, 130, 132, 243, 245. *See also* Ex Corde Ecclesiae; Theologians
Congregation for the Clergy, 108, 116, 117, 118, 131, 237, 245; role in overruling bishops, 111, 114, 169, 198, 246; organization, 126, 127; prefects, 146. *See also* Priests
Congregation for Divine Worship and the Discipline of the Sacraments, 116, 118, 126, 137, 194, 245; liturgical texts, 114, 123–124; prefects, 133, 143–147, 181, 185
Congregation for the Doctrine of the Faith, 108, 114, 116, 120, 125, 129, 161, 182, 200; prefects, 47, 52, 73, 119–120, 133, 143, 191, 194, 196, 198–199; dominance in curia, 98, 118, 134–136, 157, 184, 186, 193; and laicization, 118; members, 119–120; meetings, 122, 123, 137; and theologians, 139, 246, 250–260; and bishops, 237, 245, 246, 248; International Theological Commission, 255, 257. *See also* Theologians

Congregation for the Evangelization of Peoples, 231, 245; prefects, 47, 52, 73, 133, 143, 194; jurisdiction, 115, 116, 138; members, 118–121, 297n12; organization, 122, 123, 125–127; and other dicasteries, 130–132; finances, 204, 210, 216, 223, 227; role in appointment of bishops, 236–239, 303n10. *See also* Society for the Propagation of the Faith

Congregation for Institutes of Consecrated Life and for Societies of Apostolic Life, 116, 121, 131, 237; prefects, 47, 52, 143, 185; organization, 125–127, 148–149. *See also* Religious

Congregation for the Oriental Churches, 52; jurisdiction, 114–117, 138; membership, 119–121; meetings, 122; organization, 125–126; and other dicasteries, 130–132; prefects, 143, 144, 146, 195; finances, 224, 227; role in selection of bishops, 236–237. *See also* Catholic Near East Welfare Association

Congregation for Religious. *See* Congregation for Institutes of Consecrated Life and for Societies of Apostolic Life

Congregations and councils, 112–118; members, 118–122, 297n12, 297n14; meetings, 122–125; organization and procedures, 125–129; consultation among, 129–136; prefects and presidents, 142–147, 299n6; secretaries and undersecretaries, 147–148, 298n17, 299n7; professional staff, 148–158, 298n18. *See also* Congregation for . . . ; Council for . . . ; Curia, Roman; Papal management

Consistories, 75, 92, 104, 147, 281; history, 66–69, 108, 292n7; modern consistories, 69–74, 293n17; topics, 71. *See also* Cardinals, college of

Constantine, Emperor, 2, 11, 27, 34, 35

Consultors, Vatican, 21, 113, 129, 147, 155, 156, 158, 223; selection, 113, 129; to Congregation for the Doctrine of the Faith, 129, 198, 253, 259

Cordeiro, Cardinal Joseph, 46

Cornwell, John, 96

Council Cor Unum, 114, 125, 132, 149, 226; members, 118, 122

Council for Culture, 52, 116, 132, 133, 137, 138; members, 118, 119

Council for the Family, 114, 116, 118, 124, 182; members, 118–119, 120, 121; staff, 125, 149, 266; president, 136, 146, 147

Council for the Interpretation of Legislative Texts, 125, 144; jurisdiction, 114, 298n21; members, 118, 119

Council for Interreligious Dialogue, 125, 149, 156; president, 73, 133, 144, 146, 195; jurisdiction, 114, 116, 117; members, 118–121; and other dicasteries, 131, 132. *See also* Muslims

Council for Justice and Peace, 114, 116, 138, 149, 182, 194, 195, 266; members, 118, 121–122

Council for the Laity, 52, 60, 114, 116, 130, 149, 179, 182; members, 118–119, 120, 121

Council for Pastoral Assistance to Health Care Workers, 121, 125, 137, 144, 149; jurisdiction, 114, 116–118

Council for the Pastoral Care of Migrants and Travelers, 116, 118, 119, 121, 127, 132, 143, 149; president, 144, 195, 200

Council for Promoting Christian Unity, 127, 184, 194; jurisdiction, 114, 116–117; members, 118–121; and other dicasteries, 130–132, 135, 182, 188; presidents, 143, 145, 146, 186, 195, 196

Council for Social Communications, 116, 135, 138, 149, 156; members, 118, 121, 122; president, 135, 144, 156, 199–200

Council of Cardinals [for finances], 74, 209, 219, 223. *See also* Vatican finances

Council of Cardinals and Bishops, 236, 303n9. *See also* Congregation for Bishops

Council of the General Secretariat of the Synod of Bishops, 46–55, 289n19. *See also* Synod of bishops

Councils. *See* Congregations and councils; Council for . . . ; Ecumenical councils; Vatican II

Cuba, 3, 28, 178, 195, 209. *See also* Communism; Latin America

Curia, Roman, 106–139; history of, 106–109; tribunals, 109–112; congregations and councils, 112–125; office organization and procedures, 125–129; interdicasterial consultation, 129–136; reform of, 136–139, 171–172, 200–201, 279–283; internationalization of, 141–142; prefects and presidents, 142–147; secretaries and undersecretaries, 147–148; professional staff, 148–158; culture of, 158–171; jokes about, 80, 85, 133, 160, 161, 175, 194, 228, 288. *See also* Congregation for . . . ; Congregations and councils; Council for . . . ; Employees; Papal management; *Pastor Bonus*; Pontifical Ecclesiastical Academy; Tribunals; Vatican finances

Curran, Charles, 254, 256, 257

Daley, Brian, 30

Danneels, Cardinal Godfried, 46, 60, 97

Deskur, Cardinal Andrzej, 187, 286n16

Dicasteries. *See* Congregations and councils; Curia, Roman; Secretariat of State; Tribunals

Diocese of Rome, 5, 11–16, 19, 68, 76, 83, 106; finances of, 203–205. *See also* Bishop of Rome; Lateran Palace; St. John Lateran

Gregory X, Pope, 81–82
Gregory XII, Pope, 36
Gregory XIII, Pope, 2
Gregory XVI, Pope, 100
Gutiérrez, Gustavo, 256

Häring, Bernard, 255
Hebblethwaite, Peter, 40, 136, 181, 261
Henry IV of Germany, 230, 232–233
Henry VIII of England, 230
Herranz, Julián, 144
Hippolytus, 79
Hollenbach, David, 251–252
Humanae Vitae, 136, 247, 259, 283. *See also* Abortion; Birth control
Hume, Cardinal Basil, 46, 94, 95, 97, 267
Hurley, Archbishop Francis, 243

Inculturation, 35, 133, 273, 280, 281
Interdicasterial cooperation, 129–136, 190, 281. *See also* Congregations and councils; Papal management; Secretariat of State
Internationalization of college of cardinals, 89–92. *See also* Cardinals, college of
Internationalization of the curia, 141–142, 231. *See also* Curia, Roman
Internet. *See* World Wide Web
Interregnum, 68, 69, 76–77. *See also* Camerlengo; Cardinals, college of
IOR. *See* Vatican bank
Israel, 11, 26, 117, 195, 267. *See also* Jews; Middle East
Italian bishops' conference, 12, 14, 15; finances of, 203–205
Italian government, 206, 215; Vatican independence of, 16, 18, 22, 205, 207; and Vatican finances, 19, 21, 212, 213, 216; Vatican relations with, 21, 23, 215; and Italian church finances, 203–205. *See also* Banco Ambrosiano; Lateran Treaty; Papal states; Vatican bank
Italian politics, 15, 102, 208, 214–215, 272; and pope, 14–15. *See also* Italian government
Italian reunification. *See* Papal states
Italy, primate of. *See* Primate of Italy

Jadot, Archbishop Jean, 146, 240, 241
Jesuits. *See* Society of Jesus
Jews, 25, 121, 187, 189; and John Paul II, 72; Commission for Religious Relations with, 117, 297n10. *See also* Council for Promoting Christian Unity; Israel; Lustiger, Cardinal Jean-Marie
John XXII, Pope, 107
John XXIII, anti-pope, 36

John XXIII, Pope, 26, 183, 189; and Vatican II, 36, 244, 282; and college of cardinals, 67, 70, 89, 90–91, 102; election of, 95–98; and curia, 146, 160, 172
John Paul I, Pope, 7, 16, 174, 189, 193; election of, 76, 78, 88, 93–98, 100, 101
John Paul II, Pope, 2, 40, 189, 273, 282–283; and curia, 7, 133, 137, 170, 174; as bishop of Rome, 12–16, 204, 205; as head of Vatican City, 23; and bishops, 26, 34, 240, 243–244, 248; and synod of bishops, 43, 46–47, 49, 50, 52, 55, 59, 62, 64, 104; and consistories of cardinals, 66, 69–74; and appointment of cardinals, 81, 89–91, 97, 101; election of, 88–89, 91, 93, 95, 96, 97, 98; possible successors to, 94, 96, 98–99; management style, 98–99, 187–201; and appointments in curia, 146, 181, 185; and secretariat of state, 181, 185; and Vatican finances, 222, 226; as teacher, 260–261, 263, 272, 276, 278. See also *Catechesi Tradendae*; *Catechism of the Catholic Church*; *Evangelium Vitae*; *Familiaris Consortio*; *Pastor Bonus*; Trips of John Paul II; *Universi Dominici Gregis*
Julius II, Pope, 80
Justinian I, Emperor, 79

Kasper, Bishop Walter, 60
Keeler, Cardinal William, 121
Knox, Cardinal James, 147
König, Cardinal Franz, 93
Krol, Cardinal John, 46, 225
Küng, Hans, 249, 254, 255

Laghi, Cardinal Pio, 94, 154, 195, 239
Laicization, 117–118, 138, 198, 218, 245. *See also* Celibacy
Laity. *See* Council for the Laity; Employees, lay; Employees, women; Lay members of councils
Lateran Palace, 11, 13, 18. *See also* Bishop of Rome; Diocese of Rome; St. John Lateran
Lateran Treaty, 18, 23, 203, 204, 302n23. *See also* Papal states; Vatican City
Latin America, 222, 234, 272, 281; church in, 28, 200, 241, 273, 276, 277–278; cardinals from, 90–91, 93, 101; theologians from, 252, 255. *See also* Brazil; CELAM; Cuba; Liberation theology; Mexico; Synod for the Americas
Latin language, 3, 37, 51, 56, 57, 59, 176, 190; decline of, 50, 88, 141; in the liturgy, 79. *See also* Congregation for Divine Worship and the Discipline of the Sacraments; Lefebvre, Archbishop Marcel; Tridentine Mass
Law, Cardinal Bernard, 73
Lay members of councils, 113, 118–119, 121–122, 137. *See also* Congregations and councils

Lefebvre, Archbishop Marcel, 39, 101, 230, 248, 277, 304n26
Legionaries of Christ, 187, 188
Leo I (the Great), Pope, 16, 31, 231–232
Leo III, Pope, 17
Leo V, Pope, 80
Leo IX, Pope, 67, 101
Leo X, Pope, 80, 108
Leo XIII, Pope, 89, 95, 97, 271
Lercaro, Cardinal Giacomo, 88, 93
Liberation theology, 199, 252, 255, 265. *See also* Latin America
Libreria Editrice Vaticana, 216–217, 297n5
López Trujillo, Cardinal Alfonso, 94, 96, 97, 143, 286n16
Lorscheider, Cardinal Aloisio, 46, 93, 97
L'Osservatore Romano, 218, 297n5
Lourdusamy, Cardinal Simon, 97
Lumen Gentium, 38. *See also* Vatican II
Lustiger, Cardinal Jean-Marie, 94

Macchi, Pasquale, 183, 187
Mafia, 14, 158, 206
Mafia Emiliana, 154–155
Mafia, Polish, 185
Mahony, Cardinal Roger, 121, 209
Mandatum docendi, 249. *See also* Congregation for the Doctrine of the Faith; Theologians
Marcinkus, Archbishop Paul, 153, 206, 207
Maritain, Jacques, 102
Martinez Somalo, Cardinal Eduardo, 47, 52, 76, 94, 96, 181, 185
Mayer, Cardinal Augustin, 133, 146
McCloskey, Cardinal John, 89
McEnroy, Carmel, 256
Medeiros, Cardinal Humberto, 239
Mexico, 110, 222, 271. *See also* Latin America
Middle East, 11, 95, 176, 195, 221, 263; Oriental churches in, 115, 144, 237. *See also* Israel; Jews; Muslims; Near East Welfare Association
Missio canonica, 249. *See also* Congregation for the Doctrine of the Faith; Theologians
Modernism, 26, 89, 258, 260, 274, 275. *See also* Congregation for the Doctrine of the Faith; Theologians
Monduzzi, Bishop Dino, 154, 187, 188, 189
Muslims, 28, 72, 117, 121, 263, 265, 273. *See also* Council for Interreligious Dialogue; Middle East

Napoleon, 77, 230, 261, 272
National Conference of Catholic Bishops, 33, 73, 124, 144, 155, 188, 252; pastoral letters of, 34,

133, 252, 271; and synod of bishops, 43, 44, 53, 55. *See also* United States bishops
Navarro-Valls, Joaquin, 189–192, 299n14
Near East Welfare Association. *See* Catholic Near East Welfare Association
Neves, Cardinal Lucas Moreira, 94, 97
Nihil obstat, 179, 250, 251, 304n29. *See also* Congregation for Catholic Education; Congregation for the Doctrine of the Faith; Theologians
Noè, Cardinal Virgilio, 11, 86
North American College, 150
Nunciatures, 144, 151–153, 231, 266, 267. *See also* Nuncios
Nuncios, 108, 171–172; former nuncios in curia, 142, 144, 175, 181, 210; training and appointment of, 149–153, 175, 231, 233; role in recommending Vatican personnel, 150, 157–158; and local bishops, 177, 231, 267; role in appointment of bishops, 179, 231, 233–238, 240–242, 281; and curia, 180, 188, 250, 252, 266; and civil governments, 230–231, 263, 267. *See also* Nunciatures; Pontifical Ecclesiastical Academy; Secretariat of State

O'Connor, Cardinal John, 73, 118, 121, 206, 209, 238, 239, 241
Oddi, Cardinal Silvio, 146, 154, 198
Opus Dei, 158, 187, 188, 299n14
Ordination of women, 3, 97, 260, 276; theologians' disagreement on, 26, 252, 256, 275; bishops on, 236, 241, 243, 244; lay disagreement on, 261
Oriental churches. *See* Congregation for the Oriental Churches; Orthodox churches
Orthodox churches, 35, 278, 304n26; and the papacy, 25, 64, 138, 281; Oriental churches, 117, 130, 200; and John Paul II, 194. *See also* Congregation for the Oriental Churches; Council for Promoting Christian Unity; Patriarch of Constantinople
Ottaviani, Cardinal Alfredo, 168

Papal Household, 23, 76, 184, 187, 188–189, 216. *See also* Audiences with the pope
Papal management, 189–201. *See also* Secretariat of State
Papal representatives. *See* Nuncios
Papal states, 11, 16–18, 68–69, 107–109, 203; fall of, 11, 18, 28, 77, 87, 203, 205, 219, 282; corrupting impact of, 17–18, 87–88, 93, 233. *See also* Lateran Treaty; Vatican City
Pastor Bonus, 74, 112, 122, 131, 134, 159, 170, 199
Patriarch of Constantinople, 27, 35. *See also* Orthodox churches

Sánchez, Cardinal José, 97, 143, 239, 247
Sandri, Leonardo, 177
Schillebeeckx, Edward, 254, 255
Schotte, Cardinal Jan, 47, 49, 50, 53, 54, 57, 60, 195
Scrutineers, 84–86, 296n61. *See also* Election of popes
Secretariat of State, 174–189; two sections of, 175–180; top officials in, 180–187; relations with states, 263–268. *See also* Ambassadors to the Holy See; Nuncios; Papal management; Pontifical Ecclesiastical Academy; Secretary for relations with states; Secretary to the pope; Sostituto
Secretary for relations with states, 131, 133, 175–180, 181, 183, 191, 231, 264. *See also* Secretariat of State; Celli, Claudio; Silvestrini, Cardinal Achille; Tardini, Cardinal Domenico; Tauran, Archbishop Jean-Louis
Secretary of state, 74, 76, 77, 93, 94, 98; history of, 108; role in coordinating curia, 131, 175; role in curial appointments, 147, 148, 153; as head of Secretariat of State, 175–189, 191, 231; and bishops, 238. *See also* Casaroli, Cardinal Agostino; Cicognani, Cardinal Amleto; Gasparri, Cardinal Pietro; Secretariat of State; Sodano, Cardinal Angelo
Secretary to the pope, 183, 185–188, 189, 190, 225. *See also* Capovilla, Loris; Dziwisz, Stanislaw; Macchi, Pasquale
Seper, Cardinal Franjo, 47
Signatura, Apostolic, 110, 111–112, 246. *See also* Tribunals
Silvestrini, Cardinal Achille, 52, 94, 133, 144, 154
Siri, Cardinal Giuseppe, 78, 85, 91, 93, 95
Sixtus V, Pope, 31, 67, 69, 96, 108
Society for the Propagation of the Faith, 125, 223, 227–228. *See also* Congregation for the Evangelization of Peoples
Society of Jesus, 11, 18, 43, 44, 123, 158, 217, 251–252
Sodano, Cardinal Angelo, 195; and college of cardinals, 72, 94, 96; as secretary of state, 175, 180, 181, 185, 191, 238
Sostituto, 83, 98, 150, 153; as chief of staff, 175–177, 181–187, 191, 195, 231. *See also* Benelli, Cardinal Giovanni; Caprio, Cardinal Giuseppe; Cassidy, Cardinal Edward; Martinez Somalo, Cardinal Eduardo; Re, Archbishop Giovanni Battista; Secretariat of State
Soviet Union, 2, 178, 179, 236, 263. *See also* Communism; Russia
Spain, 37, 81, 225, 233, 261, 272; cardinals from, 80, 89. *See also* Martinez Somalo, Cardinal Eduardo

Spellman, Cardinal Francis, 121
Suenens, Cardinal Leon-Joseph, 93, 102
Swiss Guard, 7, 18, 23, 168
Synod for Africa, 45, 55, 63; membership of, 44, 45–46; preparation for, 46, 47, 48, 49, 51, 52
Synod for the Americas, 45, 47
Synod of bishops, 42–65; types and membership, 43–46, 288n9, 288n14; topics, 45, 48–49; preparing for, 49–55; procedures at, 55–58; post-synodal documents, 58–60; effectiveness of, 60–65. *See also* Council of the General Secretariat of the Synod of Bishops
Szoka, Cardinal Edmund, 22, 97, 110, 143, 207; head of the Prefecture for the Economic Affairs of the Holy See, 74, 185, 205, 209–211, 219, 221, 226–228, 300n3

Tardini, Cardinal Domenico, 175
Tauran, Archbishop Jean-Louis, 178, 191, 264
Teresa, Mother, 16, 55
Theologians, 3, 8, 26, 130, 139, 196, 199, 230, 248–263, 268, 275; and synod of bishops, 51, 60; complaints of, 99, 242, 251–252, 254–255, 257, 260, 275; in curia, 143, 156; International Theological Commission, 255, 257. *See also* Catholic Theological Society of America; Cologne Declaration; Congregation for the Doctrine of the Faith; Liberation theology; Modernism; United States theologians
Thiandoum, Cardinal Hyacinthe, 46
Third World, 44, 150, 156, 218, 288n12; debt of, 3, 106, 271; Vatican financial aid to, 8, 208, 225, 227; Catholics in 28, 267, 272, 273; cardinals from, 90, 93. *See also* Africa; Asia; Congregation for the Evangelization of Peoples; Council Cor Unum; Latin America; Society for the Propagation of the Faith
Tomko, Cardinal Jozef, 94, 195; as prefect of Congregation for the Evangelization of Peoples, 47, 52, 120, 133, 135, 191, 238; as secretary to the synod of bishops, 50, 59, 73
Tribunals, 109–112. *See also* Penitentiary; Rota, Roman; Signatura, Apostolic
Tridentine Mass, 195, 198. *See also* Lefebvre, Archbishop Marcel
Trips of John Paul II, 72, 181, 191–193, 195, 207, 240, 260, 283; statistics on, 2, 14, 192; curial reaction to, 98
Trips of Paul VI, 192, 272

United Nations, 4, 8, 73, 144, 267–268, 272, 306n71. *See also* Cairo Conference; Peking Conference

United States, Vatican attitude toward, 161, 177, 189, 252, 276

United States bishops, 13, 14, 46, 136, 243–245, 266, 271, 272, 277; appointment of, 233, 236, 239–241. *See also* National Conference of Catholic Bishops; Synod for the Americas

United States canon lawyers, 112, 127, 132, 156–157, 158, 159, 171, 242

United States cardinals, 90, 96, 101. *See also* Baum, Cardinal William; Bernardin, Cardinal Joseph; Bevilacqua, Cardinal Anthony; Keeler, Cardinal William; Krol, Cardinal John; Law, Cardinal Bernard; Mahony, Cardinal Roger; McCloskey, Cardinal John; Medeiros, Cardinal Humberto; O'Connor, Cardinal John; Spellman, Cardinal Francis; Szoka, Cardinal Edmund

United States Catholics, 177, 261, 271–272, 277, 278

United States citizens working in Vatican, 21, 126, 150, 156, 158, 166, 212. *See also* Baum, Cardinal William; Foley, Archbishop John; Marcinkus, Archbishop Paul; Rigali, Archbishop Justin; Szoka, Cardinal Edmund

United States government, 3, 233, 267, 272; Vatican opposition to foreign policy of, 3, 4, 263–265, 267. *See also* Cairo Conference; Flynn, Ambassador Raymond; Peking Conference

United States money and the Vatican, 110, 204, 208, 212, 224, 225; from foundations, 209, 210, 216, 226, 301n11. *See also* Vatican finances

United States theologians, 133, 242, 246, 250–252, 254–255, 256–257, 258–259. *See also* Buckley, Michael; Cahill, Lisa; Catholic Theological Society of America; Curran, Charles; Dulles, Avery; Fox, Matthew; Hollenbach, David; McEnroy, Carmel

Universi Dominici Gregis, 76, 78, 81–84, 87, 94, 95, 104. *See also* Election of popes

Vatican Archives, 22, 86, 147, 216, 274. *See also* Vatican Library

Vatican bank, 71, 74, 203, 204, 205–209, 224, 226–229. *See also* Banco Ambrosiano; Marcinkus, Archbishop Paul; Castillo Lara, Cardinal Rosalio José; Vatican finances

Vatican City, 5; government of, 16–24; employees of, 154, 210–213; finances of, 203–205, 209, 213–216, 217, 226–230. *See also* Employees, lay; Vatican finances

Vatican finances, 202–229, 300n3. *See also* Administration of the Patrimony of the Apostolic See (APSA); Almonry, Apostolic; Catholic Near East Welfare Association; Congregation for the Evangelization of Peoples; Congregation for the Oriental Churches; Council Cor Unum; Council of Cardinals; Employees; Peter's Pence; Prefecture for the Economic Affairs of the Holy See; Society for the Propagation of the Faith; United States money and the Vatican; Vatican bank

Vatican Library, 147, 214, 216, 274. *See also* Vatican Archives

Vatican museums, 5, 19, 21, 23, 279; finances of, 213–215, 228

Vatican Radio, 23, 158, 190, 217–218, 259, 279, 297n5

Vatican II, 36–40, 49, 60, 244, 251, 280, 283; on collegiality, 24, 29, 36; procedures at, 37–38; and the curia, 37, 42, 109, 117, 118, 141, 183, 282; and the synod of bishops, 42, 49, 60, 61. *See also Christus Dominus; Lumen Gentium;* Ecumenical councils

Vicariate of Rome. *See* Diocese of Rome

Vietnam, 3, 28, 176, 190, 195, 230, 234, 265, 267

Vigilius, Pope, 27, 79

Villot, Cardinal Jean, 180, 183, 193

Viterbo, Conclave at, 81–82, 84, 99, 100

Western Europe, 12, 115, 229; cardinals from, 90, 101. *See also* Austria; France; Germany; Great Britain; Italian bishops' conference; Italian government; Italian politics; Italian reunification; Spain

Willebrands, Cardinal Johannes, 133, 145, 146

Women, 99, 276, 283. *See also* Employees, women; Ordination of women; Peking Conference; Religious

World Wide Web, 65, 139, 214, 218, 270, 279

Wuerl, Bishop Donald, 246